Eugenio Barba

A DICTIONARY OF THEATRE ANTHROPOLOGY

SECOND EDITION

THE SECRET ART OF THE PERFORMER

Translated by Richard Fowler

Routledge
Taylor & Francis Group

LONDON AND NEW YORK

First Edition published in 1991 by Centre for Performance Research/Routledge

Second Edition published in 2006 by Routledge
2 Park Square, Milton Park, Abingdon, Oxon OX14 4RN

Simultaneously published in the USA and Canada by Routledge
270 Madison Ave., New York, NY 10016

Routledge is an imprint of the Taylor & Francis Group
Typeset in Garamond Simoncini by
Florence Production, Ltd, Stoodleigh, Devon
Printed and bound in the UK by
Scotprint, Haddington

This book is the result of research conducted from 1980 to 2005 by ISTA, the International School of Theatre Anthropology, directed by Eugenio Barba. All articles not attributed to a particular author are collaborations between Eugenio Barba and Nicola Savarese.

This book is dedicated to the memory of Katsuko Azuma, Fabrizio Cruciani, Ingemar Lindh, Sanjukta Panigrahi and I Made Pasek Tempo, founders of ISTA.

Translated by Richard Fowler and revised by Judy Barba who also translated the sections on *Eurasian Theatre, Exercises* and *Organicity*. Katie Dymoke translated the section *Nostalgia*.

Design: Nicola Savarese
Collaborator: Rina Skeel

British Library Cataloguing in Publication Data
A catalogue record for this book is available from the British Library

Library of Congress Cataloguing in Publication Data
A catalogue record for this book has been applied for

ISBN10: 0–415–37861–3
ISBN13: 978–0–415–37861–1

(Title page: A scene from Theatrum Mundi, ISTA Bologna 1990, with Balinese dancer I Made Pasek Tempo and Odin Teatret actress Roberta Carreri.)

CONTENTS

Preface
Eugenio Barba, 5

Introduction
Theatre anthropology – *Eugenio Barba*, 6
Similar principles, different performances, 6; *Lokadharmi* and *Natyadharmi*, 7; Balance in action, 8; The dance of oppositions, 10; The virtue of omission, 12; Intermezzo, 14; A decided body, 16; A fictive body, 17; A million candles, 18

Anatomy
Can the sea rise above the mountain tops? – *Nicola Savarese*, 22

Apprenticeship
Western examples – *Fabrizio Cruciani*, 24
Founding fathers and pedagogical theatre at the beginning of the twentieth century, 24; Creative process, theatre school and theatre culture, 24; Author's pedagogy, 26

An Indian example – *Rosemary Jeanes Antze*, 28
Guru as parent, honoured preceptor, 28; *Guru-kula*, study in the *guru*'s home, 29; *Guru-dakshina*, gifts and fees, 30; Ekalavya, disciple extraordinaire, 31; *Guru–shishya–parampara*, 31

Balance
Extra-daily balance, 32; Luxury balance, 32; Extra-daily technique: the search for a new posture, 35; Generalisations regarding balance, 36; Balance in action, 39; Steel and cotton, 40; Why does the performer aim for a luxury balance? What does the performer's alteration of balance mean for the spectator?, 43; Balance and imagination, 44; Brecht's unknown dance, 46

Dilation
The dilated body – *Eugenio Barba*, 52
The bridge, 53; Peripeteias, 54; The negation principle, 56; To think the thought, 57; Twin logics, 58; Seven-gated Thebes, 59

The dilated mind – *Franco Ruffini*, 62

Dramaturgy
Actions at work – *Eugenio Barba*, 66

Energy
Kung-fu, 72; Energy and continuity, 74; *Koshi*, *ki-hai*, *bayu*, 75; *Animus*, *anima*, 76; *Keras* and *manis*, 81; *Lasya* and *tandava*, 82; *Santai*, the actor's three bodies, 86; *Tame*, 84; Energy in space and energy in time, 84; Braking the action, 88; The performer's presence, 92

Equivalence
The equivalence principle, 93; *Dhanu*: archery in Indian odissi dance, 97; How one shoots an arrow in Japanese kyogen theatre, 98; Shooting with a bow, 100

Eurasian Theatre
Eurasian theatre – *Eugenio Barba*, 102
Dawn, 102; Eurasian theatre, 102; Anti-tradition, 102; Why, 103; Roots, 103; Village, 104; To interpret a text or to create a context, 104; Spectator, 104
Incomprehensions and inventions: from the Silk Road to Seki Sano – *Nicola Savarese*, 106

Exercises
Score and subscore: the significance of exercise in the actor's dramaturgy – *Eugenio Barba*, 112
A physical action: the smallest perceptible action, 112; The age of exercises, 112; Inner life and interpretation, 113; The complexity of emotion, 114; The real relationship, 116; Sport as dance, 116; The physical dialogue with the spectators, 116; The real action, 117; Meyerhold's theatre fission, 118; The exercise: a model of organic and dynamic dramaturgy, 120; Form, rhythm, flow, 120; Tacit knowledge, 121

Face and eyes
Physiology and codification, 122; The concrete gaze, 126; The action of seeing, 129; Showing that one is seeing, 130; The natural face, 134; The provisional face, 136; The painted face, 138

Feet
Microcosm, macrocosm, 140; On point, 141; Foot grammar, 146

Hands
Physiology and codification of the hands, 150; The hands: pure sound or silence, 151; How to invent hands in movement, 154; India: hands and meaning, 156; Hands and the Peking Opera, 158; Hands and Balinese dance, 159; Hands and the Japanese theatre, 160; Hands and classical dance, 161; Two examples from contemporary Western theatre, 162

Historiography
Energetic language – *Ferdinando Taviani*, 164
Henry Irving under the microscope, 165; Living marble, 166; Underneath Harlequin's costume, 168

Stanislavsky's 'system' – *Franco Ruffini*, 170
Stanislavsky's words, 170; 'The simplest human condition': the organic body-mind, 170; The mind makes demands: *perezhivanie*, 171; The body responds appropriately: personification, 171; Organic body-mind, character, rôle, 172; Conditions for meaning and the pre-expressive level, 172

Meyerhold: the grotesque; that is, biomechanics – *Eugenio Barba*, 174
A plasticity that does not correspond to the words, 174; The grotesque, 175; Biomechanics, 176

CONTENTS

Montage
The performer's montage and the director's montage – *Eugenio Barba*, 178
The performer's montage, 180; The director's montage, 180; Further montage by the director, 182

Nostalgia
Nostalgia or the passion for a return – *Nicola Savarese*, 185

Omission
Fragmentation and reconstruction, 191; The virtue of necessity, 193; To perform absence, 194; The virtue of omission, 195

Opposition
The dance of oppositions, 196; The beauty line, 200; *Tribhangi*, or the three arches, 201; The shadow test, 204

Organicity
Organic effect – *Eugenio Barba*, 206
Organicity, presence, scenic *bios*, 206; That which is organic for the actor / that which is organic for the spectator, 206

Natural and organic – *Mirella Schino*, 208
Organic and natural, 208; Performance as an organic unity, 208; Always nature, but a different nature, 209; Working languages, 210; Presence, 210; *Axé, shinmyong, taksu*, 211; *Matah, mi-juku, kacha*, 211

At work with physical actions: the double articulation – *Marco De Marinis*, 212
The first articulation, 212; The second articulation, 213; General principles, 214

Pre-expressivity
Totality and its levels of organisation, 216; Inculturation and acculturation technique, 219; Physiology and codification, 221; Codification in the East and the West, 222; The fictive body, 225; Martial arts and theatricality in the East, 227; Martial arts and theatricality in the West, 230; Body architecture, 233; The spectator's pre-interpretation, 234

Restoration of behaviour
Restoration of behaviour – *Richard Schechner*, 235
Bharatanatyam, 236; *Purulia chhau*, 237; Trance and dance in Bali, 239

Rhythm
Carved time, 241; *Jo-ha-kyu*, 243; Biological motions and the body's micro-rhythms, 244; Meyerhold: rhythm is essential, 246

Set and costume design
The costume is the set, 248; Daily clothing, extra-daily costume, 255; The water sleeves, 256

Technique
The notion of body techniques, 258
Biographical list of body techniques – *Marcel Mauss*, 258; 1. Techniques of birth and obstetrics, 259; 2. Techniques of infancy: rearing and feeding the child, 259; 3. Techniques of adolescence, 259; 4. Techniques of adult life, 260; Consumption techniques, 262; General considerations, 263

The spine: energy's helm, 264; The silent scream, 266

Pragmatic laws – *Jerzy Grotowski*, 268
Sats, 268; *Logos* and *bios*, 269

Text and stage
The culture of the text and the culture of the stage – *Franco Ruffini*, 270
The sound of two hands clapping, 270; 'Poor' text and 'rich' stage, 271; Dramaturgy, 272; Rôle type and character, 274

Training
From 'learning' to 'learning to learn' – *Eugenio Barba*, 276
The myth of technique, 276; A decisive phase, 276; Total presence, 277; The period of vulnerability, 278.

Training interculturally – *Richard Schechner*, 279

Training and the point of departure – *Nicola Savarese*, 281
Preliminary considerations, 281; Exercise models, 281; Acrobatics, 282; Training with the master, 286

Views
The view of the performer and the view of the spectator – *Ferdinando Taviani*, 288

Bibliography
Previous editions of this dictionary, 302; Collective works, 302; General bibliography, 303

Acknowledgements
ISTA: International School of Theatre Anthropology, 312; Invited artists, 312; Scientific staff and special guests, 313; Illustrations, 313; Photos, 313

Author Biographies, 314

Index, 315

PREFACE

ISTA: International School of Theatre Anthropology

Every researcher is familiar with partial homonyms and does not confuse them with homologies. For example, in addition to cultural anthropology, there also exists criminal anthropology, philosophical anthropology, physical anthropology and palaeoanthropology. In ISTA the distinction is repeatedly emphasised that the term 'anthropology' is not being used in the sense of cultural anthropology but that ISTA's work is a new field of study applied to the human being in an organised performance situation.

The only affinity between ISTA's work and cultural anthropology is the questioning of the obvious (one's own tradition). This implies a displacement, a journey, a detour strategy which makes it possible for one to understand one's own culture in a more precise way. By means of a confrontation with what appears to be foreign, one educates one's way of seeing and renders it both participatory and detached.

Let us therefore avoid equivocation: theatre anthropology is not concerned with those levels of organisation that make possible the application of the paradigms of cultural anthropology to theatre and dance. It is not the study of the performative phenomena in those cultures which are traditionally studied by anthropologists. Nor should theatre anthropology be confused with the anthropology of performance.

Again: theatre anthropology is the study of the behaviour of the human being when it uses its physical and mental presence in an organised performance situation and according to principles that are different from those used in daily life. This extra-daily use of the body is what is called technique.

A transcultural analysis of performance reveals that the performer's work is the result of the fusion of three aspects which reflect three different levels of organisation. 1) The performers' personalities, their sensibilities, their artistic intelligence, their social *personae*: those characteristics that make them unique and one of a kind. 2) The particularities of the traditions and socio-historical contexts through which the unique personality of a performer is manifest. 3) The use of physiology according to extra-daily body techniques. The recurrent and transcultural principles on which these extra-daily techniques are based are defined by theatre anthropology as the field of pre-expressivity.

The first aspect is individual. The second is common to all those who belong to the same performance genre. Only the third concerns all performers from every era and culture: it can be called the performance's 'biological' level. The first two aspects determine the transition from pre-expressivity to expression. The third is the *idem* that does not vary; it underlines the various individual, artistic and cultural variants.

The recurrent principles at the performance's biological level make the various performer techniques possible: they are the particular utilisation of the performer's scenic presence and dynamism.

Applied to certain physiological factors (weight, balance, the position of the spinal column, the direction of the eyes in space), these principles produce pre-expressive organic tensions. These new tensions generate a different energy quality, render the body theatrically 'decided', 'alive', and manifest the performer's 'presence', or scenic *bios*, attracting the spectator's attention before any form of personal expression takes place. This is, obviously, a matter of a logical and not a chronological 'before'. The various levels of organisation are, for the spectator and in the performance, inseparable. They can only be separated by means of abstraction, in a situation of analytical research and during the technical work of composition done by the actor or dancer.

ISTA's field of work is the study of the principles of this extra-daily use of the body and its application to the actor's and dancer's creative work. From this derives a broadening of knowledge that has immediate consequences on the practical, professional level. In general, the transmission of experience begins with the assimilation of technical knowledge: the performer learns and personalises. Knowledge of the principles that govern the scenic *bios* can make it possible for one to learn to learn rather than to learn a technique. This is of tremendous importance for those who choose to go, or who are obliged to go, beyond the limits of specialised technique.

Western performance study has for the most part concentrated on theories and utopias, neglecting an empirical approach to the performer's problems. ISTA directs its attention to this 'empirical territory' with the objective of going beyond the specialisations of particular disciplines, techniques or aesthetics. This is a question of understanding not technique, but the secrets of technique which one must possess before one can go beyond technique.

Eugenio Barba

Theatre anthropology

Eugenio Barba

Where can performers find out how to construct the material bases of their art? This is the question that theatre anthropology attempts to answer. Consequently it neither responds to the need to analyse scientifically what the performer's language consists of, nor does it answer the question, fundamental to those who practise theatre or dance, of how one becomes a good actor or dancer.

1–6. Similar principles, different performances: (1) Aztec dancer; (2) European jester in the Middle Ages; (3) Balinese dancer; (4) Japanese kabuki actor; (5) Indian odissi dancer; (6) classical ballet dancer.
The principles that regulate the stage behaviour of performers in various cultures are similar, but the performances are different.

Theatre anthropology seeks useful directions rather than universal principles. It does not have the humility of a science, but an ambition to uncover knowledge which can be useful to a performer's work. It does not seek to discover laws, but studies rules of behaviour.

Originally, anthropology was understood as the study of human beings' behaviour, not only on the socio-cultural level, but also on the physiological level. Theatre anthropology is thus the study of human beings' socio-cultural and physiological behaviour in a performance situation.

Similar principles, different performances

Different performers at different places and times and in spite of the stylistic forms specific to their traditions, have shared common principles. The first task of theatre anthropology is to trace these recurrent principles. They are not proof of the existence of a 'science of the theatre' nor of a few universal laws. They are nothing more than particularly good 'bits of advice', information useful for scenic practice. To speak of a 'bit of good advice' seems to indicate something of little value when compared with the expression 'theatre anthropology'. But entire fields of study – rhetoric and morals, for example, or the study of behaviour – are likewise collections of 'good advice'.

The 'bits of good advice' are particular in this respect: they can be followed or ignored. They are not inviolate laws; rather – and this is perhaps the best way to use them – one respects them so as to be able to ignore them and go further.

Contemporary Western performers do not have an organic repertory of 'advice' to provide support and orientation. They lack rules of action which, while not limiting artistic freedom, aid them in their different tasks. The traditional Asian performer, on the other hand, has a base of organic and well-tested 'absolute advice', that is, rules of art that codify a closed performing style to which all the performers of a particular genre must conform.

Needless to say, performers who work within a network of codified rules have a greater freedom than those who – like Western performers – are prisoners of arbitrariness and an absence of rules. But Asian performers pay for their greater liberty with a specialisation that limits their possibilities of going beyond what they know. A set of precise, useful and practical rules for the performer seems to be able to exist only by being absolute, closed to the influence of other traditions and experience. Almost all masters in Asian theatre enjoin their students not to concern themselves with other performance genres. Sometimes they even ask them not to watch other forms of theatre or dance. They maintain that this is the way to preserve the purity of the performers' style and that their complete dedication to their own art is thereby demonstrated. This defence mechanism has at least the merit of avoiding the pathological condition that results from an awareness of the relativity of rules: a lack of any rules at all and a falling into arbitrariness.

In the same way that a kabuki actor might ignore the best 'secrets' of noh, it is therefore symptomatic that Etienne

Decroux, perhaps the only European master to have elaborated a system of rules comparable to that of an Asian tradition, seeks to transmit to his students a rigorous shutting-off of scenic forms different from his own. For Decroux, as for Asian masters, this is not a question of narrow-mindedness or intolerance. It is an awareness that the basis of a performer's work, the points of departure, must be defended as precious possessions, even at the risk of isolation. Otherwise they will be irremediably polluted and destroyed by syncretism.

The risk of isolation is that purity might have to be paid for with sterility. Those masters who isolate their students in a fortress of rules which, in order to be strong, are not allowed to be relative and are therefore excluded from the usefulness of comparison, certainly preserve the quality of their own art, but they jeopardise its future.

A theatre can, however, be open to the experiences of other theatres, not in order to mix different ways of making performances, but in order to find basic common principles and to transmit these principles through its own experiences. In this case, opening to diversity does not necessarily mean falling into syncretism and a confusion of languages. On the one hand, it avoids the risk of sterile isolation and, on the other hand, it avoids an 'opening at any cost' that disintegrates into promiscuity. Considering the possibility of a common pedagogical basis, even if in an abstract and theoretical way, does not mean, in fact, considering a common way of making theatre. 'The arts', Decroux has written, 'resemble each other because of their principles, not because of their results'. I could add: and so it is with theatres. They resemble each other in their principles, not in their performances.

Theatre anthropology seeks to study these principles. It is interested in their possible uses, not in the profound and hypothetical reasons that might explain why they resemble each other. Studying these principles in this way, it will render a service to both the Western and the Asian performer, to those who have a codified tradition as well as to those who suffer from the lack of one.

Lokadharmi *and* Natyadharmi

'We have two words', the Indian dancer Sanjukta Panigrahi said to me, 'to describe man's behaviour: *lokadharmi* stands for behaviour (*dharmi*) in daily life (*loka*); *natyadharmi* stands for behaviour in dance (*natya*).'

In the course of the past several years I have visited numerous masters from different performance forms. With some I have collaborated at length. The purpose of my research has not been to study the characteristics of the various traditions, nor what rendered their arts unique, but to study what they had in common. What began as my own almost isolated research has slowly become the research of a group consisting of scientists, scholars of Western and Asiatic theatre and artists from various traditions. To the latter goes my particular gratitude: their collaboration is a form of generosity which has broken through the barriers of reticence in order to reveal the 'secrets' and, one could almost say, the intimacy of their professions. It is a generosity which at times has become a form of calculated temerity as they put themselves into work situations that oblige them to search for something new and that reveal an unexpected curiosity for experimentation.

7. Etienne Decroux (1898–1991), founder of modern corporeal mime.

Certain Asian and Western performers possess a quality of presence that immediately strikes the spectator and engages his or her attention. This occurs even when these performers are giving a cold, technical demonstration. For a long time I thought that this was because of a particular technique, a certain power that the performer possessed, acquired through years and years of experience and work. But what we call technique is in fact a specific use of the body.

The way we use our bodies in daily life is substantially different from the way we use them in performance. We are not conscious of our daily techniques: we move, we sit, we carry things, we kiss, we agree and disagree with gestures that we believe to be natural but that are in fact culturally determined. Different cultures determine different body techniques according to whether people walk with or without shoes, whether they carry things on their heads or with their hands, whether they kiss with the lips or with the nose. The first step in discovering what the principles governing a performer's scenic *bios*, or life, might be, lies in understanding that the body's daily techniques can be replaced by extra-daily techniques, that is, techniques that do not respect the habitual conditionings of the body. Performers use these extra-daily techniques.

In the Occident, the distance that separates daily body techniques from extra-daily techniques is often neither evident nor consciously considered. In India, on the other hand, the difference between these two techniques is obvious, even sanctioned by nomenclature: *lokadharmi* and

8–10. *Lokadharmi*: (**left**) daily behaviour of an Indian woman at her toilet (painting from the eleventh century AD); (**centre**) *natyadharmi*: the extra-daily behaviour of odissi dancer Sanjukta Panigrahi and (**right**) of an *onnagata* (an actor who plays female rôles in Japanese kabuki), both in 'mirror scenes'.

natyadharmi. Daily techniques generally follow the principle of less effort: that is, obtaining a maximum result with a minimum expenditure of energy. When I was in Japan with Odin Teatret, I wondered about the meaning of the expression which the spectators used to thank the actors at the end of the performance: *otsukaresama*. The exact meaning of this expression – used particularly for performers – is: 'you are tired'. Performers who have interested and touched their spectators are tired because they have not saved their energy. And for this they are thanked.

But an excess, a waste of energy, does not sufficiently explain the power that is perceived in the performer's life, in their scenic *bios*. The difference between the performer's life and the vitality of an acrobat is obvious. Equally obvious is the difference between the performer's life and certain moments of great virtuosity in the Peking Opera and other forms of theatre or dance. In these latter cases, the acrobats show us 'another body', a body that uses techniques very different from daily techniques, so different in fact that they seem to have lost all contact with them. But here it is not a question of extra-daily techniques but simply of 'other techniques'. There is no longer the tension of distance, the dialectic relationship, created by extra-daily techniques. There is only the inaccessibility of a virtuoso's body.

The purpose of the body's daily techniques is communication. The techniques of virtuosity aim for amazement and the transformation of the body. The purpose of extra-daily techniques, on the other hand, is information: they literally put the body '*in form*'. Herein lies the essential difference which separates extra-daily techniques from those that merely transform the body.

Balance in action

The observation of a particular quality of scenic presence has led us to differentiate between daily techniques, virtuosic techniques and extra-daily techniques. It is these latter which concern the performer. They are characteristic of the performer's life even before anything is represented or expressed. This is not easy for a Westerner to accept. How is it possible that there exists a level of the performer's art in which he or she is alive and present without either representing anything or having any meaning? For a performer,

this state of being powerfully present while not yet representing anything is an oxymoron, a contradiction in terms. Moriaki Watanabe defines the oxymoron of the performer's pure presence in this way: 'the situation of performers representing their own absence'. This might seem to be nothing more than a mental game but in fact it is a fundamental aspect of Japanese theatre.

Watanabe points out that in noh, kyogen and kabuki, there is an intermediary character between the two other possibilities (representing either a real identity or a fictional identity): the *waki*, the secondary actor in noh, who often expresses his own non-being. He engages a complex extra-daily body technique which he does not use to express himself, but which draws attention to his ability not to express. This negation is also found in the final moments in noh, when the main character – the *shite* – disappears: this actor, now stripped of his character, is nevertheless not reduced to his daily identity; he withdraws from the spectator without trying to express anything but with the same energy he had in the expressive moments. The *kokken*, the men dressed in black who assist the main actor in noh and kabuki, are also asked to 'perform absence'. Their presence, which expresses or represents nothing, draws so directly from the sources of the actor's energy and life that connoisseurs say that it is more difficult to be a *kokken* than an actor.

These examples show that there exists a level at which extra-daily body techniques engage the performer's energy in a pure state, that is, on the pre-expressive level. In classical Japanese theatre, this level is sometimes openly displayed, sometimes concealed. It is, however, always present in every performer and is the very basis of their scenic life or *bios*.

To speak of a performer's 'energy' means using a term that lends itself to a thousand misunderstandings. We give the word 'energy' many concrete meanings. Etymologically, energy means 'to be in work, at work'. How does it happen, then, that the performer's body is at work on a pre-expressive level? What other words could replace the word 'energy'?

Translating the principles of the Asian performer into one's own language involves words such as 'energy', 'life', 'power', and 'spirit', these translate terms like the Japanese words *ki-hai*, *kikoro*, *io-in*, *koshi*, the Balinese words *taksu*, *virasa*, *bayu*, *chikara*, the Chinese words *shun toeng*, *kung-fu*, and the Sanskrit words *prana* and *shakti*. The practical

11. Virtuosic techniques: acrobatic actors from the Peking Opera.

physiological condition, our age, our profession. Experiments have been done with professional actors. If they are asked to imagine themselves carrying a weight while running, falling or climbing, for example, it is found that this imagining in itself immediately produces a modification in their balance. No balance modification occurs in the body of a non-actor asked to perform the same task, since for a non-actor, imagination remains an almost exclusively mental exercise.

All this gives us considerable information about balance and the relationship between mental processes and muscular tensions, but it does not tell us anything new about the performer. In fact, to say that performers are accustomed to controlling their own presence and translating their mental images into physical and vocal actions simply means that performers are performers. But the series of micro-movements revealed in the balance experiments puts us on another track. These micro-movements are a kind of kernel which, hidden in the depths of the body's daily techniques, can be modelled and amplified in order to increase the power of the performer's presence, thus becoming the basis of extra-daily techniques.

Anyone who has seen a Marcel Marceau performance will certainly have stopped for a moment to consider the strange fate of the mime who appears alone on the stage for a few seconds, in between Marceau's numbers, holding up a card on which is written the title of the next piece. I agree, one might say mime is a mute form and even the titles, in order not to break the silence, must be mute. But why use a mime, an actor, as a noticeboard? Doesn't it mean that he is trapped in a desperate situation in which he can, literally, do nothing? Pierre Verry, a mime who presented Marceau's title cards for years, one day related how he sought to achieve the highest

meanings of the principles of the performer's life are obscured by complex terms, imprecisely translated.

I tried to get ahead by going backwards. I asked certain Asian theatre masters if, in the language they used in their work, there existed words that could translate our term 'energy'. 'We say that an actor has, or does not have, *koshi* to indicate that he has or doesn't have the right energy while performing', kabuki actor Sawamura Sojuro replied. In Japanese, *koshi* is not an abstract concept, but a very precise part of the body, the hips. To say one has *koshi*, one does not have *koshi* means one has hips, one doesn't have hips. But what does not having hips mean?

When we walk using daily body techniques, the hips follow the legs. In the kabuki and noh actors' extra-daily techniques, the hips, on the contrary, remain fixed. To block the hips while walking, it is necessary to bend the knees slightly and, engaging the vertebral column, to use the trunk as a single unit, which then presses downwards. In this way, two different tensions are created in the upper and lower parts of the body. These tensions oblige the body to find a new point of balance. It is not a stylistic choice, it is a way to engender the actor's life. It then only secondarily becomes a particular stylistic characteristic.

In fact, the performer's life is based on an alteration of balance. When we are standing erect, we are never immobile even when we appear to be so; we are in fact using many minute movements to displace our weight. A continuous series of adjustments moves our weight, first in the toes, then in the heels, now on the left side, now on the right side of the feet. Even in the most absolute immobility, these micromovements are present, sometimes condensed, sometimes enlarged, at times more or less controlled, according to our

12. Japanese noh actor: a fictive body, not a fictive character.

9

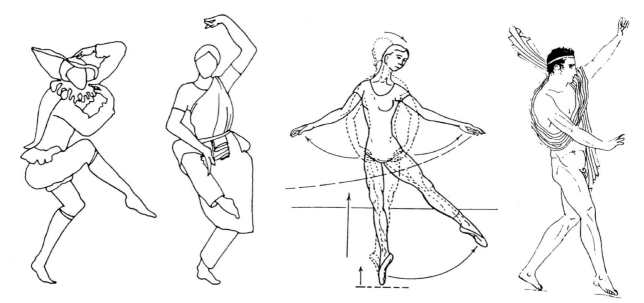

13–16. Alteration of balance: Italian commedia dell'arte actor, Indian odissi dancer, classical ballet dancer; dancer in ancient Greece in a procession in honour of Dionysus.

possible degree of scenic existence during the brief instant in which he appeared on the stage without having – and without being able – to do anything. He said that the only possible way to achieve this was to make the position in which he held the card as strong as possible, as alive as possible. In order to reach this result in his few seconds onstage, he had to concentrate for a long time to find his 'precarious balance'. His immobility became not a static immobility but a dynamic one. Not having anything else to work with, Verry had to reduce himself to the essential, and he discovered the essential in the alteration of balance.

The basic body positions of the various Asian theatre forms are likewise examples of a conscious and controlled distortion of balance. The performers of their various traditions deform the positions of the legs and the knees and the way of placing the feet on the ground, or they reduce the distance between one foot and the other, thereby reducing the body's basis and making balance precarious. 'All the technique of the dance', says Sanjukta Panigrahi, 'is based on dividing the body vertically into two equal halves, and on the unequal placing of the weight, now more on one half of the body, now more on the other half.' That is, the dance amplifies, as if under a microscope, those continuous and minute shifts of weight that we use to remain immobile and that laboratories specialising in balance measurement reveal by means of complicated diagrams. It is this *dance of balance* that is revealed in the fundamental principles of all performance forms.

The dance of oppositions

The reader should not be surprised if I use the words 'actor' and 'dancer' indiscriminately, just as I move with a certain ease from the East to the West and vice versa. The life principles that we are searching for are not limited by the distinction between what we define as theatre, dance or mime. Gordon Craig, scorning the contorted images used by critics to describe the English actor Henry Irving's particular way of walking, simply said, 'Irving did not walk on the stage, he danced on it'. The same shift from theatre to dance came to be used, but this time in a negative sense,

to deprecate Meyerhold's research. After seeing his production of *Don Juan*, some critics wrote that what he had done was not real theatre but ballet.

The tendency to make a distinction between dance and theatre, characteristic of our culture, reveals a profound wound, a void with no tradition, which continuously risks drawing the actor towards a denial of the body and the dancer towards virtuosity. To an Asian performer, this distinction seems absurd, as it would have seemed absurd to European performers in other historical periods, to a jester or a comedian in the sixteenth century, for example. We can ask a noh or kabuki actor how he would translate the word 'energy' into the language of his work, but he would shake his head with amazement if we asked him to explain the difference between dance and theatre.

'Energy', said kabuki actor Sawamura Sojuro, 'could be translated as *koshi*'. And according to noh actor Hideo Kanze, 'My father never said "Use more *koshi*" but he taught me what it was all about by making me try to walk while he grasped me by the hips and held me back'. To overcome the resistance of his father's grasp, he was forced to incline his torso slightly forwards, bend his knees, press his feet on the floor and glide them forwards rather than taking a normal step. The result was the basic noh walk. Energy, like *koshi*, is not the result of a simple and mechanical alteration of balance, but is the consequence of the tension between opposing forces.

The kyogen actor Mannojo Nomura remembered that noh actors of the Kita school said: 'The actor must imagine that above him is suspended a ring of iron which is pulling him upwards. He must resist this pull in order to keep his feet on the ground'. The Japanese term which describes this opposing tension is *hippari hai* which means 'to pull something or someone towards oneself while the other person or thing is trying to do the same'. *Hippari hai* is found between the upper and lower parts of the actor's body, as well as between the front and back. There is also *hippari hai* between the actors and the musicians, who in fact do not play in unison but try to move away from each other, alternately surprising each other, interrupting each other's tempo, yet not going so far apart as to lose the contact, the particular bond that puts them in opposition.

Expanding this concept, we could say that in this sense the extra-daily body techniques have a *hippari hai* relationship with daily techniques. We have seen in fact that although extra-daily techniques are different from daily techniques, a tension is maintained between them without their becoming isolated and separated. The performer's body reveals its life to the spectator by means of a tension between opposing forces: this is the principle of opposition. Based on this principle, which obviously is also part of the Occidental performer's experience, the codified traditions of Asia have built various composition systems.

In Peking Opera, the actor's entire dynamic pattern is built on the principle that every movement must begin in the direction opposite to that in which it will ultimately be carried out. All the forms of Balinese dance are constructed by composing a series of oppositions between *keras* and *manis*. *Keras* means strong, hard, vigorous. *Manis* means delicate, soft, tender. *Keras* and *manis* can be applied to various movements and positions of different parts of the body in a dance, and to successive movements in the same performance. This relationship is clearly visible in the basic Balinese dance position, which to the Occidental eye may appear extremely stylised. This is the result of a consistent alternation of parts of the body in the *keras* position with parts of the body in the *manis* position.

The dance of opposition characterises the performer's life on many levels. Performers use a kind of compass to orientate themselves as they search for this dance: unease. 'Mime is at ease in unease', says Decroux, and masters from all traditions have similar maxims. Japanese buyo dancer Katsuko Azuma's master told her that she could verify that a position had been correctly assumed if the position hurt. And she added, smiling, 'But if it hurts, it doesn't necessarily mean that it's right'. Indian dancer Sanjukta Panigrahi, the masters of Peking Opera, classical ballet or Balinese dance, all reiterate the same idea. Unease, then, becomes a means of control, a kind of internal radar that permits performers to observe themselves while in action, not with their eyes, but by means of a series of physical perceptions that confirm that extra-daily, non-habitual tensions are at work in the body.

When I asked Balinese master I Made Pasek Tempo what, according to him, the principal talent of an actor or dancer

might be, he replied that it was *tahan*, 'the capacity for resistance, endurance'. The same concept is found in Chinese theatre. To imply that actors have mastery of their art, it is said that they have *kung-fu*, which literally means 'the capacity to hold fast, to resist'. In the West, we might use the word 'energy' to say the same thing: 'the capacity to persist in work, to endure'. But once again, this word can become a trap.

When Western performers want to be energetic, when they want to use all their energy, they often begin to move in space with tremendous vitality. They use huge movements, with great speed and muscular strength. And this effort is associated with fatigue, hard work. Asian actors (or great western actors) can become even more tired almost without moving. Their tiredness is not caused by an excess of vitality, by the use of huge movements, but by the play of oppositions. The body becomes charged with energy because within it is established a series of differences of potential that render the body alive, strongly present, even with slow movements or in apparent immobility. The dance of oppositions is danced *in* the body before being danced *with* the body. It is essential to understand this principle of the performer's life: energy does not necessarily correspond to movement in space.

In the *lokadharmi*, the different daily body techniques, the forces that give life to the actions of extending or withdrawing an arm or leg, or the finger of one hand, act one at a time. In the *natyadharmi*, the extra-daily techniques, the two opposing forces (of extending and withdrawing) act simultaneously; or rather, the arms, the legs, the fingers, the spine, the neck, all these parts of the body are extended as if in resistance to a force which then obliges them to bend and vice versa. Katsuko Azuma explains, for example, which forces are at work in the movement – typical of both buyo dance and noh – in which the torso inclines slightly and the arms extend forwards in a gentle curve. She speaks about the forces which are acting in the opposite direction to that which one observes; the arms, she says, do not extend to make the curve, but rather it is as if they are pulling a large square box towards the chest. In this way, the arms, which appear to move away from the body, in fact push towards the body, just as the torso, pushed inwards, opposes resistance and bends forwards.

17–18. Etienne Decroux: 'mime is a portrait of work'.

11

19–23. Dance of oppositions: (**top left**) Henry Irving (1838–1905) as Cardinal Wolsey in Shakespeare's *Henry VIII*; (**bottom left**) Vsevolod Meyerhold (1874–1939) in Shentan's *Acrobats*; (**top centre**) buyo dancer Kanichi Hanayagi in *Yashima*, Bielefeld ISTA 2000; (**bottom centre**) Tom Leabhart in *A Little Thing*, Bielefeld ITSA 2000; (**top right**) kabuki actor Ichikawa Danjuro I (1660–1704).

The virtue of omission

The principle which is revealed by the dance of oppositions in the body is – in spite of all appearances – a principle that operates through elimination. Actions are isolated from their contexts, and are thereby revealed. The movements woven together into dances seem to be much more complex than daily movements. In fact, they are the result of simplification: they are composed of moments in which the oppositions governing the body's life are manifest at the simplest level. This occurs because a well-defined number of forces, that is, oppositions, are isolated, amplified and assembled, together or in succession. Once again, it is an uneconomical use of the body, because daily techniques tend to superimpose various processes, with a subsequent saving of time and energy. When Decroux writes that mime is a 'portrait of work composed with the body', what he is saying can also be assumed from other traditions. This bodily 'portrait of work' is one of the principles that preside over the life of those who then conceal this very state, such as, for example, classical ballet dancers who hide their weight and

effort behind an image of lightness and ease. The principle of oppositions, because opposition is the essence of energy, is connected to the principle of simplification. Simplification in this case means the omission of certain elements in order to put other elements into relief. These other elements then appear to be essential.

The same principles that sustain the life of the dancer – whose movements are obviously far removed from daily movements – can also sustain the life of the actor, whose movements seem closer to those used daily. Not only, in fact, can actors omit the complexity of the daily use of the body in order to allow the essence of their work, their *bios*, to manifest itself through fundamental oppositions, but they can also even omit extending the action in space. Dario Fo explains that the power of an actor's movement is the result of synthesis, that is, either the concentration of an action which uses a large amount of energy into a small space, or the reproduction of only those elements necessary to the action, eliminating whatever is considered superfluous. Decroux – like an Indian dancer – considers the body to be limited essentially to the trunk. He considers the movements

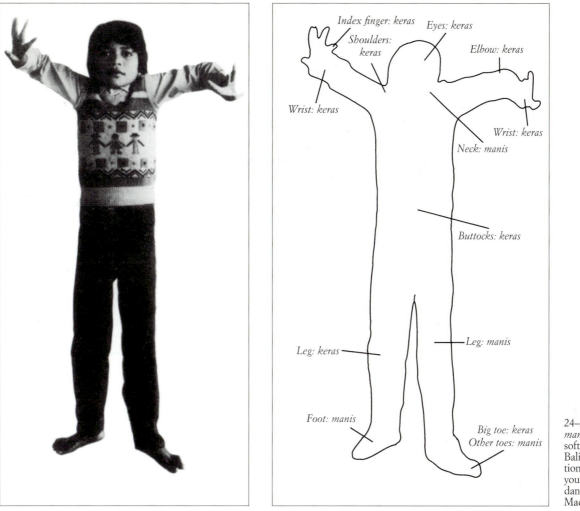

Index finger: keras
Shoulders: keras
Eyes: keras
Elbow: keras
Wrist: keras
Wrist: keras
Neck: manis
Buttocks: keras
Leg: keras
Leg: manis
Foot: manis
Big toe: keras
Other toes: manis

24–25. *Keras* and *manis* (strong and soft) principles in a Balinese dance position, illutrated by Jas, young daughter of dancer and master I Made Pasek Tempo.

of the arms and legs to be accessory (or 'anecdotal') movements, only belonging to the body if they originate in the trunk.

One can speak of this process – during which the space taken up by an action is restricted – as a process of energy absorption. It is developed from the amplification of oppositions and reveals a new and different route to the discovery of the 'recurrent principles' which can be useful to performing practice. The opposition between one force pushing towards action and another force holding back is converted into a series of rules – such as are used by noh and kabuki actors – which create an opposition between energy employed in space and energy employed in time. According to one of these rules, seven-tenths of the actor's energy should be used in time and only three-tenths in space. The actors also say that it is as if an action doesn't actually finish where the gesture has stopped in space, but continues in time.

Both noh and kabuki use the expression *tameru*, which can be represented by a Chinese ideogram meaning 'to accumulate' or by a Japanese ideogram meaning 'to bend' something which is both flexible and resistant, like a cane of bamboo. *Tameru* defines the action of holding back, of retaining. From *tameru* comes *tame*, the ability to keep energy in, to absorb into an action limited in space the energy necessary to carry out a much larger action. This ability becomes a way of describing an actor's skill in general. In order to say that an actor has or doesn't have sufficient scenic presence, the necessary power, the master tells him that he has, or doesn't have, *tame*.

All this may seem like an overly complicated and excessive codification of the performer's art. It derives in fact from an experience that is common to performers from many different traditions: the compression, into restricted movements, of the same energy which would be used to accomplish a much larger and heavier action. For example: engaging the whole body in the action of lighting a cigarette, as if one was lifting a heavy box and not a little match, or nodding with the chin and leaving the mouth slightly ajar with the same force that would be used to bite. Working in this way reveals a quality of energy which makes the performer's entire body come alive, even in immobility.

It is probably for this reason that many famous actors have been able to turn so-called 'stage business' into their greatest scenes. When these actors have to stop acting and stay on the sidelines while other actors develop the principal action, they are able to absorb, into almost imperceptible movements, the force of actions that they are not permitted to carry out. It is precisely in these cases that their *bios* stands out with a particular force and leaves its mark on the spectator's memory. 'Stage business' does not belong only to the Western tradition. In the seventeenth century, the kabuki actor Kameko Kichiwaemon wrote a treatise on the actor's art entitled, *Dust in the Ears*. He says that at given moments in certain performances, when only one actor is dancing, the other actors turn their backs to the audience and relax. 'I do not relax', he writes, 'but perform the entire dance in my mind. If I do not do so, the sight of my back is not interesting to the spectator.'

26. Synthesis sequence by Italian actor Dario Fo: moments of immobility in the extreme tension of oppositions.

The theatrical virtue of omission does not consist in 'letting oneself go' into undefined non-action. On the stage and for the performer, omission means 'retaining' that which distinguishes real scenic life and not dispersing it around in an excess of expressivity and vitality. The beauty of omission, in fact, is the beauty of indirect action, of the life that is revealed with a maximum of intensity in a minimum of activity. Once again, it is a play of oppositions that goes beyond even the pre-expressive level of the performer's art.

Intermezzo

At this point one might well ask if the principles of the performer's art which I have described do not take us too far from theatre and dance as it is known and practised in the West. Are these principles actually 'good advice', useful for performing practice? Does drawing attention to the pre-expressive level of the performer's art blind us to the

27. Japanese kabuki actor and the ikebana created by the basic lines of his position.

Western performer's real problems? Is the pre-expressive level perhaps only verifiable in theatrical cultures that are highly codified? Is the Western tradition not perhaps mainly characterised by the lack of codification and by the search for individual expression? These are undoubtedly binding questions, but rather than demanding immediate answers, they invite us to stop and rest for a moment.

So let's talk about flowers.

If we put some flowers in a vase, we do so in order to show how beautiful they are, in order to enjoy them. We can also make them take on ulterior meanings: filial or religious piety, love, recognition, respect. But beautiful as they might be, flowers have a shortcoming: taken out of their own context, they continue to represent only themselves. They are like the actor of whom Decroux has spoken: a man condemned to resemble just a man, a body imitating a body. This may well be pleasing, but to be considered art it is not sufficient that something be merely pleasing. In order to be considered art, adds Decroux, the idea of the thing needs to be represented by another thing. Flowers in a vase are irremediably flowers in a vase, sometimes subjects of works of art, but never works of art themselves.

But let's imagine using cut flowers to represent something else: the struggle of the plant to grow, to move away from the earth into which its roots sink ever deeper as it reaches up to the sky. Let's imagine wanting to represent the passage of time, as the plant blossoms, grows, develops and dies. If we succeed, the flowers will represent something other than flowers and will be a work of art, that is, we will have made an ikebana.

The ideogram for ikebana means 'to make flowers live'. The life of the flowers, because of having been interrupted, blocked, can be represented. The procedure is evident: something has been wrenched from its normal conditions of life (this is the state flowers are in when we simply arrange them in a vase), and the rules that govern these normal conditions have been replaced and analogically rebuilt using other rules. Flowers, for example, cannot act in time, cannot represent their blossoming and withering in temporal terms, but the passage of time can be suggested with an analogy in space. One can bring together – compare – one flower in bud with another already in full bloom. With two branches, one thrusting upwards and the other pointing downwards, one can draw attention to the direction in which the plant is developing: one force binds it to the earth, another force pushes it away from the earth. A third branch, extending along an oblique line, can show the combined force that results from the two opposing tensions. A composition which seems to derive from refined aesthetic taste is in fact the result of the analysis and dissection of a phenomenon and the transposition of energy acting in time into lines extending in space.

This transposition opens the composition to new meanings, meanings different from the original ones: the branch which is reaching upwards becomes associated with Heaven, the branch extending downwards, with the Earth, and the branch in the centre with the mediator between these two opposing entities: the Human Being. The result of a schematic analysis of reality and the transposition of this reality following principles which represent it without reproducing it, becomes an object for philosophical contemplation.

'The mind has difficulty in maintaining the thought of the bud because the thing thus designated is prey to an impetuous development and shows – in spite of our thought – a strong impulse not to be a flower bud but a flower.' These are words that Bertolt Brecht attributes to Hu-jeh, who adds: 'Thus, for the thinker, the concept of the flower bud is the concept of something which already aspires to be other than what it is'. This 'difficulty' in our thinking is exactly what ikebana proposes: an indication of the past and a suggestion of the future, a representation through immobility of the continuous motion which turns the positive into the negative and vice versa.

The ikebana example shows us how abstract meanings arise out of the precise work of analysing and transposing a physical phenomenon. If one began with these abstract meanings, one would never reach the concreteness and precision of ikebana, whereas by starting from precision and concreteness, one does attain these abstract meanings.

As for performers, they often try to proceed from the abstract to the concrete. They believe that the point of departure can be derived from what one wants to express, which then implies the use of a suitable technique. A symptom of this absurd belief is the diffidence shown towards codified performance forms and towards the principles for the performer's life which they contain. These principles, in fact, are not aesthetic suggestions made in order to render the performer's body more beautiful. They are a means of stripping the body of daily habits, in order to prevent it from being no more than a human body condemned to resemble itself, to present and represent only itself. When certain principles reappear with frequency, in different latitudes and traditions, one can assume that they work in our case as well.

The ikebana example shows how certain forces that develop in time can have an analogy in spatial terms. This use of analogous forces substituted for the forces that characterise the daily use of the body is the basis of Decroux's mime system. Decroux often gives the idea of a real action by acting in a way exactly opposite to the real action. He shows, for example, the action of pushing something not by projecting the chest forward and pressing with the back foot – as is done in the real action – but by arching the spine concavely, as if instead of pushing he was being pushed, and bringing the arms towards the chest and pressing downwards with the front leg and foot. This radical inversion of the forces with respect to how they could occur in the real action restores the work – or the effort – that comes into play in the real action. It is as if the performer's body was taken apart and then recomposed according to rules which are not the rules of daily life. At the end of the work of recomposition, the body no longer resembles itself. Like the flowers in our vase or like Japanese ikebana, the actor and dancer are cut from the 'natural' context in which they usually act: they are freed from the domination of daily techniques. Like the flowers and branches of the ikebana, performers, in order to be scenically alive, cannot present or represent what they are. In other words, they must give up their own automatic responses.

The various codifications of the performer's art are, above all, methods to break the automatic responses of daily life.

Naturally, this rupture of the automatic is not expression. But without this rupture there is no expression. 'Kill the breathing! Kill the rhythm!', Katsuko Azuma's master repeated to her as she worked. To 'kill' breathing and to 'kill' rhythm means to be aware of the tendency to habitually link gestures to the rhythm of breathing and music, and then to break this link. The breaking of the habitual actions of daily

28. Waves: ikebana from the Soghetsu school.

life has perhaps been most consciously and radically done in Japanese theatrical culture.

The precepts that demand the killing of rhythm and breathing, as expressed by Katsuko Azuma's master, show how the desired opposition can be brought about by the rupture of the habitual responses of the body's daily techniques. To kill the rhythm in fact implies creating a series of tensions to prevent the movements of the dance from coinciding with the cadences of the music. To kill the breathing means to hold the breath even while one is breathing out – which is a moment of relaxation – and to oppose the exhalation with a contrary force. Katsuko Azuma has said that it is actually painful for her to see a dancer following the tempo of the music, as happens in all cultures other than the Japanese. It is easy to understand why, according to the particular solutions found by her culture, a dance that follows the rhythm of the music might make her uneasy, because it shows an action which has been decided from the outside, by the music, or by daily behaviour. The solution that the Japanese have found for this problem belongs to their culture alone, but the problem itself concerns performers everywhere.

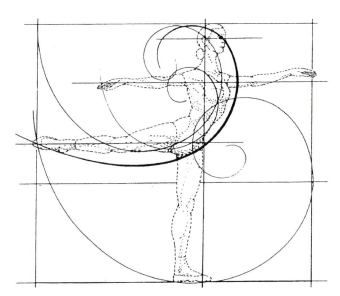

29. Schematic analysis of an arabesque, one of the basic positions in classical ballet.

30. Katsuko Azuma, Japanese buyo dancer, teaching a student to move according to *jo-ha-kyu* rhythm.

A decided body

Many European languages have an expression that might be chosen to epitomise what is essential for the performer's life. It is a grammatically paradoxical expression, in which a passive form assumes an active meaning, and in which an indication of availability for action is expressed as a form of passivity. The expression is not ambiguous, it is hermaphroditic, combining within it both action and passivity, and in spite of its strangeness, it is an expression found in common speech. One says, in fact, *essere deciso*, *être décidé*, to be decided. And it does not mean that someone or something decides for us or that we submit to decision, nor that we are the object of decision.

'To be decided' does not mean that we are deciding, nor that we are carrying out the action of deciding. Between these two opposite conditions flows a current of life that language does not seem able to represent and around which it dances with images. Only direct experience shows what it means 'to be decided'. In order to explain to someone what it means 'to be decided', we must refer to innumerable associations of ideas, to innumerable examples, to the construction of artificial situations. Yet everyone can imagine what the expression means. All the complex images and abstruse rules that are applied to actors and dancers, as well as the elaboration of artistic precepts that seem to be and are the result of sophisticated aesthetics, are the vaultings and acrobatics of an attempt to transmit an experience that cannot really be transmitted, but only lived. To explain the actor's or dancer's experience, one must use a complicated strategy to artificially create the conditions in which that experience can be reproduced.

Let us imagine once again that we can enter the intimate world of the work that takes place between Katsuko Azuma and her master. The master's name is also Azuma. When she judges that she has succeeded in passing her experience on to her student, she will also pass on her name. Azuma, then, says to the future Azuma: 'Find your *ma*'. *Ma* means something similar to 'dimension' in the spatial sense, but also 'duration' in the temporal sense. 'To find your *ma* you must kill rhythm. Find your *jo-ha-kyu*.' The expression *jo-ha-kyu* describes the three phases into which all a performer's actions are subdivided. The first phase is determined by the opposition between a force which tends to increase and another force which holds back (*jo* means 'to retain'); the second phase (*ha*, 'to break') occurs at the moment when one is freed from the retaining force, until one arrives at the third phase (*kyu*, 'speed'), where the action culminates, using up all of its force in order to stop suddenly, as if faced with an obstacle, a new resistance.

To teach Azuma to move according to *jo-ha-kyu*, her master would hold her by the waist and then suddenly release her. Azuma would work very hard to take the first two steps (while being held), bending her knees, pressing the soles of her feet to the ground, inclining her trunk slightly. Then, released by her teacher, she would advance quickly to the specified limit of the movement, at which point she would suddenly stop, as if a deep ravine had opened up a few centimeters in front of her. What she did, in other words, was to execute the movement which anyone who has seen Japanese theatre would recognise as typical. When performers have learned, as second nature, this artificial way of moving, they appear to have been cut off from the everyday space–time relationship and seem to be 'alive': they are 'decided'. Etymologically, 'to be decided' means 'to cut away'. The expression 'to be decided' has then yet another facet: it is as if it indicated that one's availability to create also includes cutting oneself off from daily practices.

The three phases of *jo-ha-kyu* impregnate the atoms, the cells, the entire organism of Japanese performance. They apply to every one of a performer's actions, to each of his gestures, to breathing, to the music, to each scene, to each play in a noh day. It is a kind of code which runs through all the theatre's levels of organisation.

René Sieffert maintains that the *jo-ha-kyu* rôle is a 'constant in humanity's aesthetic sense'. This is true in a way, even

31. The fictive body: Cristian Holder as the Chinese Conjurer in *Parade*.

16

if it is also true that a rule dissolves into something insignificant if it is universally applied. From our point of view, another of Sieffert's statements seems more important: that *jo-ha-kyu* permits the performer – as Zeami explains – to break the rule, apparently, in order to establish contact with the spectator. This is a constant in the performer's life: the building up of artificial rules goes hand in hand with their infraction. An actor who has nothing but rules is an actor who no longer has theatre but only liturgy. An actor without rules is also without theatre: s/he has only *lokadharmi*, daily behaviour with its predictability and its need for direct provocation in order to hold the spectator's attention.

All the teachings which Azuma the master passed on to Azuma the student are aimed at the discovery of the centre of the student's energy. The methods of the search are meticulously codified, the fruits of generations and generations of experience. The result is impossible to define with precision and differs from person to person.

Today, Azuma says that the principle of her life, of her energy as an actress and dancer, can be defined as a centre of gravity found at the midpoint of a line between the navel and the coccyx. Every time she performs, she tries to find her balance around this centre. Even today, in spite of her experience, in spite of the fact that she is a student of one of the greatest masters and that she herself is now a master, she isn't always able to find this centre. She imagines (using the images with which her master tried to transmit the experience to her) that the centre of her energy is a ball of steel found at a certain point on the line between the navel and the coccyx, or in the centre of a triangle formed by lines between the hips and the coccyx, and that this steel ball is covered with many layers of cotton. I Made Pasek Tempo, the Balinese master, says: 'Everything that Azuma does is *keras* covered by *manis*, vigour covered by softness'.

A fictive body

In the Occidental tradition, the performer's work has been oriented towards a network of fictions, of 'magic ifs' which deal with the psychology, the behaviour and the history of his or her person and that of the character he or she is playing. The pre-expressive principles of the performer's life are not cold concepts concerned only with the body's physiology and mechanics. They are also based on a network of fictions, but fictions, 'magic ifs', that deal with the physical forces that move the body. What the performer is looking for, in this case, is a fictive body, not a fictive personality. In order to break the automatic responses of daily behaviour in the Asian traditions, in ballet, and in Decroux's mime system, each of the body's actions is dramatised by imagining that one is pushing, lifting, touching objects of a determined weight and consistency. This is a psycho-technique which does not attempt to influence the performers' psychic state, but rather their physical state. It has, therefore, to do with the language performers use when speaking to themselves, and even more so with what the master says to the student, but does not pretend to mean anything to the spectator.

To find the body's extra-daily techniques, the performer does not study physiology. S/he creates a network of external stimuli to which s/he reacts with physical actions.

Among the ten qualities of the dancer in Indian tradition, there is one quality that has to do with knowing how to see,

32–33. The decided body: (**above**) Peking Opera actress Pei Yanling; (**below**) classical ballet dancer Martine Van Hamal.

17

how to direct the eyes in space. It is a sign that the dancer is reacting to something precise. At times, a performer's training exercises appear to be extraordinarily well executed, but the actions have no power because the way of using the eyes is not precisely directed. On the other hand, the body may be relaxed, but if the eyes are active – that is, if they see in order to observe – then the performer's body is brought to life. In this sense, the eyes are like the performer's second spinal column. All the Asian traditions codify eye movements and the directions the eyes must follow. This has to do not only with what the spectator sees, but also the performer and the way s/he populates the empty space with lines of force, with stimuli to which s/he must react.

At the end of his diary, the kabuki actor Sadoshima Dampachi, who died in 1712, writes that 'one dances with the eyes', implying that the dance one is performing can be equated with the body and the eyes with the soul. He adds that a dance in which the eyes do not take part is a dead dance, while a living dance is one in which eye and body movements work together. In Western traditions as well, the eyes are the 'mirrors of the soul' and an actor's eyes are thought of as the halfway point between physical behaviour's extra-daily techniques and extra-daily psycho-techniques. The eyes show that s/he is decided. The eyes make him/her be decided.

The great Danish physicist Niels Bohr was an avid western film fan and he wondered why, in all the final shoot-outs, the hero shot fastest even though his adversary was usually the first to reach for his gun. Bohr asked himself if some physical truth might not explain this phenomenon. He came to the conclusion that such a truth did indeed exist: the first to draw is the slowest to shoot because he decides to shoot, and dies. The second lives because he is faster, and he is faster because he doesn't have to decide, he is decided.

'True expression', says Grotowski, 'is that of a tree'. And he explained: 'If an actor has the will to express, then he is divided. One part of him is doing the willing and another part the expressing, one part is commanding and another is carrying out the commands.'

A million candles

Having followed the trail of the performer's energy, we have reached the point where we are able to perceive its nucleus:

1. in the amplification and activation of the forces that are at work in balance;
2. in the oppositions that determine the dynamics of movements;
3. in an operation of reduction and substitution that reveals what is essential in the actions and that moves the body away from daily techniques, creating a tension, a difference in potential, through which energy passes.

The body's extra-daily techniques consist of physical procedures which appear to be based on the reality with which everyone is familiar, but which follow a logic not immediately recognisable.

In noh, the term 'energy' can be translated as *ki-hai*, which means the profound agreement (*hai*) of the spirit (*ki*) with the body. Spirit here is used in the sense of spirit as *pneuma*,

34. Kathakali student practising an eye exercise.
35. Iben Nagel Rasmussen as Kattrin, the mute daughter of Mother Courage, in Odin Teatret's *Brecht's Ashes* (1982).

18

'breath'. In both India and Bali, the word *prana* is equivalent to *ki-hai*. These are inspiring images, but they are not advice that can guide us. In fact, they allude to something which is beyond the master's influence; that which is called the expression, the 'subtle charm' of the performer's art.

When Zeami was writing about *yugen*, 'the subtle charm', he used the dance called shirabioshi as an example. Shirabioshi was a dancer in the thirteenth century; she danced dressed as a man, a sword in her hand. The reason why so often, especially in the East, but also in the West, the high point of the actor's art seemed to be reached by men playing female characters or women playing male characters is because, in those cases, the actor or actress was doing exactly the opposite of what a modern performer usually does when dressed as a person of the opposite sex. The traditional cross-dressed performer is not disguised but divested of the mask of his or her sex in order to allow a soft or vigorous temperament to shine through. This performance temperament is independent of the behaviour pattern to which a man or woman must conform because of the specific culture to which they belong.

In the performances of various cultures, masculine and feminine characters are represented by those temperaments that are culturally identified as being 'naturally' appropriate to the characters' sex. Representation of the distinguishing temperaments of the sexes is therefore, in theatrical works, the most subject to convention. This representation is so profoundly conditioned that it is almost impossible to differentiate between sex and temperament. When a performer plays a person of the opposite sex, identification with the specific temperament of one sex or the other is fractured. This is perhaps the moment in which the opposition between *lokadharmi* and *natyadharmi*, between daily behaviour and extra-daily behaviour, leaves the physical plane and reaches another not immediately recognisable plane. A new physical presence and a new spiritual presence are revealed through the fracture – which in performance is paradoxically accepted – of masculine and feminine rôles.

The most apt but least usable translation of the term 'energy' emerged from one of my conversations with Indian dancer Sanjukta Panigrahi. It was the least usable because it translates the experience of a point of departure as well as a great result, but does not translate the experience of the process of achieving the result. Sanjukta Panigrahi said that energy is called *shakti*, creative energy which is neither masculine nor feminine but which is represented by the image of a woman. For this reason, in India, only women are given the title *Shakti amsha*, 'part of *shakti*'. But a performer of either sex, said Sanjukta, is always *shakti*, energy which creates.

* * * * *

After considering the dance of oppositions on which the performer's life is based and the contrasts that the performer consciously amplifies, and after examining the balance that he or she chooses to make precarious and then exploits, the image of *shakti* can perhaps become a symbol of that which we have not spoken here: the fundamental question of how to become a *good* performer?

In one of her dances, Sanjukta Panigrahi shows Ardhanarishwara, Shiva half-male, half-female. This is followed by the Danish actress Iben Nagel Rasmussen presenting *Moon and Darkness*. We are in Bonn, at the end of the International

36–38. Kabuki actor (**top**) (eighteenth-century print): performing the action of seeing requires the engagement not only of the eyes but of the whole body, which is directed towards the object in view; (**centre**) Sanjukta Panigrahi's *shakti*; (**bottom**) Kosuke Nomura's *ki-hai*.

School of Theatre Anthropology, where teachers and students from different continents have been working together for a month on the cold, technical, pre-expressive foundation of the performer's art. The song that accompanies Sanjukta's dance says:

I bow before you
You who are both male and female
Two gods in one
You whose male half has the vivid colour of a champak
    flower
And whose female half has the pallid colour
Of the camphor flower

The female half jingles with golden arm bracelets
The male half is adorned with bracelets of serpents
The female half has love-eyes
The male half meditation-eyes

The female half has a garland of almond flowers
The male half has a garland of skulls
Dressed in dazzling clothes
Is the female half
Nude, the male half

The female half is capable of all creation
The male half is capable of all destruction

I turn to you
Linked to the God Shiva
Your wife
I turn to you
Linked to the Goddess Shiva
Your husband

Iben Nagel Rasmussen sings a shaman's lament for a destroyed people. She then reappears as an adolescent stammering joyously on the threshold of a world at war. The Asian actress and the Western actress seem to be moving far apart, each one deep in her own culture. Nevertheless, they meet. They seem to transcend not only their own personalities and sex, but even their own artistic skills and show something that is beyond all this.

A performer's master knows how many years of work lie behind these moments. But still it seems that something flowers spontaneously, neither sought for nor desired. There is nothing to be said. One can only watch, as Virginia Woolf watched Orlando: 'A million candles burned in Orlando, without him having thought of lighting even a single one'.

39. Shiva Ardhanarishwara: androgynous figure (seventh century AD bas-relief, Archaeological Museum, Jhalawar, India).
40. (**opposite**) *The Wave at Kanagawa*: twentieth plate in the series *Thirty-Six Views of Mount Fuji*, by Hokusai (1760–1849).

Artaud

'The theatre is the state, the place, the point where one can apprehend the human anatomy; with the human anatomy, one can heal and direct life.'

Zeami

'In the performance of noh there are three basic elements: Skin, Flesh, and Bone.

The three are almost never found together in the same actor.

When it comes to explaining the elements of Skin, Flesh and Bone in terms of the noh, then what can be described as Bone represents that exceptional artistic strength that a gifted actor shows naturally in his performance and which comes to him of itself through his inborn ability. Flesh can doubtless be defined as that element visible in a performance that arises from the power of the actor's skill that he has obtained by his mastering of the Two Basic Arts of chant and dance. Skin, on the other hand, may be explained as a manner of ease and beauty in performance that can be obtained when the two other elements are thoroughly perfected. To put it another way: when considering the art that comes from Sight, the art that comes from Sound and the art that comes from the Heart, it can be said that Sight should be equated with Skin, Sound with Flesh, and the Heart with the Bone.'

Can the sea rise above the mountain tops?

Nicola Savarese

Anatomy is the description of life by means of its absence. Anatomy celebrates the splendour and the superior geometries of the life of corpses; therefore life can only become the object of knowledge and observation when it ceases to be life. Life is either lived or described. In mathematics, one finds reasoning by means of the absurd; in anatomy, one finds its parallel: reasoning by means of absence. (Giorgio Celli, *La Scienza del Comico – The Science of the Comic*)

In Japan at the beginning of the nineteenth century, artists such as Hokusai and Hiroshige learned and soon appropriated Italian perspective. Moreover, they mastered it to such a degree that they were able to use it to create marvellous effects, such as the elaboration of vertiginous contrasts between foreground and background. This was a totally new possibility and one which would be applied in the West only much later, when photography became free of the influence of painting and cinema free of the influence of the theatre. In fact, as can be seen in Hokusai's extraordinary painting of a wave, which goes beyond geometric perspective and becomes a visual paradox (the sea rises above the mountain top, ill.40, p. 21), the Japanese artists' way of seeing was three generations ahead of its time.

Hokusai's *Wave* not only shows how the sea can rise up above the mountain tops, it also suggests to us a way of looking the impossible, of taking an appropriate if risky point of view, between the waves. This dictionary proposes both a point of view and a risk: the performer's anatomy, the result of research into scenic *bios*, is a dissection. It is contrary to, the opposite of, spontaneity and creativity, one might even say of life in art. The carefully separated parts might not be able to be reassembled. And yet, as the great physicist Niels Bohr affirmed, opposites are complementary. This is why Eisenstein prefers to dedicate his writings to Salieri rather than to Mozart: Salieri's meticulous and obscure work – the dissection of music – was in opposition to Mozart's genius while at the same time being complementary to it.

In any case, a divided organism never regains its former life. Neither is it the task of the anatomist to recreate life. Can the life of a performer on the stage emerge from the pages of a book? Can Mount Fuji sink below the sea?

The anatomy which this dictionary seeks to reconstruct is the result of a school of seeing. The tangle of doubts, the erroneous experiments, the long journeys of approximation, all the comings and goings of investigation which precede and follow results are absent from these pages. And also missing are those contradictory aspects that make ISTA a laboratory in continuous ferment: the continuation of the school above and beyond the periods when it functions as a practical and theoretical activity; the relationship between recognised masters and auto-didactic students; the contribution of multiple cultures by way of the history of individual collaborators.

1. 'The water-seller's dance', illustration from Hokusai's *Odori hitori keiko* (*Dance Lessons for Oneself*), album printed in 1815.

Finally, the guiding motives which have permeated daily experience – the overcoming of the false differentiations between actor, dancer and mime; the confrontation/meeting between art and science; learning to see, and especially learning to learn – necessarily appear here, in the absence of motion and life, as words and images.

Can the sea rise up above the mountain tops?

Hokusai's *Wave* shows men, boats and Mount Fuji. The men and their efforts are but details in the great flux of nature. According to Zen, there are four points of view with respect to the wave:

1. Children think that the wave is a thing, a separate body of water which moves on the surface of the sea, distinct from other waves and distinct from the sea itself. When, however, one teaches them to look more attentively, they discover that they cannot make out the wave as a separate thing: the wave is a phenomenon which moves in the sea. It still makes sense to speak of the wave, but as an entity that is only theoretically separate.

2. The wave is about to crash into both the boats and Mount Fuji.

3. The wave does not crash into Mount Fuji because Mount Fuji is very far away, even though it seems to be *underneath* the wave.

4. Neither the boats nor the sea nor the mountain nor the sky are made of paper. One looks for paper but it can't be found and yet all these things are nothing but paper. In fact, there is no movement, and distance, wetness or dryness, life or death, do not exist.

In a performance – which is not made of paper – movement, distance, wetness and dryness, life and death, do exist, but only as a reflection of a fiction. And yet it has been said that not only listening to music, but also the perception of forms and reflected images can make us dance within ourselves.

In 1815, after having published his famous album, *Excerpts from the Plays*, fifty-six scenes taken from the most famous kabuki plays of the seventeenth and eighteenth centuries, in which all the great kabuki heroines reigned in delicate colours, Hokusai published another work, a small collection of drawings entitled *Dance Lessons for Oneself*.

This booklet is a series of black and white plates, each one of which shows four or five dancers: to the right and left of their arms and feet straight or curved lines indicate the complete paths of the movements begun by each limb. By studying the diagrams and the brief accompanying notes, the most popular Japanese dances could be learned: the ferryman's dance, the dance of the evil spirit, the clown's dance, the water-seller's dance (ill.1, p.22).

On the last page, Hokusai wrote, with his customary irony:

If I have made any errors in the description of the movements and steps, please forgive me. I drew as I dreamed, and a spectator's dream cannot contain quite everything. If you want to learn to dance well, learn from a master.

Although my dream cannot turn you into a true dancer, it can become an album. What I finally recommend to you, if you wish to dance, is to put your snuff-boxes and teacups somewhere safe because if you don't, no matter how careful you try to be, you'll always end up with broken pieces of china on the floor.

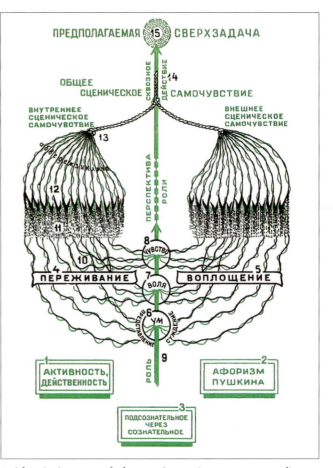

2. (**above**) Anatomy of the actor's creative process according to Stanislavsky: 1. Physical action 2. The sentence of Pushkin 3. The subconscious through the conscious technique 4. The living experience 5. Personification 6. Intellect 7. Will 8. Feeling 9. Rôle: perspective of the rôle, line of actions 10, 11, 12. Spiritual work and physical work 13. Inner and external scenic sensibility 14. General scenic sensibility 15. Principal problems.

3. (**below**) Technique disfigures anatomy: Rudolf Nureyev's foot.

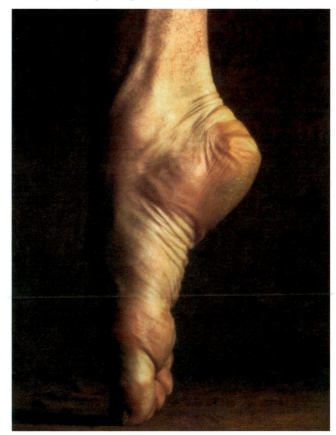

Western examples

Fabrizio Cruciani

Founding fathers and pedagogical theatre at the beginning of the twentieth century

The history of theatre in the twentieth century is not only the story of the performances. One only needs to compare the contents of any history book with what the reviews of the period say in order to see how a large part of the theatre iceberg has been submerged by historians.

Appia, Craig, Fuchs, Stanislavsky, Reinhardt, Meyerhold, Copeau: the men who are the history of twentieth-century theatre established practices and poetics that cannot be confined to one or more performances. The lines of tension have been the utopias, the continually restructured foundations of the theatre of the future, the cultural nuclei which have been consolidated around and through the theatre. It is a culture which settles like a halo around the making of theatre, lasting and penetrating, surrounding those fragile and temporal entities (the performances) in which the passion and work of theatre practitioners was manifest.

Schools, ateliers, laboratories, centres: these are the places where theatrical creativity has been expressed with the greatest degree of determination.

The practices and poetics of the great masters led to a different kind of theatre. The essential element: pedagogy, the search for the formation of a 'new man' in a different and renewed theatre and society, the search for a way of work that may keep an original quality and whose values are not measured by the success of performances but rather by the cultural tensions which the theatre provokes and defines. In such a situation, it was no longer possible to teach theatre; one had to begin to educate, as Vakhtangov emphasised. His

frenetic didactic activity was certainly a way of responding to the numerous and pressing questions being posed by young actors – as is described in his biography by Zakhava and Gorchakov – as well as being an expression of his own creative fervour.

Educating in creativity, transmitting experiences, setting up schools, establishing a teaching process: there were many fertile initiatives which were of necessity ambiguous. They had to do with both the search for rules that could concretise an operative form of training and with expressive experimentation in order to give form and substance to an idea and a cultural project. Schools are born and continue to exist not for immediate and personal reasons but in order to last and to achieve objective goals.

Academic theatre schools have teachers and courses (and thus a plan, an ideology and rules); and they were also part of Meyerhold's schools and the Proletkult schools, Copeau's Vieux Colombier and the Copiaus schools, Dullin's Atelier as well as the many different schools that sprang up in the effervescent and heretical German culture. If, on the one hand, a school (like the theatre) is a compromise with what already exists, on the other hand it is a place where utopias become realities, where the tensions that sustain the theatrical act take form and are put to the test. In an age in which the theatre of the present lives as an imminence of the possible theatre of the future, change and mutation have become *institutionalised* in theatre's micro-societies. Schools are started in order to renew the theatre, to lay the foundations of the theatre of the future and to enlarge the perspectives of the future of the theatre.

Creative process, theatre school and theatre culture

'Out of the necessity for a new organism', says Copeau in an interview in 1926, 'arises the necessity for a school, something which is no longer simply a group of students directed by a single master, but a real community capable of being self-sufficient and of responding to all its own needs.' The interviewer, Anton Giulio Bragaglia, goes on to explain with evident and polemical partiality, 'not schools: *The* Theatre School', agreeing with Copeau that 'school and theatre are the same thing'.

The problem of 'what to teach' is thus replaced by the more dynamic, artistic and hazardous problem of who teaches, and how.

In the last chapter of *My Life in Art*, 'The results and the future', Stanislavsky puts his artistic life on the balance: he first speaks of his work as actor and director and points out that he developed himself 'principally in the field of the spiritual creation of the actor' more than in the field of direction. He experimented with every form of poetics (indeed, 'all the ways and means of creative work'), from realism to symbolism to futurism, with all the means of investigation of mise-en-scène of his time; but centre stage, he sees only the talented actor in spite of the fact

1. Konstantin Sergeyevich Stanislavsky (1863–1938), a few months before his death, surrounded by students, actors and directors during a rehearsal at his studio.

that, as he writes, 'I did not succeed in finding a scenic source which helped rather than hindered artistic work' because he was searching for a simplicity that comes 'from a rich not a poor imagination'.

The central problem for Stanislavsky was that 'the actor's rules of creation have not been studied and many people consider such study superfluous and even dangerous'. The art of the theatre is based on talent but gains substance with technique, Stanislavsky says, and it is obvious that this demands the 'necessity of acquiring experience and mastery', training and virtuosity. There are no available examples or methods for the transmission of the actor's art. All the great actors, the men and women of the theatre, and scholars as well, have written about the performer's art, but it has always been a case, Stanislavsky continues, of philosophy or criticism based on results. 'There is no practical guide' beyond certain oral traditions, and yet, in order to escape from fortuitousness and dilettantism, 'elementary psycho-physical and psychological laws', as yet not studied, are necessary.

Stanislavsky writes this in 1924; young people (on the Left) reject him and he desires neither to disguise himself as one of them nor to become a useless and intolerant old man; he decides that his task is to transmit his knowledge and experience, so as to avoid both the prejudices and the discoveries of what is already known. By 1924 he had already set up the Studios in a passionate, exasperated and unsatisfied search for truth in a pedagogical situation. Then, in his book, in half a page, he reveals the treasure that he has discovered and passed on: his method of the actor's work.

Theatrical pedagogy as an expression of creativity is, in the uncertain and exhausting experience of Stanislavsky's Studios, a theatrical culture. The System, which will later be used to found theatre schools, is imparted to us through Stanislavsky's books, conceived of as a kind of didactic work that uses the technique, if not the form, of the novel in order to safeguard the vitality of the experience to be communicated.

Stanislavsky and Copeau belonged to different worlds and used different means, but both found it necessary to give the theatre meaning and dignity, and they shared a common point of departure: the struggle against the theatrical institutions of the time, their lazy conservatism, and the fight against the nonchalance of the theatrical profession. The theatre and the profession seemed to them, and not only to them, to have been reduced to false, decomposing remnants, inadequate for their necessities and their expressive aspirations and those of their time. Both were aware that, in Copeau's words, 'art and profession are not two separate things', but that the profession, like the tradition, could no longer remain what one already knew it to be and that it must logically become the search for a profession which, from time to time, and always as a singular event, declares its own ontological necessity.

Meyerhold also considers his schools as the place where different techniques are learned, techniques which are not aimed at a privileged performance system; and Reinhardt's

2–3. (**above**) Training in the Stanislavsky Studios in Moscow, following the line of physical actions; (**below**) exercises with sticks and representations of the figure of Nike (Victory).

eclecticism is fundamentally an invitation to use the most diverse techniques in a professional way, without prejudice. The freedom and commitment of the theatre practitioner are fragile, conditioned as they are by media culture and the making of performances in a specific societal context. But at the beginning of the 1900s, this freedom seemed to have been rediscovered in a new development of the creative process, by means of the expansion of methodological and technical horizons. Now, it is the practitioners of theatre themselves who, with their actions and with their words, change the mental horizon of the spectator's expectations.

The objective of the pedagogical situation is not the *dernier cri* (the 'latest thing') but rather the *premier cri* (the 'first thing') (these are Copeau's words): the willingness to build up the process of the training of creativity, the willingness to learn how to acquire the knowledge that will help one choose what to learn.

Also for this reason (as well as being an expression of the theatre culture of the century's first decades), the school is the special place where the today of the future is lived, a separate community (separate from the city, from the theatre, from the 'normal' or bourgeois world): in the experiments conducted by Stanislavsky and Sulerzhiski, with the moral pre-eminence which the latter gave to physical work; in Copeau's country retreat at the time of the first Vieux Colombier and later in Copiaus's Burgundy; in

4. Anton Chekhov (1860–1904), reading from *The Seagull* at the Moscow Art Theatre in 1899. Stanislavsky is seated on his right, Meyerhold is on the far right, and Nemirovich-Danchenko is standing on the far left.

We must give more room and deeper roots to the company spirit, we must find life styles which are favourable to the profession, an atmosphere of intellectual, moral and technical training, a discipline, traditions. The rebirth of the theatre which has been dreamed of for so long, and which is still being evoked today, seemed to me to be first and foremost a rebirth of man in the theatre.

Copeau wrote these words in 1931, in *Memories of the Vieux Colombier*. They express the opinion held by Copeau (and many others) that the new theatre was not born of the theatre and in the theatre but by the salvaging of the theatre's cultural, social and human complexity as a form of expressive communication and as a means for the realisation of human beings.

Institutionalised theatre schools had been founded and continued to be founded in response to other needs and belonged to another culture. But the studios, laboratories and masters' schools of the early 1900s were founded in order to provide the conditions for creative experience, as the theatre's workplace, as culture, as a long-term possibility. The director-teachers used these opportunities not only to train students for the theatre, or for their own theatres, but also to forge the implements of their own creativity.

In the first *Conversations for the Bolshoi School* (transcribed by Antarova), we can read how Stanislavsky, when he set up a studio, began by working on the basic problems of ethics and artistic efficacy with his students.

In the final pages of Attinger's book, we can read about the spirit of the commedia dell'arte; and in Silvio D'Amico's interview with Copeau, we read about how Copeau organised the work in Burgundy as a continuity of private, daily and artistic concerns.

We can read about the teaching methods Meyerhold used in his classes at the Borodinskaja Street studio (described in his magazine, *The Love of Three Oranges*), about his 'liberating processes' and about his catalogue of theatrical techniques.

Jaques-Dalcroze's Hellerau school with the religions of the body in nature (which took so many forms, especially in Germany); and in the final version of Laban's 'School of Art', in Truth Mountain in Ascona, with its particular ceremonies; but also in the auto-pedagogical and multi-directed diversity of the first agitprop groups and of the Bauhaus students.

Behind each of these experiences lie different schools and different poetics, but all share in common a reflection on the creative process, a reflection which is an expression of a culture and of a dynamic poetics. It must be understood that these schools and pedagogical aspirations are neither something 'apart' nor moments of crisis nor a lack of artistic creativity, as if the inability to create performances led to teaching instead. When speaking of the first decades of the twentieth century it is perhaps more useful and correct to speak of director-teachers rather than of theatrical pedagogy. The school experience is a complex phenomenon: an organic expression of their maturity and artistic creativity and a lucid demand made by their poetics.

Author's pedagogy

Copeau said that there are no rules in the theatre but that, in order to work, one must believe in them anyway. The director-teachers' search for rules is more a necessary part of *doing* than a theoretical necessity to *know*. Pedagogy as a creative act is a realisation of the need to create a theatrical culture, a dimension of the theatre which performances only partially satisfy and which the imagination translates in terms of vital tension. This is why theatre in the first decades of the century existed primarily through pedagogy (before it became organised and didactic) and why pedagogy can be seen as a red thread in the continuity of the most significant theatrical experiences of the time.

Moreover, it makes it possible for us to see certain connections with the rich and effervescent culture of the time: not only performances in relation to the theatre but also the theatre in relation to the cultural experience of a society that is living through the desperation of its own too rapid and brutal transformation.

5. Jacques Copeau (1879–1949), reading the script of *A Woman Killed by Tenderness* by Thomas Heywood in the courtyard of the Vieux Colombier Theatre. Also seen are actor Charles Dullin (1885–1949), first on the left; Louis Jouvet (1887–1951), standing, third from the right; and Suzanne Bing (1885–1967), first on the right.

6. Physical exercises for Vieux Colombier actors, led by Karl Böhm in the theatre's courtyard (Paris, 1913). Actor Charles Dullin is third from the left. Of all of Copeau's students, it was Dullin who was most responsible for the development of the physical training techniques at the school of his Atelier Theatre.

When we read Sklovskij, we get a glimmer of Meyerhold's teaching methods in the directing class at GVYRM (Advanced State Laboratories for Direction). Sklovskij also describes Eisenstein's visit to Meyerhold's class and emphasises how necessary it is to learn to create new conventions above and beyond those no longer perceived as such ('we must not forget how conventional the realistic theatre is'). He goes on to lament the fact that Stanislavsky's and Meyerhold's rehearsals had not been filmed so that new directors 'could become accustomed to learning and to being astonished'.

We have evoked them here to help us remember that in the twentieth century and in opposition to academic didactics, there existed a long-term theatrical experience, above and beyond performances, and that the theatre pedagogy of the founding fathers is artistic creation through the teaching and learning of theatre.

7. Examples of 'biomechanical' exercises invented by Meyerhold for his actors' training.

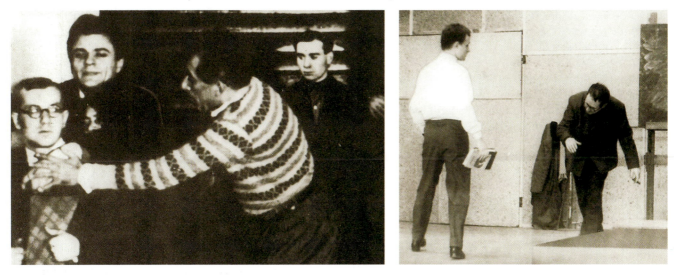

8–9. (**left**) Vsevolod Emilevic Meyerhold (1874–1939) with his actors during a rehearsal of Mayakovsky's *The Bug* (1929); (**right**) Bertolt Brecht (1898–1956) with Ekkehard Schall during a rehearsal of *The Life of Galileo* in the Berliner Ensemble's rehearsal hall.

The word 'to teach' derives from the Gothic 'taiku': sign (our word token). It is the mission of the teacher to observe what goes unnoticed by the multitude. The teacher is an interpreter of signs. (Sybil Moholy-Nagy in Paul Klee, Pedagogical Sketchbook, Faber & Faber, London and Boston, 1981)

It is the first day of work that determines the sense of one's path through theatre. (Eugenio Barba)

Pedagogy is the relationship between master and student: the secret of the transmission of art lies in the personalisation of this relationship. With few exceptions, the master–student relationship has to a large extent deteriorated in traditional Western theatre schools. But in other cultures, this living transmission of art is still practised and is the essential reason why some artistic and spiritual traditions have existed for generations and have been passed on unchanged, without losing their power.

An Indian example

Rosemary Jeanes Antze

The syllable gu *means shadows (darkness)*
the syllable ru, *he who disperses them.*
Because of his power to disperse darkness
the guru *is thus named.*
        (Advayataraka Upanishad, verse 5)

Knowledge in ancient India was oral in nature. The early religious texts, the Vedas and Upanishads, were passed on for many generations by word of mouth, only later to be committed to the written word. An oral tradition demanded a living representative – the *guru* – who both embodied and transmitted the traditional knowledge. In Vedic times it was customary for a father to pass on his learning to his son, thus perpetuating the knowledge through *parampara*, meaning lineage, progeny, uninterrupted row or series, succession or tradition. Here we have the main elements of the oral tradition: the teacher or *guru*, the student or *shishya*, and the unbroken line of knowledge or *parampara*, in which the master and disciple are individual participants in a tradition which stretches beyond both.

Continuity in the arts relies on human beings. Written texts may record certain principles, but the belief in the efficacy of the living teacher goes back to the time of the ancient sage/teacher, Narada: 'What is learnt from reliance on books and is not learnt from a teacher does not shine in an assembly'. Moreover, since dance and music communicate through non-verbal means and their nuances of expression lie beyond words, these arts are especially indebted to the living oral tradition. Students rely on their chosen *guru* as the key to the rich world of creative endeavour.

The religious *guru* is perhaps the most visible embodiment of the traditional teacher and assumes many forms, ranging from the long-haired ascetic in retreat high in the Himalayas to the jet-setting yogi with a large Western following. In India it is not unusual to seek out and follow a *guru* in spiritual matters. Often a teacher's guidance is considered essential to achieving the ultimate goal of Hindu life – *moksha* or release. Although *gurus* are generally male, there is a female example from Madras, Jnanananda, who is dubbed 'mother *guru*'. In an interview with C. White, an historian of religions, she states the rule of thumb for finding an appropriate *guru*: 'When the *chela* (disciple) is ready for the *guru*, the *guru* comes'. Her advice for subsequent behaviour towards the teacher is equally typical: 'When one finds a true *guru*, one should surrender completely.'

Guru *as parent, honoured preceptor*

Originally the *guru* was the one who performed the purificatory ceremonies over a Brahman boy and who instructed him in the Vedas. In this rôle the *guru* became a second and superior father because the ability to impart spiritual knowledge ranked higher than the capacity to give physical birth. The way that the *guru* becomes a second parent at the boy's initiation is found in the *Atharva Veda* IX: 5–8: 'When the teacher accepts the *Brahmachari* (student from the high Brahman caste) as a disciple, he treats him as an embryo within his own body. He carries him for three nights in his belly; when he is born, the gods assemble to see him.'

Even today the view of *guru* as second parent is accepted by a surprisingly large number of young people. This aptitude is documented in a recent study that dealt with the modern educational system. A questionnaire presented the following alternatives:

1. A teacher should really be like a second parent to his students and should ensure their all-round development.
2. A teacher should primarily be concerned with teaching his or her subject in the classroom and should not worry about student behaviour outside the classroom.

Over 90 per cent of high-school and college students in eight different states chose the first statement acknowledging the teacher as second parent, confirming that the ideal of *guru*, whose traditional rôle extends well beyond the classroom, is indelibly lodged in the minds of most students.

Dance *gurus* too are often viewed as surrogate parents since they give birth to the dancer in each of their students. One of the expert odissi dancers, Kum Kum Das, herself a mature woman and mother, speaks with warmth of the father–daughter relationship she maintains with her *guru*, while exponents of the temple dance tradition were actually adopted so that mother and teacher became one.

Higher than a parent, a *guru* can also be placed almost on a level with a god and revered accordingly. His blessing is essential for success in any endeavour. The following verses from the *Advayataraka Upanishad* elevate the *guru* to super-human proportions:

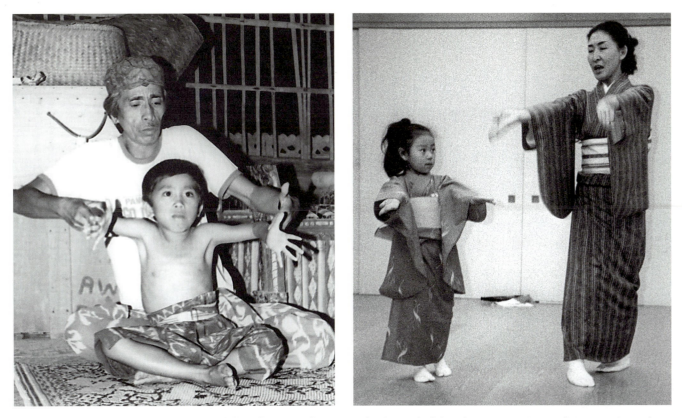

10–11. Balinese dancer I Made Pasek Tempo (**left**) and Japanese dancer Katsuko Azuma (**right**) teaching arm positions to their respective students. In Asian theatrical traditions, the student usually stands in front of the master and learns by direct imitation of the master's actions. Sometimes, however, especially at the beginning of the apprenticeship, the master stands behind the student and guides the actions directly, in order to transmit both movements and rhythms by means of physical contact (cf. ill.5 p.279).

Only the guru is transcendent Brahman
Only the guru is the supreme path
Only the guru is highest knowledge
Only the guru is the last refuge
Only the guru is the ultimate limit
Only the guru is the greatest riches.
Because he teaches that,
The guru is the highest of all.
(verses 17 and 18)

Such extravagant praise is not without its counterpart in action. In kathak dance teacher Durga Lal's practice studio in Delhi, a photograph of his late *guru*, decorated with flower blossoms and wafted with incense, hangs in a corner. Upon entering the room, each student goes first to the picture and respectfully touches her hands to the base of the portrait then immediately to her closed eyes. Next she proceeds to the present *guru*, touches his feet and bows again – in a manner similar to the obeisance performed before a deity in a temple.

The one-to-one relationship between *guru* and *shishya* is the cornerstone of the learning system, and implies a close and lasting contact between the two, based on love and devotion. Ravi Shankar names the teacher as the first of three concepts at the heart of the music tradition: *guru*, *vinaya* and *sadhana*. For a serious artist, choosing a *guru* is more important than choosing a husband or wife. Then *vinaya* follows, which is 'humility tempered with love and worship'.

Not only reverence but also fear can be part of a student's attitude towards his or her *guru* – and contribute to his or her learning. Modelled on a father–son relationship, the ideal rapport in music is intimate yet hierarchical, rather than a meeting of friends or equals. The third concept, *sadhana*,

which means practice and discipline, involves complete faithfulness to the *guru*'s tradition and absolute obedience to his instructions in art and life.

Guru-kula, *study in the* guru's *home*

It is necessary for a *guru* to be in constant contact with his student in order to be truly able to nurture the artistic skills and attitudes in his *shishya*. The ancient system arranged this through *guru-kula*, in which the student was incorporated into the *guru*'s household, almost as a family member. *Kula* is the Sanskrit word for family, lineage or house; hence, *guru-kula* means learning 'at the house of the *guru*'. This custom of going to live with the teacher, central to the system of ancient education, was the prevalent manner of learning music up to the generation now dominating the concert stage in north and south India. For most present-day students of dance, *guru-kula* belongs to an idealised past. Restrictions of time in the modern rhythm of life permit perhaps a few months of residing and learning in the *guru*'s home, but seldom the years of a full training as in the past.

A serious and celebrated dance school, Kalakshetra, founded in Madras in 1936 by Rukmini Devi, was established on principles that tried to retain the qualities and atmosphere of *guru-kula*. It is a boarding school where teachers and students live and work together for most of the year, with students staying for a minimum four-year course. The late master, Chandu Pannikar, who was the pillar of the Kalakshetra kathakali department, commanded utmost respect, demanded full attention and exacted strict discipline. Those who studied under him, including his son, say that students of today would not be up to the hardships

12–13. Sanjukta Panigrahi, age six, beginning her apprenticeship in odissi dance. 'I began to learn when I was five years old and I am still learning today. I had two masters. The first, Rukmini Devi (cf. ill.2 p.236), was perfect for technique. She was famous because in none of her students could one detect the least weak point, the least fault. My second master, Kelucharan Mahapatra, who is still my master today, says that the great artist is s/he who masters technique in order to forget it, s/he who not only charms the spectators but succeeds in changing them.'

and discipline. 'Whenever you would visit him, he would make you do some practice – eyes, *talam* (rhythm), *mudras*. It was twenty-four hours work . . . Afterwards I realised why he scolded us, why he would get angry, even if someone who was sitting and watching praised us' (Kuniraman).

The *guru* would tell even tougher stories of his own teacher, who once took him by the knot of his long hair and threw him against the wall, simply because he stopped doing the rhythm. But student life was not all trial. The close proximity with the *guru* also allowed the creativity of the master to flow whenever the mood took him. The susceptibility to mood – most critical in expressive art – was preserved and allowed within a disciplined structure of learning. Two dancers confirmed that even if inspiration came to the master in the middle of the night, he would not hesitate to call his students to him to impart his knowledge.

But the call of the *guru* did not always mean that dance instruction would be given. Another very important aspect of the *guru–shishya* relationship, especially possible in a *guru-kula* setting, is the 'service' the student performs for the master. Washing clothes, preparing and carrying hot water for a bath, giving massage and oil baths to the teacher are acts that many dancers mentioned. My odissi *guru* spoke of services he gave to his *guru*: cleaning dishes, doing shopping and conducting *puja*, or worship, in the *guru*'s house when he was away. I also saw students mending clothes and making travel arrangements for their *gurus*. Service and obedience in mundane tasks seem to demonstrate the dedication and humility in the student and worthiness to receive the knowledge and skill embodied in the teacher. As in the past, it remains an important element in the *guru–shishya* relationship today.

Guru-dakshina, *gifts and fees*

There was no prior arrangement for fees in the ancient system of education, and certain texts actually condemn teachers who stipulated payment as a condition for accepting students. However, the idea of *guru-dakshina*, gift for the *guru*, is a long-accepted and traditional practice. Early sources suggest the ideal: that the gift was simply to please the teacher, not an equivalent or compensation for the knowledge received. This ideal was based on the belief that knowledge was so sacred that even when a *guru* taught a single letter of the alphabet, he could never be adequately recompensed with worldly wealth. Nevertheless, *dakshina* was appropriate at the completion of studies. An ancient law, Manu II: 245–6, states that when the student is about to return home, 'he may offer his *guru* some wealth; the gift of a field, gold, a cow, or a horse, or even shoes or an umbrella, or a seat, corn, vegetables and clothes (either singly or together) may engender pleasure in the teacher.'

Naturally, this tradition of *guru-dakshina* has been perpetuated in contemporary situations. A *guru* who has given of his art and his love expects gratitude and respect in the form of gifts.

The major gift-giving still takes place at the time when basic training is completed, which in dance coincides with the occasion of a first performance, called *arangetram* in bharatanatyam. The standard practice was to give according to the student's abilities and the teacher's needs. The system is still fluid in concept although new expectations influence the choice and value of *dakshina* to a considerable degree. Dance *gurus* now generally receive a specified fee for their teaching services, so *guru-dakshina* becomes a source of luxury items. A new list of gifts suitable for *guru-dakshina* at the end of study could include a television set, tape recorder, moped, or the more traditional gift of clothing – perhaps a cashmere shawl or a gold necklace.

Ekalavya, disciple extraordinaire

An intriguing story of a *guru*–student relationship from the *Mahabharata*, which contains a striking example of *guru-dakshina*, seemed to be foremost in several people's minds when I tried to elicit *guru* stories. For the sake of brevity and to retain the spirit of the oral tradition, here is the version told to me by odissi *guru*, Ramani Ranjan Jena:

> Drona was the greatest of all *gurus*, and was the master of *dhanur beda*, the art of archery. He taught the sons of kings, both Pandavas and Kauravas (the two principal families of the epic who engaged in war with each other). One day Ekalavya caught sight of Drona and was filled with awe and love for the spirit of his *guru*. That power touched Ekalavya so deeply, but he was of humble and poor family so he had no rights to learn archery. Yet he was so inspired that he made an image of Drona the *guru*, practised archery before it, prayed to the *rupa* (image), and presented it with offerings. Then one fine day Drona and his students were out in the forest, and Drona caught sight of a dog, which had previously been barking and which now had an arrow piercing its snout – its nose through to its chin – that silenced the beast. Drona was astonished because only he knew the art of thus shooting an arrow, and wanted to know who was responsible. Ekalavya came forward and admitted the deed, confessing how he had taken Drona for his *guru* without the master's knowledge and how he had learnt the art. Guru Drona therefore asked for his due, *guru-dakshina*, the present offered to the teacher when training was complete. Because he feared that Ekalavya would become greater than himself, Drona asked for the thumb of the student's right hand. Ekalavya gave happily what the master requested . . . Ekalavya's mother was in tears, but the art of archery needed to be kept in the hands of the ruling class. The eager student had overstepped his bounds and gone beyond what destiny had ordained as possible in this life.

This story well illustrates many features of the *guru–shishya* relationship – though it is in itself an unorthodox situation: the dedication, intense practice, obedience and complete surrender of the student's will to the *guru*'s demands. An important detail omitted from the above version is the fact that Drona had promised his favourite student, Arjuna, that no one should be a greater archer than he. One explanation for the harsh request could be the *guru*'s wish to keep his word given to his chosen and legitimate student. The fact that Ekalavya seems to be perfectly willing to accept his *guru*'s demand demonstrates that the blessings of the *guru* are more valued than the learning of a skill. A dedicated and senior dancer-teacher told me that the respect, obedience and service rendered to a *guru* are meant to break down the ego until gradually the ego subsides and the true self emerges fully. In this light it is possible to interpret the initially shocking story of Ekalavya as one of high personal achievement in spiritual terms. Through his archery he mastered not only the bow, but also himself.

Guru–shishya–parampara

Up to this point, we have mostly considered the teacher–student relationship as a hierarchical one in the sense that a younger student owes respect to the elder master who is the source of knowledge. And yet the *guru–shishya* relationship is distinctly symbiotic in nature. An established bharatanatyam *guru*, Nana Kasar, whose classes I watched in Delhi, was quick to mention (in the presence of his students) that a good student draws out a teacher and a teacher can be inspired by and realised in his student.

The symbiotic relationship extends beyond the mutual dependence of *guru* and *shishya*. My odissi *guru* spoke one day of his belief that the *guru*, or perhaps the concept of *guru*, exists within oneself, that one holds the image and power of the *guru* in one's mind/heart. In the initial stages of the relationship, the teacher is responsible for giving birth to the artistic being of the student and for nurturing the pupil's skills by taking the rôle of second parent. Subsequently, the *guru* and his tradition are assimilated by and become contained within the disciple.

When set against the backdrop of tradition, *parampara*, the relationship between *guru* and student becomes more than just a meeting and exchange between two individuals. It serves as the vital link in the continuity of the dance. The words of three noted artists who all learnt from a distinguished bharatanatyam master, Muthukumara Pillai (1874–1960), capture a sense of the impact of a revered *guru* on the next generation: 'In his simple life, he embodied the *shastraic* concept of the real teacher, whose inspiration always remains an illumination in the minds of his students' (Mrinalini Sarabhai); 'He was the repository of a tremendous repertoire . . . For some of us the memory will remain fresh and serve as an inspiration to pass on to others what we have learnt' (Rukmini Devi); 'I know that what he imparted to me and to his other students is deathless' (Ram Gopal).

Here we see the *guru* as the inspiration that stays with the disciple and motivates further transmission. The dance continues to live and the *guru* is immortalised through his successors.

Extra-daily balance

The characteristic most common to actors and dancers from different cultures and times is the abandonment of daily balance in favour of a 'precarious' or extra-daily 'balance'. Extra-daily balance demands a greater physical effort – it is this extra effort that dilates the body's tensions in such a way that the performer seems to be alive even before he begins to express.

The performers of the various Asian traditions have codified the acquisition of a new balance and have fixed the basic positions that the student must learn and master through exercise and training. In India, for example, (ill.2) the body is bent according to a curved line that passes through the head, the trunk and the hips. This fundamental position is called the *tribhangi*, 'the three arches'. It is found in the statuary of all Buddhist temples and thus has spread throughout all cultures from Nepal to Japan (cf. *Opposition*).

Precarious balance is also found in Western theatre, as can be seen in this commedia dell'arte actor from the seventeenth century (ill.1), whose position strongly resembles the *tribhangi*. If we look at the silhouettes of these two figures, we notice that in both cases there is a deformation of the daily position of the legs and a reduction of the base of support in the foot.

Both bodies appear to have been broken and then reformed following a similar line.

In the most recent Western theatre tradition, in which the functions of actor and dancer have been separated, one finds this alteration of balance only in such strongly codified techniques as mime (ill.3) or classical dance.

Luxury balance

Why do all codified performance forms in both the East and the West contain this constant: the deformation of the daily techniques of walking, moving through space and keeping the body immobile? This deformation of daily body technique, this extra-daily technique, is essentially based on an alteration of balance. Its purpose is to create a condition of permanently

1–2. The commedia dell'arte character Frittellino (**above left**) in an engraving by Bernard Picart (1696), and odissi dancer Sanjukta Panigrahi (**above right**): cultural differences notwithstanding, the commedia dell'arte mask and the Indian dancer are transversed by analogous lines of force; likewise, the same balance principle is at work in both.
3. Etienne Decroux (**below**) in a typical mime *déséquilibre*.

unstable balance. By rejecting 'natural' balance, the Asian performer intervenes in the space by means of a 'luxury' balance, uselessly complex, seemingly superfluous and costing excess energy.

It can be said that this 'luxury' balance leads to stylisation and aesthetic suggestivity. This affirmation is generally accepted without question, with no attempt being made to find out why physical positions that alter the

natural being and the daily way of using the body have been chosen.

What exactly is happening?

Balance – the human ability to hold the body erect and to move in space in that position – is the result of a series of muscular relationships and tensions within our organism. The more our movements become complex, when we take longer steps than usual or hold the head more forward or more backward than usual, the more our balance is threatened. A whole series of tensions is set up just to keep the body from falling.

One tradition in European mime makes conscious use of this *déséquilibre*: not as a means of expression, but as a means of intensification of certain organic processes and aspects of the body's life. A change of balance results in a series of specific organic tensions which engage and emphasise the performer's material presence, but at a stage which precedes intentional, individualised expression.

(Eugenio Barba,
*Theatre Anthropology:
First Hypothesis*)

4. (**above left**) Dance opposition in jester, a German bronze from the fifteenth century (Victoria & Albert Museum, London).
5. (**above right**) Eugeni Vakhtangov (1883–1922) in a precarious balance position as the Fool in Shakespeare's *Twelfth Night* (Moscow Art Theatre Studio, 1919).
6. (**below**) Grete Wiesenthal (1885–1970) Austrian dancer of the 1930s in a position of exceptionally precarious balance, in a scene from *Donauwalzer*.

7–9. (**top**) Shiva Nataraja – Lord of the Dance, tenth century AD, bronze from southern India; (**bottom left**) the German dancer Gert Palucca; (**bottom right**) figure of Pantalone by Jacques Callot (engraving, 1616). The positions of these dancers, who are separated by great distances of time and space, are unequivocal proof of the rôle of extra-daily balance in the art of performance.

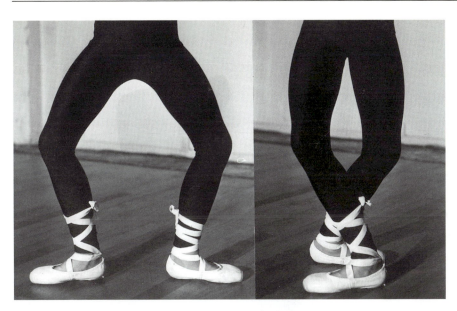

10. Precarious balance position in the classical European ballet *demi-plié*.

11–13. (**centre left**) Odin Teatret actress Roberta Carreri; (**centre right**) Purulia chhau dancer (India); (**below**) Pei Yanling, Peking Opera actress, in a precarious balance position achieved by an extreme spreading of the legs.

Extra-daily technique: the search for a new posture

In Japanese noh theatre, the actor walks without ever lifting his heels from the ground: he moves forward by sliding his heels. If one tries this, one immediately discovers that one's centre of gravity changes position, and that therefore one's balance also changes. If one wants to walk like a noh actor, the knees have to be slightly bent. This results in a slight downwards pressure from the vertebral column, and therefore from the whole body. It is exactly the position assumed when one prepares to jump.

In kabuki theatre, there are two different styles, *aragoto* and *wagoto*. In *aragoto*, the exaggerated style, the so-called law of diagonals is used: the actor's head must always be at one end of an acute diagonal line; the other end of the line is one of the feet (ill.14, p.36). The *wagoto* style is the 'realistic' style in kabuki. Here the actor moves in a way that is similar to the *tribhangi* of classical Indian dance.

In Indian odissi dance, the dancer's body is held as if the letter 'S' was passing through the hips, shoulders and head. The sinuosity of *tribhangi* is clearly visible in all classical Indian statues. In kabuki's *wagoto* form, the actor moves his body in a lateral, wave-like manner which requires a continuous action from the vertebral column. The actor's balance, and therefore also the relationship between his body weight and his base, the feet, is consequently changed.

In Balinese theatre, the actor-dancer pushes down with the soles of his feet at the same time as he lifts his toes, thus reducing his contact with the ground by almost one half. To avoid falling, he must spread his legs and bend his knees. The Indian kathakali actor pushes down with the sides of the feet, but the consequences are the same. This new base results in a fundamental change of balance: the actor stands with his legs spread and his knees bent (ill.15, p.36).

The rules for the only form of codified theatre in Europe, classical ballet, seem deliberately to force the dancer to move with precarious balance. This is true of both the basic positions and the entire range of movements such as *arabesques* and *attitudes*, where the weight of the whole body is supported by one leg, and even on the tips of the toes of one foot. One of the most important movements, the *plié*, consists of dancing with the knees bent, the best starting position for a pirouette or a jump (ill.10).

(Eugenio Barba, *Theatre Anthropology: First Hypothesis*)

Generalisations regarding balance

The balance of the human body is one of the functions of a complex system of levers made up of the bones, the joints and the muscles; the body's *centre of gravity* changes position as a consequence of the different attitudes and movements of this complex system of levers.

Muscular sense is our perception of the state of contraction or relaxation of the muscles and of the effort that the muscles make in order to hold a given weight. It is also the tactile sensation of the soles of the feet, which perceive the variations in the pressure exerted upon them by the rest of the body. This muscular sense conditions our balance in various body attitudes because it automatically indicates to us the limits within which we can move a part of the body without falling.

Statics. Mechanics teaches us that a body's *centre of gravity* is the point of balance of all the parts of that body and that the *line of gravity* is a line perpendicular to the ground from this point.

We also know that a body's centre of gravity is correctly situated when the line of gravity reaches the ground inside the perimeter of the *base of support*. This is the case for the human body when in a *standing position*. But since the skeleton is made up of so many mobile elements, the human body would not be able to stay in balance if all these elements were not held in place by the ligaments and by the work of the muscles.

One can deduce from the foregoing that in order to keep the body standing in a comfortable and symmetrical position, we need only a very slight participation from the muscles, because *the essential work is done by the ligaments.*

But if the subject under study moves from a normal standing position to a position *at attention*, the extensor muscles of the vertebral column, the gluteus maximus and the quadriceps contract immediately. In fact, in this position, the axes of the movements of extension and flexion of the joints (the joint between the atlas and the head, the joints of the vertebral column, the joints of the hip, the knee and the ankle) are seen to be in the same vertical plane as the line of gravity.

Because of the new orientation of these joints, the body is in an unstable balance position, and the various

14. Kabuki actor, Ichikawa Ennosoke, in an *aragoto* position.
15. Kathakali students from the Kalamandalam school in Kerala, India, in the basic position, the first posture learned at the beginning of apprenticeship.

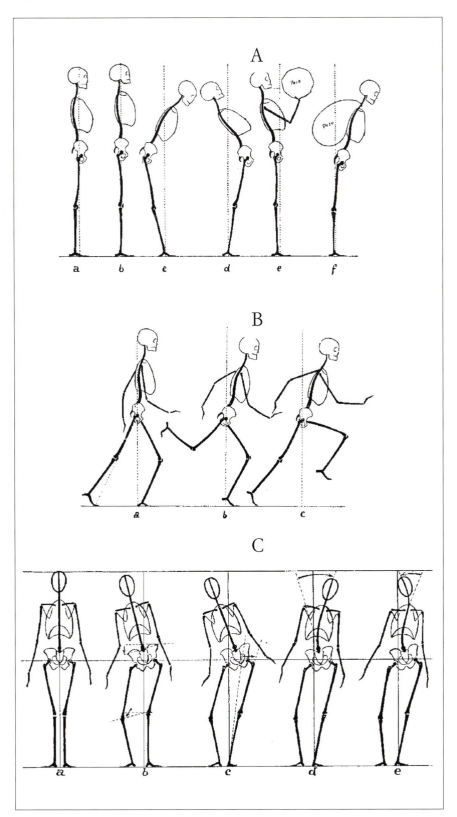

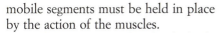

mobile segments must be held in place by the action of the muscles.

In all the positions taken by the body in which it rests on both feet, the centre of gravity will move at the same time as the body's axis, and the amount of muscular effort required to keep the body in balance will be in direct proportion to the degree of displacement of the body from the perpendicular of gravity.
(Angelo Morelli,
Anatomia per gli artisti
[*Anatomy for Artists*])

The study of balance makes it possible for us to understand how a *balance in action* generates a kind of *elementary drama*: the opposition of different tensions in the performer's body is sensed kinaesthetically by the spectator as a conflict between elementary forces. But in order to be able to move from a balance which is the result of minimum effort to a visualisation of contrary forces – and this is the image of the body of a performer who knows how to master balance – the balance must become dynamic. Muscles in action must replace the ligaments in the maintenance of the position.

16. Plates showing aspects of balance, from *Anatomia per gli artisti* (*Anatomy for Artists*), by Angelo and Giovanni Morelli. A: shift of the body relative to the line of gravity; B: the line of gravity in walking and running; C: the mechanism used to make the transition from an erect symmetrical position to an erect asymmetrical position (the line of the Indian *tribhangi* is also discernible in position (d) in this last drawing: cf. *Oppositions*).

17. Dynamic balance is clearly visible in the stationary poses of these Thai dancers: tension (and therefore dynamics) is underlined by the contrast resulting from the direction of the arms and legs (A and B) and the extreme spreading of the legs (C and D).

Balance in action

The performer's dynamic balance, based on the body's tensions, is a *balance in action*: it generates the sensation of movement in the spectator even when there is only immobility.

Artists consider this quality to be of prime importance: a painted figure which lacks this quality is, according to Leonardo da Vinci, doubly dead. It is first dead because it is a fiction and then dead again because it shows no movement of the mind or body. Modern artists have also demonstrated their preoccupation with this quality. In an interview with Charbonnier in 1951, Matisse said: 'Immobility is not an obstacle to the feeling of movement. It is a movement set at a level which does not carry the spectator's bodies along, but simply their minds'.

Actors and dancers must also be aware of the kinaesthetic consequences of their work, that is, the sensations that are experienced by the spectator witnessing the dynamic patterns of their scenic behaviour.

18–21. (**top**) Mayan dancer: mural at Bonampak (southern Mexico, ninth century AD). In the outline of the body position without costume, the alteration of balance can clearly be seen in the flexing of the head and trunk; (**centre**) the basic Balinese dance position also contains an alteration of balance created by crossing the feet; (**bottom left**) Etruscan dancer: fresco from the Triclinium tomb at Tarquinia, Italy (480–470 BC); (**bottom right**) Augusto Omolú, in the Afro-Brazilian dance of the orixás, work demonstration at Umeå ISTA, 1995.

Steel and cotton

'My master used to say that every performer has to find his own power centre. It could be imagined as a ball of steel in the centre of an triangle whose apex is the anus and whose other two angles are the corners of the pelvis at the level of the navel. The performer must succeed in centring the balance on this power point. If he finds it (but this is difficult to do, even today I sometimes don't find it), then all his movements will be powerful. But this power is not synonymous with tension or violence. My master said that the ball of steel was covered with layers of cotton, and thus resembled something soft which, deep in its centre, hides something hard. The performer's movement can be slow and soft and conceal its power, like the pulp of a fruit conceals the kernel.'

(Katsuko Azuma)

22. (**above right**) Peking Opera actor in a precarious balance position accentuated by the use of the typical black cloth boots with high white soles which are used for characters of high rank, such as emperors, generals and judges. The types of shoes worn by Peking Opera actors are based on the traditional footwear used in the Qing dynasty (1644–1911). Included among these are the *ts'ai chi'ao*, the special shoes used by women to deform their feet into the so-called 'lily feet' (cf.ill.6 p.74)
23–25. (**below left**) In kabuki, high clogs are used to increase height and modify the balance. Here the samurai Sukeroku displays his elegant costume in a characteristic *déséquilibre* position; (**below right**) jesters dancing in high shoes (eleventh-century miniature, Limoges, France).

26–29. (**above left**) Korean dancer in a painting by Kim Hong-do (eighteenth century). In the enlarged detail, the dancer's precarious balance and the line of the Indian *tribhangi* (cf. *Oppositions*) are easily discernible; (**above centre**) Katsuko Azuma in a buyo dance position: the spreading of the kimono and the simultaneous opening of the two fans visibly amplify (like a balanced letter 'V') the difficulty of the precarious position, which is nevertheless fully controlled by the dancer; (**above right**) Sogdian dancer (Tang Dynasty, AD 618–907). Sogdiana, a region corresponding today to Uzbekistan and Tajikistan and whose capital was Samarkand, was an important transit bridge between East and West on the Silk Road.

30–31. (**left**) Indian kathakali actor in a precarious balance position; (**right**) kathakali students training the same position. The young students (as opposed to the adult actor) keep the position by holding on to their big toes.

41

32–36. Dance consists of the continuous modulation of balance. Hence the apparent paradox of dances executed in kneeling positions, as in the following examples: (**top**) Balinese dancers performing the legong dance; (**centre left**) a Chinese divinity's dance with a scarf (a mural from Dunhuang, Tang dynasty, AD 618–906); (**centre right**) Susanne Linke in one of her early compositions; (**bottom**) bedhaya semang, a dance performed by women in the Javanese court in the sixteenth century, photographed at the end of the nineteenth century in the Royal Palace at Jogjakarta.

Why does the performer aim for a luxury balance? What does the performer's alteration of balance mean for the spectator?

In dancing and acting, the artist, his tool, and his work are fused into one physical thing: the human body. One curious consequence is that the performance is essentially created in one medium while it appears to the audience in another. The spectator receives a strictly visual work of art. The dancer uses a mirror occasionally; he also has at times a more or less vague visual image of his own performance; and of course as a member of a group or as a choreographer, he sees the work of other dancers. But as far as his own body is concerned, he creates mainly in the medium of the kinaesthetic sensations in his muscles, tendons and joints. This fact is worth noting, if only because some aestheticians have maintained that only the higher senses of vision and hearing yield artistic media.

All kinaesthetic shape is dynamic. Michotte has observed that 'movement seems to be essential to the phenomenal existence of the body, and posture is probably experienced only as the terminal phase of motion.' Merleau-Ponty points out that 'my body appears to me as posture'; and that, in contrast to visually observed objects, it does not have a spatiality of position but one of situation. 'When I stand in front of my desk and lean on it with both hands, the accent is all on my hands, while my entire body trails behind them like the tail of a comet. Not that I am unaware of the locations of my shoulders or hips, but they are only implied in that of my hands, and my entire posture is, as it were, readable through the hands' leaning on the desk'.

The dancer builds his work from the feelings of tension and relaxation, the sense of balance, which distinguish the proud stability of the vertical from the risky adventures of thrusting and falling. The dynamic nature of kinaesthetic experience is the key to the surprising correspondence between what the dancer creates by his muscular sensations and the image of his body seen by the audience. The dynamic quality is the common element uniting the two different media. When the dancer lifts his arm, he primarily experiences the tension of raising. A similar tension is visually conveyed to the spectator through the image of the dancer's arm.

Finally, it is essential for the performance of the dancer and the actor that visual dynamics be clearly distinguished from mere locomotion. I noted earlier that movement looks dead when it gives the impression of mere displacement. Of course, physically, all motion is caused by some kind of force. But what counts for artistic performance is the dynamics conveyed to the audience visually; for dynamics alone are responsible for expression and meaning.

(Rudolf Arnheim, *Art and Visual Perception*)

37–38. (**top**) Louis Jouvet (1887–1951), on the left, in Molière's *L'Ecole des femmes* (Paris, 1936). The *déséquilibre* in this scene is the result of Jouvet's attempt to kick the servant, and by the latter's escape. It should be remembered that the stage in the Italian-style proscenium-arch theatre was steeply sloping. This inclination, which facilitated perspective in stage design, obliged the actors to spread their legs in order to keep their balance. The use of the sloping stage in European theatre was not abandoned until towards the end of the nineteenth century; (**bottom**) Vertical section of Milan's Teatro della Scala, which was designed by Italian architect Giuseppe Piermarini (1734–1808) and completed in 1778. Note the stage's steep inclination.

Balance and imagination

In order to research the physiological bases of behaviour, experiments have been conducted that study 'the relationships between tonic postural activity (the regulating system of basic balance that makes it possible for man to maintain a standing position and keep his balance) and the motor activity that results in gesture and pantomime'. These experiments have been done with various subjects; the following text refers to those done with actors and athletes.

From the physiological point of view, the balance system is made up of several sensory-motor terminals, including externo-receptive elements (visual, auditory, tactile) and auto-receptive elements (muscular, tendonous, articular and vestibular). The proper functioning of these systems makes it possible for man to keep the projection of his centre of gravity inside the support polygon.

We know that man, whether standing or reclining, is never immobile: he oscillates following particular and complex rhythms. These rhythms are established by the various sensory-motor reflex systems which assure the regularisation of tonic postural activity. The amplitude and frequency of the oscillations of the body's axis can be measured with the stato-kinesimeter (ill.40).

During a specified period of time, the apparatus supplies certain information about the body's position:

- it localises the point of projection of the body's centre of gravity in relationship to the centre of the support polygon;
- it evaluates the amplitude and frequency of the displacement;
- it measures the phenomenon in time and in space.

While the subject is standing on the platform, the information which we obtain on the apparatus's oscilloscope, after electronic treatment, is read in two forms:

- vectorial, where the anterior, posterior and lateral displacements are registered. This is the stato-kinesogram (ill.39)
- linear, where the anterior and posterior displacements are differentiated from the lateral displacements and are registered in time. This is the stabilogram.

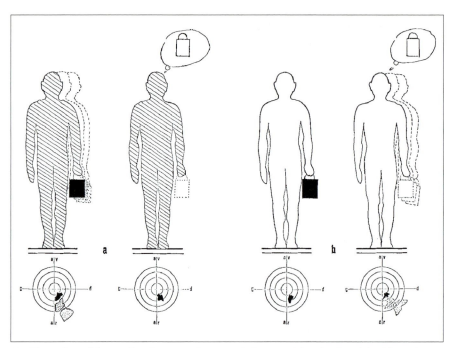

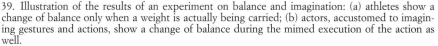

39. Illustration of the results of an experiment on balance and imagination: (a) athletes show a change of balance only when a weight is actually being carried; (b) actors, accustomed to imagining gestures and actions, show a change of balance during the mimed execution of the action as well.

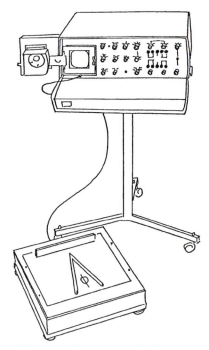

40. The stato-kinesimeter, which measures the amplitude and frequency of body axis oscillations.

41. Stato-kinesogram vector graph of changes in balance measured by the stato-kinesimeter.

42. Charles Dullin (1885–1949) as Arpagon in *L'Avare* by Molière in a position of extra-daily balance.

43–44. French mime Etienne Decroux (**above left**), and an Italian commedia dell'arte character in a seventeenth-century engraving (**above right**): the same precarious balance position.

45–46. Indian odissi dancer Sanjukta Panigrahi (**above left**), and a dancing pygmy shaman (**above right**) (drawing by French anthropologist Le Roy, 1897): the two performers have assumed a similar precarious balance position.

In the first case, the surface area covered by the 'spot' is measured (in square millimetres); in the second case, the length of the line made by the 'spot' is measured (in centimetres). The four concentric circles on the oscilloscope screen correspond to the different thresholds of pressure exerted on the platform: 5, 10 or 15 kilograms for displacements of 1, 2 or 3 centimetres in amplitude and for angular displacements on the subject's sagittal plane of 1, 2, or 3 degrees. All the oscillations of the spot that go beyond the determined threshold in the four cardinals are recorded.

In the first series of experiments, we examined the postural behaviour of two groups of subjects in good physical condition:

– a group of athletes whose physical condition is due to gesture expression adapted to reality;
– a group of actors, whose physical condition is due to mimed, 'imagined' gesture expression.

The experiment consisted in comparing the results before and during the carrying of weights (1, 2 or 3 kilograms) and during the mimed execution of the same gestures. The results (ill.39) show that:

a) in the group of athletes, the variations in displacement of the body's centre of gravity are produced in proportion to the weight when the real weight is carried, while the mimed execution of the same gesture causes no change in displacement.
b) in the group of actors, accustomed to translating an imaginary idea with the body and with gesture, there were different reactions to the two situations: carrying the weight did not practically modify the zones of displacement, while the mimed action amplified the displacements in proportion to the imagined weight.

In order to develop a motor activity, the subjects whose physical condition is determined by gesture expression adapted to reality (athletes) essentially used information based on a real and tangible stimulus. The actors, whose physical condition is determined by their more elaborated, memorised gesture expression, which they can repeat without actual physical support, can prepare the body's action essentially on the basis of the imaginary.

(Ranka Bjelác-Babíc, *The Use of a Scientific Method in the Study of Athletic and Theatrical Expression*)

Brecht's unknown dance

The influence that Brecht has had on the theatre as a director, above and beyond the influence of his theories, is due to his ability to bring out the 'life' in his actors. This was witnessed by those who saw his productions and was documented in his *Modelbucher* (*Model Books*), which were devoted to the productions he had directed.

The diary kept by Hans Joachim Bunge, Brecht's assistant on *The Caucasian Chalk Circle*, is a unique record of Brecht's use of disorientation and precision of detail, practices by which he let himself be guided while working on the level of organisation of presence, of pre-expressivity. During many of the rehearsals, he appeared to be completely unconcerned with the result, and avoided referring to anything already known or decided upon. This intuitive process – 'thoughts relate through leaps', he said, 'thoughts leaping into relationship' – confused many of his actors but helped to destroy recitative and ideological promises and caused unexpected associations and meanings to emerge from the characters and situations.

Exemplary of this process is Helene Weigel's construction of the scenic behaviour of the Governor's wife, which she began ten days before production opened. Bunge's comments on Weigel's character are particularly interesting: he remarks that the character took on a socio-aesthetic value that was not present when Weigel started to work but that resulted from the process she used to build the character.

We present a few excerpts from Bunge's diary, published in *Brecht Regista* (*Brecht the Director*), by C. Meldolesi and L. Olivi.

27.11.1953. 7th day of rehearsal

When he directs, Brecht seems to forget that it is he who has written the play. One often has the impression that he is seeing it for the first time. Sometimes he seems surprised by it and has somebody else explain the most obvious things to him. He asks the actor playing Azdak: 'But what is he really like?', and Busch answers, laughing: 'I'm sure I don't know, I'm not the author'. Brecht: 'The author, ah, well, one shouldn't always follow the author'.

8th day of rehearsal

The two lawyers present their defence arguments. Brecht gets an idea: 'It must seem like a dance, a ballet. That's why they get paid five hundred piastres'. Then he jumps up on to the stage and dances the whole scene for them, reciting some of the text. Back in his chair, he continues showing the actors how they should move, continues dancing.

16th day of rehearsal

The Governor is being taken away. Two lancers, played by extras, accompany the procession. Brecht has an experienced actor play one of the lancers, in order to show the extras how it should be done. But they still don't manage to act like lancers, their performance is colourless. Brecht suddenly says, surprised: 'That's the difference between an actor and an extra: the actor refines the smallest actions, he realises how important they are; the extra doesn't even manage to begin'.

47–49. Stanislavsky, who defined the actor as 'a master of physical actions' would have appreciated the true line of actions and counteractions in the following three actors directed by Brecht: Hans Gaugler (**top**) as Creon in *Antigone* at the Stadt-theatre Chur (1948); Leonard Steckel (**centre**) as Puntila in *Puntila and His Servant Matti* at the Berliner Ensemble (1949) and Ekkehard Schall (**bottom**) as Eilif in *Mother Courage* at the Berliner Ensemble (1952).

22nd day of rehearsal

Brecht usually gives his actors a great deal of freedom and is open to their suggestions. What has been worked on up to this point is the skeleton of the rehearsals, but nothing has been fixed yet. The constituent elements of the rehearsals are, on one hand, the characters, poetically created in action, and, on the other hand, movements rendered automatic by constant repetition. In this phase, things are fixed when they have been elaborated, but many small changes are still made. Thus, when working with Brecht, one always has the impression that nothing is final.

41st day of rehearsal

Brecht says: 'I'm afraid we'll be ready too soon'. By this he means that certain scenes and details are now considered 'final' too soon: the actors stiffen.

Brecht uses every imaginable means to keep this from happening. One scene is rehearsed until its general lines seem clear. Then the work on that scene is interrupted and another scene is rehearsed. The actors ask for more continuity in the rehearsals, so that they can set their actions and characters. Brecht does not readily give in to this request. He rehearses the scenes in sequence only when he needs to convince himself to sacrifice those moments and gestures in specific scenes which are only there because of their simple beauty.

94th day of rehearsal

Brecht rehearses the bridge scene continuously for nearly two hours. He starts from the beginning, over and over again. The actors' lines are switched around, cut, reintroduced, shortened, and finally put back where they were originally.

The gestures are likewise changed, new gestures are tried, fixed and changed again. Everything can be done in various ways. Brecht creates chaos, as usual. Is always discussing new possibilities. By the end, nobody knows what has happened. Not even Brecht himself. Now he interrupts the rehearsal: 'Let's take a break, since we don't know what to do next'. He often does this, at those moments when he doesn't manage to find a way to get what's happening on stage to go any further. From this confusion, however, more often than not, something new emerges.

112th day of rehearsal

The actress playing the Governor's wife has suddenly taken ill.

It is not certain that she will recover in time for the opening to take on the part and get it ready in the ten days that are left. Helene Weigel agrees to take over the part, she starts rehearsing it, but very circumspectly. Brecht does not ask her to do it as Kathe Reichel was doing it, he lets her try to find her own interpretation. Then a surprising thing happens: Weigel discovers a completely new way to play the part, while the servants keep the same characterisations they had had with Reichel. Reichel had seen the Governor's wife as a woman who was always on the move and worked with tremendous energy: she spoke her lines in many different ways, loudly and piercingly, softly and painfully, and had dominated the stage with many rapid movements. Weigel gave one the impression of being a born leader and achieved this effect by working in almost the opposite way.

Instead of Reichel's typical hysterical vocal leaps, Weigel chose a calm and even tone. She spoke with a low voice, but in a firm and incisive way. And instead of flying around the stage, she assumed a very still position. In nearly all the scenes, she remained seated in one place and from there dominated the entire stage. She didn't move a finger, she just gave orders.

50. Helene Weigel as the wife of the Governor in Brecht's production of his play, *The Caucasian Chalk Circle* (Berliner Ensemble, 1954). The apparent immobility conceals a nucleus of tensions, the result not only of the way in which the body's directions are divided (legs, torso, face and eyes), but also of the precarious balance caused by the (uncomfortable) sitting position, held with a curved spine.

Brecht accepted one of Weigel's ideas after he saw how well it worked on the stage: the servant must always stand tight beside his mistress, and when she signals, he must kneel and offer her his back, as if it was a chair. Reichel's governor's wife, in her hysteria, appeared to be only superficially dangerous and exhibited more than anything else the obtuse snobbism of highly born women. She is not to be taken too seriously. Weigel's governor's wife shows the seductive and brutal face of stupidity. She is clearly dangerous.

Thanks to her typical upper-class education, the Governor's wife has become a rigid, puppet-like figure. When she is dealing with servants, she does not seem human, a characteristic that is perfectly underscored by her cold, formal kindness.

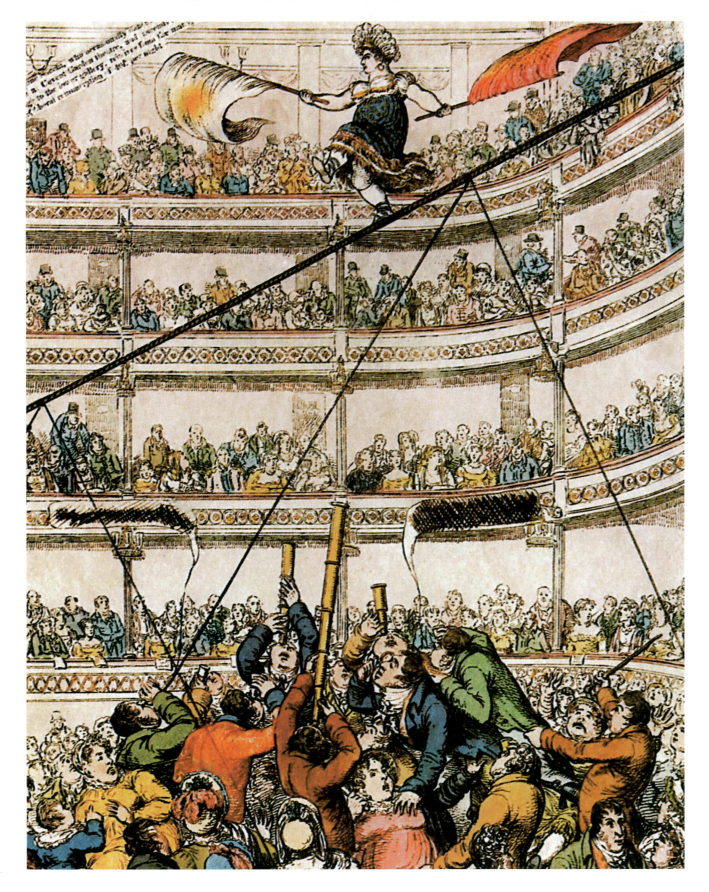

51–56. (**opposite**) Italian acrobatic dancer Sacchi at London's Covent Garden in 1816. However, the performer's search for a luxury balance is not oriented in the direction of acrobatics and virtuosity but in the direction of the extra-daily, as is demonstrated by all of the above positions from various cultures and genres: Julian Beck (**top left**) (1925–85), in Living Theater's *Six Public Acts* at the Venice Biennale, 1975; Peking Opera actress Pei Yanling (**top right**); Balinese dancer Ni Made Wiratini (**bottom left**); Isadora Duncan (**bottom centre**); and Japanese butoh dancer Natsu Nakajima (**bottom right**).

57–60. Iben Nagel Rasmussen training at Odin Teatret (1971). The exercises have an obvious effect on the body's balance (cf. *Training*)

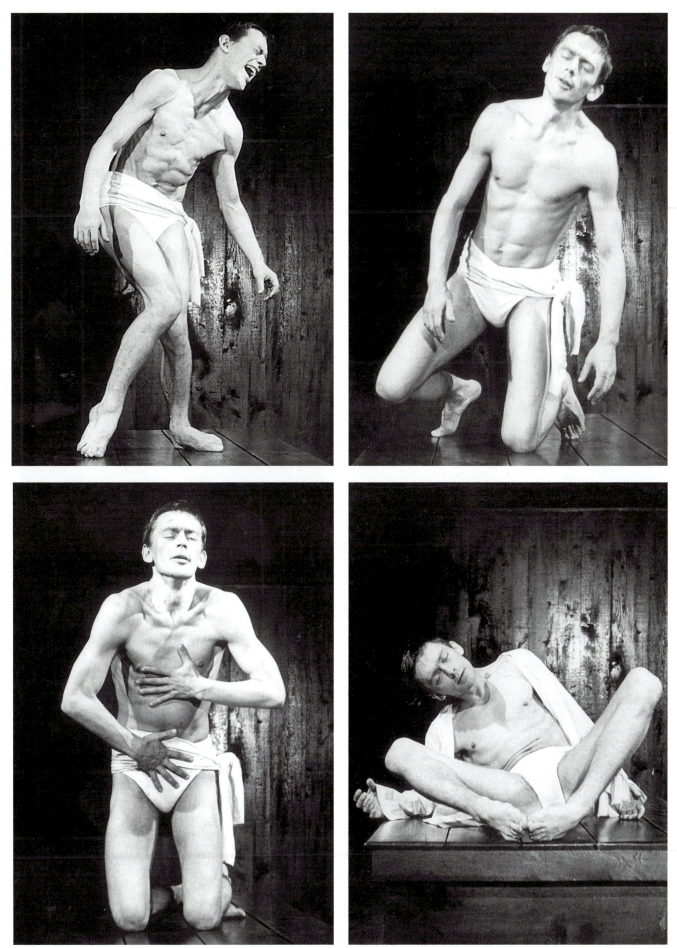

61–64. Four pictures of Ryszard Cieslak (1937–90) in *The Constant Prince* (1965), adapted from Calderon by Juliusz Slowacki and directed by Jerzy Grotowski. An example of 'theatre which dances': a contemporary actor synthesises the dance of balance in all possible positions: seated, kneeling, standing.

The dilated body

Eugenio Barba

A body-in-life is more than a body merely alive. A body-in-life dilates the performer's presence and the spectator's perception.

There are certain performers who attract the spectator with an elementary energy that 'seduces' without mediation. This occurs before the spectator has either deciphered individual actions or understood their meanings.

For an Western spectator watching an Asian actor/dancer about whose culture, traditions and scenic conventions he often knows little, this experience is to be expected. Seeing a performance whose meaning he cannot fully understand and whose manner of execution he cannot competently appreciate, he suddenly finds himself in the dark. But he must nevertheless admit that this void has a power that holds his attention, that it 'seduces' in a way that precedes intellectual understanding.

But neither seduction nor comprehension can last for very long without one another: the seduction would be brief, the comprehension would lack interest.

The Western spectator watching an Asian actor/dancer is only an extreme example. The same situation occurs every time theatre is well done. But when the observer is faced with his 'own' theatre, all that he already knows, the questions he recognises and that tell him where or how to look for answers, create a veil that conceals the existence of the 'seduction's' elementary power.

We often call this performer's power 'presence'. But it is not something which *is*, which is *there* in front of us. It is continuous mutation, growth taking place before our very eyes. It is a body-in-life. The flow of energies that characterise our daily behaviour has been re-routed. The tensions that secretly govern our normal way of being physically present come to the surface in the performer, become visible, unexpectedly.

The dilated body is a hot body, but not in the emotional or sentimental sense. Feeling and emotion are only a consequence, for both the performer and the spectator. The

1–2. Everything, from posture to costume, from facial expression to body dynamism, contributes to the dilation of the performer's presence: a dancing dervish (**above left**), and (**above right**) Helene Weigel in the title rôle in *Mother Courage*, directed by Bertolt Brecht and Erich Engel (1952).

3–4. The dilated body: Stephen Pier, in a work demonstration, and Stina Ekblad in *Medea*, at Copenhagen ISTA 1996.

dilated body is above all a glowing body, in the scientific sense of the term: the particles that make up daily behaviour have been excited and produce more energy, they have undergone an increment of motion, they move further apart, attract and oppose each other with more force, in a restricted or expanded space.

The bridge

If one questions masters of Asian and Western performance and compares their answers, one discovers that although the techniques described differ, the principles upon which they are based are similar. These principles can be combined into three lines of action:

1. alteration of daily balance in the search for precarious or 'luxury' balance;
2. dynamic opposition;
3. use of coherent incoherence.

These three lines of action imply continuous work on the reduction or amplification of the actions typical of daily behaviour. While daily behaviour is based on functionality, on economy of power, on the relationship between the energy used and the result obtained, in the performer's extra-daily behaviour, each action, no matter how small, is based on waste, on *excess*.

Now this is fascinating and at times deceiving: one tends to think that it has only to do with 'body theatre', which supposedly uses only physical and not mental actions. But a way of moving in space is a manifestation of a way of thinking: it is the motion of thought stripped naked. Analogously, a thought is also motion, an action – that is, something that mutates, starting at one place in order to arrive at another,

following routes that abruptly change direction. The performer can start from the physical or from the mental, it doesn't matter which, provided that in the transition from one to the other, a unity is reconstructed.

Just as there is a lazy, predictable, grey way of moving, there is also a grey, predictable, lazy way of thinking. A performer's actions can become heavy and blocked by stereotypes, just as the flow of thought can be blocked by stereotypes, judgements and ready-made questions. A performer who draws only upon what she already knows involuntarily immerses herself in a stagnant pool, using her energy in a repetitive way without disorienting it, without re-routing it with leaps in cataracts and falls or in that profound calm that precedes the sudden escape of water seized by a new descent. Following the analogy, thought – with the words and images that express it – can move along placid and fundamentally uninteresting channels.

One does not work on the body or the voice, one works on energy. So just as there is no vocal action that is not also a physical action, there is no physical action that is not also mental. If there is physical training, there must also be mental training.

It is necessary to work on the bridge that joins the physical and mental banks of the river of the creative process. The relationship between these two banks does not only have to do with a polarity that is part of every individual at the moment when s/he acts, composes, creates. It also links two wider, specifically theatrical polarities: the polarity between the actor and director, and the subsequent polarity between performer and spectator.

The 'dilated body' evokes its opposite and complementary image: 'the dilated mind'. But this expression should not make one think only of something paranormal, of altered states of consciousness. It also relates to the level of craft in the artistic profession.

5. Wagner, *The Flying Dutchman*, engraving by French artist Gustave Doré (1832–83).

In the course of my experience as a director, I have observed a process taking place in both myself and some of my companions: the long daily work on physical training, transformed over the years, has slowly become distilled into internal patterns of energy that can be applied to a way of conceiving or composing a dramatic action, a way of speaking in public, a way of writing. Thought has a physical aspect: its way of moving, changing direction, leaping – its 'behaviour', in fact. This aspect has also a pre-expressive level that can be considered analogous to the performer's pre-expressive work, that work that has to do with presence (energy) and that precedes – logically if not chronologically – real and actual artistic composition.

Peripeteias

Leaps of thought can be defined as peripeteias or vicissitudes. A peripeteia is an interweaving of events that causes an action to develop in unexpected ways or to conclude in a way that is opposite to how it began. A peripeteia acts through negation: this has been known at least since the time of Aristotle.

The behaviour of thought is visible in the peripeteias of stories, in the unexpected changes that occur as stories are passed along from person to person, from one mind to another. Just as happens in the creative theatrical process,

unexpected changes do not take place only in the mind of a solitary artist, but are the work of various individuals who share the same point of departure.

The Flying Dutchman was Captain Van der Decken. In his attempt to round the Cape of Good Hope, he blasphemed against God: he would not yield to the forces of storms and destiny, but insisted on continuing to try to get around the Cape until the end of his days. Thus it was that he heard a voice from Heaven repeating his own words, but now they had become a curse: 'until the last day . . . the last day'.

And so the seed of a story is sown: a captain remains at sea and never dies. A ship sails on and on. Now, this seed abandons its original context and 'leaps' into other contexts. Popular imagination superimposes the image of the captain and his eternal peregrination onto the image of Ahasuerus, the Wandering Jew, the man who never found peace.

Thus the story of Van der Decken changes. It is said that he was condemned because he had led an immoral, atheistic life: he gave the order to weigh anchor on the holy day of Good Friday, the day on which the saviour was killed.

Or: the image of the captain fades away and in its place in the imagination a ship comes into view. The ghost ship appears, suddenly: sailors see it, it is black, its sails are the colour of blood, or yellow, or they are iridescent, bewitching, changing colour ten times in an hour.

It was probably Heine who first wove the following new motif into the saga of the Flying Dutchman and his ghost ship: from time to time, Van der Decken docks at a city where he looks for love. He will be rescued from his fate when he finds a woman who will be faithful to him unto death.

In the summer of 1839, Richard Wagner was en route from Riga to London. His wife Minna was with him. He was familiar with the story of the Flying Dutchman, but he understood it only when the boat on which he was travelling was overtaken by a storm on the Norwegian reefs. The sailors then told the story of the ghost ship that always appeared before a shipwreck. After being caught in the storm for many hours, they finally managed to berth between the high cliffs of a fjord at Sandvik, a few miles from Arendal.

6. Thought in life, non-linear, non-univocal: manuscript depicting the beginning of the Aztec migration. From **left** to **right**: 1) the sovereign on an island: the hieroglyphs around the pyramid represent his name and that of his tribe; 2) the crossing: the hieroglyph in the rectangle represents the date; 3) footprints indicate the march towards the city of Colhuacan, represented by the large hieroglyph; 4) eight more tribes await the sovereign: each tribe is represented by a hieroglyph and by the figure of a talking man. Drawing from *Le Geste et la parole* (*Gesture and Word*) by anthropologist André Leroi-Gourhan (1911–86).

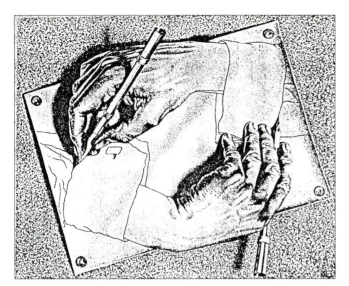

7. To think the thought: *Dessiner*, (*To Draw*), 1948, lithograph by Maurits Cornelis Escher (1898–1972).

When the voyage was over and Wagner had arrived safely in London and then made his way to Paris, he talked about the storm along the Norwegian coast, saying that the wind was sinister and demonic as it howled in the stays. He told of having seen a sail emerge from the darkness and of believing that he could make out the Dutchman's ship.

It probably happened – according to those who are fond of anecdotes – that while in Sandvik, Wagner, a guest in the house of a Norwegian captain, became interested in the young girl who was serving at table. He heard her called *jenta* (girl, servant) and thought that this was her real name. Later, he changed her name to Senta, a name not used in Norway, or only in the Norway imagined by Wagner for *Der Fliegende Holländer*.

Wagner takes the theme of the love that redeemed the Dutchman, but turns it around. He accepts Heine's version and at the same time negates its meaning.

Senta does in fact love the Dutchman and swears to be faithful to him unto death. But the Dutchman has overheard a conversation between Senta and Erik (Senta had also once sworn to be faithful to Erik unto death). Now, taken by her destiny, irrevocably bound to the Dutchman, Senta must renege on her promise to Erik. The Dutchman decides to return to sea: salvation seems impossible, since it is impossible that he will find a woman who will be faithful to him unto death. It will in fact be he who will save Senta, and not the other way around: he fears that Senta will betray him just as she has betrayed Erik. And women who betray him are condemned for eternity. The theme of a curse that can be reversed by a woman turns into a theme of a new destiny of condemnation that now falls also upon women in love.

The Dutchman, then, flees in order to save the woman who should have saved him. He flees what he believes to be a false love, but Senta is in fact faithful to him unto death: when the ship sails, Senta throws herself into the sea and, dying, remains faithful to her promise. The ship then slowly sinks, and as the sun rises, Senta and the Dutchman ascend to Heaven.

And so now a new metamorphosis: the story, as transformed by Heine and developed by Wagner through a series of oppositions, is now taken up by Strindberg. He releases all the potential energy contained in the final variations introduced by Wagner. And as this potential energy is released, it inverts the meaning of the story: now the central theme is one of infidelity, of the pain that a woman inflicts on the man who loves her. It is a theme to which Strindberg returns continuously and which he confronts here using the plot inherited from Wagner.

He also uses it by negating it, by turning it inside out: every seven years, the Dutchman must meet and love a woman. This is the condition for his salvation, not because the woman will redeem him, but because of her infidelity.

The theme of love, which had been introduced as an opposite pole to the theme of condemnation, the Dutchman's never-ending voyage, now leaps to a new opposite and superimposes itself onto the theme of the sea voyage, becoming its spiritual equivalent. The Dutchman's true punishment is the continual failure of love. Love no longer releases him from punishment, as in Heine and Wagner, but is itself the punishment. It redeems and transforms even the ghost ship, changing it from a damned prison to a cross.

Let us recall the original story: Strindberg seems closer to it than his predecessors. Yet he is very far from it. The essential element of the story, although it still has its original value, has gone deeper. The torment of physical wandering is dilated by its spiritual double and the sailor, who had become similar to the Wandering Jew, to *Faust*, to *Don Juan*, returns to being a lonely sailor abandoned by a woman in every port.

When one thinks about variations on a theme, one thinks of virtuosity, of sophisticated artistry. But the variations in the story of the Dutchman are not mere variations: with each of the transitions, a change of state has taken place.

It is easy to observe the *leaping* behaviour of thought when it manifests itself in the peripeteias of a famous story. It is more difficult to be so flexible as *not to impede* the manifestations and disorientations of this behaviour in the placid flow of one's own thinking.

8. To think the thought: drawing by Romanian caricaturist Saul Steinberg, used by Sergei Eisenstein (1898–1948) in his book *The Non-Indifferent Nature*, 1947.

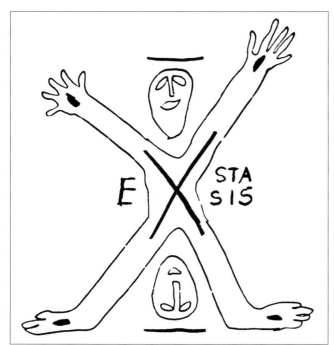

9–10. *Extasis*, (**top**) drawing made by Eisenstein during his stay in Mexico in 1931. *Ex-stasis*: to go out of oneself. It is not the actor who must enter ecstasy, but the spectator who must 'go out of himself', who must, that is, transcend the limits of the direct and literal perception of what the actor is doing in order 'to see' behind the screen of the obvious and the known; (**bottom**) Augusto Omolú in a work demonstration at Copenhagen ISTA, 1996.

The negation principle

There is a rôle that performers know well: begin an action in the direction opposite to that to which the action will finally be directed.

This rule recreates a condition essential to all those actions which in daily life demand a certain amount of energy: before striking a blow, one draws one's arm back; before jumping, one bends one's knees; before springing forward, one leans backwards: *reculer pour mieux sauter*.

In the performer's extra-daily activity, such behaviour is applied even to the smallest actions. It is one of the means that the performer uses to dilate his physical presence.

We could call it the 'negation principle': before carrying out an action, the actor negates it by executing its complementary opposite.

The 'negation principle' becomes a formalistic void if its soul – that is, its organic quality – is lost. Often in the theatrical and non-theatrical use of trivial declamation, the 'negation principle' becomes a way of *inflating* gesture. A parody, in fact, of *dilated* action.

What is the internal logic that determines the power of the 'negation principle'? On the one hand, the nervous and physical dynamics by means of which every energetic action begins with its opposite; on the other hand, a mental attitude.

One of the clearest descriptions of this recurrent mental attitude is contained in Arthur Koestler's *The Sleepwalkers*. The book is dedicated to 'the history of the changes of man's vision of the universe'. Koestler shows how every creative act – in science, in art, or in religion – is accomplished through a preliminary regression to a more primitive level, through a *reculer pour mieux sauter*, a process of negation and disintegration that prepares the leap towards the result. Koestler calls this moment a creative 'pre-condition'.

It is a moment that seems to negate all that is typical of a search for a result: it does not determine a new orientation but is rather a voluntary disorientation that demands that all of the researcher's energy be put in motion, that his senses be sharpened, like when one walks in the dark. The dilation of the actual potentialities costs dearly: one risks losing control of the meaning of one's own action. It is a negation that has not yet discovered the new entity that it affirms.

The performer, the director, the researcher, the artist ... all often ask themselves: 'What does what I do *mean*?' But in the moment of the 'negation of action', or of the creative 'precondition', this is not a fruitful question. At this point it is not the meaning of what one is doing that is essential, but rather the precision of the action that prepares the void in which a sense – an unexpected meaning – can be captured.

Theatre artists, obliged to create in a way that nearly always involves the collaboration of many individuals, are often impeded by a fetishistic need for meanings, by the apparently 'natural' need to agree at the outset on the results to be achieved.

An actor, for example, executes a certain action that is the result of an improvisation or a personal interpretation of a character. It is natural that she gives the action a very precise value, that she associates it with specific images or a specific thought. If, however, the meaning which the action has for the actor is made inappropriate or incomprehensible because of the context in which the action is placed, then the actor thinks that this action fragment should be dropped and forgotten. She believes, in short, that the marriage between the action and its associated meanings is indissoluble.

If one says to an actor that her action can remain intact while its context (and therefore its meaning) is completely changed, she usually feels that she is being treated as inert matter, that she is being 'exploited' by the director. As if the soul of the action was its meaning and not the quality of its energy.

Many directors have the same pre-conceived idea: they tend to believe that a specific image or sequence of images can obey only one simple dramatic logic, can only transmit such and such a meaning.

But the principle of 'negating the action' points in the very opposite direction, freeing one from the pre-established order, from dependence on the result that one *wants* to obtain. It is as if the point of departure is transformed, by means of its opposite, into a drop of energy that can develop real expressive potentialities by *leaping* from one context to another.

In practical theatre work, this has to do with the peripeteias to which an action or an idea are subjected from the moment they take form to the moment they are placed in the completed production. Like the Flying Dutchman, condemned to travel from country to country, from epoch to epoch, the original meanings of the actions' nuclei die even while continuing to live: they leap from meaning to meaning without getting lost. Creative thought is actually distinguished by the fact that it proceeds by leaps, by means of an unexpected disorientation that obliges it to reorganise itself in new ways, abandoning its well-ordered shell. It is the thought-in-life, not rectilinear, not univocal.

The growth of unexpected meanings is made possible by a particular disposition of all our energies, both physical and mental, perching on the edge of a cliff just before taking flight. This disposition can be achieved, distilled, through training.

Physical-training exercises make it possible for the performer to develop a new behaviour, a new way of moving, of acting and reacting: s/he thus acquires a specific skill. But this skill stagnates and becomes unidimensional if it does not strike deep, if it does not reach down into the performer's being, made up of mental processes, the psychic sphere, the nervous system. The bridge between the physical and the mental causes a slight change of consciousness that makes it possible to overcome inertia, the monotony of repetition.

The dilation of the physical body is in fact of no use if it is not accompanied by a dilation of the mental body. Thought must tangibly pass through the *obvious*, inertia, the first thing to present itself when we imagine, reflect, act.

To think the thought

A physicist is walking along a beach and sees a child throwing stones into the sea, trying to make them skip. Each stone makes no more than one or two little skips. The child is perhaps five years old, and the adult, the physicist, remembers that he too, in his childhood, bounced stones over the water. Indeed, he was very good at it. So the adult shows the child how it is done. He throws the stones, one after another, showing the child how to hold them, at what angle to cast them, at what height over the surface of the water. All the stones that the adult throws skip many times, seven, eight, even ten times.

'Yes', the child then says, 'they skip lots of times. But that isn't what I was trying to do. Your stones are making round circles in the water. I want mine to make square circles.'

We know this story because the physicist told it to Einstein. Einstein reacted in an unexpected way when his young friend told him about meeting the child: 'Give him my compliments and tell him not to worry if his stones don't

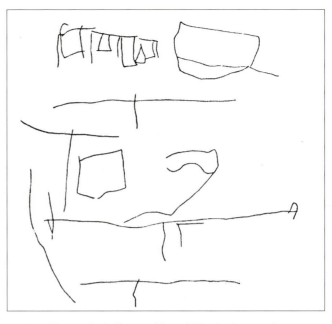

11. Jens (three and a half years old): a children's playground.

make square circles in the water. The important thing is to think the thought'.

The questions that have given rise to many of the most important scientific discoveries are, when examined closely, as useless or gratuitous as that of the child busy throwing his stones in the water.

'Why does incandescent iron become red?', the fifty-year-old Max Planck asked himself; 'What would a man see if he could ride a ray of light?', Einstein asked himself. The fact these questions led to great scientific discoveries should not blind us to the fact that they were leaps into the dark, rapid ideas which escaped one's grasp.

To think the thought implies waste, sudden transitions, abrupt turns, unexpected connections between previously unrelated levels and contexts, routes that intersect and vanish. It is as if different voices, different thoughts, each with its own logic, were simultaneously present and began to collaborate in an unplanned way, combining precision and fortuitousness, enjoyment of the game for its own sake and tension towards a result.

This image of research is similar to that of a pack of hounds pursuing a prey that may or may not be ahead of them. The hounds run together, break up and disperse, get in each other's way, rush into thickets and ravines that severely test their abilities and energies and, when they emerge, they run in circles, discouraged at having lost the trail, are forced to turn back. But sometimes the dispersed hounds join up again and the reassembled pack tracks the prey down, discovers the idea.

It is not certain that the idea to be discovered will be there waiting for us, willing to be pursued and captured. It is a pure potentiality. We do not know what it's about nor what it might be used for. Sometimes, it all comes to nothing. Other times, something new presents itself, like a surprise that obliges us to become involved in an unexpected area. Some scientists change their field of research; some writers give up the story they have been working on and follow the new peripeteias of characters who have practically imposed themselves; in the midst of work on a production, one becomes aware that in reality *another production* is leading us by the hand, without yet knowing where it is leading us.

Sometimes one has the impression that it is not we who are 'thinking the thought', and that all we can do is silence the prejudices that prevent the thought from being thought.

At first, this is a painful experience. Before becoming a feeling of freedom, of an opening to new dimensions, it is a fight between what one has decided a priori, what one aspires to, and – on the other hand – the mind-in-life.

The danger of falling into chaos is obvious. When one succeeds in establishing this creative 'pre-condition', one can even have the feeling that one is possessed or that one is being taken out of oneself. But it is a feeling that remains anchored to the terra firma of craftsmanship, of one's trade.

When Eisenstein sat down at his moviola, he succeeded in creating a condition for his work in which it was the material itself, and not results that had been previously decided upon, that dictated its own unexpected logic. He – who had worked out his film frame by frame, who had composed it in his designs before ever doing so on the set – succeeded in sitting down in total ignorance in front of the material that he himself had created. The programming that had guided him up to that moment was now of no more use and he spoke of the 'ecstasy of montage'.

'To think the thought', the 'mind-in-life', the 'ecstasy of montage' . . . these expressions all refer in a figurative way to the same kind of experience: various fragments, various images, various thoughts are not connected due to a precise direction or according to the logic of a clear plan, but belong together because of 'consanguinity'.

What does consanguinity mean in this context? That the various fragments, images, ideas, alive in the context in which we have brought them to life, reveal their own autonomy, establish new relationships, and connect together on the basis of a logic that does not obey the logic used when we imagined and sought after them. It is as if hidden blood-ties activate possibilities other than those which we think are useful and justified.

In the creative process, the materials with which we work have both a utilitarian life and a second life. The first, left to itself, leads to clarity without profundity. The second risks leading us into chaos because of its uncontrolled power.

But it is the dialectic between these two lives, between mechanical order and disorder, which leads us towards what the Chinese call *li*, the asymmetrical and unforeseeable order that characterises organic life.

Twin logics

A dialectic relationship does not exist in and of itself. It is born of the willingness to control forces that, left to themselves, would only conflict with each other.

Dialectics is a learned way of thinking and acting. In creative work, the asymmetrical order of *li* is something that is above all an artificial work. The search for oppositions, for differences, must paradoxically be the other face of the search for unity and wholeness.

How can one intensify the difference between the performer's way of seeing and the spectator's way of seeing? How can one reinforce the polarity between director and actor? And thus, how does one search for a stronger relationship between the various forces in question? The possibility of dilating the body of the theatre depends on the answers to these questions.

At times, in the course of work on a production, an actor's actions begin to come alive, even if the director doesn't understand why the actor is acting in that particular way. It can happen that the director, who is the first spectator, does not know how to explain rationally, within the framework of the production, the meaning of what the actor is doing.

Directors can admit the difficulty they have in accepting this spark of unknown life, can ask for explanations, can request that the actor become coherent. But they thereby jeopardise the collaborative relationship: they are trying to eliminate the distance that separates them from the actor, they demand too much, and at the same time, too little, demand a consensus, an agreement about intentions, about what is on the surface.

When one speaks of actors' work, their technique or their art, their 'interpretation', one often forgets that theatre is a relationship. All actors' extra-daily techniques correspond, from the spectator's point of view, to a primary need: the waiting for that moment in which the veil of daily life is torn and the unexpected breaks through. Something known is suddenly revealed as new.

Even spectators' deepest reactions, the matrices of their appreciation or their clearly formulated judgement, are secret, unforeseeable.

The power of theatre depends on one's ability to safeguard the independent life of other logics beneath a recognisable mantle. Logic – that is, a series of motivated and consequent transitions – can exist even if it is secret, incommunicable, even when its rules cannot extend beyond a single individual's horizon.

There is a preconceived notion that only that which obeys a shared logic is logical. Another aspect of this preconceived notion would have us believe that the personal, secret, intimate world is ruled by chance, by automatic associations, by chaos: a magma in which there are no *leaps* but rather inconsequent oscillation.

What we call irrationality might be this oscillation left to the mechanical repetition of our fixations and obsessions which disappear and reappear, agitatedly, without development. But it might also be a rationality which is ours alone, a *raison d'être* that does not help us to be understood but to communicate with ourselves.

There are also collaborative relationships, fertile or hollow, in each individual's mental theatre.

When adults try to copy the way children draw, they usually do no more than draw badly, they try to renounce the logic of their own way of seeing, impoverish it, leave their hand to chance, avoid precision, imitate infantile ways of drawing. And so it becomes infantile.

To the adult, in fact, children's drawings appear to lack something, are badly done or scribbled. But they actually adhere to an iron-clad logic. A child does not draw what s/he sees or how s/he sees it, but what s/he has experienced. If s/he experiences an adult as a pair of long legs with a face that suddenly bends over him/her, s/he will draw this adult as a circle on top of two sticks. Or s/he may paint a 'self-portrait' with enormous feet because s/he is happy with some new shoes. If the mother is more important than the father, when drawing the parents the mother will appear bigger than the father.

For those who study children's drawings, those scribblings called first drawings, which very small children make, are also the result of direct experience. They are not representations, but rather actions of the hand in relationship to a mental picture: here is a running dog.

It is the presence of only one logic that makes children's drawings infantile, not their approximate or primitive nature.

However, 'good' drawings by older children or adults also adhere to only one logic. The fact that they are now more recognisable, that they demonstrate an adherence to shared rules, does not make them less banal.

In the works of a true painter, *numerous logics* act simultaneously. They fit into a tradition, they use its rules or consciously break them in surprising ways. In addition to transmitting a way of seeing, they also represent a way of experiencing the world and translate onto the canvas not only the image but also the *gestus*, the quality of motion that has guided the brush.

Thus one can say that the painter has 'kept the child in herself', not because she has kept her innocence and ingenuousness, not because she has not been domesticated by a culture, but because, in the precision of her craft, she has woven together 'parallel' or 'twin' logics, without substituting one for the other.

Being-in-life is the negation of the succession of different stages of development; it is simultaneous growth by means of ever more complex interweavings. Perhaps this is why Meyerhold accepted an actor only when he could discern in the adult the child that once was.

Seven-gated Thebes

'But why do people go to the theatre?'. Béla Balàzs once asked himself and his readers this useless question. The value of useless questions, of the words with which each of us has a dialogue with oneself, is never valued highly enough.

But why do people do theatre?

I was fifteen years old when I went to the theatre for the first time. My mother took me to see *Cyrano de Bergerac*. The hero was played by Gino Cervi, a very popular Italian actor. But it was neither he nor the other actors who impressed me, nor the story they were telling, which I followed with interest but without amazement. It was a horse. A real horse. It appeared pulling a carriage, according to the most reasonable rules of scenic realism. But its presence suddenly exploded all the dimensions which until then had reigned on that stage. Because of this sudden interference from another world, the uniform veil of the stage seemed torn before my very eyes.

In the theatres to which I went in the following years, I searched in vain for the disorientation that had made me feel alive, for that sudden dilation of my senses. No more horses appeared. Until I arrived in Opole in Poland and Cheruthuruthy in India. Today it is obvious to me that there exists a parallel that was already discernible in Grotowski's work: the dilation of the actor's presence and the spectator's perception corresponds to a dilation of the *fabula*, the plot and its interweavings, the drama, the story or the situation represented. Just as there is an extra-daily behaviour for the performer, there is also an extra-daily behaviour in thinking a story.

During the first few years of my work in the theatre, I interfered with the text, which was the point of departure for the production, by creating unexpected changes of direction, breaking the text's linear development and composing the general action through the montage and interweaving of

12–14. Twin logics; children's drawings: (**top**) Alasdair (four years old) – the cat is all whiskers; (**centre**) Chloe (six years old) – the cat has both whiskers and a tail; (**bottom**) cat seen by a fifty-nine-year-old adult: *Kitten's Monologue* (1938), drawing by Paul Klee (1879–1940).

15–16. Twin logics: Drawings by a child and an adult. (**above**) Maria, four years old, changes a man into a two-room apartment; (**right**) *The House Becomes a Chinese*: animated film from 1911 by French filmmaker Emile Cohl (1857–1938), who Walt Disney called 'the father of animation'.

two or more simultaneous actions. The text, in these cases, was like a wind blowing in one direction. The production sails against the wind, in the opposite direction. But it is still the power of the wind that is the motive force.

Later, another possibility was revealed, and accepted not without fear and resistance: to follow the logic of the material that surfaced in the course of improvisation, moving away from the point of departure and discovering only at the end of the process what the nature of the production might be, what meaning it might have for me and for the spectator.

Before beginning *The Gospel According to Oxyrhincus* with Odin Teatret, I realised that these experiences, which at first I believed to be the fruit of personal temperament and of the material circumstances that had conditioned my activity, instead corresponded to an objective necessity: the thought that passed through the actors' pre-expressive presence also passed ever more clearly through the way of conceiving a production.

In the devising of the story for a new production, what could the mental equivalent of the actor's pre-expressive level be? The mental pre-expressivity could be an image ready to take flight.

I thought: a person, on a mountain, in a desert. Who is it? A man? A woman? A child? What is he or she doing? Waiting for someone? Or is it a hermit? Does he or she see a burning bush? Is it the Old Man of the Mountain? And what is the mountain called? Tabor? Ararat? Kilimanjaro? Which desert is it? Scott's pack ice or the desert of the Tartars?

An image such as this cannot, however, be the equivalent of the actor's pre-expressive level or what we call the 'pre-expressive nucleus'. It is nothing more than a good improvisation stimulus for myself and for the actors. A pre-expressive nucleus must be something that dilates and mutates yet retains its identity, like the metamorphoses of the story of the Flying Dutchman and his ghost ship.

At the beginning of 1984, I asked each of my actors to choose a character from a different story and to write a scenario, adapting the story's peripeteias, its events and vicissitudes. We thus had six stories which, together with mine, would become the seven different gates into one single production.

The six characters were: Sabbatai Zevi, the Jew who presented himself as the Messiah and became a Muslim; Antigone; Joan of Arc; a young Brazilian outlaw, a *cangaceiro*; the Grand Inquisitor of Seville; and a Hassidic Jew. These characters built the production *The Gospel According to Oxyrhincus*.

They were not casually chosen. They responded both to the individual actors' interests and to other logics that were simultaneously and independently in motion.

In fact, in 1982 we had begun work on a project whose point of departure was a story by Borges, 'The Dead Man'. A young Argentinian outlaw, Beniamin Otalora, joins Aureliano Bandeira's Uruguayan band, demonstrates his courage, saves Bandeira's life and ends up seducing his woman and becoming her lover. The old Bandeira tolerates all this without reacting. His position becomes weaker by the day. Otalora usurps the command ever more obviously.

One evening, after a new success, when all the bandits are seated around the table, Otalora openly sits in his leader's place. Bandeira sits at the other end of the table, ignored by all. Beside Otalora stands the woman who formerly was his leader's lover and who is now his.

Old Bandeira's next-in-command approaches Otalora and draws his pistol. Suddenly Otalora understands that his ascent has been tolerated and honoured by all because Bandeira had condemned him to death the moment he first arrived. He alone had been ignorant of the fact that he was already a dead man. Bandeira's next-in-command fires.

From this tale came the seventh story for *The Gospel According to Oxyrhincus*, my story. Borges's text had set in motion two different series of associations. The band of outlaws reminded me of the Brazilian *jaguncos* and *cangaceiros* as they are described in books by Euclides da Cunha, Eduardo Barbosa and Billy Jaynes Chandler, or in the films of Ruy Guerra and Glauber Rocha.

But the outline of the story (the older leader who has a young man killed, the last supper, the shadow of incest) had made my imagination leap to other contexts: the Keeper of the Law who kills those who revolt; Creon, who had his son killed, and Antigone, the bride he had promised to his son; Judas, who died along with his messiah; the Prodigal Son; God the Father, who caused his son's death.

Modelled on the story of Aureliano Bandeira and Beniamin Otalora, the vicissitudes of God the Father and the

Son coincided with the gnostic interpretation of Christianity, which saw in the God of the Law, in Jahveh, an evil demiurge, fighting against the forces of light.

The Brazilian *sertao* thus became populated with voices coming from the Hellenic city of Oxyrhincus (modern-day Behnesa in Egypt) where, in 1903, three gnostic manuscripts were discovered.

The two trails – *cangaceiros* and gnostics – met and other themes established channels between them. One of these themes came from the story of Antonio Conselheiro, reconstructed by Mario Vargas Llosa in his novel, *The War of the End of the World*: *cangaceiros* congregated in the 'New Jerusalem' of Canudo, the Holy City built by a new Messiah in the *sertao* desert. They were rebels who, in the name of their God, defeated many of the military expeditions sent against them but were finally massacred to the last man.

Could the exterminating angels of the end of time, found in religious mythologies, be represented in the garb of *cangaceiros* assembled at Canudo? Or did these bandits believe themselves to be angels who had come down to earth to bring about the age of justice?

And who was this Hassidic Jew who appeared among the characters chosen by the actors? A Jew who had crossed the *sertao* in search of the Messiah, just as the anarchic Galileo Gall, in search of the Revolution, had done in Vargas Llosa's novel?

Meanwhile, the theme of Antigone and of the revolt buried alive was developing autonomously, following its own logic. What would happen if, at the foot of the cross, on Calvary, these figures were to meet: the men and women of the revolt, saints and nihilists, Buddha and Antigone, Francis of Assisi and Sabbatai Zevi, Mohammed and Jacob Frank, Captain Ahab and Zarathustra?

But over each mental panorama there lay a wavering cloud that formed and deformed the paternal face of Sosso Dzhugashvili, known as Joseph Stalin. And he was laughing, laughing and dribbling blood.

These tumultuously coexisting associations and images could take on a meaning and could attain a unity because there was another logic contemporaneously in motion which had to do with the work of the whole group and which imposed a certain order.

The point of origin was always Borges's 'The Dead Man'. Each actor had made a scenario from the story which he or she presented as a director, leading the company through it. There were, then, several production sketches, very different from each other, even though all had the same point of departure. Each production sketch, even though an embryo, contained fragments with their own power. Taking these fragments out of context, I began to weave them together, making a montage, building an ulterior production, still with Borges's theme.

This work process was not related to a production, it was only an internal study. But its logic presented itself again when, in 1984, we began to work on *The Gospel According to Oxyrhincus*.

From the seven stories linked to the six characters chosen by the actors and myself, both an autonomous text and a unitary production emerged. They have nothing to do with what my companions and I had foreseen, but they are the result of our disorientations and reorientations.

There are seven gates, but there is only one Thebes. The audience will enter Thebes through one of the gates: a production about the manifestations of faith in our time and about the revolt which is buried alive. But the other six gates into Thebes remain open.

Who can tell the dancer from the dance?

17. The dilated body: *The Death of Laocoon and His Sons*, marble group from the end of the second century AD (Vatican Museum, Rome).

The dilated mind

Franco Ruffini

In order to speak about the dilated mind, it is necessary to begin with the general notion of the pre-expressive level. The pre-expressive level can be defined as the level at which the performer constructs and directs his/her presence on the stage, independent of and before his/her final goals and expressive results.

'Presence' in this definition is free of any metaphorical connotation. It is literal.

The performer's presence, his/her way of being on stage, organically, is obviously a physical and mental presence.

Pre-expressivity, while being physical, is also manifested in a mental dimension.

Using the terminology proposed by Eugenio Barba in *The Dilated Body*, where dilated body and dilated mind are respectively the physical and mental aspects of scenic presence, one can say that scenic presence is related to a dilated body and a dilated mind in reciprocal interdependence.

Scenic presence is both physical and mental, therefore a dilated mind exists. But what proof do we have of its existence? And what do we know about how it functions?

As with all questions concerning the theatre, the answers to these questions are best looked for not by vanishing into the world of one's (own) ideas but by turning to the world of facts, by confronting the theatre practitioners of yesterday and today.

The theatre practitioner I will try to use here in the search for the dilated mind is Stanislavsky, and particularly the Stanislavsky of *Robota aktëra nad soboj v tvorceskom protsesse perezhivanie. Dnevnik ucenika* (*An Actor Prepares*) and *Robota aktëra nad soboj tvorceskom protsesse voplostcenia. Dnevnik ucenika* (*Building a Character*).[1] For the sake of brevity, these two works will here be given the collective title *Robota aktëra*.

The convictions amassed by historiography concerning Stanislavsky's system are so well rooted that it is necessary to begin with certain rather pedantic observations.

First of all, the actor's work described in *Robota aktëra* is explicitly and unequivocally described by Stanislavsky as not having to do with the interpretation of rôles, even if, obviously, it is the basis of that interpretation. The direct and declared objective of the actor's work according to Stanislavsky is the recreation of organicity. By means of the system, the actor learns to be organically present on the stage, before and independently of the rôles that he will have to perform. The actor's work described in *Robota aktëra* is, therefore, work at the pre-expressive level.

Second, *perezhivanie* (which could be translated as 'return to life', in an almost biological sense, as when a frozen seed 'returns to life') is neither the aim of the system nor its only (and privileged) aspect. It is only the psycho-mental part of a more comprehensive work, whose physical aspect is personification. *Perezhivanie* activates internal scenic sensibility and personification activates external scenic sensibility. But the actor must achieve a general scenic sensibility: the synthesis, not the sum, of the two scenic sensibilities, internal and external.

For Stanislavsky, the stage is actually a second nature because, as in *nature*, there can be no physically coherent scenic action which is not also psychically coherent (justified) and vice versa. It is also a *second* nature because, as opposed to what happens in nature, physical coherence and psychical coherence must be constructed by means of the two aspects of the actor's work on himself.

Since the actor's work on himself is work at the pre-expressive level, and since this work is developed by means of personification and *perezhivanie*, *perezhivanie* is its mental aspect.

Stanislavsky's *perezhivanie* is the concretisation of the actor's dilated mind.

How is this *perezhivanie* acquired and how does it work? According to a widely accepted preconception, *perezhivanie* is equivalent to identification with the character, as if this identification was an assortment of techniques aimed at making the feelings of the character come alive.

To refute this preconception it is sufficient to turn to the dictionary and to semantics.

In the dictionary, *perezhivanie* is defined as 'to feel strongly'; semantically, (which is very important to consider when dealing with an analytical language such as Russian), the prefix *pere* placed before 'to live' means an excess. Therefore, rather than translating *perezhivanie* as 'return to life', one ought to speak of a vitalisation of the mental

18–19. Stanislavsky in (**above**) Goldoni's *Locandiera* (1898) and (**opposite**) in Molière's *Le Malade imaginaire* (1913).

horizon. In any case, *perezhivanie* refers more to the idea of activity and tension than to abandon, which is the meaning almost synonymously evoked by identification.

But, linguistic considerations aside, let us take an example of *perezhivanie* from *Robota aktëra*. Torzov, Stanislavsky's spokesman in the novel, is working with his favourite student, Kostia. Kostia must play the part of an oak on a hillside. Realising that his student is bewildered, Torzov begins to bombard him with *ifs*. 'If I was an oak on a hill . . . One among many or alone?

Alone, because the surrounding trees have been cut down.

But why have they been cut down? So that the oak can be used as a lookout from which to watch for enemies . . . '

And in this way, because of being bombarded with the given conditions proposed by both the master and the student, Kostia's mind begins to be vitalised. Many lives have been sacrificed for the oak: his task is not only important, it is even sanctified by sacrifice. Now the oak is no longer a lookout post, it is the lookout itself. And it sees enemies approaching menacingly. It trembles with fear . . . the battle begins. The oak is anxious, consumed by the terror of being burned . . .

Kostia is ready to act. Has he identified himself with his character? If so, *this* identification has nothing to do with the current idea of identification. If we wish to continue to speak of identification, we must at least consider it in concrete terms.

Perezhivanie in Stanislavsky's system is the construction of a substitute psycho-mental apparatus that supplants both the daily apparatus (using which it would be impossible to play the rôle of an oak on a hill) and the apparatus of interpretative cliches (using which the actor would begin to rustle, to wave in the wind, as occurs in so many so-called improvisations).

It is a *cold* construction which, however, produces *heat*, an increase of temperature, a surplus; it causes the actor to vitalise his own mind, rather than re-live something in his own mind.

The Stanislavskian actor's mind in *perezhivanie* is really a dilated mind. This dilated mind induces and justifies coherent physical action executed by a dilated body, exactly as occurs in nature: but due to conscious work.

The example of the oak on the hill is an eloquent one, since the character with which one must identify is not a human being and therefore not a character whose psychology one can adopt. But all the other examples of *perezhivanie* in *Robota aktëra* (that of the burnt money comes to mind), if examined without prejudice, also reveal the same pattern.

Actors, having a scenic task, fashion a substitute psycho-mental apparatus: in the same way that, in parallel and interdependently, they fashion a substitute physical apparatus, that is, a dilated body.

The existence of a form of mental behaviour connected to the pre-expressive level in Stanislavsky's system obliges us to continue the investigation of the characteristics of the dilated mind. One could say that it is an excess mind: just as the dilated body is a body distinguished by an excess of energy.

This can also be the starting point for the search for other possible analogies with the dilated body, that is, with the physical aspect of the pre-expressive level.

Eugenio Barba has made significant suggestions in this regard in *The Dilated Body*. The 'creative pre-condition' (the dilated mind) is, according to Barba, characterised by three modalities:

- peripeteia;
- disorientation;
- precision.

Our strategy should now be clear. We wish to see if, once the connections between dilated body and dilated mind have been ascertained, these connections can be found in Stanislavsky's system. The verification of this 'historical case' is not accidental, in so far as we can now consider it given that in the system the so-called 'return to life' is nothing other than the dilated mind, the mental aspect of the performer's pre-expressivity.

There can no longer be any doubt that the characteristics of the dilated mind that Barba has drawn attention to are analogous to those that have been theoretically and experimentally determined as pertaining also to the dilated body.

The mental perpipeteia corresponds to the 'leap' of the action-in-life, that is, the 'negated action' as Barba has defined it in *Silver Horse*.[2] The energetic leap which is in opposition to inertia and which renders an action unexpected could even also be called a physical peripeteia, fully respecting the Aristotelian meaning of the term.

The dilated mind's precision corresponds to the elimination of redundance in the dilated body's physical action.

Mental disorientation (to which I will return) is the correlative of that negation of the (well-)known which obliges the performer's body-in-life to surprise and be surprised with unpremeditated actions, with actions born immediately.

These mental processes are applied to something that is not the creative result but rather the route that makes this result possible.

Hence the methodological importance of the 'historical case' represented by Stanislavsky. In *Robota aktëra*, it is the process itself, leading to the dilated mind (to *perezhivanie*, in Stanislavsky's terminology), which is described and not its results. As far as the results are concerned, there is only Torzov's 'I believe it' or 'I don't believe it'.

I will not dwell on the description of this process but rather will attempt to investigate what is not described. Not something concealed (or occult) but something so obvious that it is not seen as the description of a process. This is a bit like what happens when one doesn't notice a picture frame even though it is exhibited just as much as the picture is, or like the purloined letter which can't be found, in Edgar Allen Poe's story.

If when referring to both *Moja zhizn' v iskusstve* (*My Life in Art*)[3] and *Robota aktëra* one can speak in general of *narrative form*, as far as *Robota aktëra* itself is concerned it is necessary to specify that the novel form (the diary of an imaginary student in Torzov-Stanislavsky's school) is also (and significantly) developed by means of dialogues between the master and the students. The tensions that animate these dialogues, as well as the rhythm and modulation present, bring Plato's *Dialogues* immediately to mind.

If *Moja zhizn' v iskusstve* has a generic narrative form, *Robota aktëra* is particularly characterised by the narrative form of Platonic dialogue.

Once the Platonic dialogue form has been recognised, one must ask oneself whether this form only frames the content or whether it is an integral part of the content.

I maintain that the Platonic dialogue form is not the form within which the treatise arguments are developed: it is an argument of the treatise, and perhaps its principal argument, since it has been so well protected that it is displayed as the very picture frame of the argument.

Socrates, in Plato's *Dialogues*, behaves with his interlocutors in exactly the same way that Torzov-Stanislavsky behaves with his students. He urges them, he probes them with continual questions, until the *idea* emerges from the student, like something which was already there and which only needed the maieutic power of the dialogue to come to light.

Maieutics, which means 'the art of the midwife', is the art of *bringing thought to life* and therefore of making thought breathe. For Socrates, maieutics was not so much a teaching method as the teaching itself, even though it was hidden (protected) as a frame.

One must say the same of Torzov-Stanislavsky. The master does not teach the *perezhivanie* technique, that is, the technique of the dilated mind. Or better: along with the techniques (use of emotive memory, given conditions, etc.), he teaches *the technique of all techniques*.

This *technique of all techniques* is the maieutics in the Platonic dialogue form, that is, Socratic questioning. Torzov's student learns that the dilated mind (*perezhivanie*) is only acquired by means of implacable questioning and by believing in the idea that will emerge from the answers. Moreover, he learns that the memories, the images, and the stories drawn out by means of *perezhivanie* will only transform the idea into truth if he believes in the idea.

In Stanislavsky's second nature, one does not believe in something because it is true: on the contrary, something is true because one believes in it.

If maieutics is the dilated mind's technique par excellence, what can we learn from maieutics about the dilated mind itself? What can we learn about the processes that activate the dilated mind and that determine how it works, even if only with respect to the historical case of Stanislavsky?

A great deal, if one reveals immediately that perpeteia, precision and disorientation are the specific and fundamental characteristics of Socratic questioning. In maieutics, one intentionally changes the direction of questioning suddenly, not in order to *confuse* but in order to *disorient* the train of thought and free it from the commonplace.

Mental peripeteia, leaps in the train of thought, disorientation ... all presuppose precision. It is the precision of detail, the face-to-face confrontation, not the far-off battle in the name of a hidden truth which causes the collapse of the resistances that prevent thought from flowing with multiform but coherent and truthful life.

If these are the modalities of Socratic questioning, one must remember that the actor who questions himself in

20–22. Stanislavsky in Griboyedov's *Wit Works Woe* (1906), (**opposite top**) in Shakespeare's *Othello* (1896) and (**opposite bottom**) in Chekhov's *Uncle Vanya* (1899).

the search for *perezhivanie* is at one and the same time the questioner and the answerer.

Changing the question changes the answers; disorienting, one becomes disoriented oneself; insisting on precision, one becomes obliged oneself to respect the detail that makes one's idea believable, that is, true.

If Platonic dialogue is the primary technique for the inducement of *perezhivanie* in the student of the system, we can say that the Platonic monologue is the mental state of actors who search for *perezhivanie* by themselves (which is nearly always the case).

The mind in *perezhivanie*, the Stanislavskian actor's dilated mind, is therefore characterised by peripeteia, disorientation, precision.

And so our strategy has come full circle.

The dilated mind, with its own specific means, is based on the same principles as those that define the dilated body. It is really and concretely the mental dimension of the pre-expressive level.

The dilated mind corresponds to the dilated body in so far as both are aspects of an undivided and indivisible presence: physical and mental presence. The dilated body and the dilated mind are the two faces of the same process, which has to do with the actor's body/mind-in-life.

Notes

1 *Robota aktëra nad soboj v tvorceskom protsesse perezhivanie* and *Robota aktëra nad soboj v tvorceskom protsesse voplostcenia* are the second and third volumes of the Russian edition of Stanislavsky's works. These two texts, as I indicated in parenthesis, are referred to respectively as *An Actor Prepares* and *Building a Character*, but they are not exactly the same thing. In fact, the two American texts are edited editions of the respective Russian texts and, moreover, are organised using a set of arguments that is not present in the original edition. This organisation, in addition to amputating the continuity of the Russian text, also obscures the narrative dialogue form, which is however of fundamental importance for a correct reading of Stanislavsky's work. The Italian edition *Il lavoro del'attore* (Bari, Laterza, 1975, 2 volumes) is more trustworthy since, even though it combines the second and third volumes of the Russian edition into a single text, it is complete, and there is no manipulation of the internal organisation.

2 *Silver Horse* is the transcription of a seminar for choreographers held by Eugenio Barba in Mexico in 1985. It is published in a special issue of *Escenica* 1986, the theatre magazine of the National Autonomous University of Mexico, edited by Patricia Cardona. An English translation can be found in E. Barba, *The Paper Canoe: A Guide to Theatre Anthropology*, Routledge, London and New York 1993.

3 *My Life in Art* is an edited edition of *Moja zhizn' v iskusstve* (the first volume of the Russian edition of Stanislavsky's works). The French edition, with a preface by Jacques Copeau, is taken from the American edition. The Italian edition, *La mia vita nell'arte* (Turin, Einaudi, 1963) is, however, complete.

Actions at work

Eugenio Barba

The word 'text', before referring to a written or spoken, printed or manuscripted text, meant 'a weaving together'. In this sense, there is no performance which does not have 'text'.

That which concerns the text (the weave) of the performance can be defined as 'dramaturgy', that is, *drama-ergon*, the 'work of the actions' in the performance. The way in which the actions work is the plot.

It is not always possible to differentiate between what, in the dramaturgy of a performance, may be 'direction' and what may be the author's 'writing'. This distinction is clear only in theatre which seeks to *interpret* a written text.

Differentiating between autonomous dramaturgy and the performance per se dates back to Aristotle's attitude towards the tradition of Greek tragedy, a tradition already well in the past even for him. He drew attention to two different fields of investigation: the written texts and the way they are performed. The idea that there exists a dramaturgy which is identifiable only in an autonomous, written text and which is the matrix of the performance is a consequence of those occasions in history when the memory of a theatre has been passed on by means of the words spoken by the characters

in its performances. Such a distinction would not even be conceivable if it were the performances in their entirety that were being examined.

In a performance, actions (that is, all that which has to do with the dramaturgy) are not only what is said and done, but also the sounds, the lights and the changes in space. At a higher level of organisation, actions are the episodes of the story or the different facets of a situation, the arches of time between two accents of the performance, between two changes in the space – or even the evolution of the musical score, the light changes, and the variations of rhythm and intensity which a performer develops following certain precise physical themes (ways of walking, of handling props, of using make-up or costume). The objects used in the performance are also *actions*. They are transformed, they acquire different meanings and different emotive colourations.

All the relationships, all the interactions between the characters or between the characters and the lights, the sounds and the space, are actions. Everything that works directly on the spectators' attention, on their understanding, their emotions, their kinaesthesia, is an action.

The list could become uselessly long. It is not so important to define what an action is, or to determine how many actions there may be in a performance. What is important is to observe that the actions come into play only when they are woven together, when they become texture: 'text'.

1–2. Text becomes action; (**above**) page from the notebook kept by Edward Gordon Craig (1872–1966) for the mise-en-scène of Shakespeare's *Hamlet* at the Moscow Art Theatre, 1909–10: Act V, scene 2: the duel between Hamlet and Laertes; (**right**) model of the Moscow Art Theatre stage: using this scale model and cardboard cut-outs, Craig explained his concept for the direction of *Hamlet* and his ideas for the movements of the characters to Stanislavsky and his actors. In the picture, the duelling figures of Hamlet and Laertes (Act V, scene 2) can be seen on the right side of the stage.

3. Mise-en-scène diagrams drawn by Stanislavsky for the appearance of the travellers in the second act of Chekhov's *The Cherry Orchard* (1904).

The plot can be of two types. The first type is accomplished through the development of actions in time by means of a *concatenation* of causes and effects or through an alternation of actions which represent two parallel developments. The second type occurs only by means of *simultaneity*: the simultaneous presence of several actions.

Concatenation and *simultaneity* are the two dimensions of the plot. They are not two aesthetic alternatives or two different choices of method. They are the two poles whose tension and dialectic determine the performance and its life: actions at work – dramaturgy.

Let us return to the important distinction – investigated especially by Richard Schechner – between theatre based on the mise-en-scène of a previously written text, and theatre based on a performance text. This distinction can be used to define two different approaches to the theatrical phenomenon and therefore two different performance results.

For example: while the written text is recognisable and transmissible before and independently of the performance, the performance text exists only at the end of the work process and cannot be passed on. It would in fact be tautological to say that the performance text (which is the performance) can be extracted from the performance. Even if one used a transcription technique similar to that used for music, in which various horizontal sequences can be arranged vertically, it would be impossible to pass on the information: the more faithful one tried to make it, the more illegible it would become. Even aural and visual mechanical

recording of the performance captures only a part of the performance text, excluding (at least in the case of performances that do not use a proscenium stage) the complex montages of actor–spectator distance–proximity relationships, and favouring, in all those cases in which the actions are simultaneous, a single montage from among many. It reflects in fact only *one* observer's way of seeing.

The distinction between theatre based on a written text, or in any case on a text composed a priori and used as the matrix of the mise-en-scène, and theatre whose only meaningful text is the performance text, represents rather well the difference between 'traditional' and 'new' theatre. This distinction becomes even more useful if we wish to move from a classification of modern theatrical phenomena to a microscopic analysis or an anatomical investigation of scenic *bios*, of dramatic life: dramaturgy.

From this point of view, the relationship between a performance text and a text composed a priori no longer seems like a contradiction but like a complementary situation, a kind of dialectic opposition. The problem is not, therefore, the choice of one pole or another, the definition of one or another type of theatre. The problem is that of the balance between the *concatenation pole* and the *simultaneity pole*.

The only prejudicial thing that can occur is the loss of balance between these two poles.

When a performance is based on a text composed of words, there is a danger that the balance in the performance will be lost because of the prevalence of linear relationships (the plot as concatenation). This will damage the plot understood as the weaving together of simultaneously present actions.

If the fundamental meaning of the performance is carried by the interpretation of a written text, there will be a tendency to favour this dimension of the performance, which parallels the linear dimension of language. There will be a tendency to consider as ornamental elements all the interweavings that arise out of the conjunction of several actions at the same time, or simply to treat them as actions that are not woven together, as background actions.

The tendency to underestimate the importance of the simultaneity pole for the life of the play is reinforced, in the modern way of thinking, by the kind of performance which Eisenstein in his time was already calling the 'real level of theatre', that is, the cinema. In the cinema, the linear dimension is almost absolute and the dialectic life of the interwoven actions (the plot) depends basically on two poles: the concatention of actions and the concatenation of an abstract observer's attention, the eye-filter which selects close-ups, long shots, etc.

The cinema's grip on our imagination increases the risk that the balance between the concatenation and simultaneity poles will be lost when we make theatre performances. The spectator tends not to attribute a significant value to the interweaving of simultaneous actions and behaves – as opposed to what happens in daily life – as if there was a favoured element in the performance particularly suited to establishing the meaning of the play (the words, the protagonist's adventures, etc.). This explains why a 'normal' spectator, in the West, often believes that he doesn't fully understand performances based on the simultaneous weaving together of actions, and why he finds himself in difficulty when faced with the logic of many Asian theatres, which seem to him to be complicated or suggestive because of their 'exoticness'.

If one impoverishes the simultaneity pole, one limits the possibility of making complex meanings arise out of the performance. These meanings do not derive from a complex concatenation of actions but from the interweaving of many dramatic actions, each one endowed with its own simple meaning, and from the assembling of these actions by means of a single unity of time. Thus the meaning of a fragment of a performance is not only determined by what precedes and follows it, but also by a multiplicity of facets whose three-dimensional presence makes it live in the present with a life of its own.

In many cases, this means that for a spectator, the more difficult it becomes for him to interpret or to judge immediately the meaning of what is happening in front of his eyes and in his head, the stronger is his sensation of living through an experience. Or, said in a way that is more obscure but perhaps closer to the reality: the stronger is the experience of an experience.

The simultaneous interweaving of several actions in the performance causes something similar to what Eisenstein describes in reference to El Greco's *View of Toledo*: that the painter does not reconstruct a real view but rather constructs a synthesis of several views, making a montage of the different sides of a building, including even those sides that are not visible, showing various elements – drawn from reality independently of each other – in a new and artificial relationship.

These dramaturgical possibilities apply to all the different levels and all the different elements of the performance taken one by one, as well as to the overall plot. The performer, for example, obtains simultaneous effects as soon as he breaks the abstract pattern of movements, just as the spectator is about to anticipate them. He composes his actions ('composes' used here in its original meaning, deriving from *cum-ponere*, 'to put together') into a synthesis that is far removed from a daily way of behaving. In this montage, he segments the actions, choosing and dilating certain fragments, composing the rhythms, achieving an equivalent to the real action by means of what Richard Schechner calls the 'restoration of behaviour'.

The use of the written text itself, when it is not interpreted only as a concatention of actions, can guide elements and details, which are not themselves dramatic, into a simultaneous interweaving.

We can draw from *Hamlet*, for example, certain information: traces of the age-old strife between Norway and Denmark are to be found in the conflict between Hamlet's father and Fortinbras's father; England needing to pay taxes to Denmark echoes the days of the Vikings; the life of the Court recalls the Renaissance; the allusions to Wittenberg reflect Reformation issues. All these various historical facets (which we can really *use* as *different* historical facets) can be various choices by means of which the play can be interpreted: in this case, one chosen facet will eliminate the others.

They can also, however, be woven together into a synthesis with many simultaneously present historical elements, whose 'meaning' as it relates to the interpretation of *Hamlet* – that is, what the play will show to the spectators – is not foreseeable. The more the director has woven the different threads together, according to his own logic, the more the meaning of the performance will appear surprising, motivated and unexpected, even to the director himself.

Something similar can also be said for the play's protagonist, for Hamlet. The concatenation of Shakespeare's assembled actions (his montage) usually results in an image of Hamlet as a man in doubt, indecisive, consumed by melancholia, a philosopher ill-suited to action. But this image does not correspond to all the single elements of Shakespeare's total montage. Hamlet acts resolutely when he kills Polonius; he falsifies the message from Claudius to the King of England with cold decisiveness; he defeats the pirates; he challenges Laertes; he quickly notices and sees through the stratagems of his enemies; he kills the King. For an actor (and a director), all of these details, taken one by one, can be used as evidence with which to construct a coherent interpretation of Hamlet. But they can also be used as evidence of different and contradictory aspects of behaviour to be assembled into a synthesis which is not the result of a previous decision about what kind of character Hamlet is going to be.

As can be seen, this simple hypothesis brings us much closer to the creative process (that is, composition process) of many of the great actors in the Western tradition. In their daily work, they did not and do not begin with the interpretation of a character, but develop their work following a route not based on *what?* but on *how?*, assembling aspects that would at first seem incoherent from the point of view of habitual realism, and ending up with a formally coherent synthesis.

Actions at work (dramaturgy) come alive by means of the balance between the concatenation pole and the simultaneity pole. There is a risk of this life being lost with the loss of tension between the two poles.

While the alteration of balance for the sake of weaving through concatenation draws a performance into the somnolence of comfortable recognisability, the alteration of balance for the sake of weaving in the simultaneity dimension can result in arbitrariness, chaos. Or incoherent incoherence. It is easy to see that these risks are even greater for those who work without the guide of a previously composed text.

Written text, performance text, the concatenation or linear dimension, the simultaneity or three-dimensional dimension: these are elements without any value, positive or negative. Positive or negative value depends on the quality of the relationship between these elements.

The more the performance gives the spectator the experience of an experience, the more it must also guide his attention in the complexity of the actions which are taking place, so that he does not lose his sense of direction, his sense of the past and future – that is, the story, not as anecdote, but as the 'historical time' of the performance.

All the principles that make it possible to direct the spectator's attention can be drawn from the life of the performance (from the actions that are at work): the interweaving by means of concatenation and the interweaving by means of simultaneity.

To create the life of a performance does not mean only to interweave its actions and tensions, but also to direct the spectator's attention, his rhythms, to induce tensions in him without trying to impose an interpretation.

On the one hand, the spectator's attention is attracted by the action's complexity, its presence; on the other hand, the spectator is continuously required to evaluate this presence and this action in the light of his knowledge of what has just occurred and in expectation of (or questioning about) what will happen next.

As with the performer's action, the spectator's attention must be able to live in a three-dimensional space, governed by a dialectic which is his own and which is the equivalent of the dialectic that governs life.

In the final analysis, one could relate the dialectic between the interweaving by means of concatenation and the interweaving by means of simultaneity to the complementary (and not the opposing) natures of the left and right hemispheres of the brain.

Each Odin Teatret production uses the scenic space in a different way. The actors do not adapt to given spatial dimensions (as happens on the proscenium stage) but model the architecture of the space according to the specific dramaturgical demands of each new production.

But it is not only the respective spaces occupied by the actors and spectators that change from production to production. During a given single production, the actors sometimes work on the sides of the performing area, at other times in the middle; thus certain spectators experience certain actions in close-up, as it were – when the actors are but a few centimetres from them – while other spectators see the whole picture from a much wider angle.

These same principles are used in outdoor performances, which take place in squares and streets, on balconies and on the rooftops of cities or villages. In this case the environment is given and apparently cannot change, but the actor can use his presence to make a dramatic character spring out of the architecture, which we are normally no longer able to see because of daily habits and usages and which we no longer experience with a fresh eye.

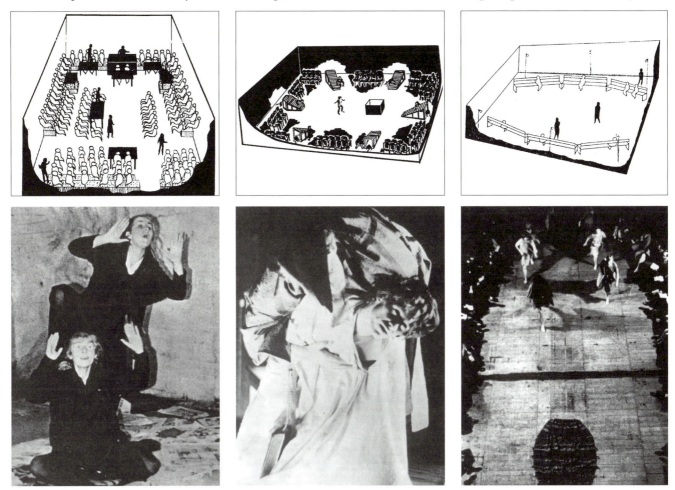

4–9. The organisation of the scenic space: placing the actors and spectators in the space and creating a relationship between them is one of the most important actions in the concatenation–simultaneity pole of the performance text. Examples of actor–spectator proximity relationships in various Odin Teatret performances: (**left**) *Ornitofilene*, 1965; (**centre**) *Kaspariana*, 1967; (**right**) *Ferai*, 1969.

10–11. Odin Teatret outdoor theatre work in relation to space: performances in Salento, Italy.

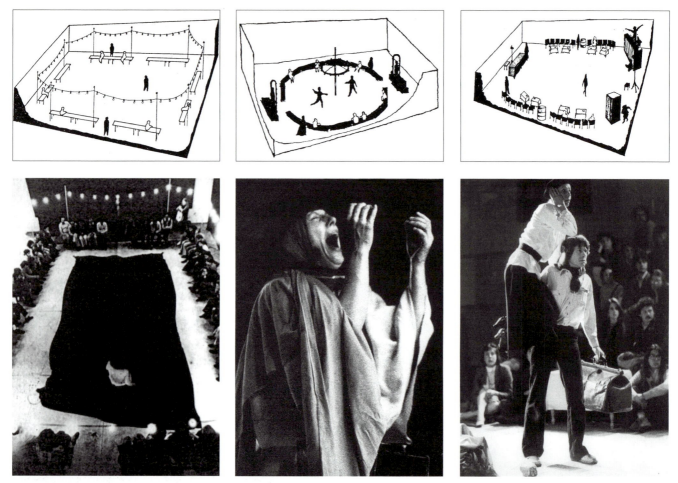

12–17. (**left**) *Min Fars Hus*, 1972; (**centre**) *Come! And the Day Will Be Ours*, 1976; (**right**) *Brecht's Ashes*, 1982.

18–21. Odin Teatret outdoor theatre work in relation to space: performances in Peru and Chile.

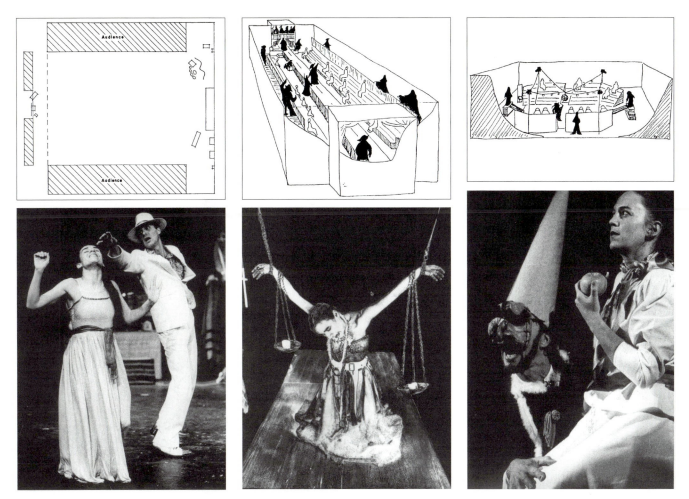

22–27. (**left**) *The Million*, 1979; (**centre**) *The Gospel according to Oxyrhincus*, 1985; (**right**) *Talabot*, 1988.

28. *The Book of Dances*, Peru, 1978.

Energy: power, force; capacity for doing work. (Penguin English Dictionary, Penguin Books, Harmondsworth, England, 1984).

Performers' energy is a readily identifiable quality: it is the performer's nervous and muscular power. The mere fact that this power exists is not particularly interesting, since it exists, by definition, in any living body. What is interesting is the way this power is moulded in a very special context: the theatre. At each moment of our lives, consciously or otherwise, we model our energy. In addition to this daily use of energy, however, there is also a surplus use of energy which we do not use to move, to act, to be present and to intervene in the surrounding world, but which we use to act, to move, to be present, in an effective theatrical way. Studying the performer's energy therefore means examining the principles which performers can use to model their muscular and nervous power according to non-daily modalities.

The various constellations of these principles are the basis of the techniques of various traditions: from Decroux to kabuki, from noh to classical ballet, from Delsarte to kathakali. But they are also the basis of various individual techniques: from Buster Keaton to Dario Fo, from Totò to Marcel Marceau, from Ryszard Cieslak to Iben Nagel Rasmussen.

(F. Taviani, *The Actor's Energy as Premise*).

Kung-fu

Every theatrical tradition has its own way of saying whether or not the performer functions as such for the spectator. This 'functioning' has many names: in the West, the most common is energy, life, or more simply, the performer's presence. In Asian theatrical traditions, other concepts are used, as we will see, and one finds expressions like *prana* or *shakti* in India; *koshi, ki-hai* and *yugen* in Japan; *chikara, taxu* and *bayu* in Bali; *kung-fu* in China.

To acquire this power, this life, which is an intangible, indescribable and unmeasurable quality, the various codified theatrical forms use very particular procedures. These procedures are designed to destroy the inert positions of the performer's body, in order to alter normal balance and to eliminate daily movement dynamics.

It is paradoxical that this elusive quality is arrived at by means of concrete and tangible exercises. This paradox is typified by the word *kung-fu*, which is both the name of a specific exercise and the phrase used to describe the impalpable dimension which we call the performer's presence.

In Chinese, *kung-fu*, known in the West as a combat technique, literally means 'the ability to resist'. It has, however, a number of other meanings: it is the name of the national martial art, but also refers to any discipline, capacity or ability which is mastered only by continuous effort. It can mean work that is carried out and completed, and power, but it can also stand for a scholar's work (the name of the Chinese philosopher Confucius is a Western adaptation of *kung-fu-tsu*). Thus, the term does not have one

1–2. Mei Lanfang (1894–1961) specialised in Peking Opera female rôles. His son Mei Baoju is a performer in the same genre. Mei Baoju is seen here in performance and daily-life situations: (**top**) demonstrating a *tan* (female) rôle at the Holstebro ISTA (1986) and (**below**) walking in the countryside around Holstebro.

single meaning: its meaning depends on the context in which it is used. *Kung-fu* is often a generic expression used in reference to exercise; thus, every master of an art or science can be said to have *kung-fu*.

The term is in fact applied to a series of complementary concepts, from exercise or training to the results of these activities. For performers, to have *kung-fu* means to be in form, to have practised and to continue to practise a particular training, but it also means to possess that special quality which makes them vibrate and renders them present, and which indicates that they have mastered all the technical aspects of their work.

3–4. Mei Lanfang (1894–1961), the famous Chinese female impersonator; (**above**) late in his life and in everyday clothes demonstrating a Peking Opera movement and (**below**) as he appeared at the beginning of his career playing women warrior characters.

Energy and continuity

An extremely rare photograph from 1935 (ill.6) shows a Peking Opera student learning to master the use of the *ts'ai chi'ao* and to acquire *kung-fu* with his master's assistance. *Ts'ai chi'ao* are special shoes that deform the foot in such a way that all the body's weight is supported by the toes. These shoes were traditionally worn by women whose feet were stunted by being wrapped in tight bandages from birth, and were later adapted to the normal feet of *tan* actors, who play female rôles.

In his autobiography, Mei Lanfang (1894–1961), who was without doubt the greatest Peking Opera actor ever, famous in both China and the West, describes the way he trained and acquired *kung-fu* during his apprenticeship:

There are certain basic movements for the *chingyi* (respectable woman) rôle which must be practised over a long period of time before accuracy can be achieved. These include the walk, opening and closing the door, the hand movement, pointing the fingers, swinging the sleeves, touching the hair at the temples, pulling on a shoe, throwing up a hand to call to Heaven, swinging the arm to bewail something, pacing round the stage, and fainting into a chair.

I remember using a long bench for exercises when I was quite young. A brick was placed on the bench and standing on it with little stilts attached to my feet I tried to remain on the brick for the time it takes to burn a stick of incense. When I first started, my legs trembled and it was torture. I could not stay up for more than a minute before it became unbearable and I had to jump down. But after some time, my back and legs developed the proper muscles and I gradually learned to stand on the brick quite steadily.

In the winter I practised fighting and pacing around on ice while wearing short stilts. At first I slipped often, but once I became accustomed to walking on stilts over the ice, it was effortless to go through the same motions on stage without the stilts. Whatever you do, if you go through a difficult stage before reaching the easy ones you'll find that the sweetness is well worth the bitter trouble.

5. *The Wrestler*, Olmec sculpture (National Museum of Anthropology, Mexico City). In spite of the immobility of the pose, the figure has a seemingly crushing tension and possesses a power which leaps from the stone. Or, as put by Octavio Paz, a contemporary Mexican: 'The immobility is the embrace of two lovers'.
6. Peking Opera School (1925): training with the *ts'ai chi'ao*, the shoes for deformed feet used in feminine rôles. The master guides and assists the student: the stick which the master holds under his arm speaks for itself.

7–8. (**left** and **centre**) Katsuko Azuma, buyo dancer, demonstrating the typical way of walking used in classical Japanese theatre, and in a position of energy in time (Volterra ISTA, 1981). The ways of holding the arms in a fixed position, of bending the legs and of sliding the feet wearing the *tabi*, the bifurcated white slippers, are clearly visible in these photos without costume.
9. (**right**) Jas, young Balinese dancer, in precarious balance on tip-toe, immobilises the dance in a moment of energy in time.

I used to get blisters on my feet when I was practising on stilts and suffered much pain. I thought my teacher should not have made a boy in his teens go through such severe trials and felt bitter about it. But today when in my sixties I can still do feminine warrior poses in such operas as *The Drunken Beauty* and *The Mountain Fortress*, I know that I am able to do so only because my teachers were severe with me in my basic training.

(Mei Lanfang, *Autobiography*)

Koshi, ki-hai, bayu

In Japan, even though each of the different theatrical traditions (noh, kyogen, kabuki) has its own particular terminology, there is one single word which all the traditions use to define the actor's presence: *koshi*.

In Japanese, *koshi* refers to a very specific part of the body: the hips. When we walk normally, the hips follow the movement of the legs. But if we want to reduce the movement of the hips – that is, to create a fixed axis within the body – we have to bend the knees and move the trunk as a single unit (ill. 7–8).

By blocking the hips and preventing them from following the movements of the legs, two different levels of tension are created in the body: in the lower part (the legs which must move), and in the upper part (the trunk and the vertebral column, which is engaged by pushing on the hips).

The setting up of these two opposing tension levels within the body necessitates the adoption of a special balance position, involving the head and the muscles of the neck, trunk, pelvis and legs. The actor's entire muscular tonus is altered. He uses much more energy and must make a greater effort than when walking according to his daily technique.

(Eugenio Barba,
*Theatre Anthropology:
First Hypothesis*)

In noh theatre in particular, we find a more general term for the performer's energy: *ki-hai*, which means 'the profound accord (*hai*) of the spirit (*ki*, in the sense of *pneumo* and *spiritus*, 'breath') with the body'. *Ki-hai* is equivalent to the Sanskrit term *prana*, meaning *pneuma* and *spiritus* and is used by performers both in India and in Bali.

In Bali, there are three words used to define the performer's presence: *cesta kara*, *taksu* and *bayu*. *Cesta kara* is the power that the performer acquires with regular and rigorous training. *Taksu*, on the other hand, is a kind of independent divine inspiration which takes possession of the performer and which is not under his control. A performer might say, 'There was *taksu* tonight' or 'There was no *taksu* tonight', but the presence or absence of *cesta kara* depends entirely on him.

Bayu, 'wind', and 'breath' (*spiritus*), is however the term normally used to describe the performer's presence; the phrase *pengunda bayu* refers to the correct distribution of his energy. Like *ki-hai* in Japanese, the Balinese term *bayu* is a literal description of the increase and decrease of a force which elevates the body and whose complementarity generates life.

Animus, anima

Venilia and Selacia were two Roman goddesses: one was the goddess of the waves that lap the shore, the other was the goddess of the waves that return to the open sea. Why two goddesses, if the water that comes in to the shore and the water that moves seaward again is the same water? The substance and the force may be the same, but the direction and quality of the energy are different, opposite. The wave's energy, the dance of the two goddesses, can be discovered in the performers' pre-expressive sub-stratum, in the blending of the two profiles of their double-edged energy, the vigorous *animus* energy and the soft *anima* energy.

Before being thought of as a purely spiritual entity, before being made platonic and Catholic, the soul was thought of as a wind, a continuous flux that animated the motion and life of animals and humans. In many cultures, not only in Ancient Greece, the body was and is compared to a percussion instrument: its soul is the heat, the vibration, the rhythm.

10–11. In every man there is a woman and in every woman a man. This commonplace – or universal – truth does not help the performer to become aware of the double and sharp-edged nature of individual energy, the existence, that is, of *anima* and *animus* energy. It would be a mistake to speak of masculine or feminine energy or to equate these with *animus* and *anima* energy. It would be equally misleading to think that a performer is driven by only one of these energies: they are always both present, and an experienced performer knows how to equilibrate their use, accentuating now one and then the other.

The use of this alternation of the flow of energy is very clear when one thinks of such universally known performers as (**top**) Charlie Chaplin (1889–1980), in *Shoulder Arms* or (**bottom**) Anna Magnani (1908–1973) in a shot from Luchino Visconti's *Bellissima* (1951). Chaplin's energy quality is soft, typically *anima*, yet no one would dream of saying that he is feminine. An actress such as Anna Magnani shows a prevalently *animus* energy quality, and likewise, no one would claim that she is masculine.

The alternation between *animus* and *anima* energy is clearly discernible in Indian, Balinese or Japanese actors and dancers, particularly when they are telling or dancing stories that involve many characters; this alternation is similarly clearly discernible in Western actors, dancers and mimes who have also undergone a training that does not differentiate between the sexes. Their ability to model the complementarity of their energy has made it possible for many actors to fascinate and surprise by contradicting stereotypical male–female social behaviour. In film, for example, one need only consider the *animus* aspect of such actresses as Greta Garbo, Katherine Hepburn and Bette Davis, or the *anima* emanations of such actors as Marlon Brando, James Dean, Montgomery Clift or Robert de Niro.

This wind – vibration and rhythm – can change face by means of a subtle mutation of its internal tension. Boccaccio, commenting on Dante and summarising the attitudes of a millenarian culture, said that when *anima*, the living and intimate wind, is drawn towards and desires something, it becomes *animus* (in Latin *animus* means 'air', 'breath').

Soft energy, *anima*, and vigorous energy, *animus*, are terms that have nothing to do with the distinction between masculine and feminine, nor with Jungian archetypes or projections. They describe a very perceptible polarity, a complementary quality of energy difficult to define with words, and therefore often difficult to analyse, develop and transmit.

By means of techniques passed on by tradition, or through the building of a character, performers acquire an extra-daily form of behaviour. They dilate their presence and consequently also sharpen the spectator's perception. They are body-in-life in the fiction of the theatre or dance. Or they aspire to be so. To this end, they have repeated the same actions over and over, they have trained rigorously. To this end, they use mental processes, magic 'ifs', personal subtexts. To this end, they imagine that their body is the centre of a network of physical tensions and resistances, unreal but effective. They use an extra-daily body and mind technique.

12. (**top**) In Bali, energy is defined by the term *bayu* ('wind'), in Japan, the term used is *ki-hai* ('spirit', 'breath'), in theatre anthropology, the term *animus* (Latin for 'air', 'breath') is used. But what are the actual means used to raise this wind which animates the performer's actions? It has to do with the mastery of certain precise positions, based on a well-articulated differentiation between soft and strong tensions, observable here in the Balinese dancer, Desak Made Suarti Laksmi (from a demonstration at the Holstebro ISTA, 1986). All the forms of Balinese dance are based on and constructed according to a series of oppositions between *keras* (strong) and *manis* (soft).

13. (**below**) I Made Bandem, Balinese dancer, as Hanuman, the monkey king in the *Ramayana*. In the Indonesian *Wayang Wong* stories, Hanuman is given the name Bayuatmaja, 'Son of the Wind'. Not only is he the son of the wind god but himself possesses tremendous speed and superhuman powers. There are three elements in Balinese art and religion which are considered to be fundamentally interconnected: *bayu*, *sabda*, and *idep*, 'action', 'word', and 'thought' respectively. When a Brahman priest prays, he has the prayer in his mind, the words on his lips and the actions in his hands (cf. *Hands: mudras*), all at the same time. The same three elements are also present in performing, where they serve to fuse intentions, movements and gestures with the spoken dialogue.

14–15. (**left**) Kanichi Hanayagi now in the rôle of a samurai doing a demonstration at the Holstebro ISTA (1986). (**right**) Actor K. N. Vijayakumar performing a female rôle from kathakali theatre at the Holstebro ISTA (1986).

On the visible level, it seems that they are expressing themselves, working on their body and voice. In fact, they are working on something invisible: energy.

The concept of energy (*energeia* = 'strength', 'efficacy', from *én-érgon*, 'at work') is a concept both obvious and difficult. We associate it with external impetus, with an excess of muscular and nervous activity. But it also refers to something intimate, something that pulses in immobility and silence, a retained power which flows in time without dispersing in space.

Energy is commonly reduced to imperious and violent behaviour models, but it is actually a personal temperature-intensity which the performer can determine, awaken, mould and which above all needs to be explored.

The performer's extra-daily technique, their scenic presence, derives from an alteration of balance and basic posture, from the play of opposing tensions that dilate the body's dynamics. The body is rebuilt for the scenic fiction. This 'art body' – and therefore, 'unnatural body' – is neither male nor female. At the pre-expressive level, sex is of little import. Typical male energy and typical female energy do not exist. There exists only an energy specific to a given individual.

The performer's task is to discover the individual propensities of his or her energy and to protect its potentialities, its uniqueness.

It is an apparently inoffensive point of departure to learn to perform according to one of two clear perspectives, both of which are related to the distinction between the sexes. It does, however, have a consequence: the introduction, without justification, of rules and habits from daily reality into the extra-daily territory of the theatre.

On the final level, the performance, the level of results, the performer's presence takes form in a scenic figure, a character, in which masculine or feminine characterisation is inevitable and necessary. It is however both unnecessary and damaging when this masculine or feminine characterisation is also dominant on a level in which it does not belong: the pre-expressive level.

During apprenticeship, individual differentiation passes through the negation of the differentiation of the sexes. The field of complementarity dilates. This is seen in the West (in modern dance and mime) when in training – work on the pre-expressive level – no account is taken of what is masculine or what is feminine, and in the East when a performer takes on both masculine and feminine rôles. The double-edged nature of energy becomes tangibly evident. The balance between the two energy poles, *animus* and *anima*, is preserved.

In this context, the Balinese speak of a continuous interweaving of *manis* and *keras*. The Indians speak of *lasya* and *tandava*. These terms do not refer to women and men or to masculine or feminine qualities, but to softness and vigour as aspects of energy. The warrior god Rama, for example, is often represented in the 'soft' manner: *lasya*.

Anima and *animus* refer to the two sides of a pair of scales, a *concordia discors*, an interaction between opposites which brings to mind the poles of a magnetic field or the tension between body and shadow. It would be arbitrary to particularise them sexually.

(Eugenio Barba, *Animus-Anima*)

16–19. Peking Opera actress Pei Yanling as herself (**bottom right**) and in three rôles: the Monkey King (**top left**), a heavenly spirit (**top right**), a warrior (**bottom left**). Three different but clear examples of *animus* energy, three male characters made extraordinarily alive by Pei Yanling, the most famous performer of male rôles in contemporary China (demonstration at the Holstebro ISTA, 1986).

20. Kabuki actor Kanichi Hanayagi as a young geisha and (see ill. 14 on page 78) as a samurai. When kabuki first began, towards the middle of the sixteenth century, it was performed uniquely by actresses, but when their performances became too licentious, the shogun's government, in the interests of public morality, prohibited them and declared that all female rôles should henceforth be performed by men only. These actors were called *onnagata*. As a result of, and thanks to this stipulation, the *onnagata* were able to develop a series of refined and elaborate techniques for the interpretation of female rôles, achieving such a degree of perfection that even today, the fascination exerted by kabuki is to a large extent due to their skills. The by now ancient and well-established Japanese tradition of female rôles being played by male actors – also typical of other traditional Asian theatres, such as the Peking Opera and kathakali (see ill.15 on page 78) – demonstrates how the interpretation of a rôle depends not on the performer's sex, but rather on the way s/he models energy.

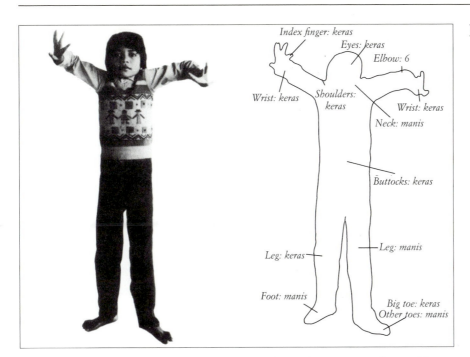

21. *Keras* and *manis* (strong and soft) principles in a Balinese dance position, illustrated by Jas, young daughter of dancer and master I Made Pasek Tempo.

22. Javanese choreographer Sardono W. Kusumo teaching the *keras* and *manis* positions during a demonstration at the Balinese seminar at Odin Teatret (Holstebro, 1974).

Keras *and* manis

In Bali, energy is defined using the term *bayu* ('wind'), in Japan, *ki-hai* ('spirit', 'breath'), in theatre anthropology the terms *animus* and *anima* (from the Latin, meaning 'air', 'breath') are used. It is a wind that animates the performer's actions. But how does one make this wind blow? By mastering precise body positions that are based on a well-articulated distinction between soft and strong tensions. We can observe these positions in Balinese dance: all the forms of Balinese dance are in fact constructed on a series of oppositions between *keras* and *manis*.

Keras means strong, hard, vigorous. *Manis* means delicate, soft, tender. *Keras* and *manis* can be applied to various movements, to positions of different parts of the body in a dance, to successive movements in the same performance. This relationship is clearly visible in the basic Balinese dance position, which to Western eyes may appear extremely stylised. In any case, it is the result of a consistent alternation of parts of the body between the *keras* and *manis* positions.

(Eugenio Barba,
Theatre Anthropology)

If we examine the typical step position taken by Jas, the youngest daughter of Balinese dance master I Made Pasek Tempo, we can see the alternations of *keras* and *manis*. The extended diaphragm is also a *keras* position and is typically found throughout Asia, often emphasised by costume. In both China and India, strips of cloth or tight belts are used underneath the costume to keep the diaphragm compressed. In Japan, the traditional *obi*, which ties the *kimono* between the chest and the hips, is bound much more tightly when it is part of a theatrical costume than when it is used in daily life.

23–24. One of the first commedia dell'arte Harlequins, Italian actor Tristano Martinelli, and the character Scaramouche, played by famous Italian actor Tiberio Fiorilli, Molière's master, reveal a surprising analogy with the basic Balinese position (where the neck is sunk down between the shoulders, cf. preceding illustrations). Assuming this position creates a series of tensions not only in the shoulders but throughout the performer's body.

Lasya *and* tandava

In the Indian tradition as well, one works on energy within the energy polarity and not in relation to the correspondence between the character and the performer's sex. Indian dance styles are in fact divided into two major categories, *lasya* (soft) and *tandava* (vigorous), based on the way these styles are executed in movements, irrespective of whether the performer is male or female.

The distinction between these two aspects of dance is ancient and derives from a myth associated with the god Shiva, Lord of the Dance, in his manifestation as Ardhanarishwara, literally, the 'Lord who is half woman'. The image of Ardhanarishwara is typically a figure which is half man, Shiva himself, and half woman, Shiva's wife Parvati (ill.39 p.20). This image is considered to be an expression of the reciprocal action of the male and female elements in the cosmos. The first dance created by Shiva Ardhanarishwara was crude and wild (*tandava*) while the dance created by his Parvati half, who imitated his movements, was delicate and gentle (*lasya*).

Indian dance has made use of these two aspects of Shiva's unity: not only the style but also every element of it (movement, rhythm, costume, music) is defined as *tandava* if it is strong, vigorous, tumultuous or as *lasya* if it is light, delicate and gentle. For this reason, the interpretation of characters is not based on the performers' sexual identities but on the modelling of energy in a strong or delicate direction.

For example, there is a tradition which survived until very recently in village temples in the province of Orissa. Pre-adolescent male children, dressed and made up as women, were trained to interpret a completely female dance. The *gotipuas*, as they were called, were professionals, and performed not only in the temple, but also for a much wider public: during religious festivals, local nobles often asked them to perform outside the temples. On these occasions, they would present episodes from *Krishna-lila* or other mythological stories, as an integral part of the religious celebrations.

25–27. Guru Kelucharan Mahapatra (1926–2004), actor, dancer and choreographer, considered the most important architect of contemporary odissi dance, together with a *gotipua* student. Guru Kelucharan Mahapatra began his apprenticeship when very young, learning female rôles in the gotipua tradition (cf. following illustrations). Today he is known not only as a great performer of female rôles in odissi dance, but also as the master who, with his student Sanjukta Panigrahi, has restored odissi style, with the result that it is now a form of classical Indian dance appreciated worldwide.

28–31. Gautam, an eleven-year-old gotipua student, made-up and costumed as a woman, being guided in various training exercises by *guru* Kelucharan Mahapatra (demonstration at the Holstebro ISTA, 1986).

Tame

In addition to the concept of *koshi*, both noh and kabuki have another concept which defines, in a complementary way, the creation of a new quality of energy. In physics, energy must be neither degraded nor lost; similarly in theatre and dance. Performers must retain the energy which they continuously produce and renew. They do this by building an obstacle, 'a dam'. This is *tame*.

Both noh and kabuki use the expression *tameru*, which can be represented by a Chinese ideogram meaning 'to accumulate' or by a Japanese ideogram meaning 'to bend' something which is both flexible and resistant, like a cane of bamboo. *Tameru* defines the action of holding back, of retaining. From *tameru* comes *tame*, the ability to keep energy in, to absorb into an action limited in space, the energy necessary to carry out a much larger action. This ability becomes a way of describing an actor's talent in general. In order to say that an actor has or doesn't have sufficient scenic presence, the necessary power, the master tells her that she has, or doesn't have, *tame*.

(Eugenio Barba, *Theatre Anthropology*)

Katsuko Azuma (ill. 32), even though her body is hidden by her *kimono*, shows the opposition that is created by the power that is pushing her forward and the power that is holding her back. This opposition is visible in the neck and hands, but the energy's hidden structure is found in the curve of the spinal column, in the arms and in the legs, which are contracted like a tight spring. In the position of a fall forward that 'never takes place', the performer suspends the visual action but continues to show the energy which is travelling through her. *Koshi* and *tame* are in fact this ability of the performer to transform immobility into action and to achieve a dilated body (cf. *Pre-expressivity*), not by means of the amplification of movements but by means of tensions inside the body.

Energy in space and energy in time

My entire body is engaged, I am ready, prepared to act in a very precise way: to grasp the bottle on the table in front of me. My postural muscles are activated and there is a slight displacement of my body which, although almost imperceptible, mobilises the same energies that would be necessary for the real action. I am executing an action, not in space, but in time – that is, I am engaging my postural muscles, but not those displacement muscles that would move my arms, nor the manipulation muscles that would help my fingers grasp the bottle.

There is a rule in noh theatre that says that three-tenths of any action should happen in space and seven-tenths in time. Usually, if I want to grasp this bottle, I engage just that energy which is necessary to carry out the action, but in noh, seven times more energy is engaged, not to carry out the action in space, but to hold it within the actor and retain it (energy in time). This means that for any action, the noh actor uses more than twice as much energy than is necessary for the action in space alone. On one hand, the actor projects a quantity of energy in space; on the other hand, he retains more than twice as much within himself, creating a resistance to the action in space.

(Eugenio Barba, *Theatre Anthropology: First Hypothesis*)

32. Katsuko Azuma, buyo dancer, shows a *tame* (position of retained energy) during a demonstration at the Bonn ISTA (1980).

Energy in time is thus manifest by means of an immobility which is traversed and charged by a maximum tension. It is a special quality of energy that is not necessarily the result of an excess of vitality or displacements of the body. In Oriental traditions, a master is someone who is 'alive' in this immobility. In martial arts in particular, immobility is the sign that one is ready for action. In *t'ai chi*, it is said that 'to meditate actively is a hundred, a thousand, a million times better than to meditate at rest'. In Western theatre this situation is very rare: only great performers succeed in using this type of energy.

Peking Opera performers suddenly stop in certain positions, interrupting an action at the height of tension and retaining this tension in an immobility which is neither static nor inert but dynamic. As a Chinese actor expressed it in his basic English: 'movement stop, inside no stop'. The dance of opposition in these poses, called *shan-toeng* or *lian-shan* (literally, 'to stop the action'), is danced *in the body* and not *with the body*.

33–34. (**top left** and **right**) Odissi dancer Sanjukta Panigrahi: stillness in motion.
35–36. Katsuko Azuma performing a male rôle (**bottom left**) and a female rôle (**bottom right**) in buyo dance. Energy in space and energy in time do not depend on male or female categories.

Santai, *the actor's three bodies*

Noh has always been performed exclusively by men, who also play women. Sometimes the woman may be young and presented with grace and gentleness; other times, she is old and even though her actions are more contained, they are nevertheless fluid and soft. On other occasions, the woman leaves the stage and then returns as a ghost and behaves as if possessed, like a fury or a demon, using an energy that seems more fitting to a warrior. How can the same performer give life to such prodigious changes?

The answer to this question is given by Zeami, the founder of noh, in his treatise entitled *Shikadosho*:

An actor who is beginning his training must not overlook the Two Arts (*nikyoku*), and the Three Types (*santai*, literally, three bodies). By the Two Arts I mean dance and chant. The Three Types refer to the human forms that constitute the basis of rôle impersonation: an old person (*rotai*), a woman (*nyotai*), a warrior (*guntai*).

The three basic types of which Zeami speaks are not, however, rôle types – as they are generally translated – but *tai*, that is, *bodies* that are guided by a particular energy quality which has nothing to do with sex. The three types are in fact different ways of using the *same* body, giving it different lives by means of different types of energy. One of the other meanings of the expression *tai* is 'appearance'.

To understand how this is possible, one must not look at 'extreme' bodies – the woman and the warrior – but at the body of the old person, such as it is described in the treatise *Nikyoku Santai Ezu* (*Two Arts and Three Types with Illustrations*). Here Zeami gives concrete instructions as to how to embody the three *tai* and illustrates the instructions with drawings:

1. Old Person type: serenity of spirit, distant gaze.
2. Woman type: its substance is spirit, strength is excluded.

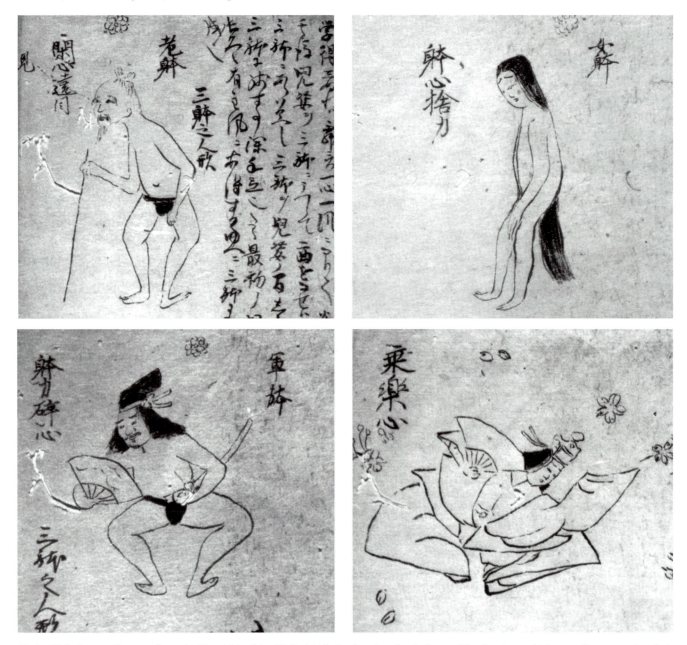

37–44. Noh theatre rôle types drawn by Zeami Motokiyo (1363–1444), the founder of noh theatre. The drawings, which according to certain scholars were not made by Zeami himself but rather by his brother-in-law Komparu Zenchiku, are taken from *The Two Basic Arts* and the *Three Rôle Types*, a brief treatise on the art of performing written by Zeami. This work is a summary of concepts more fully developed in Zeami's best-known book, *The True Path Towards the Flower*. The figures of the Old Man, the Woman and the Warrior, drawn without costume (ill.37, 38, 39) in order

3. Warrior type: its substance is strength, the spirit is found in details 'delicacy within strength'.

Zeami then draws the three *tai*, without costume, and this makes it possible for us to discover the *substance*, that is, the position of the spinal column. It is interesting to note that in the drawing of the old person, who is leaning on a cane, Zeami takes care to indicate the upward direction of the character's gaze. This is in contrast to the bent posture of an individual who is so weak that he must lean on a cane. A tension is thus created in the neck and the upper part of the spinal column.

This drawing reveals the secret of the *three bodies*: by means of an old person's body, the performer consciously manipulates the two faces of energy – *animus/anima* – which are both alive in him. He thus causes the real *hana* to bloom. *Hana* is the flower which, according to Zeami, characterises the great performer:

Playing the rôle of an old man represents the very pinnacle of our art. These rôles are crucial, since the spectators who watch can gauge immediately the real skills of the actor. [...] In terms of stage deportment, most actors, thinking to appear old, bend their loins and hips, shrink their bodies, lose their Flower, and give a withered, uninteresting performance. Thus there is little that is attractive in what such actors do. It is particularly important that the actor refrain from performing in a limp or weak manner, but bear himself with grace and dignity. Most crucial of all is the dancing posture chosen for the rôle of an old man. One must study assiduously the precept: portray an old man while still possessing the Flower. The results should resemble that of an old tree that puts forth flowers.

(Zeami, *Fushikaden*)

to show the body positions better, represent the three basic noh theatre rôle types. Note that in the drawing of the Old Man (ill.37, p. 86, **top left**), the line drawn upwards from the eyes creates an opposition to the tendency of the body of an old man to bend and slouch. Other drawings by Zeami show the other noh theatre rôle types: the dance of a heavenly being (ill.40); a child (**above left**); a warrior (**above right**); a woman (**below left**); and a devil (**below right**).

Braking the action

The use of energy in time and in space can also be applied to the *bios* and rhythm of the whole performance: Meyerhold defined this operation as 'braking the rhythms'. 'Braking the rhythms' is overtly seen in two of Meyerhold's productions: *Bubus, the Teacher*, in 1925, and *The Government Inspector*, in 1926.

The playing area for *Bubus, the Teacher* is a large plateau, on which the actors move against a background of continuous music made up of forty-six pieces by Chopin and Liszt. The actors' way of speaking is based on combinations of long and short rhythms. In 1926, in *October in the Theatre*, Gausner and Gabrilovitch described the results as follows:

The braking of the rhythms in *Bubus* makes it possible for us to discover that combinations of segments of time can acquire meaning. We were thus offered a new theatrical procedure of extreme importance. [. . .]

We see the *tempo* actor Okhlopkov, who is so far almost unique in this genre. With his segments, his longs and shorts, he performs *in time*. This is how he has built the rôle of General Berkovetz in *Bubus*, which is completely made up of these alternations. Assembled, they give the impression of feelings: alarm, joy, despair, lust. Mime is only added as auxiliary material.

In the scene where the General is called to the telephone by Van Kamperdaf, the capitalist, the mimed elements are: the work of the face and the hands and the succession of body sketches which would express nothing if they were not sustained by the *tempo*. It is the *tempo* which gives these mimed elements all their meaning.

So the General is called to the telephone. With a brusque movement, he lifts his head and looks at the servant: eight seconds. His face is expressionless. The length of the pause reveals his alarm. He suddenly rises up from his chair and stands immobile: ten seconds. The tension of the alarm mounts: fourteen seconds. He slowly nods: fifteen seconds. He slides his hand inside his dolman and then rapidly withdraws it again: four seconds. The contrast between the *tempo* of the preceding gradation and the rapid final discharge (the removal of the hand from

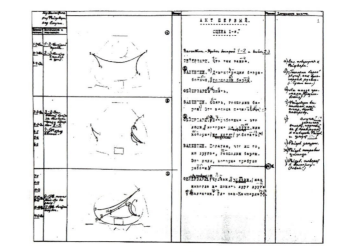

45. A scene from Meyerhold's production of A. Faiko's *Bubus, the Teacher* (1925).
46. A sketch by I. Slepjanov of the circular set design for Meyerhold's *Bubus, the Teacher*.
47. The first page of the director's score for *Bubus, the Teacher* reconstructed by Tsetnerovitch (1926). The different columns from the left describe: the time in seconds for each action; the tempo of each action; a sketch of the actor's movement in space, segmented and numbered in different phases; the author's text in which the length of pauses and the speed of speeches are inserted; the relation between music and text; and finally an exact indication of the way in which certain words should be pronounced or certain movements performed.

48. 'A beautiful recurrence': the fourteenth scene in Meyerhold's production of Gogol's *The Government Inspector* (1926): a close-up of the set's central platform.
49. Set design sketch by P. Kiselëv for Gogol's *The Government Inspector*, based on a series of doors. The position for the mobile platform is indicated in the centre of the sketch.
50. Sketch of the sloping mobile platform which Meyerhold used in the mise-en-scène of *The Government Inspector*.
51. *Jesus among the Doctors* (1506) by Albrecht Dürer (1471–1528). This painting, which Meyerhold saw in Rome in the Palazzo Barberini, was the model for the condensed composition of the relations in *The Government Inspector*.

the dolman) announces that the telephone call will be disagreeable.

The body mime (very reduced) and the gestures (sketched) play only a secondary rôle. They are signals which underline the succession of the time segments. [...] There is no doubt that this performing genre – using *tempo* – has a more powerful effect than mime.

In 1926, when Meyerhold presented his mise-en-scène of *The Government Inspector*, he explained the use of the musical background as a restriction of time. The music not only regulated the intonations and timbre of the speeches, but was also an accompaniment to the actors' dialogues. Sometimes the music was a melodic variation of the dialogues, at other times it was a contrast to the dialogues. Each character had its own musical theme, like a Wagnerian leitmotif.

But this restriction in time was also accompanied by a restriction of the space. The playing area for *The Government Inspector* was no longer the large plateau used for *Bubus*, but was a semi-circular area onto which fifteen red doors opened. There was a small platform in the centre (3.55 by 4.25 metres). The entire performance was concentrated on this small platform area.

This restricted scenic area obliged the actors to be extremely conscious of both their most detailed movements and the performance's general rhythm, so as not to break the unity of the musical and scenic tensions. Meyerhold comments:

In *Bubus*, a musical background was created which functioned as a form of self-control. An actor might have wanted to make a pause, but the music forced him to continue. Or, an actor might have wanted to let himself go into improvisation, but no, everything was perfectly orchestrated on planes of continuous unities, to such an extent that many people saw the performance as a dramatic ballet.

In *The Government Inspector*, it will be necessary to gather all the actors into an area of no more than three square metres. To concentrate them in a very confined area and to light this area with full light, even when the scene is set at night. The mimed performing will thus be seen better. The characters will be seated on a divan. But the important thing is that the floor will be very sloping. It will be difficult to walk on. Even the furniture will be inclined towards the public. There will be a wooden table in front of the divan, so that the people seated on the divan will only be seen from the waist up. One will be able to glimpse the actor's legs underneath the table; above the table, their faces and hands will be visible. The surface of the table will be dark: there we can place the actors' hands and show them to the public. So we'll have a parade of hands and faces, the actors will smoke pipes of various sizes, big and small. A group of people smoking, puffing away, dozing and even sleeping.

(*Meyerhold at rehearsal*, 20 October, 1925)

On stage, it is not at all a question of static groups, but of an action: the action which time exerts on the space. Above and beyond the plastic principle, the performing is determined by the time principle, that is, by rhythm and music.

If you look at a bridge, you see that it is a sort of leap set in the metal. In other words, it is not immobility, but movement. The essential part of a bridge is not the decoration which ornaments its railings but the tension which it expresses. The same applies to performing. Using another kind of comparison, I could say that the actor's performing is like the melody and the mise-en-scène is like the harmony.

(Alexander Gladkov, *Meyerhold speaks*)

52–58. Italian actor Ermete Zacconi (1857–1948) in *The Telephone Call* by French author André de Lorde, the most acclaimed Grand Guignol playwright (called Prince of Terror). The play, capitalising on the recent invention of the telephone, ends with a horror scene in which the hero, making a telephone call to his family, 'hears' the rape and murder of his wife and children. This scene required a crescendo of emotional reactions and thus a use of energy in time very similar to that demanded by Meyerhold for General Berkovetz's telephone scene in *Bubus, the Teacher* (cf. preceding page).

53

54

57

58

The performer's presence

Kung-fu, understood as exercise, and as the presence of energy in action both in time and in space, is clearly discernible in this sequence of photographs of an actress from a different tradition and in a different work context.

Odin Teatret actress Iben Nagel Rasmussen is seen using various ways of walking, of stopping, and of using a prop that belong to her daily training, based on exercises which she herself has elaborated. But we find here the application of all the principles of extra-daily technique.

In the immobile position (ill.59), energy in time, the actress stops, but on tip-toe, in a position of precarious balance accentuated by the *keras* position of the neck, similar to that of a hanged man. It is this *keras* position of the neck that lifts the arms upwards.

Energy in space (ill.60): the way of walking, the spreading of the legs, which increases the distance between the feet, with a twisting of the trunk which recalls the Indian *tribhangi*.

And finally (ill.61), the running movement and dynamic action with a precarious balance which rests on one foot only, with the knees slightly bent (in a posture which Odin technical terminology calls *sats*, that is, 'preparation for action, for impulse, *to be about to* . . .'). The position of the head alters balance and breaks the body line.

The Odin Teatret term *sats*, that is, the impulse to action which is energy in time corresponds to what Stanislavsky defined as 'standing in the correct rhythm':

> Stanislavsky persisted: "You are not standing in the correct rhythm!"
>
> To stand in rhythm. How – to stand in rhythm! To walk, to dance, to sing in rhythm – this I could understand, but to *stand*!
>
> "Pardon me, Konstantin Sergeyevich, but I have no idea whatsoever what rhythm is". "That is not important. Around that corner is a mouse. Take a stick and lie in wait for it: kill it as soon as it jumps out . . . No, that way you will let it escape. Watch *more attentively* – more attentively. As soon as I clap my hands, beat it with the stick . . . Ah, see how late you are! Once more. Concentrate more. Try to make the stroke of the stick almost simultaneous with the clap. Well then, do you see that now you are standing in a completely different rhythm than before? Do you feel the difference? To stand and watch for a mouse – that is one rhythm: to watch a tiger that is creeping up on you is quite another one".
>
> (V.O. Toporkov, *Stanislavsky in Rehearsal*)

59–61. Odin Teatret actress Iben Nagel Rasmussen in a street performance in Sardinia (1975).

To translate the invisible wind by means of the water which it sculpts as it passes by (Robert Bresson)

Equivalence: to have the same value and yet be different (from a dictionary)

Art is the equivalent of nature (Picasso)

For example, in The Barrier Gate (Sekinoto) *(1784), when 'Ki ya bo . . .' written with characters meaning 'living', 'wild', and 'evening', is sung, the actor ignores these meanings and instead mimes 'tree' (ki also means tree in Japanese), 'arrow' (ya also means arrow), and 'pole' (bo also means pole)* (James Brandon, *Form in Kabuki Acting*)

The equivalence principle

If we observe a hand in daily life, we immediately notice that each finger is animated by a tension that is different from the tensions that animate the other fingers. By means of a codification which specifies the position of the elbow, the bending of the wrist and the articulation of the fingers, the Asian performer has constructed an equivalent to the variety of tensions in daily life. Great artists have always been inspired by the idea of art as an equivalent to nature rather than as a reconstruction of nature. The various tensions in the wrist and fingers of Michelangelo's *David* animate the marble with that perpetually vibrant energy characteristic of life (ill. 1–2).

The *belle courbe* demonstrated by Ingemar Lindh (ill.10–13, p.97) is a good example of the play of extra-daily tensions in the body of a Decroux mime. Analysing the *belle courbe* will help us understand how one succeeds in creating an equivalence by using counterweight and will also clarify the respective functions of the various parts of the performer's body.

The trunk and the legs never change position – *la belle courbe* – but the position of the arms is variable. The legs divide the body weight, respecting the counterweight principle: the leg which is extended backwards (ill.4) supports balance only (counterweight), while the forward leg, bent, carries all the body's weight. This forward leg is traversed by an imaginary plumb line which begins at the shoulders and ends in the middle

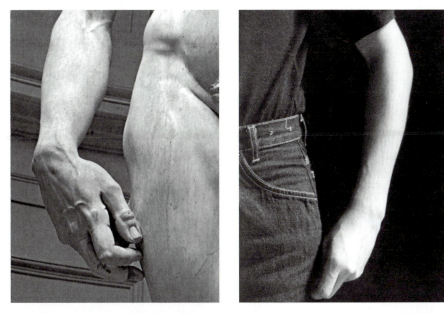

1–3. (**top left**) Detail of the right hand of Michelangelo's (1475–1564) *David* (1503), and (**top right**) of the left arm of Japanese kyogen actor Kosuke Nomura in the basic *kamae* position (cf. *Pre-expressivity*); (**bottom**) Detail of Pablo Picasso's *Guernica* (1937), Picasso Museum, Madrid.

of the metatarsal arch. The extended back leg, which functions as a counter-weight, can move or even be lifted without compromising either the body's position or its balance (ill.5).

The *belle courbe* is not a position which the mime has arbitrarily chosen in order to give his body a precarious balance. Rather, it is the result of both a technical demand made by the performer and a precise observation of the reality which he proposes to represent. Let us see what happens.

When one pushes something in daily reality (ill.6), the body's weight is normally supported by both the rear leg and the arms which are pushing forward. This is a familiar image, used to represent both a first degree lever and the effort of human work. When the 'pushing' is being done by a mime (ill.7) the effort cannot be made in the same way because the absence of the concrete opposition causes one of the two support bases to disappear. Nevertheless, as can be seen, the same tension of effort can be found in Ingemar Lindh's position: he shows that he is pushing. He has simply found an equivalent position in his body.

Equivalence, which is the opposite of imitation, reproduces reality by means of another system. The tension of the gesture remains, but it is *displaced* into another part of the body. In this case, the force is moved from the arms to the forward leg. It is the pressure of this leg on the ground (ill.7) and not that of the arms that makes the concrete effort.

What does the spectator see?

The spectator sees a fiction, suggested to him by the mime. Nevertheless, the force is not simulated. By convention, the mime works by eliminating all material reality, every object with which an action can be made. But, because of the same convention, he cannot make an abstraction of the reality which constitutes the sphere of comprehension between the spectator and himself, and without which his gestures would be gratuitous and sterile. This negation of one reality leads to his technique of indirect imitation, the search for an equivalent by means of the only reality at his disposal, that is, the organic use of his own body.

The principle remains the same when the mime enters the less realistic area of *abstract mime*, or when, using the same equivalence procedure, creations and inventions are found that are neither arbitrary nor fortuitous.

4–5. The right leg, which can be lifted from the floor, is the counterweight; the left leg supports the body's weight. Demonstration at the Volterra ISTA (1981) by Swedish mime Ingemar Lindh, student of Decroux.

6–7. Diagram of the direction of force when a weight is actually being pushed (**centre left**) and when the weight is mimed (**centre right**): it can clearly be seen that mime uses an equivalent to the actual force.

8–9. (**bottom**) In these drawings by painter Valentine Hugo, based on the ballet *Le Sacre du printemps* (1913), choreographed by Nijinsky to music by Stravinsky, the dancer keeps the same positions in the legs and the torso but the introverted or extroverted arms suggest different stories.

By means of personal interpretation, the mime thus seeks to suggest to the spectator the concrete nature of effort, but the objective of this force, what it wants to 'tell', depends, however, on the arms. We remarked above that in this sequence (ill.10–13) the trunk never changes position, while the arms assume various positions without altering the basic position. This means that the opposition of tensions that make the body's energy manifest is found entirely in the trunk; the arms are only the anecdote, the literature. In other words, the essence of the gesture is found in the position of the trunk and of the legs that support it.

This phenomenon, seemingly paradoxical since it is a more mental than visual concept and leads us to consider the arms and the hands as symbols of the action, is well known in Asian theatres (cf. *Hands*), but also in certain examples of Western art. As anyone who frequents classical museums will affirm, Greek and Roman statues, decapitated and armless, often have a remarkable tension, even though they are but fragments. A great deal has been written about the position of the arms in the Venus de Milo; the position of the rest of the body has given rise to no plausible conjecture whatsoever.

Let us recall a remark made by the poet Rilke concerning Rodin's sculptures. Wanting to give his sculptures a bold and primordial quality, Rodin tried to embody them with the same power that he had observed in fragments of ancient statues: he violently amputated many of his figures, reducing them to torsos. He did this, for example, with *L'Homme qui marche* (*The Walking Man*) (ill. 14). He once jokingly said that the head is of no use for walking. Rilke appreciated these amputations and this method of work, which reminded him of Eleonora Duse playing D'Annunzio's *La Gioconda* without using her arms (ill. 15).

10–15. (**top and centre**) The Decroux image of the mime's *belle courbe*, demonstrated by Ingemar Lindh: the arms, which can change position, are the anecdote, while the essence of the gesture, or rather, its life, lies in the trunk, which never changes position; (**bottom left**) the walking man: detail of a statue by Auguste Rodin (1840–1917), Sculpture Museum, Barentin, France; (**bottom right**) Eleonora Duse (1858–1924) in D'Annunzio's *La Gioconda* (1899).

16–24. Sanjukta Panigrahi demonstrating the use of a bow and arrow in odissi dance (Volterra ISTA, 1981).

Dhanu: *archery in Indian odissi dance*

The bow and the arrow are absent (cf. *Omission*), and yet, when we look at a sequence of static images (ill.16–24), we are able to perceive an equivalent to the tensions and forces necessary for the shooting of the arrow. In the search for equivalence, the performer dilates her body to the maximum so that the visual image that she offers at each moment of the action can be as dynamic and expansive as possible (cf. The shadow test in *Opposition*). Each of the positions is intended to underline and amplify the actions as if the performer was working with a real bow and a real arrow: the force used to draw the bow, the direction of the shot and the concentration needed to aim.

The performer does not show someone who is shooting an arrow. Rather, she recreates a dialectic person–bow–arrow relationship: the static position of the archer versus the release-speed of the arrow. This relationship is illustrated by the series of oppositions that are created: the twisting of the vertebral column to take the bow from the quiver (ill. 17–18), displacement of the body's weight in the second phase of the action, to notch the arrow (ill. 19–21). The effort needed to draw the bow is recreated by means of the work of the left (forward) leg, which supports the body's weight, and the work of the curved arm, which seems to echo the large curve formed by the head, the spinal column and the right leg (ill.23). And finally, the culmination of the action, the shot itself, is represented by the sudden propulsion of the body forwards

(ill.24), corresponding to the arrow which flies towards a timid and defence-less doe (ill. 25, below).

If we did not know the theme of these actions, we would have difficulty in understanding that they had to do with archery, and it would be difficult to make the value of the equivalences appear. However, even without knowing the theme, we understand, because of the forces that become present and that are irradiated from the performer's body. This is demonstrable in the smallest details, from the very beginning of the actions: when Sanjukta Panigrahi, after having placed her bow in front of her, turns, and by the way she uses her eyes, makes us see the arrow she takes from the quiver (ill.18–19), or when, drawing the bow, she shows us the extreme tension of the fingers of her right hand (ill.22–23).

25–26. (**left**) Sanjukta Panigrahi: fawn position and *mudra* (cf. *Hands*); (**right**) Ida Rubenstein (1885–1960) as Saint Sebastian in *Le Martyre de Saint Sébastien* (1911), written by D'Annunzio and scored by Debussy. Two equivalent positions: the body extended towards the right, the head and eyes in the opposite direction, the weight on the left leg, the right leg supported by only a part of the foot. Cultural differences aside, the performers' scenic bodies seem to be equivalent, but while for Rubenstein the bow is purely ornamental, representing no more than what it is (an object which the actress is using to support herself), Sanjukta Panigrahi's *tribhangi* (cf. *Oppositions*) position contains a play of oppositions that results in a clearly perceptible tension in the bow.

How one shoots an arrow in Japanese kyogen theatre

It is interesting to note that although this actor is kneeling and his stature is reduced, he must still displace his weight from one leg to the other, as if he was standing. But he cannot work on the displacement of balance from one foot to the other in the same way as the odissi performer. In spite of this limitation, the actor respects the equivalence principle: he exploits the only possibility he has and displaces his balance on his knees, while the feet are used as a third, precarious support. Their support is precarious because it is the point of the foot and not the heel that rests on the ground.

The shooting of the arrow is represented by the 'flight' of the arms (ill.37–39) and the hitting of the target is represented by the rapid dropping of the arms and the noise made by the palms when they strike the thighs. This noise is the finishing touch to the guttural sound that the voice has been making during the action of drawing the bow.

While respecting the basic rules of Japanese archery tradition, the actor breaks the automatism of the daily gesture and creates an equivalent by transforming the visual stimuli into sounds that are just as effective. As Eisenstein aptly put it, in Japanese theatre one 'hears' movement and 'sees' sound.

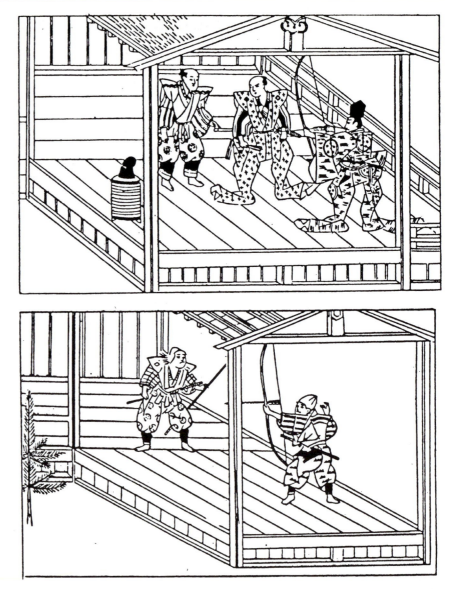

27–28. Use of bow and arrow in two kyogen farces: *Gan Tsubute* (*A Goose and a Pebble*) and *Fumi Yamadachi* (*The Cowardly Bandits*). Humorous skits performed in between noh dramas, kyogen farces use the traditional noh stage but are done in a more realistic style. Nevertheless, kyogen actors use few props; like noh actors, they make extensive use of fans to represent various objects. In these prints, however, bows and arrows have been deliberately included for the purposes of clarity and legibility.

29–31. Positions from the demonstration on page 99 (ill.34–36), done with costume and prop. One notices how the actor's body is almost camouflaged by the *kimono*: the costume conceals the upwards tension effected by the pelvis and the way in which the toes are bent downwards. Nevertheless, the tight folds of the *akama* (the elegant pant-skirt which Japanese men wear over the *kimono*) and the rectangularity of the large sleeves seem to restore, by means of yet another equivalence, the tension of the action. The fan is not only ornamental but alludes to the bow, just as in dozens of other situations where it is used, almost like a magic wand, for an infinite variety of equivalent purposes.

Since we have evoked the world of cinema and montage, let us draw attention to another detail. Observing the position taken by Kosuke Nomura (ill.37), one might think that in order to reproduce the movement of the arrow's release, the right hand would have to be drawn backwards, as happens in reality. Instead, the actor cuts the action: he passes to the subsequent positions (ill.39) which, linked together by rapid movement, evoke the flying ascent of the arrow and prevent the mechanical reproduction of the retraction of the arm.

32–39. Kosuke Nomura demonstrating the use of a bow and arrow in kyogen style (Volterra ISTA, 1981).

Shooting with a bow

This exercise from Meyerhold's bio-mechanics not only illustrates the equivalence principle, but also clearly demonstrates how one of its objectives was a continuous variation of the 'archer's' posture resulting in a veritable 'dance of balance'.

Erast Garin, one of Meyerhold's actors in 1922, describes the exercise 'Shooting with a bow' as follows:

'An imaginary bow is held in the left hand. The student advances with the left shoulder forward. When he spots the target he stops, balanced equally on both feet. The right hand describes an arc in order to reach an arrow in an imaginary belt behind his back. The movement of the hand affects the whole body, causing the balance to shift to the back foot.

The hand draws the arrow and loads the bow. The balance is transferred to the front foot. He aims. The bow is drawn with the balance shifting again to the back foot. The arrow is fired and the exercise completed with a leap and a cry.

Through this, one of the earliest exercises, the pupil begins to comprehend himself in spatial terms, acquires physical self-control, develops elasticity and balance, realises that the merest gesture – say with the hand – resounds throughout the entire body, and gains practice in the so-called 'refusal'. Thus, in this exercise the 'pre-gesture', the 'refusal', is the hand reaching back for the arrow. The étude is an example of the 'acting sequence' which comprises intention, realisation and reaction.'

(*Meyerhold on Theatre*,
ed. by Edward Braun)

40–51. (**opposite**) Shooting an arrow: sequence from one of Meyerhold's biomechanical exercises (1922) executed by Gennadi Bogdanov – a pupil of Meyerhold's actor, Nicolai Kustov – at Copenhagen ISTA, 1996.
52–55. In each tradition we find scenes or exercises in which the actor shoots with a bow. The bow is the embodiment of a play of oppositions. The aim is not only to illustrate the release of the arrow, but to recreate in the body the dynamics that characterise the tensions of the bow: (**top left**) Karsavina in *Coq d'Or* (1914), choreography by Mikhail Fokin; (**top right**) Ted Shawn in *Grossienne* (1923); (**bottom left**) Martha Graham, untitled solo piece (1924); (**bottom right**) Mary Wigman in *Dream Figure* (1927), part of her solo dance cycle *The Visions*.

Eurasian Theatre

Eugenio Barba

The influence of Western theatre on Asian theatre is a well-recognised fact. The important effect that Asian theatre has had and still has on Western theatre practice is equally irrefutable. But there remains an undeniable embarrassment: that these exchanges might be part of the supermarket of cultures.

Dawn

Kathakali and noh, onnagata and barong, Rukmini Devi and Mei Lanfang – they were all there, side by side with Stanislavsky, Meyerhold, Eisenstein, Grotowski and Decroux when I started to do theatre. It was not only the memory of their theatrical creations that fascinated me, but above all the detailed artificiality of the actor-in-life as created by them.

The long nights of kathakali gave me a glimpse of the limits which the actor can reach. But it was the dawn that revealed these actors' secrets to me, at the Kalamandalam school in Cheruthuruty, Kerala. There, young boys, hardly adolescents, monotonously repeating exercises, steps, songs, prayers and offerings, crystallised their *ethos* through artistic behaviour and ethical attitude.

I compared our theatre with theirs. Today the very word 'comparison' seems inadequate to me since it separates the two faces of the same reality. I can say that I 'compare' Indian or Balinese, Chinese or Japanese traditions if I compare their epidermises, their diverse conventions, their many different performance styles. But if I consider that which lies beneath those luminous and seductive epidermises and discern the organs that keep them alive, then the poles of the comparison blend into a single profile: that of a Eurasian theatre.

Eurasian theatre

Eurasian theatre does not refer to the theatre contained within one geographic area, on the continent of which Europe is a peninsula. It suggests a mental and technical dimension, an active *idea* in modern theatrical culture.

It includes that collection of theatres which, for those who concentrated on the performer's problems, have become the 'classical' points of reference of research: from Peking Opera to Brecht, from corporeal mime to noh, from kabuki to Meyerhold's biomechanics, from Delsarte to kathakali, from ballet to butoh, from Artaud to Bali . . . This 'encyclopedia' has been put together by drawing on the repertoire of the European and Asian scenic traditions.

When we speak of Eurasian theatre we are recognising the existence of a unity sanctioned by our cultural and professional culture. We can cross its borders but we cannot ignore them. For all those who in the twentieth century have reflected in a competent way on the performer, the borders between 'European theatre' and 'Asian theatre' do not exist.

Anti-tradition

It is possible to consider the theatre in terms of ethnic, national, group or even individual traditions. But if in doing so one seeks to comprehend one's own identity, it is also essential to take the opposite and complementary point of view and to think of one's own theatre in a transcultural dimension, in the flow of a 'tradition of traditions'.

All attempts to create anti-traditional forms of theatre in the West, as well as in the East, have drawn from the tradition of traditions. Certain European scholars in the fifteenth and sixteenth centuries forsook the performance and festival customs of their cities and villages and rescued the theatre in Athens and ancient Rome from oblivion. Three centuries later the avant-garde of the young romantics broke with the classical traditions and drew inspiration from new, distant theatres: from the 'barbarous' Elizabethans and the Spaniards in the *Siglo de Oro*, folk performances, the commedia dell'arte, 'primitive' rituals, medieval mysteries, and 'Oriental' theatre.

These are the theatrical images that have inspired the revolutions led by all anti-traditional Western theatres in the twentieth century. Today, however, the Asian theatres are no longer approached through tales but are experienced directly.

Every ethnocentricity has its eccentric pole, which reinforces it and compensates for it.

Today, in the Asian countries, the value of autochthonous tradition is emphasised vis-à-vis the diffusion of foreign models or the erosion of cultural identity. Nevertheless, Stanislavsky, Brecht, agitprop, and 'absurd' theatre continue to be means of repudiating scenic traditions that are inadequate to deal with the conditions imposed by recent history.

In Asia, this breach with tradition began at the end of the nineteenth century: Ibsen's *A Doll's House*, the plays of Shaw and Hauptmann, the theatrical adaptations of Dickens's novels or of *Uncle Tom's Cabin* were presented not as simple imports of Western models, but as the discovery of a theatre capable of speaking to the present.

In the meeting between East and West, seduction, imitation and exchange are reciprocal. We in the West have often envied the Asians their theatrical knowledge, which transmits the actor's living work of art from one generation to another. They have envied our theatre's capacity for confronting new themes and the way in which it keeps up with the times. They have longed for the Western flexibility that allows for personal interpretations of traditional texts, often having the energy of a formal and ideological conquest.

On the one hand, then, stories that are unstable in every aspect but the written; on the other hand, a living art, profound, capable of being transmitted, and implicating all the physical and mental levels of actor and spectator, but anchored in stories and customs that are forever old. On the one hand, a theatre that is sustained by *logos*, reflection and

1. The contacts between performative genres and traditions are often seen through inter-cultural categories and more rarely through intra-cultural ones. The renewal of European theatre coincided with the rediscovery of the classical Graeco-Roman theatre, the commedia dell'arte and the popular forms of circus, cabaret and music-hall. The photo shows an unusual event: noh actor Akira Matsui improvising with Kanichi Hanayagi, a nihon buyo dancer (Bielefeld ISTA, 2000). Japanese scholars and performers describe the aversion and hostility between actors from the two great noh and kabuki traditions. But there is also documentation of reciprocal secret visits in order to spy on their respective artistic and technical exploits.

reasoning. On the other hand, a theatre that is above all, *bios*, organic forms.

Why

Why in the Western tradition, as opposed to what happens in Asia, has the actor become specialised: the actor-singer as distinct from the actor-dancer and, in turn, the actor-dancer as distinct from the actor-interpreter of texts?

Why in the West does the actor tend to confine himself within the skin of only one character in each production? Why does he not explore the possibility of creating the context of an entire story, with many characters, with leaps from the general to the particular, from the first to the third person, from the past to the present, from the whole to the part, from persons to things? Why, in the West, does this possibility remain relegated to masters of storytelling or to an exception such as Dario Fo, while in the East it is characteristic of many theatres and types of actor, both when he acts-sings-dances alone and when he is part of a performance in which the rôles are shared?

Why do so many forms of Asian theatre deal successfully with that which in the West seems acceptable only in opera, that is, the use of words whose meaning the majority of the spectators cannot understand?

Clearly, from the historical point of view there are answers to these questions. But they only become professionally useful when they stimulate us to imagine how we can develop our own theatrical identity by extending the limits that define it against our nature. It is enough to observe from afar, from countries and uses that are distant, or simply different from our own in order to discover the latent possibilities of a Eurasian theatre.

Roots

The divergent directions in which Western and Asian theatres have developed provokes a distortion of perception. In the West, because of an automatic ethnocentric reaction, ignorance of Asian theatre is justified by the allegation that it deals with experiences that are not directly relevant to us, that are too exotic to be useful to us. This same distortion of perception idealises and then flattens the multiplicity of Asian theatres or venerates them as sanctuaries.

A deeper knowledge of one's own professional identity implies overcoming ethnocentricity to the point of discovering one's own centre in the 'tradition of traditions'.

Here the term 'roots' becomes paradoxical: it does not imply a bond that ties us to a place, but an *ethos* that permits us to move about. Or better, it represents the force that causes us to change our horizons precisely because it roots us to a centre.

This force is manifest if at least two conditions are present: the need to define one's own traditions for oneself; and the capacity to place this individual or collective tradition in a context that connects it with other, different traditions.

Village

ISTA, the International School of Theatre Anthropology, has given me the opportunity to gather together masters of many traditions, to compare the most disparate work methods and to reach down into a common technical substratum – whether we are working in traditional or experimental theatre, mime, ballet or modern dance. This common substratum is the domain of pre-expressivity.

It is the level at which the actor engages his own energies according to an extra-daily behaviour, modelling his 'presence' in front of the spectator. At this pre-expressive level, the principles are the same, even though they nurture the enormous expressive differences that exist between one tradition and another, one actor and another. They are *analogous* principles because they are born of similar physical conditions in different contexts. They are not, however, *homologous,* since they do not share a common history. These similar principles often result in a way of thinking that, in spite of different formulations, permits theatre people from the most divergent traditions to communicate with each other.

The work of forty years with Odin Teatret has led me to a series of practical solutions: not to take the differences between what is called 'dance' and what is called 'theatre' too much into consideration; not to accept the character as a unit of measure of the performance; not to make the sex of the actor coincide automatically with the sex of the character; to exploit the sonorous richness of languages, which have an emotive force capable of transmitting information above and beyond the semantic. These characteristics of Odin Teatret's dramaturgy and of its actors are equivalent to some of the characteristics of Asian theatre; but Odin's were born of an autodidactic training, of our situation as foreigners and of our limitations. This impossibility of being like other theatre people has gradually rendered us loyal to our diversity.

For all these reasons I recognise myself in the culture of a Eurasian theatre today. That is, I belong to the small tradition of a group theatre which has autodidactic origins but grows in a professional 'village' where kabuki actors are not regarded as being more remote than Shakespearian texts, nor the living presence of an Indian dancer less contemporary than the American avant-garde.

To interpret a text or to create a context

It often occurs in this 'village' that the actors not only analyse a conflict, let themselves be guided by the objectivity of the *logos* and tell a story, but dance *in* it and *with* it according to the growth of the *bios*. This is not a metaphor.

Concretely, it means that the actor does not remain yoked to the plot, does not interpret a text, but creates a context, moves around and within the events. At times the actor lets these events carry her, at times she carries them, other times she separates herself from them, comments on them, rises above them, attacks them, refuses them, follows new associations, or leaps to other stories. The linearity of the narrative is shattered by constantly changing the point of view, by anatomising the known reality and by interweaving objectivity and subjectivity (i.e. expositions of facts and reactions to them). Thus the actor uses the same liberty and the same leaps of thought-in-action, guided by a logic which the spectator cannot immediately recognise.

The characteristics that have often created misunderstandings about Asian theatre, confusing it with 'archaic' ritual or making it appear as perfect but static forms, are the same ones that bring it closest to our epoch's most complex concepts of time and space. It does not represent a phenomenology of reality, but a phenomenology of thought. It does not behave as if it belonged to Newton's universe. It corresponds instead to Niels Bohr's subatomic world.

Spectator

Eurasian theatre is necessary today as we move into the twenty-first century. I am not thinking of Asian stories interpreted with a Western sensibility, nor am I thinking of techniques to be reproduced, nor of the invention of new codes. Even the complex codes that seem to make sense of many Asian performances remain unknown or little known to the majority of spectators in India as well as in China, Japan and Bali.

I am thinking of those few spectators capable of following or accompanying the actor in the dance of thought-in-action.

It is only the Western *public* that is not accustomed to leaping from one character to another in the company of the same actor; that is not accustomed to entering into a relationship with someone whose language it cannot easily decipher; that is not used to a form of physical expression that is neither immediately mimetic nor falls into the conventions of dance.

Beyond the public there are, in the West as well as in the East, in the North as in the South, specific *spectators.* They are few, but for them theatre can become a necessity.

For them theatre is a relationship that neither establishes a union nor creates a communion, but ritualises the reciprocal strangeness and the laceration of the social body hidden beneath the uniform skin of dead myths and values.

2. Lisa Nelson and Steve Paxton improvising at the Copenhagen ISTA (1996).

3–4. Kazuo Ohno (butoh) and Sanjukta Panigrahi (odissi dance) improvise at Odin Teatret's thirtieth anniversary in Holstebro (1999). Eurasian theatre has a practical and theoretical dimension. It allows us to consider as an entity diverse performative genres and techniques that are connected not only by exchanges and intersections, but most of all by a common professional identity.

Incomprehensions and inventions: from the Silk Road to Seki Sano

Nicola Savarese

The distances that separate the East from the West, the two extremes of the Eurasian continent, are enormous. Yet, since prehistoric times, the people of Europe and Asia have tried to overcome this remoteness through a net of itineraries known as the Silk Road and stretching from the northern steppes to the highlands of central Asia. The great migrations, the continuous military conquests and the routes relentlessly opened by merchants have been at the origin of ideological, technical and artistic exchanges, resulting in real fusions of cultures. In historical times, the Greeks and above all the Romans favoured commerce and communication with Asia, as proved by the precious silk fabrics from China from the beginning of the Roman imperial epoch. Later, in the thirteenth century, the Mongol empire tried to re-establish these bonds after the long period of isolation due to the Arabic conquests. Also after the era of the 'great discoveries' and the opening of the Atlantic routes, the caravan paths between Asia and Europe continued to be conspicuous rivers of men and women, commodities, techniques, ideas and fantasies that the European colonial society absorbed and redistributed.

On the itineraries of the Silk Road, among the endless travellers who followed them, together with soldiers, merchants, messengers and pilgrims, we find those who earned their living as jugglers, acrobats, musicians and dancers. They were people who brought with them, 'sewn into their bodies', their own techniques and histories. According to Plutarch, hundreds of Greek performers reached the confines of India, following the army of Alexander the Great. Equally, mimes from Syria, together with crowds of harpists, trumpeters, buffoons, jugglers and dancers arrived at the huge theatres in Rome to satisfy the Romans' fashion for exotic shows, as Horace, Juvenal and other writers from Augustus' epoch record.

Similarly, on the opposite side, the rich Tang empire (618–907), stretching in its apogee from Mongolia to central Asia, made Chang'an (today Xian) its capital, transforming it into a cosmopolitan metropolis open to the West. The Chinese courtiers' life in Chang'an was marked by luxury, the search for pleasure and relaxation, where tolerance and a liking for the exotic had a central place. Countless objects from this society, recovered from graves, as well as a lot of terracotta statuettes represent actors, musicians, dancers and storytellers from Tibet, central Asia and from those same regions that had supplied mimes to the Roman empire. This phenomenon, known as 'Tang exoticism', left as a legacy the performances of the 'one hundred games' which are at the origin of Chinese Opera with its singing and acrobatic techniques.

In the centuries when Cordoba was in rivalry with Byzantium and built the Alhambra and the Alcázar, the Arab musician and composer Ziryab (789–857) arrived in the Spanish city. He had worked for Harun ar-Rashid, the great Abbasid caliph, the hero of *The Thousand and One Nights*, who had made Baghdad the richest and most cultured town in the world. Ziryab became an arbiter of fashion in Moorish and Catholic Spain, with a lot of followers. We owe to him many culinary recipes and the wearing of different clothes according to the seasons. He improved the local music,

introducing new rules and instruments, perhaps even the lute which is the precursor of all European string instruments. The Arabs are also believed to have introduced the shadow theatre (later inexplicably called 'Chinese shadows') to the West. These are some of the ancient underground roots of that vision that was often called *oriental theatre*.

To avoid confusion, however, and in order to proceed in a historically correct way, we need to consider at least four phases in the knowledge, interpretation and appropriation of the performance genres of East and West, both by Western as well as Asian artists. From the point of view of the West, these four phases or perspectives, may be defined as *oriental theatres*, *Asian theatres*, *East–West*, and *Eurasian theatre*. These definitions are not in conflict with each other, nor are they schools of thought, but have their origin in different historical situations of information and study.

The perspective of the *oriental theatres* developed in the eighteenth century when the West became aware of the existence of the non-European civilisations. Thus Orientalism was born: the ramification of the studies of and interests in Asian civilisations. Thanks to these orientalistic studies, the Europeans discovered manifestations of a spectacular character in Asia that could be compared with Western theatre forms. This happened already with the first translations of dramatic texts. The Chinese play of the thirteenth century, *The Orphan of the Family Zhao*, translated by French Jesuits, and *Sakuntala* by Kalidasa, a Sanskrit author of the fourth century AD translated into Latin by the English scholar William Jones, were widely diffused and imitated. But since the plot of these two texts involved royal characters, European scholars considered them as 'tragedies', the literary genre which, according to the Aristotelian canons of the epoch, was appropriate for noble and illustrious subjects. This is just one of the many misunderstandings with which the history of the respective knowledge between East and West is paved. The Chinese text was in fact just a libretto for actors, and the Indian play could not be a tragedy since, in classical India, the concept of the tragic does not exist, and Sanskrit plays always have a happy ending.

These translations, however, did not awake any curiosity for the Asian performances' structure or their performers' technique. Everyone neglected the fact that the abovementioned plays had, in China and India, a mise-en-scène in which dance, music and the performers' skill played a fundamental rôle. The lack of direct experience of Asian performances generated further misunderstandings, concealing for the Europeans the genuine theatrical and non-literary nature of Asian theatres. This ignorance or indifference lasted up to the beginning of the twentieth century when Asian performers began to tour in Europe, particularly on the occasion of World Exhibitions. European audiences, scholars and theatre people could see for the first time live Asian performances, even if perceived through the veil of the dominating exotic fashions.

The American and European tours of the Japanese ex-*geisha* Sada Yacco and her husband Kawakami Otojiro made them famous, turning them into living emblems of Japanese fashion and infatuation. They were, however, not interpreters of a traditional theatre form but, on the contrary, of a sort of break-up, which in Japan was defined 'new wave' (*shimpa*), a fragmentary synthesis of kabuki and Western exoticism. Despite the fame achieved in Europe, Sada Yacco and Kawakami Otojiro were not appreciated in their own country and their westernised extrovert mise-en-scènes aroused scandal in traditional Japanese milieux.

A certain notoriety also befell Hanako, another Japanese dancer of more obscure origins, whose manager was the

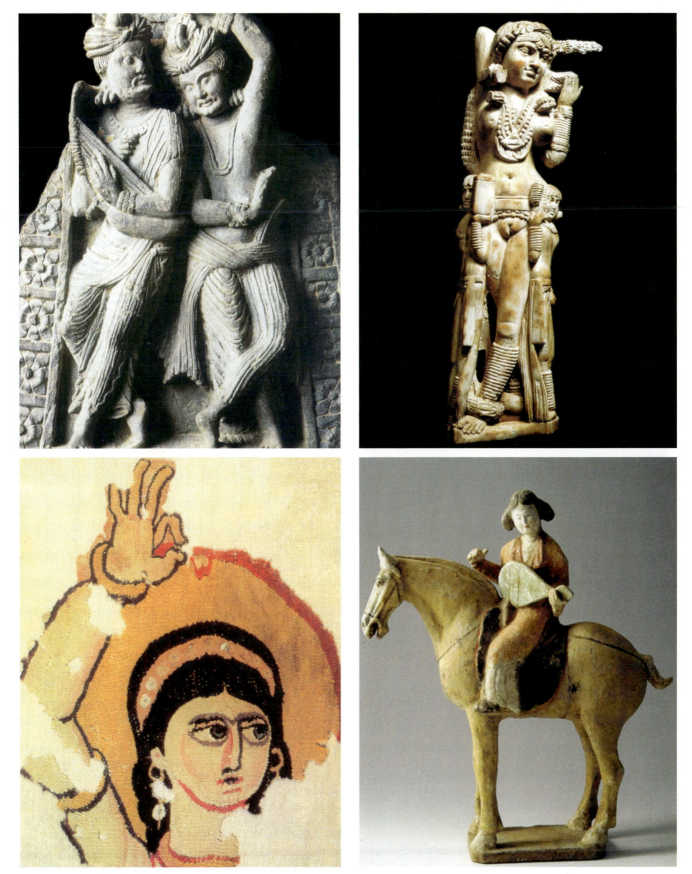

5. (**top left**) Two elegantly clad men perform a ceremonial dance: bas-relief of Indo-Greek art or Gandhara (today's northern Pakistan). Gandhara art is proof of the diffusion of Greek culture to Asia. Notice the dynamic posture and the folds of the garments similar to the plissé of many Greek Hellenistic statues. 6. (**top right**) Indian dancer. This ivory figurine, found during excavations in Pompei, destroyed in AD 79, testifies to the antiquity and the profusion of exchanges between India and the Roman Empire. 7. (**bottom left**) Coptic dancer with raised hand (fragment of Egyptian tapestry of Coptic epoch, fourth to fifth century AD). This gesture corresponds to the Indian *mudra katakamukha*, still used today in various traditional dances, meaning, among other things, 'to gather flowers', 'to make a garland'. 8. (**bottom right**) Musicians on horseback from the city of Chang'an, (today Xian), the splendid ancient capital of China (enamelled terracotta of the Tang dynasty, AD 618–907). During their journeys on the Silk Road, rich merchants and especially aristocrats were often accompanied by a company of actors or musicians travelling with them on camelback. According to the chronicles, also Alexander the Great, in his expedition to India in 324 BC, was accompanied by numerous actors and dancers for the amusement of his army.

enterprising American dancer Loie Fuller. Hanako became a friend of the great sculptor Rodin who made numerous portraits of her. To these artists we have to add ensembles such as the Siamese dancers who visited St Petersburg in 1900 and left their mark on Mikhail Fokin's and Léon Bakst's work, respectively choreographer and stage/costume designer of Diaghilev's *Ballets Russes*; or the Cambodian King's *corps de ballet* which performed in France during the 1906 World Exhibition in Marseilles and once again was a source of inspiration for Rodin.

The case of Michio Ito (1892–1961) is exemplary. He left his native Japan to learn dance from Isadora Duncan in Europe. Instead he was chosen by W. B. Yeats to interpret his 'dancing plays', based on ancient Irish sagas. The result was a mixture of European-Japanese mythology that stunned the rich cosmopolitan living rooms in London. Michio Ito emigrated to the USA and exploited his fame, teaching his own dance style, halfway between noh and kabuki. The story of Uday Shankar (1900–77) is analogous. This young Indian came to Europe to study painting, but was convinced by Anna Pavlova, the great international star of classical ballet, to become her partner in a sequence of dances inspired by India. Uday Shankar not only accepted the challenge but subsequently founded his own company of 'traditional' Indian dance which nevertheless filled Hindu traditionalists with indignation.

As we have seen, many of these Asian performers were not representative of their theatrical traditions but interpreters of the cultural renewal that was emerging in Asian countries and had as a point of reference an exoticism addressed to the West. Therefore, even in these cases, Westerners were not confronted with the genuine face of traditional Asian theatres. The sharp gaze of Gordon Craig, who was an admirer of Asian cultures, perceived immediately these misunderstandings and wrote about them with firmness to such an extent that Ananda Coomaraswamy dedicated to him the English translation of *Abhinaya Darpana* (*The Mirror of Gestures*), an ancient Sanskrit treatise on dance technique. Single playwrights such as Paul Claudel or directors such as Meyerhold or Dullin also recognised at once the Asian performers' rigorous technique which demanded consideration and study.

Asia's theatres were no longer the echo of a 'mysterious Orient' but a patrimony to explore and from which to learn. Such an attitude did not avoid new misunderstandings, although fertile. Some theatre artists, attracted by the refined Asian stage practice, concentrated on the performers' techniques, relegating to the background the social and cultural context in which they had originated. For example, when Artaud wrote about the Balinese dancers in the Colonial Exhibition in Paris in 1931, he did not make any mention of Bali's specific culture. He did not know anything about the island, then a Dutch colony, nor did he show any interest in it. The only thing that struck Artaud when he happened to see the Balinese dances in the Dutch pavilion of the Exhibition was the fact that these embodied *the theatre* as he would have liked to do. For him the Balinese dances were the expression of an exemplary theatrical language founded upon the performer's body-hieroglyph and not upon words.

Can we say that Artaud's point of view was limited and characteristic of a dominator whose way of looking was degenerated by colonialism? Such an affirmation would not be appropriate. Artaud did not want to defraud or denaturalise a foreign culture, but to grasp its deep essence. Artaud, although ignorant of Bali's history and culture, knew how to recognise its living kernel, its *bios*, in the dancers' codified forms.

Another misunderstanding with fertile consequences rose from the famous meeting that took place in Moscow in 1935 between the Chinese actor Mei Lanfang and the Russian theatre intelligentsia – among others Stanislavsky, Meyerhold, Eisenstein and Tretiakov. Bertolt Brecht was also present, and after Mei Lanfang's demonstration, he theorised his *Verfremdung* effect, his distancing technique, stating that such procedure is the foundation of the Chinese actor's art. However, in his biography, Mei Lanfang explained at length the importance for an actor to identify himself with the character, thus contradicting Brecht's interpretation.

The incursions of the Asian theatre forms into Europe had a corresponding analogous dynamic in Asia. The influence of Western theatre consisted mainly in the adoption and creation of the so-called spoken drama. This type of performance, whose form was absolutely new with respect to the Asian classical traditions, was radically innovatory with its civil and social contents. The whole modern and contemporary theatre in Asia is the result of the appropriation of the Western drama canons, which were also efficient vehicles of ground-breaking political ideas.

In China, Zhang Pengchun, who had studied in the USA, took advantage of his direct acquaintance with Western theatre and founded the Nankai's Company of the New Play in 1914 in Tiajin. His experiments became the model for the exponents of the new theatre and for the spoken drama's playwrights. The latter had espoused the theses of the 'May 4th' cultural movement, whose name stemmed from the day in which a massive demonstration was held in China in 1919 to favour the substitution of feudal values with democratic ones originating in the West. Playwrights such as Ouyang Yu-qian, Tian Han and Hong Shen (who in 1928 proposed the definition 'spoken drama') were authors of civil plays in a realistic style. In this stream of renewal (which also included the art of the actor) Cao Yu, considered the most prominent author of *huaju* (spoken drama) did not hesitate to stage a vast assortment of Western models: Chekhov, Ibsen, Oscar Wilde, O'Neill as well as Shakespeare and the Greek classics. This melting pot of experiences inspired the young Huang Zuolin to study in England in the beginning of the 1930s where he met George Bernard Shaw and Michel Saint-Denis, the well-known disciple of Copeau. There he also became acquainted with Stanislavsky's system and Brecht's ideas.

The spreading of Stanislavsky's and Brecht's theories and practice in Asia, and their many original adaptations, would require a vast research (up to now never undertaken in its totality). Let us briefly name two emblematic cases. The first is Huang Zuolin, who promoted Brecht's epic theatre in Shanghai People's Theatre which he directed after his return from England. The second one is the Japanese Seki Sano. After having been active in a proletarian theatre in Tokyo, Seki Sano went to Moscow and for several years studied Stanislavsky's system and Meyerhold's techniques. In 1937 he was forced to flee to Mexico where he taught generation after generation of Latin American theatre artists who contributed to the development of a professional and national identity in their respective countries.

In Japan, as in republican China, a movement of theatrical renewal (*shingeki*), inspired by the West, developed in the 1920s after the 'new wave' inaugurated by Kawakami. Among its leading personalities we find Tsubouchi Shoyo, who introduced numerous plays by Shakespeare as well as Ibsen's *A Doll's House*, and Osanai Kaoru, who after a compromise between the new theatre and kabuki, founded a free theatre on Antoine's model, devoted to European

9. (**above left**) Indian dancer or *nautch-girl*, as Englishmen living in India called her (English painting from the eighteenth century). In the West such a dancer was called *bayadera*, from the Portuguese 'bailadera' or dancer. 10. (**above right**) Exotic costume for the character of Idamé in *The Orphan from China* (1755), a play by Voltaire imitating *The Orphan of the Family Zhao*, a Chinese text of the thirteenth century translated by French Jesuits. 11. (**bottom left**) Morocco's ambassadors attend a performance at the Comédie Italienne in Versailles (painting from the beginning of the eighteenth century by Antoine Coypel, 'the first official painter of the king'). 12. (**bottom right**) Tightrope walkers and men on stilts perform at a public feast in a square of Istanbul together with dancers, buffoons and musicians (Turkish miniature from the seventeenth century). From Istanbul, via Venice and Genoa, many itinerant players entered Europe, including the manipulators of shadow theatre.

playwrights, from Ibsen and Hauptmann to Wedekind and Pirandello. There is no doubt that the centre of the new Japanese theatre movement was the Tsukiji Shogekijo (the Small Theatre of Tsukiji) opened by Hijikata Yoshi in Tokyo in 1924. This theatre was a laboratory concentrating on Western styles (symbolism, expressionism) and the experiments of the European avant-garde.

In India, an English colony since the end of the seventeenth century, there had been several presentations of European theatre long before the arrival of Indian performers in Europe. Small English theatres existed in Calcutta – still a military fortress – to which the great actor Garrick sent used sets and even some actors and actresses from London. These amateur performances were soon emulated locally and, under the direction of a Russian traveller, a certain Lebedev, English and Bengali actors played together. The imposition of the English language in Indian colleges and schools – where upper-class children were educated – on the one hand obliged the students to study Shakespeare, and on the other created an awareness of the existence of a national Indian culture. Theatre contributed to this awareness with plays that imitated English models, but also with research into indigenous forms. The great poet Rabindranath Tagore encouraged both tendencies. He wrote successful plays in a Western style, and he also rescued the traditional dance of the *devadasi*, making it part of the curriculum for girls of good family attending the University of Santiniketan which he had founded.

In the beginning of the twentieth century, European theatre people began to make performances with the director as their absolute creator, and the actor as an active partner in this process. The East–West perspective proposed the example of a total actor able to dance, sing, improvise, be an acrobat, play musical instruments, compose and interpret texts, as performers had previously done in commedia dell'arte and still do in kabuki. To realise this goal, any example, model or stimulus that could feed this ideal and renew the bases of the acting craft was taken into consideration. Similarly, the young generations of theatre artists in the various Asian countries were searching for models and incentives to build a modern and national theatre, capable of expressing the conditions and needs of their society.

The source of inspiration was multiple: new technologies, the visionary manifestos of futurism and the various avant-gardes, the participatory rituals of distant cultures described by the recent 'science' of anthropology, Asian theatres and those traditions that had become 'myths' in the West: commedia dell'arte, Elizabethan theatre, the Spanish Siglo de Oro, fairground shows, the circus, and the Greek performances of the origins. The curiosity and fascination were both inter-cultural and intra-cultural. All these forms were a patrimony accessible through historical documentation and the classics – Shakespeare, Lope de Vega, Gozzi – interpreted with fantasy and contemporary sensibility for social conditions. Yet, in addition to books, Asian theatres had the advantage of presenting live performances. By going back to history's exemplary theatres, European performers and directors attempted to re-examine the technical basis and artistic goals of their craft and to heal the original 'wound' when, in the sixteenth century, dancers, musicians and acrobats broke away from the text-centered literary theatre, giving life to distinct performative genres (cf. *Nostalgia*).

Curiosity and fascination remained alive and active up to the Second World War. Thereafter, the Oriental theatres went beyond the stadium of 'patrimony of inspiration' and became autonomous fields of studies as Asian theatres. A few scholars, mostly from the USA, took to travelling throughout Asia.

Their journeys could have different purposes, as for instance Faubion Bowers who was a censor in occupied Japan after the Second World War. Bowers realised the foolishness of censoring the kabuki texts, considered to be feudal and militaristic, since these were not a primary element in the performance. What really mattered in kabuki was the performer's art. However, in censoring the texts, the performer's art which is closely tied to them would be smothered and the world would lose a unique art form. So Bowers, the censor, contributed to abolishing censorship in kabuki and is acknowledged today as its 'saviour'. Also other American scholars have actively contributed to the knowledge of Asian classical theatre forms, freeing them from their exotic veil. Among these should be mentioned Adolphe Clarence Scott, Donald Keene, James Brandon and Leonard Pronko who was the first to suggest the idea of an East–West total theatre.

At the end of the twentieth century, Edward Said stigmatised Orientalism as unjustifiable and the cause of problems, misunderstandings and deceptions. Orientalism is a partial and ethnocentric perception that distorts and renders banal the genuine aspects of the Asian cultures. Today, well aware of the gaps in the East–West approach, we must recognise that this historically conditioned point of view helps us to reconstruct the history of the theatrical relationships between Europe and Asia. This approach induced curiosity and enthusiasm, stimulated the imagination and encouraged research and studies because the East was always an alter ego for Europe, 'the other' par excellence, the most direct option of comparison even after the discovery of America. Similarly, the West and its mythicised culture and technology have played an analogous rôle in the artistic practices and in the sensibility of the various social layers of Asian societies.

Today, as yesterday, the many realities of what we call theatre absorb impulses from Asia, Europe and all other continents, from the past and the present, from religious ceremonies and scientific experiments, from folklore to political manifestations, turning them into personalised new scenic practices. These practices do not explain history although they originate from history. Like the vision of Oriental theatres, the perspective of Eurasian theatre will also provoke misunderstandings. This is inevitable when we try to analyse and put into words complex historical processes and facts.

Careful observation is necessary in order to understand. We need to scrutinise closely the performers' practices to grasp their sense. Today there is a clear difference between those who study theatre through books, and those who, in addition to books, also follow the performers' creative process. Today, at the beginning of the third millennium, this is the principal distinction between theatre scholars.

The Eurasian theatre begins here, from the awareness of technical principles and a pragmatic knowledge shared by the various theatre cultures of the Eurasian continent. In this professional 'middle territory', the iridescent traditions of Asian classical theatres – noh, kabuki, Indian and Balinese dances, Peking Opera – cohabit with European and Western traditions – classical ballet and modern dance, mime, opera, political theatre and theatre laboratory. This territory of practice and theatrical thought witnesses the convergence of Euripides and Kalidasa, Shakespeare and Zeami, Aristotle's *Poetic* and the *Natyashastra* as parts of a patrimony of common insight. This professional territory is explicit today not only for Asian and European artists, but for whoever confronts the materiality of the craft and the challenge to find through it a personal sense in the society in which he or she lives. But exchanges, interactions, misunderstandings and fusions began many centuries ago, on the Silk Road.

13. Sada Yacco (1871–1946) as Ophelia. Back in Japan after her European tour, the Japanese actress played this rôle in *Hamlet*, directed by her husband Kawakami Otojiro; 14. The dance of Sada Yacco in a sketch by the young Picasso (1900); 15. Kawakami Otojiro (1864–1911) as the father's ghost in his production of *Hamlet*; 16. Bronze mask by Rodin of the Japanese dancer Hanako (1868–1945); 17. Seki Sano (1905–66), the Japanese director who studied in Moscow and influenced Mexican and Latin American theatre; 18. The Japanese dancer Michio Ito (1892–1961) interpreting the hawk's spirit in *At Hawk's Well* by W. B. Yeats (1916); 19. Rabindranath Tagore (1864–1941) performing in his play *Visarajan* (*Sacrifice*) at the Empire Theatre in Calcutta; 20. A Cambodian dancer at the Paris World Exhibition (1889); 21. The Balinese ensemble welcomes the French and Dutch authorities outside the Dutch Pavilion at the Colonial Exhibition in Paris (1931). These are the very same dancers who Artaud saw and wrote about.

Score and subscore
The significance of exercises in the actor's dramaturgy

Eugenio Barba

In the twentieth century a revolution of the invisible has taken place. The importance of hidden structures was disclosed in physics as in sociology, in psychology as in art or myth. A similar revolution also happened in theatre, with the peculiarity that the invisible structures, in this case, were not something to be discovered in order to understand how reality functioned, but rather something to be recreated onstage to give an effective quality of life to scenic fiction.

The invisible 'something' which breathes life into what the spectator sees is the actor's subscore. By subscore I do not mean a hidden scaffolding, but a very personal process, often impossible to grasp or verbalise, whose origin may be a resonance, a motion, an impulse, an image or a costellation of words. This subscore which belongs to the basic level of organisation supports still further levels of organisation in the performance. These levels extend from the effectiveness of the presence of the individual actor to the interweaving of their relationships, from the organisation of space to dramaturgical choices. The organic interaction between the different levels of organisation brings out the meaning that the performance assumes for the spectator.

The subtext – as Stanislavsky called it – is a particular type of subscore. The subscore does not necessarily consist of the unexpressed intentions and thoughts of a character, of the interpretation of his or her motivations. The subscore may consist of a rhythm, a song, a certain way of breathing or an action which is not carried out in its original dimensions but is absorbed and miniaturised by the actor who, without showing it, is guided by its dynamism even in immobility.

A physical action: the smallest perceptible action

Stanislavsky, who was considered by many to be a master of psychological interpretation, analysed characters and motivations with the meticulous perspicacity of a novelist. His aim was to deduce from the intricate web of the subtext a series of supporting points for the life of the 'physical actions'. And when he spoke of 'physical actions' he meant above all a succession of attitudes or movements possessed of their own inner life.

If I have to define to myself a 'physical action', I think of a gentle breath of wind on an ear of corn. The corn is the attention of the spectator. It is not shaken as by a gust in a storm, but that gentle breath is just enough to upset its perpendicularity.

If I have to indicate a physical action to an actor, I suggest recognising it by elimination, distinguishing it from a simple movement or gesture. I tell him or her: a 'physical action' is the 'smallest perceptible action' and is recognisable by the fact that even if you make a microscopic movement (the tiniest displacement of the hand, for example) the entire tonicity of the body changes. A real action produces a change in the tensions in your whole body, and subsequently a change in the perception of the spectator. In other words, it originates in the torso, in the spinal cord. It is not the elbow that moves the hand, not the shoulder that moves the arm, but each dynamic impulse is rooted in the torso. This is one of the conditions for the existence of an organic action. It is obvious that the organic action is not enough. If, in the end, it is not enlivened by an inner dimension, then the action remains empty and the actor appears to be predetermined by the form of the score.

I do not think there is a unique method to generate inner life. I believe the method is one of negation: not to impede the development of one's inner life. This can be learnt on condition that you act *as if* it cannot be learnt.

The age of exercises

The revolution of the invisible marked, in theatre, the age of exercise. A good exercise is a paradigm of dramaturgy, i.e. a model for the actor. The expression 'dramaturgy of the actor' refers to one of the levels of organisation of the performance, or to one aspect of the dramaturgical interweaving. Indeed, in every performance there are numerous dramaturgical levels, some more evident than others, and all necessary for the recreation of life on stage.

But what is the essential difference between an exercise (which I have defined as a 'paradigm of dramaturgy') and dramaturgy in the traditional sense: comedy, tragedy or farce? In each case it is a question of a well-contrived web of actions. But whereas comedies, tragedies and farces have a form and a content, exercises are pure form, dynamic developments without a plot, a story. Exercises are small labyrinths that the actors' body-mind can trace and retrace in order to incorporate a paradoxical way of thinking, thereby distancing themselves from their own daily behaviour and entering the domain of the stage's extra-daily behaviour.

Exercises are like amulets which the actor carries around, not to show them off, but to draw from them certain qualities of energy out of which a second nervous system slowly develops. An exercise is made up of memory, body-memory. An exercise becomes memory which acts through the entire body.

At the beginning of the twentieth century when Stanislavsky, Meyerhold and their collaborators invented exercises to train actors, they gave birth to a paradox. Their exercises were something quite different from the training followed by students at theatre schools. By tradition, actors practised fencing, ballet, singing and above all the recitation and acting of particular fragments of classical plays. The exercises, on the other hand, were elaborate scores, codified down to the smallest detail and an end in themselves.

All this is evident when we scrutinise the oldest of the exercises passed down to us, those which Meyerhold conceived and called biomechanics and whose aim was to teach 'the essence of scenic movement'.

1–3. Three illustrations from Michael Chekhov's book *To the Actor* (published for the first time in English by Harper & Row, New York, 1953) which describes a wealth of exercises.

Inner life and interpretation

Several characteristics distinguish an exercise and explain its effectiveness as dramaturgy reserved for the non-public work of the actors, i.e., the work on oneself:

1. Exercises are primarily a pedagogical fiction. The actor learns not to learn to be an actor, or in other words learns not to learn to act. Exercises teach how to think with the entire body-mind.
2. Exercises teach how to carry out a real action (not 'realistic' but real).
3. Exercises teach that precision in form is essential in a real action. An exercise has a beginning and an end, and the path between these two points is not linear but fraught with peripeteias, changes, leaps, turning points and contrasts. Even the simplest exercises presuppose a multitude of variations and tensions, sudden or gradual modifications of intensity, rhythm acceleration, and the use of space in different directions and on different levels.
4. The dynamic form of an exercise is a continuity constituted by a series of phases. In order to learn the exercise precisely it is divided up into segments. This process teaches how to think of continuity as a succession of minute but well-defined phases that are perceptible actions. An exercise is an ideogram made up of strokes and, like all ideograms, must always follow the same succession. But each single stroke can vary in thickness, intensity and impetus.
5. Each phase of an exercise engages the entire body. The transition from one phase to another is a *sats*.
6. Every phase of an exercise dilates, refines or miniaturises certain dynamisms of daily behaviour. In this way these dynamisms are isolated and 'edited', becoming a montage and underlining the play of tensions, contrasts, oppositions – in other words, all the elements of basic dramaticity that transform daily behaviour into the extra-daily behaviour of the stage.
7. The different phases of the exercise make you experience your own body not as a unity but as a centre for simultaneous actions. In the beginning, this experience coincides with a painful sense of expropriation of one's own spontaneity. Later, it turns into the fundamental quality of the actor: a presence ready to be projected in diverging directions and capable of attracting the attention of the spectator.
8. Exercises teach how to repeat. Learning to repeat is relatively easy as long as it is a question of knowing how to execute a score with ever greater precision. It becomes demanding in the next phase. Here the difficulty lies in continuous repetition without becoming dull, which presupposes discovering and motivating new details, new points of departure within the familiar score.
9. The exercises make you assimilate, through action, a paradoxical way of thinking, go beyond the daily automatisms and adjust to the extra-daily performance behaviour.
10. The exercises are the way of refusal: they teach renunciation through fatigue and commitment to a humble task.
11. The exercises force you to surpass the stereotypes and the conditioning of your own male/female cultural behaviour.
12. An exercise is not work on the text, but on oneself. It puts the actor to the test through a series of obstacles. It allows you to get to know yourself through an encounter with your own limits, and not through self-analysis.
13. The exercises lead to self-discipline or autonomy in relation to the expectations and habits of the craft. They represent a new beginning, the birth of a scenic body-mind, independent of the demands of performance, but ready to implement them.

Exercises teach how to work on what is visible through repeatable forms. These forms are empty. At the beginning they are filled with the concentration necessary for the successful execution of each single phase. Once they have been mastered, either they die or they are filled by the capacity for improvisation. This capacity consists in varying the execution of the diverse phases, the images behind them (for example: to move like an astronaut on the moon), their rhythms (to different music), the chains of mental associations.

In this way a subscore develops from the score of the exercise.

The value of the visible (the score) and the invisible (the subscore) generates the possibility of making them carry on a dialogue, creating a space within the design of movements and their precision.

The dialogue between the visible and the invisible is precisely that which the actor experiences as inner life and in some cases even as meditation. And it is what the spectator experiences as interpretation.

The complexity of emotion

When we speak of dramaturgy we should think of montage. The performance is a complete system in itself integrating diverse elements, each obeying its own logic and all interacting amongst themselves and with the exterior.

The dramaturgy of the actor means above all the capacity to construct the equivalent of the complexity that characterises action in life. This construction, which is perceived as a character, must have a sensorial and mental impact on the spectator. The objective of the actor's dramaturgy is the capacity to stimulate affective reactions.

There is a naive conception according to which emotion is a force which takes hold of and overwhelms a person. But an emotion is a complex pattern of reactions to a stimulus.

This complex web of reactions expressed by the term 'emotion' is characterised by the activation of at least five levels of organisation which inhibit each other in turn but which are all simultaneously present:

1. a subjective change, which we normally call 'feeling': for example, fear (a dog comes up to me in the street);
2. a series of cognitive evaluations (I consider: the dog seems well behaved);
3. the manifestation of involuntary autonomous reactions (acceleration of the heartbeat, of the breathing, sweating);
4. an impulse to react (I want to walk away quickly);
5. the decision on how to behave (I force myself to walk calmly).

It is the complexity of the emotion and not a vague feeling that the actor must reconstruct. We must therefore work on all the different levels that we have identified as characterising an 'emotion', which – although belonging to the world of the invisible – are nevertheless physically concrete. Moreover, each of these levels is guided by its own coherence.

The complexity is achieved by interweaving simple elements in opposition or in harmony, but always simultaneously. All this offers infinite possibilities, theatrically speaking. I can construct my reactions towards the dog by working separately with the different parts of my body: my legs behave courageously, for example; my torso and arms, slightly introverted, reveal assessment and reflection; my head reacts as if to move away; while the rhythm of the blinking of my eyelids reconstructs the equivalent of the autonomous involuntary reactions.

The complexity of the result is attained by working on simple elements, each one separate, then put together level by level, interwoven, repeated, until they melt into an organic unity that reveals the essence of the complexity that characterises every living form.

It is this passage from the simple to the 'simultaneous multiplicity' that the exercise teaches: the non-linear development of minute perceptible actions, subject to peripeteias, changes, leaps, turns and contrasts, through the interaction of clearly defined phases.

In a word, by artificially reconstructing complexity, the exercise encounters *drama*.

4. Ryszard Cieslak (1937–1990): Grotowski's plastic exercises (1970).
5. The Italian clown Romano Colombaioni teaching acrobatics (1969).

114

6

7

8

9

6. Exercise at the Jaques-Dalcroze Institute at Hellerau (1911–14).
7. Georges Carpentier (1894–1975) was the greatest European boxer between 1908 and 1925, world middleweight champion in 1920. Etienne Decroux dedicated to him this homage: 'Vigour and grace; force and elegance; radiance and thought; readiness to risk and smile. He would never have imagined that he was the inspirational image of our corporeal mime'. Boxing was the sport that most fascinated European theatre reformers. It was part of the training in Meyerhold's school even when his actors and actresses no longer executed biomechanical exercises. Eisenstein studied it, and a boxing match became the climax in his production *The Mexican* (1921) based on a short story by Jack London. Brecht, besides writing several poems on boxing champions whom he defined as 'machines of human fighting', wrote a biography of the German boxer Samson-Körner. Cf. Franco Ruffini: *Teatro e box. L'atleta del cuore nella scena del novecento*. Il Mulino, Bologna, 1994.
8–9. Rudolf Bode's gymnastic exercise (1922). Pupil of Jaques-Dalcroze, the German Rudolf Bode (1881–1970) elaborated a method of 'expressive gymnastics'. The human body was considered as an organism and each movement involved it in its entirety. 'A natural movement is a movement of the whole body'. Bode's main theoretical points were the principle of totality (each movement always affects the body's totality) and the principle of the centre of gravity (a movement, of any part of the body, always originates from the centre of gravity). Eisenstein knew about 'expressive gymnastics' and wrote an essay in 1922 together with the playwright S.M. Tretjakov commenting on Bode's book *Ausdruckgymnastik* (*Expressive Gymnastics*). Kazuo Ohno also studied Bode's method in his youth.

10–12. (**above left**) Rudolf Bode's exercises (1922); (**centre**) Meyerhold's biomechanical exercise (1922); (**above right**) fighting with sticks: exercise at Odin Teatret (1968).

The real relationship

Theatre is the art of relationships that are manifested through dialogue with or without words. Scenic relationships are feigned. Therefore, in order to infuse into them a persuasive force, it is essential to find their muscular system, a physical web of actions and reactions. Sports based on fighting provide the elementary conditions for the play of actions and reactions between individuals. They are the natural gymnastics of relationships.

Sports based on fighting constitute the gymnastics of the physical dialogue. The dynamics of attack, of feint, of parrying and riposting train the logic of acting-reacting, calibrating this logic not on fictive, but on real circumstances. Boxing has a value, in this context, not as an exercise of strength, but as an elementary level of physical dialogue.

This explains the importance of martial arts in the actor's training in European and Asian traditions. In the syllabus of European theatre schools, the sport of fencing was omnipresent. It was usually justified by the demand of the actors to interpret duel scenes in plays of the classical repertory: for example, *Romeo and Juliet*, *Hamlet* and *Cyrano*. Behind these justifications lies the tacit awareness that fencing moulded the basis of physical dialogue.

In spite of appearances, even acrobatics, which at times are included in the actor's training, may be considered a variant of fighting. The difficulty and the relative dangerousness of the exercise are not intended to transform actors into acrobats. They teach them to react in a decided way, in readiness and according to a succession of push and counterpush which continuously change the floor or the prop into an adversary capable of striking, and thus punishing the least lack of precision. In this sense acrobatics are also gymnastics of relationships. They transform weight, balance and unanimated objects into critical partners of a live dialogue of actions and reactions.

Sport as dance

The syllabus of the reformers' school – Jaques-Dalcroze, Meyerhold, Copeau or Dullin – besides exercises that they invented, also included gymnastics, athletics and a few specific sports such as fencing, tennis, boxing and discus-throwing.

In tennis, fencing and boxing, the athlete stands with his legs apart in a posture favouring a state of alert. He is ready to react, unable to foresee what will happen next: the necessity to move forward, backward or to one side. At times he takes the initiative, at others reacts adapting to an external stimulus. Sometimes he is totally immobile, attentive and vigilant, prepared to release all his tension, to spring in defence, attack or parry (accuracy, force and physical intelligence are necessary to strike an adversary or to smash a ball to the end of the court). The weight is moving incessantly from one leg to another, animated by a varied stream of impulses, with small jumps, gliding or darting steps, 'staccato', 'pizzicato', 'legato' (those 'gait's ornaments' that the students learned in Hellerau). It is a dance whose principle is a continuous and irregular pendulum of the weight from one leg to the other.

Tennis, fencing and boxing are a ballet of energy in action, precise and functional. These – and no others – were the sports that the reformers privileged because they were based on a unending flow of *sats*, on responses to concrete stimuli presupposing real actions.

In discus-throwing, on the other hand, the athlete whirls around himself and then hurls the discus, carefully controlling his balance and stopping within the limit of a line which must not be crossed. The same principle can be found in many dance exercises as well as in Decroux: a succession of actions whose rapid acceleration is suddenly frozen in a dynamic immobility that contains the direction towards which they aimed.

The physical dialogue with the spectators

The relationship between the actors and the spectators is based on what Coleridge called the 'suspension of disbelief'. In order to become efficient, this relationship, which is supported by a web of illusions, must rest on a solid ground, i.e. on a physical consistency.

This physical consistency can be called 'kinaesthetics', i.e. the sense which allows the spectators, in spite of their apparent inactivity, to perceive within their own body physical impulses corresponding to the movements onstage.

In this case too, sports, gymnastics and acrobatics become useful reference points for the performing craft. They indicate one of the muscular substrata which relate the actor to the spectator.

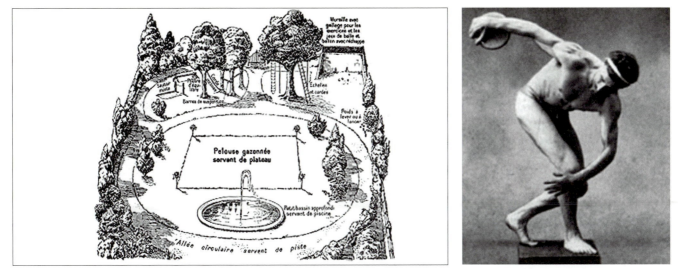

13. (**above left**) Georges Hébert: a garden adapted as a family sports stadium. In the garden can be seen a circular running track, a swimming pool, a wall in the background for climbing over or bouncing a ball against, ropes and ladders for climbing, beams at a certain height from the ground for walking and balancing. 14–15. (**right** and **above right**) Herbert's exercises: discus throwing and tug-of-war.

The athletic and acrobatic feat entertains the spectator with a primary relationship of a kinaesthetic nature: a web of actions and reactions, a sort of physical dialogue that precludes any meaning. Circus and acrobatic performances, built up exclusively on physical attractions, attain on this elementary level a power which was often lacking in elaborate theatre performances, in spite of their intellectual, aesthetical and literary force. Therefore circus artists and mountebanks became a model for the twentieth-century theatre reformers and avant-garde, beginning with the futurists. They made it possible to imagine a theatre able to embody even the deepest tragedies and the most refined poetry with the vitality and the almost electrical discharge of the performances based upon the physicality of acrobats and athletes. Artaud dreamed of an 'athlete of the heart'. This should happen in a theatre where dialogues and encounters between characters would possess the bare and live necessity of the actions in a boxing match.

The real action

A few gymnastic methods and sports are directly related to stage practice because they contribute towards developing an ability of immediate reaction

which affects the spectator's kinaesthetic sense. Moreover, they teach the actor to master the craft's physical and dynamic foundations in its individual dimension (the use of energy), in its dialogical dimension (the relationship to partners) and in its public dimension (the relationship with the spectators).

Although the actor's actions take place in a context characterised by fiction, they must be *real* in their substance, true psycho-physical actions and not just empty gestures. At the primary level of scenic *bios*, their efficacy depends on being material work which shapes the mental and physical energy into a perceptible act capable of influencing the spectators' nervous system and sharpening their attention. The actor can profit by the principles of those gymnastics that consist in adapting the effort and logic of an action to an obstacle or an arduous task. Theatre reformers were aware of this when they applied the methods of physical training of Georges Hébert or Rudolf Bode (Cf. *Apprenticeship* and *Training*).

Georges Hébert (1875–1957) called 'natural gymnastics' his method of physical training which he liberated from the gym exercises and pieces of equipment and developed according to actions necessary to overcome 'natural' obstacles. For Hébert, the ideal stadium was a garden. In its

limited space it was possible to reproduce the variety of a vast natural landscape in which to swim, run, jump and climb. Like a theatre stage, it was an area for testing oneself in real actions, not for pretending.

Hébert was a marine officer. During his travels he had observed how people from so-called primitive societies kept their body fit, and had compared their way of doing this with the artificiality of the gymnastic exercises in his own society. He noticed that gymnastics based on exercises and pieces of equipments in venues such as the gym, correspond to abstract criteria which risk becoming an aesthetical goal in themselves. He wished to overcome his own limits and to discover the harmony of an action whose vigour and economy are determined by the obstacle's nature.

For these reasons, Hébert's gymnastics were chosen by Jacques Copeau as the foundation for his actors' training, preferring it to dance and Jaques-Dalcroze's eurhythmics. Similar considerations were the point of departure for Meyerhold's and Decroux's research on biomechanics and corporeal mime. The aim was always to oppose the tendency inherent in scenic fiction to transform itself into falsity or inauthenticity. This is theatre's woodworm: the risk that fiction deteriorates into an inefficacious and innocuous pretence.

Meyerhold's theatre fission

It was Meyerhold who identified in his work a way to create a sort of fission in theatre practice, unleashing the potential energies for those who do theatre as well as for those who watch it. The first step had the characteristics of a humble craftsmanlike invention. Meyerhold explained how and why the actor's 'plastic actions' did not have to harmonise with the words of the character. He pointed out how in daily life there exists a complementarity, or independence, between words and gestures. Words represent explicit intentions, whether sincere, conventional or false, in relationships between individuals. But often gestures, attitudes, proximity, looks and silences that accompany words do not only underline the relationships that they express, but reveal the real nature of these relationships, both from an emotional and a social point of view. Meyerhold showed how the actor could consciously shape these two levels of behaviour, outlining his/her movements according to a logic that interwove new relations with the words, without having to illustrate them.

It was a technical procedure whose effects enabled the spectator not to stop at the surface but to consider contemporaneously the multiple dynamics that are at work within the various realities of the individual and his or her relations with society. The gap between the two performing levels – that of behaviour and that of speech – gave depth to the spectators' vision, making them perspicacious.

The search for perspicacity concerns both the spectator and the actor. This does not mean that both of them see and understand in the same way, nor that both undergo the same experience of an experience when watching or performing a theatrical action. An actor can carry out his or her own exploration and search for a meaning in and with the microcosm of his or her body-mind. This meaning, however, remains independent with regard to the meaning perceived and the exploration carried out by the spectator watching the performance. The same performance can become a veritable anthropological exploration for both the actor and the spectator, but it is not necessarily the *same* expedition for both of them.

The fission operated by Meyerhold in the core of theatre practice is the premise for dealing with dramaturgy in its complexity. Dramaturgy, as 'performance text' is an organism which is made up of various level of organisation, each having an autonomous life and interacting with the others like the lines of different instruments in a musical composition.

There is the narrative level of organisation, with its plots and peripeteias – most thoroughly explored by traditional text-centred theatre.

Another level of organisation is that of organic dramaturgy, which composes the dynamics of the actions and the flow of impulses directed at the spectators' senses. This level of 'theatre that dances' gives the actions a coherence that does not stem from the meaning but from the capacity to keep alert, stimulate and persuade the spectator's senses like music that is not aimed at the hearing but at the actor's and spectator's nervous system.

Lastly, there is the level of that which, for want of a better expression, I call the 'dramaturgy of changes of states'. I could define it as the totality of knots or dramaturgical short circuits that radically alter the meaning of the story and plunge the spectator's senses and understanding into an unexpected void that condenses and disorientates their expectations. Meyerhold continually emphasised the importance of this third level of dramaturgical organisation, using and expounding the concept of 'grotesque'. His disciple Eisenstein applied the principles of the grotesque to film montage. He spoke of ecstasy, intended in the literal meaning, as *ex-stasis*, a leap beyond the ordinary dimension of reality.

The density resulting from the manipulation and intertwining of the three levels of dramaturgical organisation is not only meant to have an impact on the spectator's perception. It is also useful for the actor in his work on himself. In this case, the dramaturgy does not generate a performance but a score called 'exercise'. Meyerhold's biomechanical exercises are theatrical organisms composed for the doers, not for the observers. They are more than physical training, they are incorporated forms of a way of thinking.

History has saved a fragment of a film with a few biomechanical exercises composed by Meyerhold and performed by his actors. This document conveys to us, in a coded language, Meyerhold's thought-in-action. It is as one could see it, alive, face to face. Meyerhold maintained that the actor had to know how 'to live in the precision of a design'. The document allows us to verify it with our own eyes. We see clearly how the actors live the exercises instead of simply performing them. Everything happens as though the design was a code that comes to life and blossoms in the organic nature of a specific individual.

The organic quality comes from the actor, but the design is Meyerhold's. It is the trace of a thought that lives through counter-impulses and contrasts, dilating certain details and simultaneously assembling them together with others that 'normally' belong to successive stages of the action. This thought invents peripeteias such as a series of swerves in relation to a foreseeable line of conduct. The peripeteia does not only concern the development of a story, but becomes physical behaviour, dynamic design, a dance of balance and contrasting tensions. Each exercise lasts only a few seconds, yet long enough to condense the vision and the realisation of the theatre as a discovery and laying bare of the skeleton hidden behind the appearances of what is visible.

The biomechanical exercises are not training patterns, but sensory metaphors showing how thoughts move. They train thought. They are action that distils the way in which what we call 'life' reveals itself to different levels of organisation, from that of pre-expressive presence and scenic *bios* to the expressive and dramaturgical, the social and political. They show Meyerhold as a creative visionary in a historical theatre. He does not depict the colours of the places and the times, nor does he devote himself to the interpretation of historical events, but he plunges his gaze into the distant roots of what is to be.

The 'design' of the exercises restores Meyerhold to us better than any photograph or portrait.

(Eugenio Barba,
Grandfathers and Orphans)

16. (**above**) Scene from *Antigone* by Sophocles, directed by Meyerhold in his studio in 1914. Already during this period Meyerhold concentrated on the fission of the movement attempting to reconstruct on stage a dynamic that could affect the spectators' nervous system. This scene from Sophocles' tragedy clearly anticipates bio-mechanics (**left**).

18–19. (**below left** and **below right**) Gennadi Bogdanov as Lucky in Samuel Beckett's *Waiting for Godot* interpreted according to biomechanical principles (Copenhagen ISTA, 1996).

The exercise: a model of organic and dynamic dramaturgy

An exercise can be considered as a model of organic or dynamic dramaturgy. Dramaturgy is a succession of linked events. Its technique consists in providing a peripeteia to each action of the work. By peripeteia we mean a change of direction and tension. Dramaturgy does not refer only to dramatic literature, the words or the narrative plot.

There exists also an organic or dynamic dramaturgy which orchestrates the composition of rhythms and dynamisms affecting the spectator at a nervous, sensorial and sensual level. The exercises invented and practised in the course of the twentieth century – from Stanislavsky and Meyerhold to Grotowski, the Living Theatre, the Open Theatre or Odin Teatret – are an active way to incorporate the principles of scenic presence. These principles induce a performer to think or act with the whole body-mind, and they are fundamental to the development of his or her organic dramaturgy in a performance.

Dramaturgy is a way of thinking. This embodied thought makes itself evident by means of a technique which organises a series of simultaneous actions: a score. Phase by phase, the score establishes, uncovers and interweaves links and relationships. It is a process that transforms a multitude of fragments in a unitary organism in which the various details and components are no longer distinguishable as separate entities. To execute an exercise means to infuse life into a structured form that does not narrate anything. The pupil learns the exact shape of each phase, the succession and simultaneity of its diverse details and the precise changes of direction and intensity. Through repetition, the pupil restores an organic unity characterised by an ever-changing rhythm and flow.

Form, rhythm, flow

Form, rhythm and flow are the names of three diverse perspectives in relation to the performer's action. They do not indicate different technical principles or aspects of the composition. They designate three faces of the same reality. We can distinguish them temporarily and operationally, well aware that this distinction is a fiction that is useful to research.

An improvised or fixed score, a series of exercises or a dance may be treated as:

a) a form, a design in space and time resulting from a montage;

b) a scansion and alternation of *tempi*, accents, speed and various energy colours and nuances;

c) a river bank that allows the energy's organic flow.

The final result makes it impossible to distinguish between the action's flow, rhythm and shape. In the same way, it is impossible to separate the physical action from the mental, the body from the voice, the word from the intention, the performer's pre-expressive level from his or her expressive efficaciousness, and the actor's dramaturgy from that of a fellow actor or the director.

20–25. 'Tre-tre', a sequence of exercises by Roberta Carreri and Julia Varley (demonstration at Montemor ISTA, 1998). The 'tre-tre' sequence is executed by two or more actors who undergo its various phases synchronising the *sats*, the impulses and the shape of each action and posture. This chain of exercises is based on dynamic immobility, interrupted by 'transitions'. Another characteristic of the 'tre-tre' is the centripetal and implosive attitude of the postures. These exercises, invented by Odin Teatret's senior actors after more than thirty years of training, do not underline a vital exuberance which spreads in space, but a stillness in tension which radiates energy.

Tacit knowledge

Every type of corporeal training tends to strengthen certain patterns or plans of action which enable us to act without having to think about *how* to put them into practice. It is as if the body itself, a hand, a foot, the spine were doing the thinking, without involving the head. In the same way, for example, after a period in which every movement must be understood, learned and memorised, we learn to drive a car. In the end we are able to drive without having to call to mind every single procedure, reacting appropriately and immediately if something unexpected happens, while at the same time we may be listening to music, speaking with a passenger or following a train of thought.

The ability to react appropriately and immediately does not mean automatically following a memorised pattern of actions. It consists in knowing how to imagine a new and unforeseen pattern and executing it even before you are aware of where it is leading, according to a behaviour whose precise rules have been incorporated.

To learn the actor's craft means to incorporate certain competences, skills, ways of thinking and behaving that, on stage, become 'second nature', to use the words of Stanislavsky and Copeau. For the trained actor, scenic behaviour becomes just as 'spontaneous' as daily behaviour. It is the result of a re-elaborated spontaneity. The aim of this 're-elaboration of spontaneity' is a capacity to perform actions decisively so that they become organic and effective to the senses of the spectator.

Re-elaborated spontaneity is not simply an unconstrained, free and easy manner that *simulates* spontaneous behaviour. It is the result of a process that rebuilds a dynamic equivalent to that which governs our daily behaviour within the extra-ordinary realm of art: the balance between that which we are aware that we know and that which we know without knowing it: our tacit knowledge.

Or, according to Michael Polanyi's terminology, it is the relationship between 'focal knowledge' and 'tacit knowledge'.

(Eugenio Barba,
Tacit Knowledge: Heritage and Waste)

Physiology and codification

The illustration (ill.1) shows the pupil movements of a subject who is looking for the first time at a drawing based on Paul Klee's *Picture of an Old Man*. The black areas represent the subject's visual fixations and the numbers give the order of the fixations on the drawing during a period of twenty seconds. The lines between the black areas represent the *saccades* or rapid eye movements between one fixation and another.

The eyes are the most active of all human sense organs. Other sensory receptors, such as the ears, accept rather passively whatever signals come their way, but the eyes are continuously moving as they scan and inspect the details of the visual world. [...]

During normal viewing of stationary objects the eyes alternate between fixations, when they are aimed at a fixed point in the visual field, and rapid movements called *saccades*. Each *saccade* leads to a new fixation on a different point in the visual field. Typically there are two or three *saccades* per second. The movements are so fast that they occupy only 10 per cent of the viewing time.

Visual learning and recognition involve storing and retrieving memories. By way of the lens, the retina and the optic nerve, nerve cells in the visual cortex of the brain are activated and an image of the object being viewed is formed there. [...] The memory system of the brain must contain an internal representation of every object that is to be recognised. Learning or becoming familiar with an object is the process of constructing this representation. Recognition of an object when it is encountered again is the process of matching it with its internal representation in the memory system. [...]

The most informative parts of a line drawing are the angles and sharp curves. The angles are the principal features the brain employs to store and recognise a drawing. When a subject views a picture, his eyes usually scan it following – intermittently but repeatedly – a fixed path,

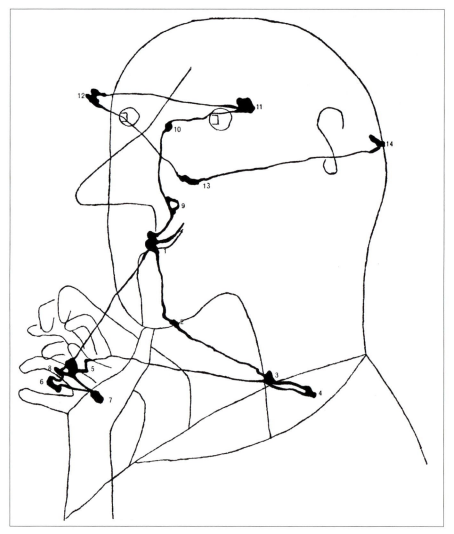

1. Eye movements made by a subject viewing for the first time a drawing adapted from Paul Klee's *Picture of an Old Man* appear in black. The numbers show the order of the subject's visual fixations on the picture during part of a twenty-second viewing. The lines between the numbers represent *saccades*, or rapid movements of eyes from one fixation to the next.

2. Kathakali student doing eye exercises.

3–5. Kathakali students doing eye exercises in relation to hand movements or *mudras*.

the 'scan path'. Scan paths appear in the subject's eye movements during the learning phase, and during the recognition phase his first few eye movements on viewing a picture (presumably during the time he was recognising it) usually follow the same scan path he had established for that picture during the learning phase.

(David Noton and Lawrence Stark, *Eye Movements and Visual Perception*)

This continual eye movement provides very special information to the performer who must *show that he is looking*: as the *saccades* demonstrate, the eye is never still. In exactly the same way that in the most apparently static balance position, we are continually shifting our weight from one part of the foot to another, micro-movements are always occurring in the most fixed gaze. Asian performers have constructed an equivalent to this eye movement: partly by creating artificial tensions and directions to give emphasis to the way the eyes are used (ill.2), but above all by forcing the eyes to move and then fix on specific points in the surrounding space, on the hands or the horizon (ill.4–5).

We normally look straight ahead and about 30 degrees downwards. If we keep the head in the same position and raise the eyes 30 degrees, a muscular tension will be created in the neck and trunk that will alter our balance.

The kathakali actor follows his hand *mudras* with his eyes, slightly above his normal field of vision. The Balinese actor looks upwards. In the Peking Opera *lian shan* (actor's 'frozen positions'), the eyes look upwards. Noh actors describe how they lose all sense of space, and how they have difficulty keeping their balance, because the eye holes in their masks are so tiny. This is one explanation for their particular sliding gait, in which the feet never leave the floor – somewhat like blind men who slide along, feeling their way, always ready to stop in case of unforeseen obstacles.

All these performers use a field of vision when performing that is different from the one they use in daily life. Their whole physical attitude is changed: the torso's muscle tone, the pressure on the feet, the balance. A change in the normal way

of looking brings about a qualitative change of energy. By one simple change in the daily way of looking, these performers are able to give impetus to a whole new level of energy.
(Eugenio Barba, *Theatre Anthropology: First Hypothesis*)

Once again, codification (that is, formalisation) of physiological processes helps the performer destroy daily automatisms in the use of the eyes. Directing the eyes is therefore no longer a mechanical reaction but is transformed by the performer into an action, the *action of seeing*.

6–7. Italian actor Giovanni Grasso (1873–1930) (**above right**) as Turiddu in Giovanni Verga's *Cavalleria rusticana* (1912). The body full front, the fists closed, the eyes grim. But the impression of menace is in fact mostly due to a particular torsion of the spinal column. One notices how Grasso, in order to show his eyes to the spectators, does not stand in profile but frontal and is therefore constrained to keep his pupils in the corners of his eyes in order to look at his adversary. Meyerhold saw Giovanni Grasso during a tour the latter made in Russia and, according to Gladkov, commented: 'I became aware of many of the rules of biomechanics when I saw the magnificent Sicilian tragic actor, Grasso, perform'. (**bottom**) The Spanish dancer Tórtola Valencia in her exotic interpretation of *The Africana* at the beginning of the twentieth century. Contrary to what one might think, also for dancers the eyes are of fundamental importance.

8. The dance of oppositions: Kazuo Ohno in *Admiring La Argentina* (1977). In butoh, even the act of seeing follows the principle of oppositions. In order to look within him/herself, the dancer performs with an unfocused gaze.

The concrete gaze

If one observes the various methods that Asian performers have for the use of their eyes and gaze, one is immediately struck by their particular way of rolling the eyes and of directing their gaze in very precise directions. But if one follows the direction of the gaze, one realises that it is fixed on a point which is . . . empty. This in no way detracts from the concrete nature of the gaze and even serves to establish a precise spatial quality for the spectator and to make historical and theatrical characters and animals come alive, even though they are physically non-existent on the stage. Moreover, this concrete gaze is accompanied by a constant dialectic between *manis* (soft) and *keras* (vigorous) tensions (cf. *Energy*) which make it possible for the spectator to follow both the performer's interior and exterior life.

Both in Bali (ill.13–14) and in the Peking Opera (ill.9–10), the eyes are directed, as we have seen, higher than they normally are in daily life. We can see the passage from *keras* to *manis* in young Jas's eyes and in the way that Lin Chun-Hui has of beginning with the eyes focused in one direction in order to finish with the eyes focused in the opposite direction (cf. *Opposition*). Indian dancer Sanjukta Panigrahi uses her fingers and arms to underline the wide opening of her eyes and her radiant expression: the eyes thus become the apex of a triangle formed by the arms and fingers, which extend the curve of the superciliary arch (ill.11–12).

Katsuko Azuma's downcast gaze (ill.15) becomes intense and penetrating thanks to the fan, which stresses the gaze of a single eye, catching and directing the spectator's attention at will (ill.16).

126

9–16. Ways of directing the eyes and drawing the spectator's attention to eye movements in various Asian theatrical cultures: Lin Chun-Hui, Peking Opera (p. 126 **top** and **centre**); Sanjukta Panigrahi, Indian odissi dance (p. 126 **bottom**); young Jas, Balinese legong dance (**top** and **centre**); Katsuko Azuma, Japanese buyo dance (**bottom**).

17–18. (left) Kabuki actor in an eighteenth-century Japanese print: notice how the action of looking forwards is accompanied by a corresponding movement backwards with the spinal column; (right) A Comédie Française actor at the beginning of the twentieth century expressing terror: the expression is accentuated by the tension in the spinal column.

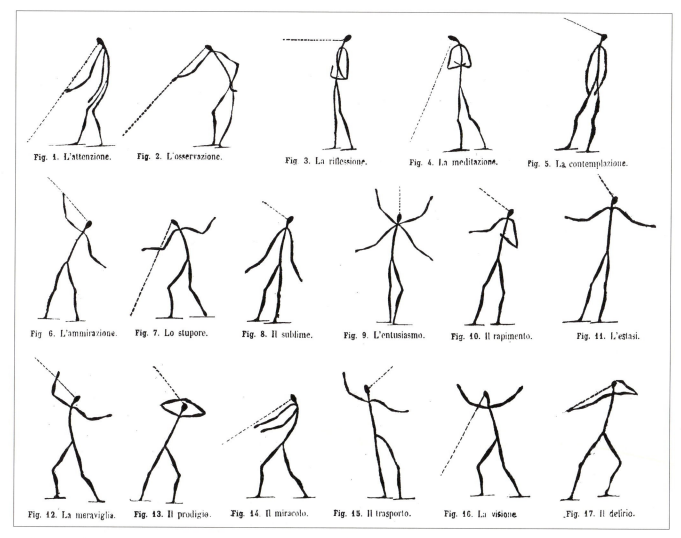

Fig. 1. L'attenzione.   Fig. 2. L'osservazione.   Fig. 3. La riflessione.   Fig. 4. La meditazione.   Fig. 5. La contemplazione.

Fig 6. L'ammirazione.   Fig. 7. Lo stupore.   Fig. 8. Il sublime.   Fig. 9. L'entusiasmo.   Fig. 10. Il rapimento.   Fig. 11. L'estasi.

Fig. 12. La meraviglia.   Fig. 13. Il prodigio.   Fig. 14. Il miracolo.   Fig. 15. Il trasporto.   Fig. 16. La visione.   Fig. 17. Il delirio.

19. Direction of the eyes and the emotions in diagrams by Italian dancer and dance theorist Carlo Blasis (1795–1878), taken from *L'uomo fisico, intelletuale e morale* (*Physical, Intellectual and Moral Man*, Milan, 1857): 1. Attention; 2. Observation; 3. Reflection; 4. Meditation; 5. Contemplation; 6. Admiration; 7. Amazement; 8. Sublimity; 9. Enthusiasm; 10. Rapture; 11. Ecstasy; 12. Wonder; 13. Fascination; 14. Awe; 15. Rapture; 16. Vision; 17. Delirium. Notice how each change in the direction of the eyes corresponds to a change in the position of the spinal column.

The action of seeing

When Siddharta left his father's palace and went in search of the ultimate truth, he spent six years studying philosophy and living an ascetic life in a hermitage lost in the mountains. But enlightenment did not come. As time passed, Siddharta began to despair and doubt. One day, he lifted his eyes and saw the morning star. Its rays pierced him and he found enlightenment. He left the hermitage and began to travel the world to make his experience known so that others could share the freedom which he now enjoyed.

You have looked at the stars thousands of times. But you suddenly see a star in a new way that leads to that type of understanding which is a total experience. This is the action of seeing: reacting to this action, you discover yourself and the 'other' is revealed to you.

(Eugenio Barba in conversation with actors at ISTA, Bonn, 1980)

The eyes can see everything except themselves: therefore the performer must see with a second pair of eyes. This is what Zeami is suggesting when he says: *mokuzen shingo*, 'the eyes in front, the heart behind'. What does he mean? Performers on stage can see what is on their left, on their right, in front of them; but, unlike the spectator, they cannot see behind themselves. There is

therefore only one possibility open to them: to dilate their field of vision and to use their heart (*kokoro*) to see behind them. They must work on two opposing levels: ahead with the eyes, behind with the heart. *Mokuzen shingo*.

Accepting Zeami's poetic definition of the performer's sixth sense, we also discover that it is a metaphor for a physical truth. For performers, seeing behind themselves implies being attentive to something that is happening behind their backs. This 'being on the lookout' creates a tension in the spinal column, an impulse ready to be released. At the same time, an opposition is created in the performer's body between looking ahead and being attentive to what is happening behind. Tension and opposition engage the spinal column, as if it was ready to act, to turn. This is how performers see with a second pair of eyes, that is, with their spinal columns. They are ready to act: to react.

This is very clear in the figure of the Japanese actor (ill.17): he is looking ahead, but the position of his body, of his legs, and especially of his extended and curved torso, gives one the distinct impression that he is ready to stand up. The back is pulled backwards while the gaze is directed forward. The hands, fanned open, seem to underline the 360-degree circular nature of the tension which traverses the spectator. There is no doubt that this actor, at this moment, is seeing with his *heart*.

The eye spinal column equivalence is not unknown in Western theatre. In Zeami, this equivalence is hidden behind the veil of a poetic paradox which renders it practically incomprehensible to the uninitiated; in the West, the practice of this equivalence is confused, strangled by the problem of expressivity understood in a more psychological than physical way.

Let us examine the drawings by the Italian choreographer, dance and pantomime master Carlo Blasis (1795–1878). These drawings and their captions describe the various body attitudes that express emotion: e.g. attention, astonishment, enthusiasm, wonder, ecstasy (ill.19). But they can also be read in a completely different way: when the eyes work precisely and fix on something, the gaze immediately modifies the position of the spinal column. The eyes and the spinal column work in co-relation, irrespective of what is *behind* the body. One could say that these figures look in a certain way *in order to express* the various emotions. But the opposite might also be true: that it is the way of looking which creates expression. For a performer, seeing is not looking with the eyes; it is an action that engages the entire body.

Alexander Gladkov attributes the following to Meyerhold:

I can always distinguish a genuine from a poor actor by his eyes. The good actor knows the value of his gaze. With only a shift of his pupils from the line of the horizon to the left or right, up or down, he will give the necessary accent to his acting, which will be understood by the audience. The eyes of poor actors and amateurs are always fidgety, darting here and there to the sides.

20–21. Sanjukta Panigrahi shows two *rasa*, two representations of emotion, from odissi dance: fear (**left**) and disgust (**right**). The nine *rasa* (love, heroism, compassion, wonder, laughter, sorrow, anger, fear, tranquillity) are common to all traditional forms and styles of Indian dance-theatre, and depend largely on facial expression. While it is true that the rest of the body, the arms, and the hands, underscore the representation of feeling, their use is not determined by the way feeling is expressed with the face. There is a noticeable dialectic relationship between the direction of the eyes and that of the trunk and the spinal column: the action of seeing is already a reaction of feeling.

Showing that one is seeing

In the past, when the only illumination in kabuki (and also Western) theatre was candles and oil lamps, the actors performed almost in the dark. A long way from the mystical Wagnerian gulf. And so a stage servant would follow the protagonist around the stage, carrying a long pole with a candle in a little dish at one end. Thus the actor's face, upper torso and arms were illuminated without the assistant being visible to the spectators. In spite of this contrivance, it was necessary to give the spectators time to take in the actor's expression, at least in the most crucial moments; it was even more difficult to catch this expression in the twilight given that the spectators were often occupied with other activities: eating, drinking tea, gossiping.

One might suppose that this situation gave birth to the kabuki actors' custom of stopping, or better, of *cutting* as they describe it, a *mie* (literally, 'to show'). Why cut? The actor's pose could be described as stopping the film in that particular frame where the actor is showing a special tension: hence the meaning of cutting the action and of blocking a living immobility. We have already encountered this phenomenon, in the chapter on *Energy*, when referring to the Peking Opera position called *lian-shan*: 'to stop the action'.

Mie is still practised in kabuki theatre, even though today the stage is fully lit. *Mie* is in fact one of the kabuki actor's most spectacular techniques, a virtuosity understood and appreciated by the spectators. But what exactly is a *mie*?

One could say that a kabuki performance is a transition from one *mie* to another, that is, from one summit of tension to another. The time between these poses is fluid because in fact the poses occur at the end of each scene. Sometimes, it is even a case of a super-pose, of a great *tableau vivant* in which all the secondary actors and stage servants participate by means of a series of attentive and silent actions: they assist the principal actors, arranging a *kimono* sleeve, lifting a train, changing the position of a prop (a long sabre, a flowering branch), creating a series of concentric rays around the actor who is executing the *mie*. The term *mie* refers, however, only to the principal actor's pose; the centre of this pose, the fulcrum of the entire ensemble, is the eyes, which inevitably attract the spectators' attention. Why?

22–24. Examples of *mie* (showing the eyes): an eighteenth-century print by painter Sharaku (1794) (**bottom left**), and by contemporary kabuki actors.

For a kabuki actor, to cut a *mie* means to stop suddenly, in the middle of a vortex of activity, after having made expansive arm movements and after having opened his eyes wide: the pupils cross, the eyes twist as if they were about to pop out of the actor's head. But what could seem no more than a bizarre artifice for 'showing' how an actor can see is in fact a much more subtle dramatic device. One or both of the pupils cross, depending on where the actor wants to direct his, and therefore the spectators', attention. The pupils function like a telephoto lens zooming in.

25–28. (**top left**) Eighteenth-century Parisian poster for a performance of grimaces and physiognomic displays. Many 'actors' of the time became very popular in highly successful performances which consisted of nothing more than the presentation of a series of grimaces: in a darkened room, lit only by candlelight, which accentuated facial features and concentrated the spectators' attention on facial expression, the actors mimed all the various passions that could possibly be expressed by the human face; (**below left**) A stage servant illuminates the actor's face with a candle attached to the end of a bamboo pole, a convention known as *tsura akari*, 'face light' (nineteenth-century Western engraving); (**top right** and **below right**) Kabuki actors in a *mie* showing the eyes.

For example, a servant is seated to the right of a samurai and tells him about some careless thing he has done, something irremediable and dangerous to his master. To underline his disapproval and to fix it in the *mie*, the actor playing the samurai directs his left eye to the servant seated on his right while his right eye continues to stare straight ahead, towards the spectators. If the situation required both the samurai and the servant to act at the same time, they would look towards each other. It sometimes happens that several characters freeze in the *mie*. The result is a fantastic crossing of eyes in an extravagant triangulation.

The focusing of attention and the tension produced in the actor are communicated to the spectators, underlined not only by the suspension of all other scenic action – all the actors not involved in the particular action stop and wait for its denouement – but also by the clapper blows made by a stage hand: two blows to indicate the beginning of the movement which leads to the pose, then a hail of blows during the *mie* immobility, and finally two blows to announce that the *mie* is finished. These blows intensify the emotion and arouse the spectators during the dramatic phase. Today, the spectators usually applaud the actors because they have caught both the actors and themselves at the peak of the *climax*. This peak is expressed by a tension which is about to explode and which is nevertheless retained. Even though immobile, the actor's body is never inert.

But the most important thing is the scenic use of the eyes. Using a deformation of his optical apparatus, the actor physically shows us the dramatic vicissitudes in the relationships between the characters.

If, as has been said, theatre is 'showing the relationships between people', kabuki confirms that it has to do with an act which passes exclusively through the actor's body.

(Nicola Savarese,
Il teatro nella camera chiara
[*Theatre in the Lightroom*])

29–32. Examples of energy in time with the eyes: Etienne Decroux (**top left**); Dario Fo (**top right**); Chinese actor Mei Lanfang (**centre**); Charles Dullin (**bottom**).

132

33–35. Three facial expressions of Odin Teatret actress Roberta Carreri in her solo performance *Judith* (1987).

The natural face

As part of his study of certain faculties innate in both man and animals, the ethologist Eibl-Eibesfeldt draws attention to the fact that the gesture of showing the teeth is common to both man and anthropomorphs. This is particularly true of the canine teeth, even though 'our upper canines have diminished in size'. This means that the 'motor module has survived the reduction of the organ which used to be shown'. Eibl-Eibesfeldt's illustrations (ill.38) show a baboon, a kabuki actor miming anger and an angry young girl. By using the expression miming anger, the ethologist unintentionally underlines the transformation of a daily technique into an extra-daily technique: these facial gestures are in fact the equivalent of a kabuki actor's *mie*.

The expression 'to show one's teeth' is so rich in meaning that it has passed from physiology to proverb. Everyone knows that the eyes, the facial muscles, the mouth and even the ears (when they redden) are important indicators of the intentions and feelings of living beings, but this should not make us lose sight of another observation: as is demonstrated by the kabuki actor who is miming anger, a spectator will automatically recognise intentions and feelings in an actor irrespective of what the actor himself is feeling and experiencing, as long as he makes his eyes and facial muscles assume a precise position.

This is one of the numerous implications of pre-expressivity familiar to both the Asian and Western performers, as evidenced by the plates in Aubert's *L'Art du mime* (*The Art of Mime*, 1901) and the masks used in Japanese theatre (ill.36–37). The mask becomes a face and the face a mask. It is not the psychology of feelings but the anatomy of forms which is being dealt with here.

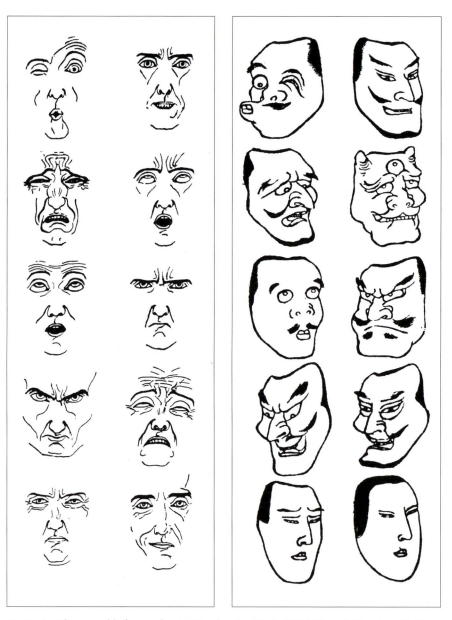

36–37. Facial mime: table from Aubert's *L'Art du mime* (Paris, 1901) (**above left**) and profile drawings of popular Japanese noh and kyogen masks (**above right**). The similarity between the expressions drawn by Aubert and those of the Japanese masks is remarkable. Moreover, it is worth noting that the first exhibitions of old noh masks in Europe, at the end of the nineteenth century, were carefully studied not only by artists and art critics but also by doctors and scientists, who found them to be exceptionally accurate anatomically.

38. The innate ability of animals to 'show their teeth' (the canines) is also found in humans, in spite of the reduced size of the dental apparatus: in order to demonstrate this, ethologist Eibl-Eibesfeldt compared a baboon, a kabuki actor and an angry child.

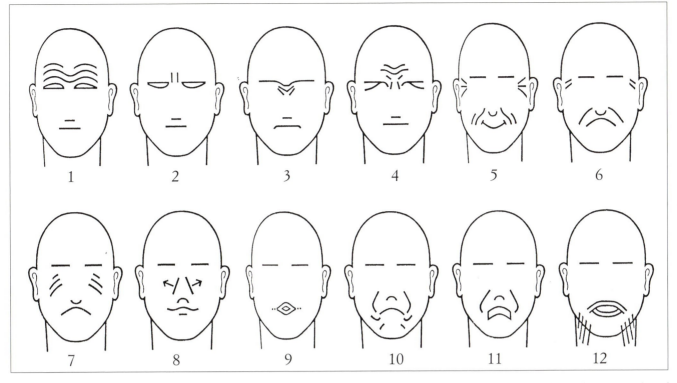

39. Although the facial muscles do not work independently of each other, facial expression is determined by the prevalence of one or another of these muscles over the others. In this table from his *Anatomy for Artists*, French anatomist Duval shows what effects would be created if the facial muscles could function independently. The resulting expressions clearly show that pure physiological movement has in itself an effect on the spectator's perception. Expressions: 1. *frontalis*: attention, surprise; 2. *orbicularis oculi*: reflection, meditation; 3. *procerus*: severity, menace, aggression; 4. *corrugator*: dislike, sorrow: 5. *zygomaticus major*: laughter; 6. *levator labii superioris et alae nasi*: discontent, affliction; 7. *levator labii*: extreme affliction, crying; 8. *compressor naris*: attention, sensuality: 9. *orbicularis oris*: pouting; 10. *depressor anguli oris*: scorn; 11. *depressor labii inferioris*: disgust; 12, *platysma*: sorrow, torture, extreme force.

40. Painted face of an Indian teyyam dancer (Kerala, India).

The provisional face

On the one hand, there is an attempt to theatricalise, that is, dramatise, the performer's face by dilating it; on the other hand, in the case of precise codification, there is the need to respect the rules of life: we have already seen this when describing how the eyes are lifted 30 degrees above the normal horizon in order to modify the tensions of the spinal column. But there is yet another possibility, another way of giving the face an extra-daily dimension: the mask.

When performers put on a mask, it is as if their body has suddenly been decapitated. They give up all movement and expression of facial musculature. The face's extraordinary richness disappears. There is such a resistance created between the *provisional* face (*kamen* in Japanese) and the performer that this conversion of the face into something apparently dead can actually make one think of a decapitation. This is in fact one of the performer's greatest challenges: to transform a static, immobile, fixed object into a living and suggestive profile.

Theatres such as the noh have taken the use of masks to an extreme, discovering and adapting laws for expression and developing an extremely refined construction technique which makes noh masks veritable masterpieces of sculpture. When wisely animated with the use of an appropriate tension in the spinal column and with delicate tremblings that exploit the play of light and shadow, this object, seemingly dead, acquires a miraculous life (ill.44).

Today, Western theatre often rejects the mask as something artifical which represses the performer. Even when a performer, like the Decroux mime, wants to cancel the face (Decroux maintains that the face and hands are 'the instruments of lies and the apostles of gossip'), he uses neutral masks or transparent cloth and not a provisional face, or even half-masks which only cover part of the face (usually the upper part, as in commedia dell'arte or Balinese theatre) and give the performer a certain freedom.

But it would be a mistake to think that if a performer wears a mask it means that the face is forgotten. According to Balinese custom, the face under the mask must act. Further, if one wants the mask to live, the face must take on the same expression as the mask (ill.43): the face must laugh or cry

41. I Made Bandem, Balinese dancer and theatre scholar, showing the correlation that the actor must find between his 'real' and 'false' faces if he wishes to make a mask come alive.

42. Half-mask from *topeng* (Balinese mask theatre), used by I Made Pasek Tempo in a demonstration at the Volterra ISTA (1981).

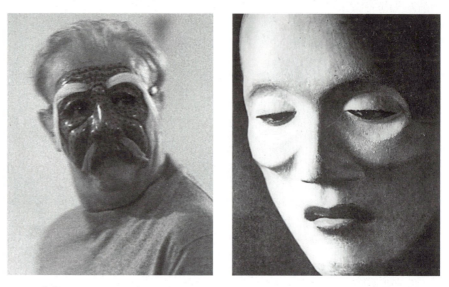

43–44. (**left**) Dario Fo in a demonstration at the Volterra ISTA (1981), using a Balinese *topeng* mask reminiscent to that used by Pantalone in commedia dell'arte; (**right**) noh mask of an old man.

with the mask. This is not an excess of zeal. Performing with a mask, using it to express reactions and feelings, and being able to orient oneself in space in spite of a restriction of the field of vision, requires actions which force the rest of the body to work in a particular way. Anyone who has performed with a mask knows that the use of the body is totally different when one is wearing a mask, even if the actions one does are the same.

45–46. The face alive like a mask: (**left**) Meyerhold (seated) during a rehearsal of the final scene of *The Government Inspector* by Gogol. The Russian director is showing his actor how to freeze the face in the final expression; (**below**) actors Zbigniew Cynkutis and Ryszard Cieslak in a scene from *Akropolis*, a classical text by Polish playwright Stanislaw Wyspianski (1869–1907), adapted and directed by Grotowski (Theatre Laboratory of the Thirteen Rows, Opole, 1962). The actors kept the same mimed expressions throughout the entire performance: facial compositions which became actual masks because of the use of particular muscles.

The painted face

All theatrical cultures have sought to dramatise the facial features by accentuating, deforming or enlarging them. Kathakali actors practise a special exercise designed to strengthen the eyeball muscles and to augment the mobility of the pupil (ill.2 p. 122). In addition, before a performance, they insert a grain of red pepper under the eyelid: blood flows into the eye area because of the irritation caused by the pepper grain and makes the blue and green faces of the heroes and demons look supernatural.

Peking Opera make-up transforms the actor's face into a veritable mask (ill.48–49) and informs the spectator about the rôle and its dominant characteristic: courage, cleverness, wisdom, stupidity, wickedness ... The colour combinations that accentuate the facial features produce striking effects. Female rôles are characterised by a vivid pink colour which emphasises the wide open eyes (it is customary to pull up the skin of the forehead in order to widen the eyes).

The same striking colours are found on the faces of kabuki actors (ill.50), and the effect is increased by the distorted gaze of the *mie*. The hairstyles make the forehead recede back to the middle of the skull so that the eyebrows can be painted high up, making the eyes seem larger.

Mimes use a special technique to pull the facial muscles and to carry expressivity beyond the limits of daily and conventional behaviour.

Exercises of this kind, the use of make-up, special hairstyles and artificial colours make it possible for the performer to modify expression completely and to use it in a conscious extra-daily way. An actual geometrical system is used in both Japan and China to calculate the design of make-up according to facial dimensions. The sweat on the performers' faces gives the matt colours of the make-up a shiny and brilliant patina which increases the illusion of life. This effect does not appear at all unnatural to the spectator, since the face keeps all its mobility.

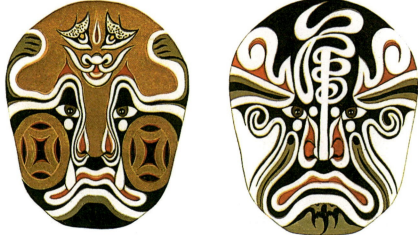

47. Kathakali actor M.P. Sankaran Namboodiri's facial make-up, in a demonstration at the Holstebro ISTA, 1986.
48–49. Line and colour proportions in two Peking Opera make-ups.

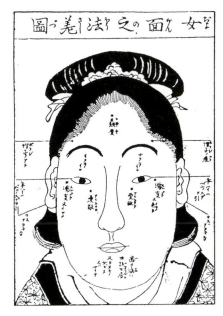

50. Facial make-up of a kabuki actor making a *mie*: notice how this extra-daily make-up requires that even the inside of the mouth be coloured.

51–52. (**left**) This engraving, found in a book on Japanese kabuki theatre published in 1802, shows the 'cartography' of the face of an *onnagata*, the actor who plays female rôles. This 'cartography' must not only transform a male but must also heighten the sensuality of the eyes. The face is first covered with a thick layer of white paste: the notes on the engraving indicate the areas which must then be coloured. A reddish shadow, the first sign of sensuality, is drawn on the ear lobes, which are usually hidden by wigs, and on the eyebrows, whose form varies according to the rôle (they are also often shaved). The pink colour turns to red under the eyebrows in order to avoid creating a violent contrast with the black line on the white background. Then come the most 'erogenous' areas of the face: the fire-red mouth, always small but with a full lower lip, and the corners of the eyes. The eye is painted like a wide erotic tear: the red hue is extended in the outside corner, lifting the lower edge of the eye and rising gently outwards. Below the eyes, on the sides of the nose, is the area of natural charm, of grace without malice, blending with the sensual. The teeth are painted black for married women, evil women and women who run houses of prostitution; (**right**) an *onnagata's* face made up: the famous actor Banda Tamasaburo.

139

Microcosm, macrocosm

All the principles of extra-daily technique, as well as what we have defined as the actor's pre-expressivity (cf. *Pre-expressivity*), can be found in the Balinese and Kathakali performer's basic foot position (ill.1):

- the alteration of balance;
- the opposition of directions;
- the destruction of the weight and force of inertia by means of the play of *keras* and *manis* tensions (cf. *Energy*) which recreate an equivalent to the tensions of the big toe in daily life.

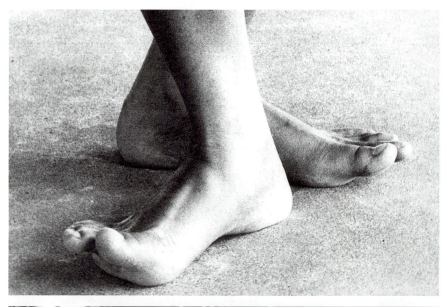

The foot exemplifies a particular type of life, as if in a microcosm. The life which is continuously flowing through the bodies of newborn babies is clearly seen mirrored in the constant movements of their toes. The foot position taken by the Balinese and Indian performer seems to suggest that he is trying to discover an equivalent to the life he had as a newborn child, when the foot was not accultured by a way of walking and by shoes.

It is, however, interesting to note how this life has been reconstructed by means of a new acculturation of the foot. It is said that the modern dance revolution was born when dancers began to dance barefoot. The foot's freedom was proclaimed by the abandonment of stiff satin shoes. And so it is: all Indian dancers and actors (kathakali, bharatanatyam, odissi) perform barefoot, as do dancers in south-east Asia from Cambodia to Indonesia. With the exception of a few specific rôles, the feet of Japanese and Chinese actors are covered only with special stockings that allow them to slide their feet.

But we should not be misled by the fact that the bare foot at first seems 'free': in all forms of codified theatre, the bare foot is constrained to adapt to deforming positions as if wearing very particular kinds of shoes. These deformations of the foot result in variations of balance, special ways of walking and the maintenance of a different tension in the entire body.

Whether deformed by special shoes or left free, the feet determine the body's tone and its dynamic in space.

1. (**top**) Basic foot position in Balinese dance: notice the tension in the big toe, tensed upwards.
2–3. (**centre** and **bottom**) Basic foot position in kathakali: notice how the toes are turned in and how the weight is supported on the outside edges of the foot.

140

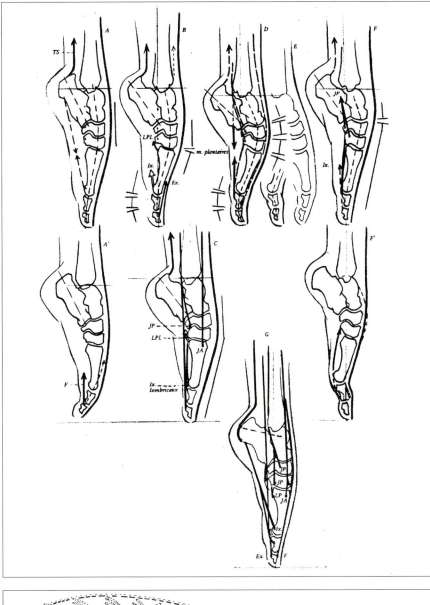

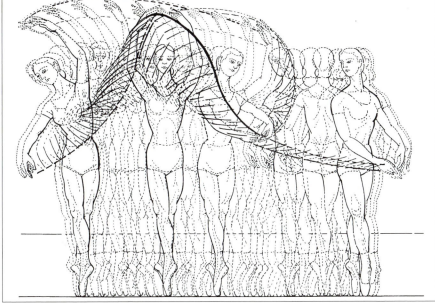

On point

Petipa, the great French choreographer and founder of a particular style of classical dance, claimed that staying 'on point' gave 'the final touch to the whole picture'. In fact, this virtuosity, characteristic of ballet dancers and almost a symbol of classical ballet, is only the last of a series of proposals for the use of the foot. It was first seen in 1880, when Carlo Blasis developed new dance techniques with the aid of specially constructed, reinforced shoes.

To dance 'on point', required by many of the steps and moves in classical dance, is evidence of major work by a tradition on a specific part of the body and of an attempt to exploit and improve the body's potential. In *Lettres sur la danse* (1760), Noverre established the seven fundamental ballet movements: *to bend, to stretch, to rise up, to jump, to slide, to leap, to turn*. Since that time, all ballet dancers and choreographers have added to, interpreted or corrected the French tradition in their own ways. Noverre's encouragement of the free movement of the body and, especially, his fixing of rules for this movement, are of prime importance, but even more revolutionary is his having established a fundamental principle that none of his successors have been able to refute: one cannot understand the seven movements in isolation, one cannot establish rules for each part of the body if these parts are considered separately.

The anatomy of the human body is structured in such a way that even a single movement of one individual part results in a kind of muscular echo in all the other parts. Consequently, the rules that govern the feet in classical dance as well as in all other forms of codified theatre, can only be considered in relation to the rest of the body. Such an essential and basically simple consideration would seem obvious and yet it is a distinguishing characteristic of great ballet masters and dancers. It differentiates those who are only concerned with technique and the rules that organise the different parts of the body and its movements from those who master the technique and are able to co-ordinate the action of the body and to create a personal synthesis, their own style.

4. (**top**) The anatomy of the foot of a classical ballet dancer 'on point': the diagrams show that that there are various ways of being 'on point', depending on the articulation of the big toe.
5. (**bottom**) Diagram of movement 'on point' taken from Kirstein's classical dance manual. Accompanied by arm gestures, the dancer's body moves in space through a series of almost imperceptible changes in the position of the big toes. Normal or daily movement, one leg following another, is supplanted: the body seems to float across the stage.

6. One of the ways of walking used by the actors in Wyspianski's *Akropolis*, directed by Grotowski (1962). The scenic action took place on several levels; the spectators were seated between these various levels (their faces can be seen in the background). Thus the actors' legs and feet (deformed by large wooden shoes) were often directly in the spectators' line of vision. The rhythm and way of walking evoked the exhausting labour of prisoners in a Nazi concentration camp, the setting chosen by Grotowski for his production of this early twentieth-century Polish classic.

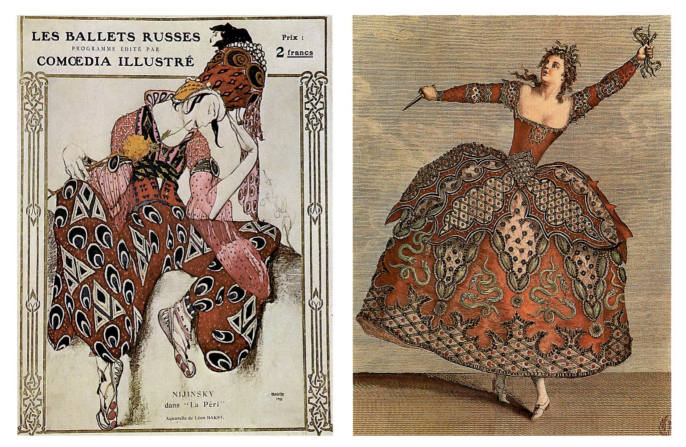

7–8. The way of walking in classical ballet with a new acculturation of the feet: (**left**) Bakst programme design for Les Ballets Russes production of *La Péri*; (**right**) lavishly costumed dancer in Jean-Philippe Rameau's (1683–1764) tragic opera-ballet *Hippolyte et Aricie*.

9–10. (**top**) Nineteenth-century print of famous Viennese classical dancer Fanny Essler (1810–84). The way of walking in classical ballet is based on the same opposition principles found in other theatrical cultures (cf. opposite, ill.11–18). Before 1880, the footwear used in classical dance was a simple slipper with no metal reinforcement. The foot was not constricted in any way and the sole of the foot was in full contact with the floor. In spite of the upwards tension and desire for lightness typical of classical dance, the position of the foot was similar to that seen in many Asian dances: one foot flat on the floor, the other on point; (**below**) Diagram of an *entrechat* (literally, 'interlacing'), drawn by Friederich Albert Zorn. Zorn was the author of *Grammatik der Tanzkunst* (*Grammar of the Art of Dance*, Leipzig, 1887), a prestigious manual which synthesised all the technical information on dance that had accumulated between 1660 and 1885. The *entrechat* is a typical classical ballet jump: the diagram shows an increasing number of beats of the calves. Dancers today manage up to eight beats; Nijinsky was able to do ten. It was through the evolution of this jump, which is a way of showing that the dancer is 'weightless', that classical ballet in the era of Romanticism definitively took off from the floor.

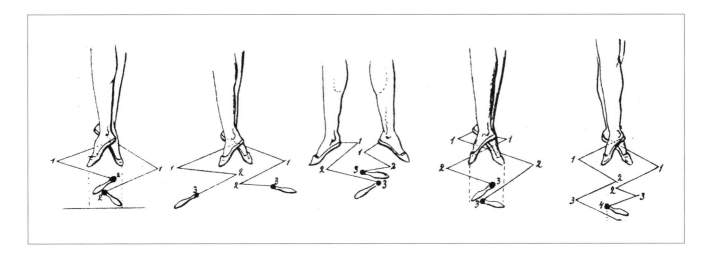

11

12

13

14

15

16

11–18. Way of walking in Balinese dance, illustrated by the young dancer Jas at the Volterra ISTA, 1981. Each step is accompanied by a change of tension in the arms and hands; every change in the lower part of the body is accompanied by a corresponding change in the upper part of the body. This way of walking becomes an extra-daily technique thanks to the *keras*, the force used in placing the foot on the floor (ill.14–15). Lifting the toes while walking (ill.11) results in a tension which lifts the knee higher than is the case in daily walking. The *keras* tension in the ankle lifts not only the foot but also the rest of the leg, and to a much greater height than normal (ill.16).

17

18

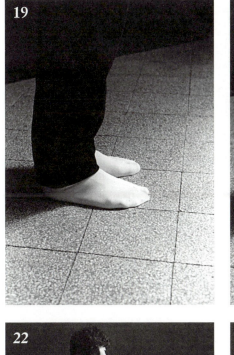

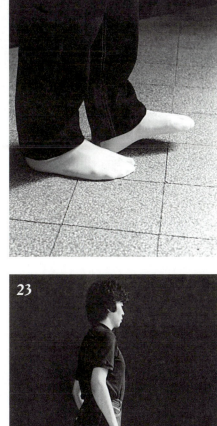

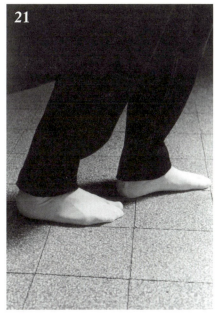

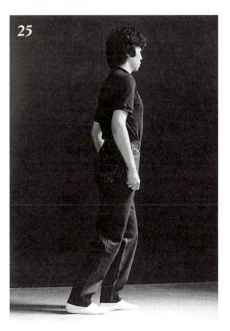

19–26. Way of walking in kyogen theatre, demonstrated by Kosuke Nomura. The feet are never lifted from the floor but slide along it, obliging the body to find a lower position so that the knees can be bent. The result is a very particular gait, in which the shoulders are neither lifted nor lowered as they are in daily walking. The kyogen actor moves smoothly forward: changes in speed do not alter the overall body architecture. Dressed in a capacious *kimono* which conceals all but his feet, the actor seems almost to float along the floor.

Foot grammar

The way in which the feet are used is the basis of a stage performance. Even the movements of the arms and hands can only augment the feeling inherent in the body positions established by the feet. There are many cases in which the position of the feet determines even the strength and nuance of the actor's voice. An actor can still perform without arms and hands, but to perform without feet would be inconceivable.

Noh has often been defined as the art of walking. The movements of the actor's feet create the expressive environment. The basic use made of the feet in noh consists of a shuffling motion. The actor walks by dragging the feet, turns around in a shuffle-like motion and strikes a rhythm with his feet in the same way. The upper parts of his body are practically immobile; even the movements of his hands are extremely limited. Whether the actor is standing still or in motion, his feet are the centre of interest. These feet, encased in *tabi* (white bifurcated socks) provide one of the most profound pleasures of noh, as they move from a position of repose forwards and backwards, left and right, up and down with their own independent rhythm. Such patterns of foot motion can be created out of the intimate relationship of the feet of the actor with the surface of the noh stage. The very life of the art depends on the fixing and deepening of the relationships of the feet to the stage in order to render the expressiveness of foot movements all the more compelling. In fact, this kind of ambulatory art is involved in all theatrical performance.
(Tadashi Suzuki, *The Way of Acting*)

After having attended a Moscow Art Theatre performance, a Japanese theatre critic at the beginning of the twentieth century claimed that the Japanese would never be able to perform Western authors well: according to him, it was useless to continue to attempt 'translated' theatre because 'we Japanese have shorter arms and legs than Westerners'. It may seem curious that this first criticism of the Japanese imitation of European theatre is based on a physical observation, but a more complex reality is concealed here.

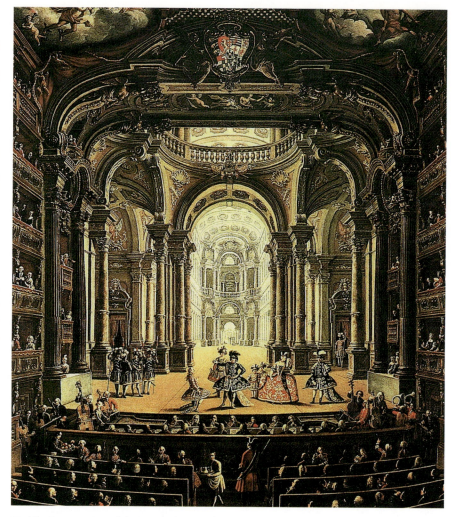

27. The inauguration of the Royal Theatre of Turin, 26 December, 1740, in a painting by Pietro D'Oliviero. The deep-perspective stage was designed by Bibiena.
28–29. Actor from the Tadashi Suzuki Company in two different gaits from their training of walking.

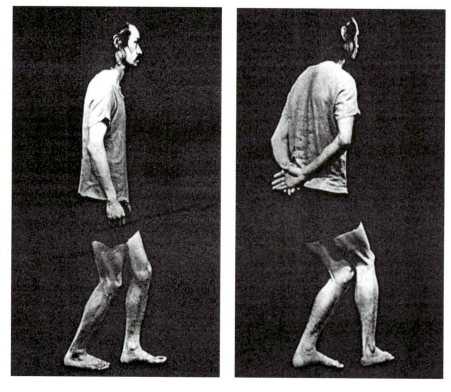

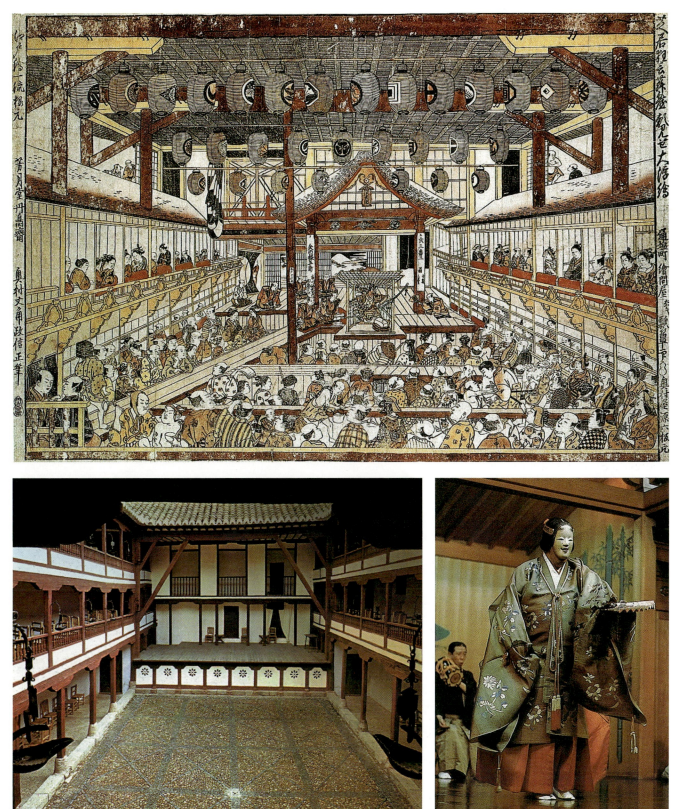

30–32. Print (1740) (**top**) by painter Okamura Masanobu of the interior of a kabuki theatre. One can see the arrangement of the stage and of the so-called *hanamichi* ('flower path') passageway which divides the audience in two and which the actors use for entrances and exits, executed with very particular flamboyant techniques. The print shows not only the theatre's internal architecture but also the performance and the social phenomenon of which it is a part: the spectators eat, drink and converse during the show. The *mon*, the coats of arms of the principal actors, are painted on lanterns hung at the back of the stage. The titles of the performances and dances in the evening's programme are painted on signs hung on pillars to the left and right of the main playing area. The figures on the sides at the top right and left are the theatre attendants who control the amount of light coming into the room by opening or closing sliding panels: until the end of the nineteenth-century, performances in Japan took place only during the day; (**below left**) the only wooden *corral* or performance courtyard still standing, in Almagro, Spain. There is a remarkable similarity between the *corral* and the kabuki stage (the placement of spectators and stalls, the roof over the stage, the illumination from above, and even wooden pillars of the same colour). Nevertheless, the two scenic spaces are different, create different relationships between the performer and the spectator; (**below right**) noh actor. Paul Claudel has written: 'In the Western drama something happens, in noh someone arrives.'

The first Japanese actors who introduced Western plays to Japan, part of the tremendous effort at 'Westernisation' taking place in the whole nation, strove to imitate European theatre's realism and naturalism by copying surface, daily actions: the ways of smoking, eating, using handkerchiefs, greeting or walking. All these actions were new for them and had no point of reference in their daily lives. This external imitation must have seemed just as ridiculous as our efforts to use chopsticks or to sit on our heels, with the knees bent (as the Japanese do).

But as Tadashi Suzuki, one of the contemporary Japanese theatre men most interested in the confrontation of actor techniques, writes:

The art of stage performance cannot be judged by how closely the actors can imitate or recreate ordinary, everyday life on the stage. An actor uses his words and gestures to try to convince his audience of something profoundly true. It is this attempt that should be judged. In these terms, most Japanese actors, whether their arms and legs are short, fat, or whatever, are capable of giving performances that might suit translated plays in quite another way. An actor, however long his arms and legs, will appear clumsy if he cannot project a sense of profound truth to his audience. The actor's nationality is irrelevant.

Since the coming of the modern theatre to Japan, however, the artistic use of foot movements has not continued to develop. This is too bad, because realism in the theatre should inspire a veritable treasure house of walking styles. Since it is commonly accepted that realism should attempt to reproduce faithfully on the stage the surface manner of life, the art of walking has more or less been reduced to the simplest forms of naturalistic movement. Yet any movement on the stage is, by definition, a fabrication. Since there is more room within realism for a variety of movements than in noh or in kabuki, these various ambulatory possibilities should be exhibited in an artistic fashion. One reason the modern theatre is so tedious to watch, it seems to me, is because it has no feet.

(Tadashi Suzuki, *The Way of Acting*)

On Japanese stages, the feet, protagonists of the art of walking, have a long route at their disposal: in both noh and

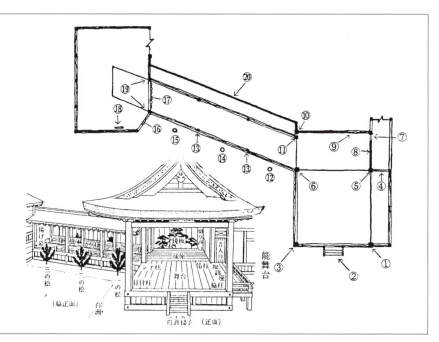

33–34. Floor plan of a noh theatre (**top**) and front view of the stage: notice the *hashigakari*, the bridge which the actor must cross, in full view of the public, on his way from the 'mirror room', where he finishes dressing, to the stage itself. The numbers indicate the essential reference points on a noh stage: 1. *Waki* (supporting actor) pillar; 2. Stairs; 3. Orientation pillar (for masked actors); 4. Door used by noble characters; 5. Flautist's pillar; 6. *Shite* (lead actor) pillar; 7. Sliding door for entrance of chorus; 8. Side wall; 9. Rear wall, on which a pine tree is always painted; 10. Stage assistant pillar; 11. Kyogen (comic actor) pillar; 12. First pine tree; 13. Pillar which defines the playing area; 14. Second pine tree; 15. Third pine tree; 16. Window through which the action on stage can be watched; 17. Curtain; 18. Mirror, in the 'mirror room'; 19. Pillar of the curtain door; 20. Outside bridge wall; (**bottom**) Open air noh theatre: Nishi Honganji Temple, Kyoto, one of the oldest noh stages in Japan.

kabuki (ill.30, 33), a bridge connects the forestage and backstage areas. Characters enter via this bridge and it is here that the *dilated* body appears, giving the spectator the possibility of appreciating the actor's extra-daily dimension. It is not by accident that the long bridge in kabuki is called *hanamichi*, the flower path: it is on this path that the *marvellous Flower*, the supreme degree of the actor's career and art of which Zeami spoke, takes form.

While they did not have an expedient similar to the bridge on the Japanese stage, Western actors used an artifice by means of which they were able to show the extra-daily nature of space and their movement in this space. They came on stage from the wings but they did not come down to the apron in a straight line (ill.39). Instead, they followed an oblique, even tortuous, route.

The *horizontality* of the Japanese stage (also characteristic of the first European stages (ill.31) became *depth* in Western theatre, accentuated by the set designs in trompe-l'oeil perspective (ill.27). In both cases, however, the actor's art of walking is rigorously respected.

A

B

35–39. (**top left**) Set design used by Meyerhold and Sololev for their lessons on commedia dell'arte at the Borodinskaya Studio (1915–17); (**centre left** and **bottom left**) diagrams (A) and (B) show the movements of the actors in two scenes from Cervantes' *The Salamanca Grotto*: (A) entrances for the appointment scene; (B) entrances for the final curtain call – the three arches indicate the actors' lineup for their bows; (**top right**) drawing of a *Ciaccona* dance for Harlequin presented in London in 1730, showing the circular, tortuous pattern which the character must follow when he enters the stage; (**bottom right**) entrances and tortuous routes for different rôles according to Jelgezhuiz's theatre treatise *Theoretische lessen over de gesticulatie en mimik*, Amsterdam 1827.

The hands are loquacious, the fingers are tongues, their silence is clamorous.
(Aurelius Cassiodorus)

Everywhere the hand goes, the eyes follow, and where the eyes look, thought follows, and where thought goes, feeling follows, and where feeling goes, one finds rasa.
(Nandikeshwara)

Physiology and codification of the hands

Codification (the fixing of gestures, poses and movements into a code) can be considered as the transition from a daily technique to an extra-daily technique by means of an equivalent (cf. *Equivalence*). This becomes obvious when one studies the codification of the hands in the various traditional Asian theatres: the hand, whether it has a meaning, as in Indian *mudras*, or whether it has no meaning (or has lost its meaning), as in the case of Balinese dancers or pure Indian dance (*nritta*), tends to recreate the dynamism of the 'hand-in-life'.

The hands, and above all the fingers, like the eyes, are continuously changing tensions and positions, both when we speak (gesticulating) and when we are acting or reacting in order to take, to push, to support ourselves, to caress. In the case of an action or reaction, the positions and tensions of the fingers change accordingly as soon as the eyes have transmitted the relevant information, as occurs, for example, when one is about to pick up a shard of broken glass or a bread crumb, or if one must hold a heavy dictionary or an inflated balloon. The asymmetry of the fingers' organic movements is a sign of credibility: this is manifest by means of the tensions of the manipulatory muscles, which are ready to act according to the weight, the fragility, the temperature, the volume, and the value of the object towards which the hand is extended, but also by means of the emotional state that the object itself elicits.

1–2. (**left**) Buddha presenting his doctrine: drawing taken from a seventh-century wall painting (Bezeklit, India). The detail of the right hand shows the *mudra* or sign for *vitarka*, indicating reasoning, the expounding of a doctrine or the telling of a story. (**above**) The same gesture as in the preceding illustration, but taken from Bulwer's *Chirologia* (London, 1644), here meaning 'to distinguish between opposites', that is, 'to know how to reason'.

3–5. (**centre left**) Cheyenne Indian sign language: table taken from *Gesture* by Hacks (Paris, 1890). From the upper left: 'friend', 'dying person', 'not true', 'the sun', 'nearly dead', 'killed'; (**centre right**) alphabet for deaf-mutes in a nineteenth-century Danish manual by A.C. Nyegaard (*De Dövstummes haandalphabet* [*Sign Language for Deaf-Mutes*], Copenhagen, 1898); (**bottom**) Secret signals used by members of the Parisian underworld: 'he's a traitor', 'let's meet outside', 'we're in trouble' (from T. Brun, *The International Dictionary of Sign Language*, London, 1969).

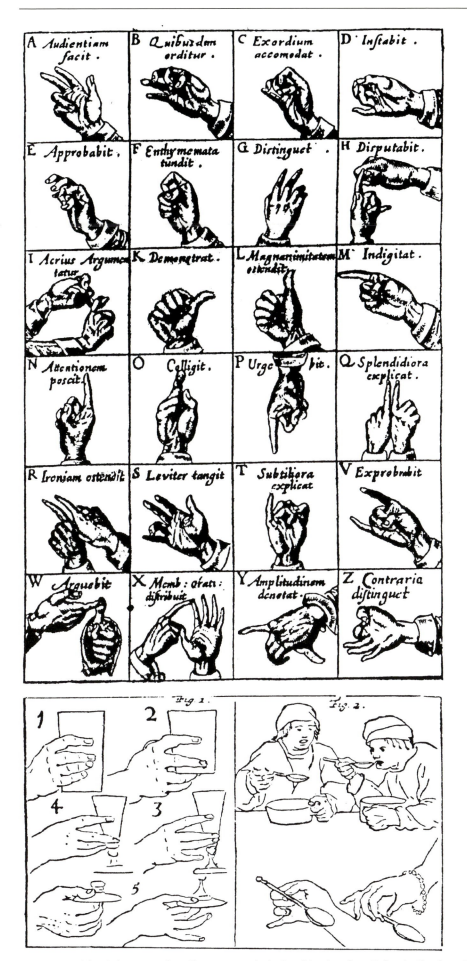

The hand acts, and acting, speaks. This speaking can be as literal as a word which represents something, or it can simply be like a sound, a pure vocal dynamic, which when produced by the voice is the result of the continuous change of tensions and articulations of the vocal apparatus (lips, tongue, vocal cords). The hand is articulated like a sound which says nothing.

Hands that can have a meaning – both inside and outside the theatre – are used by North American Indians (ill.3), deaf-mutes (ill.4) and criminals (ill.5). In the theatre, the Indian codifications called *hasta mudra* are the most elaborate.

The hands: pure sound or silence

Due to the complexity of the hand's anatomical structure and of its articulation possibilities, there are, in the movements of the fingers alone, infinite possible modifications of form and behaviour. Due to its communicative qualities, the hand has been exploited not only theatrically: many people, fascinated by the hand's potential, have, at various times, attempted to create a universal language, developing an artificial codification of daily gestures.

In 1644, J. Bulwer, an Englishman, published *Chirologia* – a very advanced work at the time – which contained a collection of more than 200 images of gestures executed by the hands. He found these gestures in Greek, Roman and Hebrew traditions, with the intention of creating a language that everyone could understand. This is the first Western example in the modern era that considers the hand as more than an instrument for counting (ill.6).

In his *The Discovery of Chironomia*, 1797, Vincenzo Requeno, a Spanish monk living in Italy, examined Greek and Latin authors, and particularly those texts devoted to the ancient art of pantomime, and attempted to popularise a 'lost art' and to restore it to use (ill.8). But his illustrations do not go beyond a certain literary, neo-classical taste, and show nothing more than hands indicating numbers, as was done in the classical tradition of the fifteenth and sixteenth centuries (ill.8–10).

6–7. **(top)** Table of chirograms (literally, written with the hands), taken from Bulwer's *Chirologia* (London, 1644); **(bottom)** Habitual, daily proletarian and bourgeois drinking and eating gestures, drawing by Gerard de Lairesse in *Groot Schilderboek*. Gerard de Lairesse (1641–1711) was a painter of picturesque genre scenes and published this book on painting in Amsterdam in 1707. The book became so popular that it actually influenced eigthteenth-century gesture.

In 1806, Gilbert Austin, another Englishman, intended his *Chironomia* to be used by actors, dancers and political orators, in order to provide them with a codified rhetoric of gestures drawn from the treatises of Quintilian and Cicero. And a year later, Henry Siddons, son of actress Sarah Siddons, adapted *Ideen zu einer Mimik* (*Ideas about Mimicry*) by Engel, a German, with the same goal of making this work available for theatrical and oratorial use.

There are only a few examples of attempts made in the West to codify the hand and its gestures, examples in which theatrical interest appears, however, most explicit on the theoretical and literary levels, and rarely influences contemporary practice. In fact, it is possible to say that while in Asian theatre the behaviour of the hands has been recreated, acquiring actual symbolic meaning value, the only accurate codification in the West has been the sign language used since ancient times by the deaf, and internationally systemised only in the past century. But this codification belongs to the daily sphere.

In the past ten years, however, theatre for the deaf has begun to be performed. This theatre is fascinating for those spectators who do not understand the sign language alphabet because of the pure dynamics of hands speaking in silence, just as we Westerners are fascinated by the Indian *mudras* without understanding what they mean.

By means of this limited example, we can understand what was defined above as the hand's 'speaking' with a 'pure sound'. We can find a theatrical equivalent to the dynamics and language of the hands in daily life. This equivalent makes it possible for the hands both to speak (transmit concepts) and to exist as a 'pure sound'. But when there is no precise code, we are tempted to pay attention only to the hands' expressivity, forgetting that the hands' attributes are equally the result of a series of tensions and articulations which, although they are not fixed, nevertheless follow specific principles that give form to expressivity.

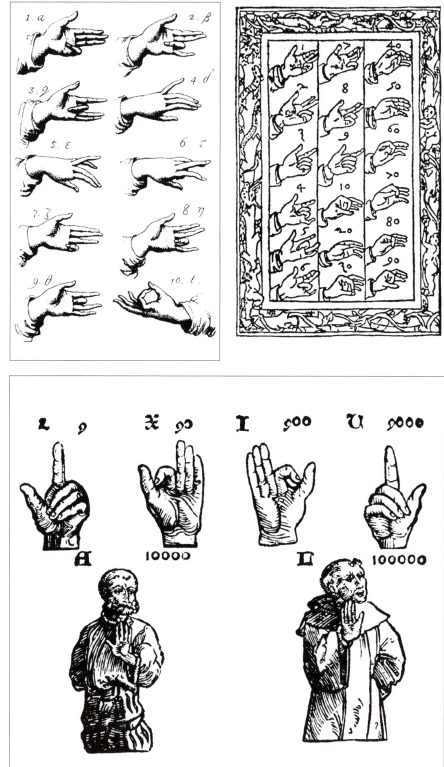

8. (**above left**) Table from *The Discovery of Chironomia* by Vincenzo Requeno (Parma, 1797).
9. (**above right**) Digital numeration in *De arithmetica* by Filippo Catandri (Florence, 1491).
10. (**bottom**) Digital numeration in a sixteenth-century Abacus for merchants.

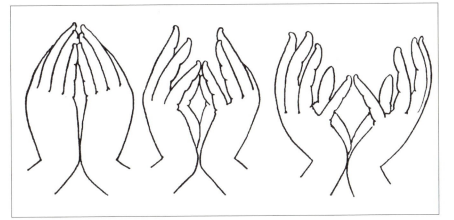

11. (top) Statue of Buddha in the Todaiji Temple (Nara, Japan). Even though this is the largest bronze statue in the world, more than 15 metres high, the artist has paid great attention to detail: the tensions in the fingers have been conscientiously respected; the vitality and delicacy of the hands has been brought fully alive.

12–13. (above) Two joined hands opening outwards, the kathakali lotus flower *mudra*. The same gesture can take on other meanings in other contexts: in daily Western gesticulation, for example, it could mean 'prayer' or 'sphere'. (right) Detail of Rodin's *Cathedral* (Rodin Museum, Paris): the cathedral is represented by the two hands joined in prayer. Speaking about this work, Rodin said that the ogive was for him the essential element of gothic architecture and that he had found in these two joined hands, which have an ogival shape, a form equivalent to that of a cathedral.

How to invent hands in movement

The best hand actions do not necessarily need to be faithfully copied from reality. In fact, pictorial logic, the demands of the drawing and the work's overall concept impose certain conditions. Anyone who has seen the expressive and interpretative solutions found by Leonardo, Michelangelo, Grünewald or Rodin will be able to understand the artist's need to create forms that respond to his intuitive impulse. A good point of departure for drawing the hand in action in an original and personal way is to sketch or even to copy any image of the hands' numerous gestures. It is not necessary that this sketch show behaviour that is already precise and neither is it necessary that there be a strong resemblance to the desired result. The sketch can merely be a point of departure on the basis of which one develops one's own personal vision.

In the sketch (ill.15), one notes how a simple up-and-down movement of the index finger can express a sense of excitement as well as various other meaning nuances. Changes in the positions of the little finger give further emotional nuances to the movement. In this drawing, each change of the finger modifies the meaning of the gesture. One should study these drawings and experiment with different emotional meanings by moving the drawings into different positions.

(Burne Hogarth,
Drawing Dynamic Hands)

These statements by the American artist Burne Hogarth, famous for his Tarzan illustrations (ill.16), are taken from a drawing course for students at the New York School of Visual Arts, of which Hogarth himself is a founder. The interesting thing for us here is that the study proposed by Hogarth, the anatomical analysis of movement, does not compromise expressivity. On the contrary, certain anatomical details, such as the little finger's change of position, 'coldly' determine the drawing's expressivity.

Let us consider another example of the hand's pre-expressivity taken from a manual for cartoonists' animation, *Cartoon Animation*, by Preston Blair. The aim of this manual – to show how one animates – is similar to the

14. (**top**) Hand animation for comics and cartoons; table taken from Preston Blair's *Cartoon Animation* (Laguna Hills, Calif., 1994), a manual for animators.
15–16. The movement of the hand (**bottom left**) in Burne Hogarth's drawings: analysis of the movement, and (**bottom right**) a drawing from a Tarzan cartoon.

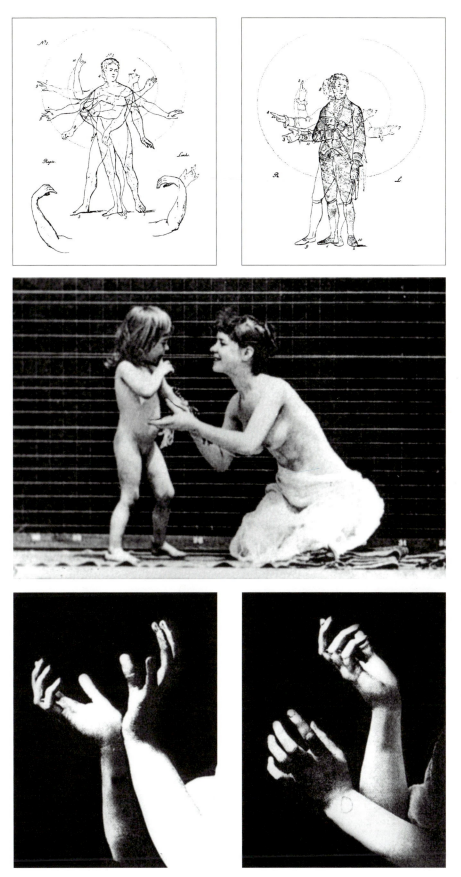

interest of the performer who has no codification (ill.15).

The cartoonist's drawings and notes contain at least three precise pieces of information. Above all, the omission of one of the three middle fingers: the removal of this finger eliminates a superfluous element and puts the essential elements into relief (cf. *Omission*), without causing the reformed hand to lose its 'hand' identity. Second, there is a slight emphasis placed on one part of the hand – the base of the thumb – drawing attention to its importance for articulation and for the dialectic between the thumb and the other fingers. Finally, there is the repeated exclusion of uniformity: in these drawings, as in the theatre, onstage, the fact that just a finger changes destroys monotony and breaks automatism. The transition of one finger from *keras* to *manis* (cf. *Energy*) which causes one's perception of the entire hand to change.

Among the acute and minute observations made by François Delsarte (1811–71) concerning the hand's expressive gestures, there are certain details that refer to the behaviour of a single finger. For years, Delsarte, walking through the Luxembourg Gardens, compared the gestures of women bending down towards children: if the woman was a nurse and did not love the child, she extended her arms but the thumb of the hand was turned inwards; if, however, she loved the child, the thumb was lifted. If the woman was the child's mother, the thumb was extended to the maximum (ill.19). Delsarte noted that in Michelangelo's work, will and energy are expressed by the outward extension of the thumb; cadavers in a morgue, on the other hand, have the thumb turned inwards. This is the life of the hands which the actor must confront, with or without codifications.

17–18. Long-arm movement in tragedy (**top left**) and short-arm movement in comedy (**top right**); table by Jelgerhuis in *Theoretische lessen over de gesticulatie en mimik* (*Theoretical Lessons on Gesture in Mime*), Amsterdam, 1827. Jelgerhuis was an experienced German actor who gave lessons in theatrical practice; he later published these lessons in two volumes. In one of these volumes, he presented more than 100 extremely clear drawings to explain the grammar of stage movement in various dramatic genres. In the part of the book devoted to the hands, he explains the function of the arms relative to the hands: hand gestures are in fact identical in tragedy and in comedy but the gestures used in comedy seem to be different because of the impression of distance from the body created by a different way of opening the arms.

19. (**centre**) A mother reaches towards her child (photo taken by Muybridge). Notice how the thumbs, extended upwards, confirm Delsarte's hypothesis concerning the connection between the opening of the thumbs and the mother's relationship to her child.

20–21. (**bottom**) The 'dance of hands', a solo performance created by American Loie Fuller (1862–1928).

India: hands and meaning

In Sanskrit, *hasta* (hand, forearm) and *mudra* (seal) refer to hand gestures whose use dates back to sacred performances during the time of the Vedas (around 1500 BC), when the gestures were used by the priests while they repeated the *mantras*, the religious formulae. There was also a traditionally fixed list of six *mudras*, which represented Buddha's gestures and corresponded to moments in his life.

The introduction of the *mudras* to dance, beginning in the classical period of Indian art, is described and codified in innumerable treatises (many still in manuscript form) on the basis of which the various genres of Indian dance were founded, from bharatanatyam, to kathakali and odissi dance and all the other less known but diffuse forms found in nearly all parts of India (cf. *Restoration of Behaviour*).

Although the *mudras* usually have the same positions in all the dance forms, they have different names and uses. For example, in bharatanatyam, there are twenty-eight (or thirty-two) root *mudras*, while in kathakali there are twenty-four and odissi dance uses about twenty in common with other forms, which also have their own *mudras*. Based on these root *mudras*, kathakali has developed the greatest number of *mudra* combinations, divided into three possibilities: *sanyukta*, the same *mudra* in both hands; *asanyukta*, a *mudra* in one hand only; *misra*, a different *mudra* in each hand. Using these *mudras* in different ways in the space, in relationship to body and facial expression, the kathakali performer can create a vocabulary consisting of about 900 words.

But the *mudra* characteristic which is perhaps most interesting from the point of view of pre-expressivity is that used in relationship to the two principle categories into which all Indian dance-theatre and the very roots of codification are subdivided. In interpretative dance (*nritya*), the *mudras* have the real language value of which we have spoken, that is, they have literal word meanings; in pure dance (*nritta*), which is always included in every dance performance, the *mudras* have a purely decorative value and are used as 'pure sound'. Moreover, based on codification into precise signs – *hasta/mudra*: 'hand/seal' – there is a classification called *hasta prana*, the life of the hands, which specifies the principle positions

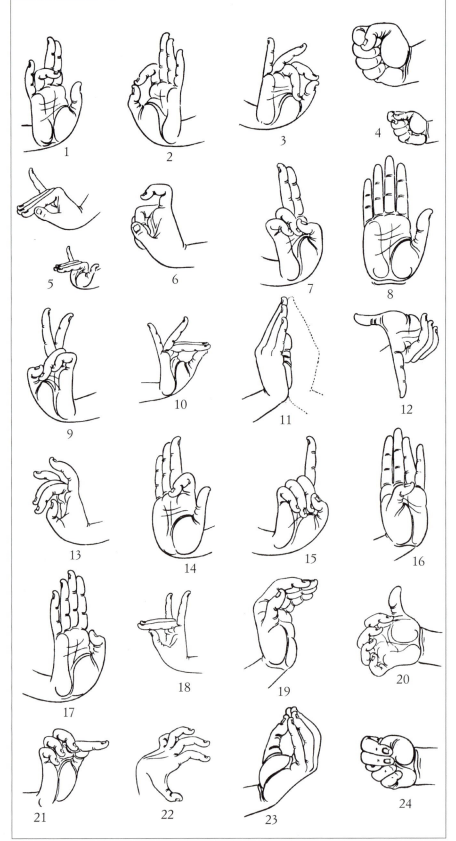

22. The twenty-four kathakali root *mudras*: 1. *Pataka*; 2. *Mudrakya*; 3. *Kataka*; 4. *Mushti*; 5. *Kartarimukha*: 6. *Sukhatunda*; 7. *Kapitthaka*; 8. *Hamsapaksha*; 9. *Sikhara*; 10, *Hamsasya*; 11 *Anjali*; 12. *Ardhachandra*; 23. *Mukura*; 14. *Bhramara*; 15. *Suchikamukha* or *Suchimukha*; 16. *Pallava*; 17. *Tripataka*; 18. *Mrigasirshsa*; 19. *Sarpasirsha*; 20. *Vardhamanaka*; 21. *Arala*; 22. *Urnanabha*; 23. *Mukula*; 24. *Katakamukha*. Taking only the first *mudra*, *Pataka*, as an example, here are the various possible meanings it can have: (1) with two hands: sun, king, elephant, lion, bull, crocodile, arch creeper, flag wave, road (or street), *patala* (underworld), earth, loin, vessel (i.e. ship), palace, evening, midday, cloud, anthill, thigh, servant, feet, disc (Vishnu's weapon), seat, lightning, gateway, cold, cartwheel, peaceful, hunched or crooked, door, pillow, canal, top of the foot, bolt: (2) with one hand: day, daytime, going, tongue, forehead, body, as, like, this, sound, messenger, beach, sandy place, tender leaf.

in which the hands can be placed. Here is the list of the *hasta prana*:

– *kuncita*: fingers bent inwards;
– *prerita*: fingers bent backwards;
– *recita*: rotating hands;
– *apavestita*: palm face downwards;
– *udvestita*: palm face upwards;
– *punkhita*: wavering fingers;
– *vyavrtta*: fingers turning backwards;
– *bhujanga*: serpentine movements;
– *prasarana*: relaxed or separated fingers.

It is this precise pulsation, created by tensions that vary continuously from one intention and dynamism to another, which establishes the life of an actor's hands, above and beyond all cultural codification.

23–26. (**top** and **centre left**) Students at the Kalamandalam kathakali school in Cherutteruthy, Kerala, India, learning the *mudras*; (**centre right**) kathakali actor M.P.S. Namboodiri demonstrating a *mudra* at Holstebro ISTA 1986; (**bottom**) examples of two-handed *mudras* in odissi dance.

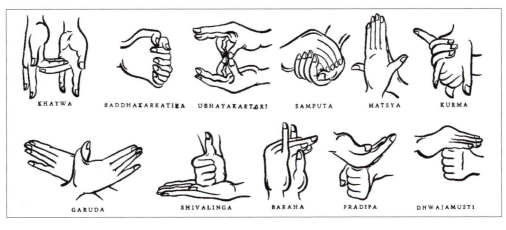

KHATWA   BADDHAKARKATIKA   UBHAYAKARTARI   SAMPUTA   MATSYA   KURMA

GARUDA   SHIVALINGA   BARAHA   PRADIPA   DHWAJAMUSTI

Hands and the Peking Opera

In Chinese theatre, there are more than fifty conventional hand positions, based on the need to be able to differentiate between the various rôles into which Peking Opera characters are divided. Specifically, they are a way of distinguishing male characters and female characters, which until recently were performed exclusively by male actors. In addition to having special make-up and costumes, it was also necessary to reconstruct a behaviour of the hands appropriate to the character's sex and social status. Women, for example, gesture with a tapered hand, while young characters gesture discreetly keeping the thumb hidden, and old characters and warriors lift the thumb to emphasise the gesture's power.

As the number of positions demonstrates, Chinese actors' hands are regulated by conventions that tend to repeat and amplify daily gestures. Moreover, the Chinese actor, in order to perform complex emotions that cannot be expressed by a simple gesture or by one of the numerous body positions,

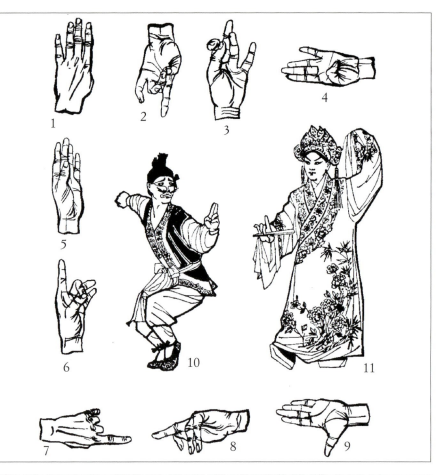

27–28. (top) Examples of hand-use conventions in Peking Opera: 1. Embarrassment (male rôles) 2. Oneself (pointing the index finger towards the chest, male and female rôles); 3. Beginning of a gesture to express defence; 4. Unwillingness (similar to gesture 1, showing the palm with the thumb hidden); 5. Uncertainty (female rôles); 6. One of the twenty ways of showing something (female rôles); 7. To exclude someone from a conversation, the index finger of one hand is pointed towards the other arm, which is raised; 8. Gesture of defence, accompanied by a rapid movement of the cape towards the right; 9. A hopeless situation (thumb pointed downwards, male rôles, both protagonists and antagonists). The central drawings (10–11) of the two Peking Opera characters, a clown and a youth, show that a hand gesture is an action executed with the whole body; (below) Mei Lanfang, great Peking Opera actor and master, shows a student correct finger tension.

158

turns his back to the spectators or hides his face behind one of the water sleeves which artificially elongate the costume (cf. *Set and Costume*).

Finally, one should not forget that, in contrast to Indian or Balinese performers, Chinese actors speak and sing at length: the hands are thus used to define a particular pose or to underline words, but they do not take the place of the words.

Hands and Balinese dance

The dynamics of the hands are expressed by Balinese dancers through the position *keras* and *manis* (cf. *Energy*), the strength and softness of the fingers, of the palm and of the wrist. It is this opposition between principles governing the whole body of the actor that gives to the hands – when they have lost their original meaning – the dynamism of 'pure sound'.

It is interesting to note that the constant changes in the tensions of the hands causes a continuous change in the position of the arms; in their turn they influence the trunk of the body and the head where the accent is on the gaze.

29–30. *Keras* (strong) and *manis* (soft) in a Balinese dance position illustrated by I Made Bandem at Salento ISTA,1987; (**bottom**) the index finger stresses the tension *keras* (strong) in the hands of the Balinese dancer I Wayan Bawa at Seville ISTA, 2004.

Hands and the Japanese theatre

From the bending of the hand in the basic body position, *kamae* (cf. *Pre-expressivity*), to its use in connection with props and other scenic objects, and to its active participation in dynamic poses and more realistic gestures, what the performers of every type of Japanese theatre and dance tend to show is the organity and essential nature of the hand's position. While reproducing each variation, each dynamic of the hand in life, the positions of the hand are dictated by economy, each superfluous detail having been removed. The codification of Japanese performers' hands does not express words but rather precise meaning (cf. *Views*). This is the result of a process whose purpose is to retain only what is essential and can be considered as an example par excellence of the transition from daily technique to extra-daily technique.

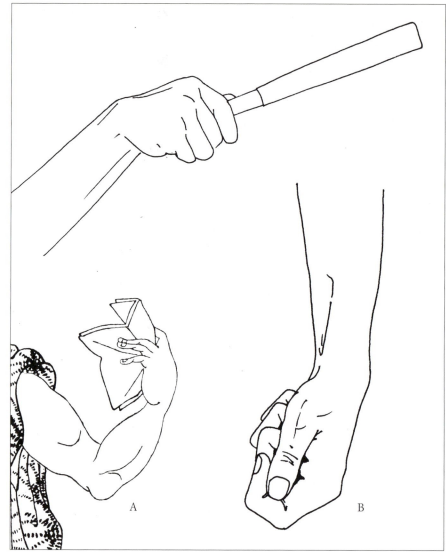

A   B

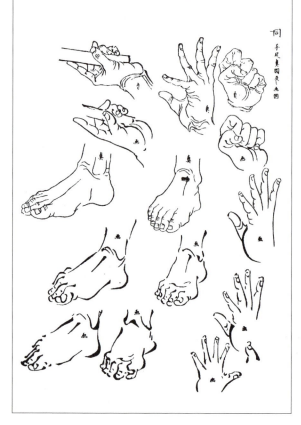

31–33. (**top**) Kabuki actor hand positions: the particular way of bending the wrist in the basic *kamae* position (B) results in one of the typical tensions that make the hands of Japanese actors both alive and extra-daily. One notices in this illustration from an eighteenth-century manual for actors (A) how the simple act of folding a piece of paper becomes a complex sleight of hand; (**bottom left**) study of hands and feet by Japanese painter Kyosai. In Japanese painting, which is essentially graphic in nature (there are, for example, no shadows such as are found in Western painting), much importance is given to the study of detail and line which must, as in the case of these hands, express the tensions found in life; (**bottom right**) Katsuko Azuma as the mythical lion, Shishi.

Hands and classical dance

While in classical dance, as in Japanese and Balinese theatre, there exists a precise codification of the positions of the hand, the Western dancers' hands express only pure dynamics and have no specific meaning.

This study has been made with the sole aim of showing how the mechanism of the arm and hand is precise, exact. The movement of the arm, an extension and accompaniment of the rhythm of the body and hand, expresses the nuances, indicates the meaning of the movement. One must work on these nuances and meanings with reflection and sensitivity in order to avoid transforming them into gesticulation, which the great freedom of the articulatory movements lead to.

(Georgette Bordier, *Anatomie appliquée à la danse* [*Anatomy Applied to the Dance*])

34. (**top**) The hands in modern dance: Carolyn Carlson in a work demonstration at Copenhagen ISTA, 1996.
35. (**bottom left**) Hands and arms in classical ballet: table taken from *Anatomie appliquée à la danse* (*Anatomy Applied to the Dance*) by G. Bordier (Paris, 1980).
36. (**bottom right**) The use of hands and arms in eighteenth-century classical ballet: engraving by Pierre Rameau in *Le Maître à danser* (*The Dancing Master*) (Paris, 1725).

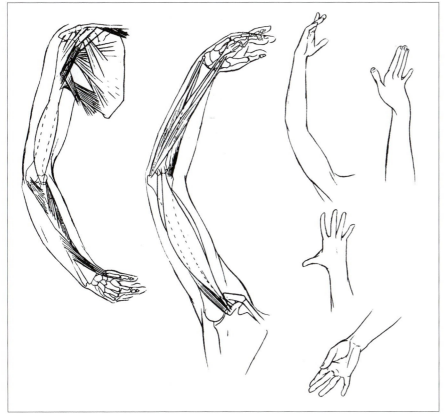

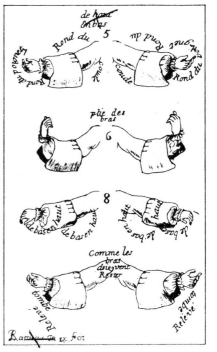

Two examples from contemporary Western theatre

The use of the hands is codified in the Asian performer, expressive for the spectator even when 'coldly' demonstrated. The same effect of the 'life' of the hands, varied in such a way as to recreate the tensions of the hand in life; is achieved in Western performers by means of an individual, often psycho-technical process, through improvisations. But even though based on personal improvisations, the process must be 'fixed' without losing its vitality. (ill.37–38, 39–40).

37–38. (**top**) Canadian actor Richard Fowler in *Wait for the Dawn* (1984); (**below**) Norwegian actress Else Marie Laukvik in Odin Teatret's *Come! And the Day Will Be Ours* (1978).

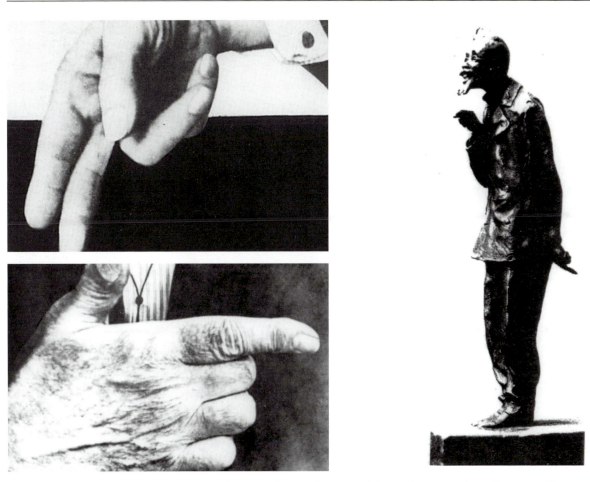

39–41. (**above right**) Stanislavsky as Doctor Stockmann in Ibsen's *The Enemy of the People*, 1900: sculpture by S. N. Sudbinin. It is only by means of such rare images as this that today we are able to imagine the physical behaviour and typical gestures of this character (ill.39–40), which was one of Stanislavsky's best performances. His biographer David Magarshack writes:

As a producer, Stanislavsky taught his actors the method of reaching to the inner nature of their parts through the external idiosyncracies of any person they knew in life who seemed to approach most closely their mental picture of the character they had to represent. He even went so far as to encourage them to make up as the person they had in mind for the model of their parts. Stanislavsky himself took the composer Rimsky-Korsakov as his model for the make-up of Dr Stockmann. In this part, Stanislavsky found that his stage comportment and gestures seemed to come to him by themselves. But it only seemed so. When he came to analyse his acting, he discovered that while he assumed that Stockmann's gestures, gait and deportment had come to him intuitively, they had really emerged hand-made from his subconscious mind where he had stored up a great number of impressions of people he had met in life and then unconsciously picked out those that were most characteristic and typical of Dr Stockmann. Thus Dr Stockmann's short-sightedness, his hurried gait, his manner of walking with the upper part of his body thrust forward, and particularly the expressive use he made of his fingers – forefinger and middle finger thrust out and the two other fingers folded with thumb on top – were all taken from life. [. . .] As for his way of 'sawing the air' when engaged in a heated argument, with his thumb stretched out and forefinger and middle finger as well as third finger and little finger held close together and the two sets of fingers held apart like the blades of a pair of scissors, he got it from Maxim Gorky, who always drove home his point that way.

(David Magarshack, *Stanislavsky*, London 1950)

Meyerhold used to say: 'How are characters born? First an arm appears, then a shoulder, then an ear, then a gait.' (In *Théâtre en Europe*, n. 18, 1988).

42–43. Italian actress Franca Rame in one of her one-woman performances (1984). The hands underline the words and amplify the vocal action. The right hand opens like a mouth in a vigorous action which contrasts with the gentle action of the left hand (**above**); this complementarity is also found in another image: the words escaping from the lips are underlined by the action of the whole body, the open upper hand causing the lower hand to vibrate (**left**).

In the following texts, a comparison is made between the two arts of memory: on the one hand, 'empirical memory', which is handed down orally by means of a particular terminology, certain physical and vocal rhythms and the professional biography of the individual actor or dancer at the moment of passing experience on to someone else; and on the other hand, 'written memory', or historiography, based on the description of events and relationships, on documents, notes, stories and recollections, etc., all the various visible and verifiable relics, in an attempt to reconstruct, penetrate and connect fragments of the past. Historiography, not as a succession of events, but as a way of presenting this succession, is a memory based on choice and becomes interpretation through description. Historiography thus preserves a past reconstructed from the writer's point of view and degree of experience. This reconstruction is a continuous succession of reinterpretations: historiography not as the memory of what is no longer visible, but as a 'way of seeing'.

Energetic language

Ferdinando Taviani

The expression 'energetic language' is metaphoric and has an ironic flavour. It is metaphoric because it applies a term to the performer's pre-expressive level which derives from certain esoteric traditions, traditions that believe in the existence of a primordial and effective language (a language, that is, that can transform and not only name). This primordial language is called 'energetic language' or 'the language of the birds'. The expression is used ironically because although the performer's effectiveness often seems to depend on mysterious, inexplicable forces, we can, by adopting a scientific attitude and by using experimental methods, study this language. It is also used ironically because it is no more imprecise than those attempts at definition that apply 'scientific' concepts to the theatre and the performer inexactly. The result is only an illusion of exactness. A conscious imprecision is already a form of precision. An illusory precision, however, is the height of confusion.

We use the expression 'energetic language' here to draw attention to what we know about the performers that can be of use to render them alive onstage, to construct their extra-daily presence in a performance situation. From Stanislavsky on, the practices used by the performer to construct his presence have been the object of explicit scientific consideration, that is, they have been investigated according to their general principles. This research has currently led to theatre anthropology and the concept of pre-expressivity on which it is based. But work on pre-expressivity existed, on the practical if not on the theoretical level, long before it became the object of scientific consideration.

This practice was humble: not only because it was yet to be theoretically

postulated and thus ennobled as a technique justified by science, but also because it had to do with the less noble aspects of the performer's art. That is, it was concerned neither with the interpretation of character nor with that particular expressive and creative force that made the performer an artist, a creator, and not merely an executant. The performer's pre-expressive practices were art's 'kitchen'. It is therefore natural that when explaining their work, performers spoke about these practices rarely or not at all. To find traces of this hidden knowledge, we must become archaeologists and dig among the papers and documents that performers have left behind.

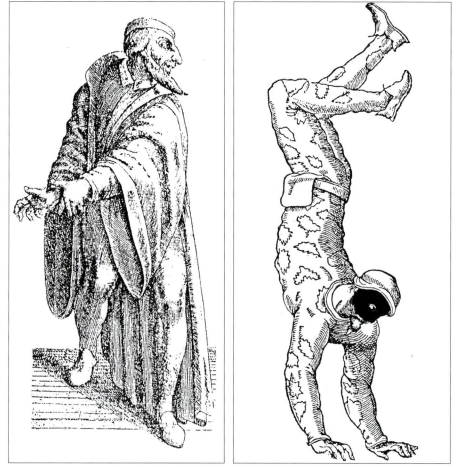

1–2. The 'energetic language' of Pantalone and Harlequin: details from prints in the *Recueil Fossard*, an album of sixteenth-century engravings, all having to do with commedia dell'arte masks, collected by a certain Monsieur Fossard for Louis XIV. The *Recueil Fossard* remained forgotten until the beginning of the twentieth century when Agne Beijer discovered it among the uncatalogued archives at the Stockholm Museum. It was published for the first time in 1928, in Paris, by Pierre Louis Duchartre, one of the first historians of commedia dell'arte companies.

3. Harlequin's 'energetic language': details from anonymous prints in the *Recueil Fossard*.

Theatre anthropology, then, becomes a method for the study of the performer in the past rather than an area of experimental investigation. From the excavations, there emerge traces of certain practices that can in turn become useful instruments for the performer's work. The circle of knowledge is thus established, from empirical work to theoretical instruments. These instruments help to clarify certain zones which up until now have not been given much attention in the history of performers and which can, if one wishes, become new points of departure for practical experimentation.

The following are examples of actors who, lacking a well-codified tradition, invented their own personal pre-expressive technique: a kind of hidden dance (hidden from the spectator) which made their scenic presence live.

Henry Irving under the microscope

Irving was born in 1838 and died in 1905. In 1930, Gordon Craig published a book on Irving (*Henry Irving*, Longmans, Green & Co., New York and Toronto). I will quote from pages 67–77.

Craig considered Irving his master, the man who introduced him to the exactness of theatrical art. According to Craig, Irving was particularly important because he cleared the field of the false naturalness/artificiality opposition:

"But was he natural?" is always being asked. Indeed he was – natural like lightning – but not natural like the ape. [. . .]

Irving was natural, yet highly artificial. [. . .] He was artificial, as certain plants seem artificial. He was as artificial – as an orchid – as a cactus – exotic and stately, forbidding, and so curiously composed as to be what we may call architectural, attractive as are all shapely things.

To understand Irving's secret, one must penetrate the form of his interpretations and discover the hidden structure of presence that lies hidden beneath it. We have to examine him as if under a microscope. Craig reproached the critics for their incompetence in this regard. They only looked at the results, they ignored the processes. He particularly reproached William Archer, who in 1883 had published *Henry Irving, Artist and Manager: A Critical Study*. Archer wondered, for example, how one could define the unusual way of walking that characterised Irving on stage. He spoke of it in vague terms, almost as if it was an eccentricity. Craig responds:

Had he asked me what he should say of Irving's walk, and "how to describe it?" I should have said: "My dear Archer, describe it, if you must speak of it at all, as a whole language!" I should have been obliged to add: "If you know what I mean." [. . .] No; the good William Archer would not have understood what it was I meant by saying that Irving's walk was a whole language. He understood nothing about Irving, and passed along this misunderstanding to his friend, Mr. Bernard Shaw. But Archer always tried to speak the truth.

But why did Irving walk so strangely?

I think that there is no one who saw him in a street or a room, in private life, who denied that he walked perfectly. [. . .] Irving walked perfectly naturally – but only in private life. As soon he stepped upon the boards of his theatre, at rehearsal, something was added to the walk – a consciousness. [. . .] At night, Archer, excluded from rehearsals, was allowed to come into the theatre for a couple of hours, provided he sat down in a seat on the other side of the footlights. Archer is wringing his hands and crying: "What can I say of his walk? It isn't walking!".

My dear old Archer, you were right for once. It wasn't walking. It was dancing!

Irving's hidden dance was not handed down to him by a tradition. Irving – as Stanislavsky will do later – turns to the text for information as to how to construct his presence. But

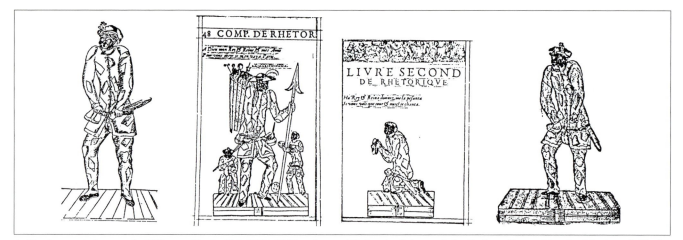

4. The 'energetic language' of Tristano Martinelli (c.1556–1630), a famous Harlequin. Prints and details from *Composition de rhétorique de M. don Arlequin*, a seventy-page booklet which Martinelli had printed in 1601 for Henry IV, and of which a single copy remains, kept in the National Library in Paris. A curious detail, an indication of the author's bizarre personality: of the booklet's seventy pages, fifty-nine are blank.

the difference between Irving and Stanislavsky is that Irving does not ask questions about the character:

> Not having a home in which to train himself, Irving did as many other great actors of England have done – he took Shakespeare as his guide and master. [. . .]
>
> And Shakespeare helped him, for in Shakespeare is a great, a curious rhythm, and it was this he captured. [. . .] Irving had caught the most difficult Shakespearian rhythm, and was suiting the action to the word. [. . .] And thus it came about that Irving positively designed (as M. Fokin had designed) dances which fitted perfectly to the speeches given him by Shakespeare.

Compared to Stanislavsky's 'subtext', Irving's (hidden) dance is revealed as the result of a completely different technique that nevertheless follows substantially analogous criteria. It answers the same professional question: how does one reconstruct the organicity of the actor's scenic presence? What Irving finds in Shakespeare is a parallel to the text's 'meanings'. This parallel provides him with a pre-expressive score that can also be developed in contexts that have nothing to do with Shakespeare:

> When he came to melodrama, to *The Bells*, *The Lyons Mail*, or *Louis XI*, he realised that a good deal more dance would be needed to hold up these pieces – and then it was that, putting out all his skill, he wiped the floor with the rôle and danced it like the Devil. When it was Shakespeare he was dealing with, he had merely to wipe the beautiful glass window-panes. His movements were all measured. He was forever counting – one, two, three – pause – one, two – a step, another, a halt, a faintest turn, another step, a word. (Call it a beat, a foot, a step, all is one – I like to use the word 'step.') That constituted one of his dances. Or seated on a chair, at a table – raising a glass, drinking – and then lowering his hand and glass – one, two, three, four – suspense – a slight step with his eyes – five – then a patter of steps – two slow syllables – another step – two more syllables – and a second passage in his dance was done. And so right through the piece – whatever it might be – there was no chance movement; he left no loose ends. All was sharp cut at beginning and end, and all joined by an immensely subtle rhythm – the Shakespearian rhythm.

By the time Craig writes his book on Irving, the research done by Stanislavsky and Meyerhold has already established a new way of approaching the actor's art. It is therefore probable that Craig projected this new way of seeing onto the recent past, using it to discover his old master's secret logic.

The chapter on Irving's way of performing is a veritable essay on theatre anthropology *avant la lettre*. For example, one is struck by how much importance Craig attaches to the opposition between daily body technique and extra-daily technique and, above all, by the method he uses to analyse Irving's hidden dance. It is hidden not only because it is not exhibited, but particularly because it leaps from one part of the body or the voice to another. It is not gesture composition but an energy pattern that can be dilated or restricted in space, that can at one moment guide the way of walking and at another moment direct an impulse of the hand or a tiny movement of the eyes or the way of pronouncing a word by breaking it up.

Living marble

The performer's 'energetic language' is in reality the dance of energy. Since energy can dance, the performer does not concentrate directly on the energy, but on the channels that convey it. Similarly, when a fountain architect wants to make water dance, he or she is certainly not so foolish as to try to change water's nature, but builds channels according to the rules of hydraulics. These channels are not the dance, but, as the water passes through them, it begins to dance.

The research conducted by Stanislavsky and Meyerhold, like the theory-less practices of the great European actors, is a response to a fundamental requisite: to make it possible for the actor to work following two parallel lines. The first line has to do with interpretation, with the construction of meaning; the second, deeper and less obvious to the spectator, has to do with 'energetic language', with the construction of *presence*. In order to function, this line must be detailed, that is, composed by means of a succession of micro-actions, each one of which has a very precise beginning and an even more precise end. The end of one micro-action is the beginning of the next. These actions can be the various steps of a hidden dance (as with Irving) or the various sequences of internal images that the actor projects as a kind of mental

5–6. (**top**) Three illustrations taken from Italian actor Antonio Morrocchesi's treatise on the art of performing, *Lezioni di declamazione e d'arte teatrale* (*Lessons in Performing and Theatrical Art*, Florence, 1832); (**below**) *The Death of Socrates*, oil on canvas, 1771, by Jacques-Louis David (Louvre Museum, Paris).

film (as Stanislavsky sometimes taught). There are innumerable techniques, but the fundamental exigency to which they respond is always substantially the same: to define a line of action that is relatively independent of interpretative work and that can be broken down into very precise segments.

To this end, certain actors use actual figurative clichés. We can find a good example of this technique in a book by an Italian actor, Antonio Morrocchesi. He was the greatest tragic actor in Italy at the turn of the eighteenth century. He died in 1838 (the year Irving was born). At the end of his career, he founded a theatre school and published a treatise on the art of performing, *Lezioni di declamazione e d'arte teatrale*, (Florence 1832, *Lessons in Performing and Theatre Art*).

To his spectators, Morrocchesi seemed to be an impetuous, passionate actor. At times he seemed to be 'possessed' by the character. In his book he reveals how the material of his art was, on the contrary, classical, premeditated in all its details, like the work of a sculptor. He chooses and explains certain excerpts from the most famous works he interpreted. For each segment of a sentence, sometimes for each individual word, he designs a figure, a pose, in a statue-like attitude, similar to the heroes painted by Jacques-Louis David. Seen as a whole, these designs reproduced by Morrocchesi seem to illustrate his way of performing. In reality, they are not at all the representation of the actions that the actor carried out on stage: rather, they are an X-ray of the actions. One need only consider the *speed*. The time needed to say a word, a fragment of verse, a segment of a sentence, is short. This means that the two, three, or four poses that succeed each other in a single section of the text can only be isolated in the abstract. They can be separated only when the actor's action is submitted to an analytical view that breaks it down into its parts and when the actor composes the action detail after detail. But when the action is actually done, the individual poses disappear and what appears to the spectator is a single, often vortical, action.

On reading the book and looking at the drawings, one is led to think that the different positions are above all pauses in the action. But this is not the case. One understands why Morrocchesi seemed impetuous and spontaneous to the spectators, while in his eyes, in his mental vision, he was performing a composition (a dance) based on neo-classical attitudes.

Clichés appear to the spectator as clichés, that is, as conventional attitudes, only when they are recognisable, when they can be distinguished one from the other. Paradoxically, the actor seems artificial (in the negative sense of the word) when he uses few clichés. If he uses many clichés, he becomes 'natural'. A great many clichés become a channel through which energy, life, rushes.

In this case as well, (one example among many) the actor deduces his own hidden dance from the text, using a personal technique. He establishes a line of action that does not take the meaning of the interpretation into consideration, but only the effectiveness of presence. It is of course true that the actor uses words to find the various positions, the various clichés, but it is also true that these clichés are not then used to represent the words and are burnt up in the speed of the action.

Faced with actors who work with personal techniques of this type, certain spectators – such as the poets Musset and Lamartine – testify to having experienced 'living marble', a statue that is contradictorily transversed by heat and the flow of life. The actor, using Craig's words, 'was natural, yet highly artificial'.

Underneath Harlequin's costume

A fascinating story yet to be written is the story of the silent earthquake that occurred in European theatre with the separation of the art of acting from the art of dance (and song). This separation took place not only on the theoretical level, but also in practice. Up until the end of the seventeenth century, codified dances guided the performer's behaviour: the actor hid these dances, the dancer displayed them. But the same physical knowledge was basic to the work of both.

The dance master will stay beside the actor in the following centuries as well. He will often be one of the actor's teachers. But from the beginning of the eighteenth century on, the dance master's teachings will be used only to give grace and decorum to the actor's movements. They will be used more on the surface of the actions than in their intimate structure.

If, however, we go further back in time, to that period during which the first great professional Italian companies were formed, those companies which today are called commedia dell'arte, we discover a very different interpenetration between acting and dance.

Let us take a look at the drawings of Italian actors which are part of the *Recueil Fossard*, a collection of prints today kept in Stockholm and published for the first time by Agne Beijer in 1928 (the most recent edition was published in 1982 by Librairie Théâtrale, Paris). These drawings show actors performing at the French court from 1575 to 1589. The most astonishing thing one notices in the pictures of these actors drawn during scenic action is the scant emphasis placed on their ridiculous appearance. To become aware of this, it is sufficient to compare these drawings with the illustrations by Callot in *I balli di Sfessania*. The actors in the *Recueil Fossard* prints are characterised by gestures which dilate organic tensions and demonstrate, in an energetic way, the forces that regulate a body in movement. The dilation of the gesture is used for more than the construction of a caricature: it gives energy to the actor's scenic presence.

This is particularly evident in the character of Pantalone: he is an old man, but the actor composes the figure with wide and vigorous gestures. He does not, for example, imitate a bent old man's gait, but reconstructs it by means of a contrast that transmits the idea of the old man without reproducing his weakness. The back is bent, but so bent that it becomes as powerful as a compressed spring. Each step is bigger than a normal step, so that the old man's precarious balance is reconstructed by means of a *déséquilibre* which implies an *abundance* rather than a *lack* of energy.

If we cover the face of one of these Pantalones from the *Recueil Fossard*, we discover that when the mask and the long beard are no longer part of the image, nothing is left of the *chenu veillard* (the hoary old man) who the actor is playing. The actor's physical good looks and muscular vigour become clearly visible.

We can make the same experiment with Harlequin: if we use our imaginations to strip away the patched costume and keep only his silhouette, we can no longer distinguish him from a tragic character. We see poses that resemble the poses of classical sculpture (dying heroes, men begging for mercy, warriors).

Even in immobility and in the least animated actions, the basic postures of the actors playing Pantalone and Harlequin keep the investment of energy that acrobats use for their feats of strength and agility. The pre-expressive level manifested by these actors seems to derive from carnival dances, sword dances, fight dances, acrobatics. The same quality of energy is present, but here it is withheld, transformed into hidden dance.

The fascination that commedia dell'arte first had for spectators all over Europe was probably due to the way Italian actors managed to create a tension between the expressive and pre-expressive levels of their acting: a comic, farcical scenic expression designed so as to make the spectators laugh. This technique, however, grew out of an energetic, vigorous, 'acrobatic' sub-stratum, 'acrobatic' understood in the original sense of the word, that is, 'moving on the extremities', on tip-toe, but also pushing each tension to its extreme, searching for unstable balance.

At the beginning of the history of the modern actor, in the commedia dell'arte which so profoundly inspired the theatre reformers of the nineteenth century, we find special proof of an ability to maintain two different levels of organisation and to reassemble this dichotomy into a living contrast.

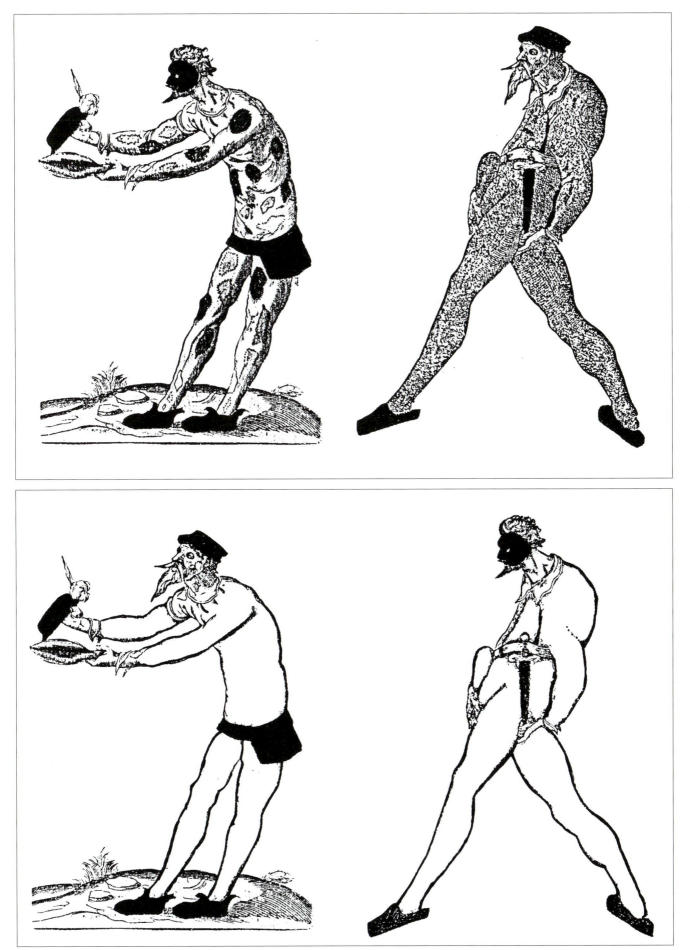

7–8. (**top**) Harlequin and Pantalone: details from a engraving in the *Recueil Fossard*. (**bottom**) Switching the figures' heads and removing Harlequin's patched costume helps to draw attention to Pantalone's vigorous physical form and to Harlequin's tragic bearing. The basic postures of the actors who play Pantalone and Harlequin are determined by a pre-expressive body posture which is in stark contrast to their rôles.

Stanislavsky's 'system'

Franco Ruffini

Stanislavsky's words

In *An Actor Prepares*,[1] Torzov (Stanislavsky's spokesman in the novel) says to his students at the end of two year's work:

All that you have learned in these two years now lies confused in your minds. It will not be easy to assemble and fix all the elements which we have analysed and extracted with our sensibility, one by one. Yet what we have found is nothing more than the simplest, most normal human condition. [. . .] It is disconcerting to realise how something so common, something which is usually spontaneously created, vanishes without a trace as soon as the actor sets foot on the stage, and that to re-establish it, so much work, study and technique is necessary. [. . .] Because of the individual elements of which it consists, general scenic sensibility *is the simplest and most natural human condition.* On stage, in the inert world of the set, in the wings, among the colours, the cardboard, the prop man's furnishings, general scenic sensibility is the voice of human life, of reality.

There are many biases concerning Stanislavsky's 'system': it has to do only with identification with character; it is useful only for naturalistic or realistic actors; it is the consequence of a particular poetics, and so on.

But Stanislavsky is not of this opinion, as we have seen. He says that the purpose of the 'system' is to construct 'general scenic sensibility', that is, to recreate, on stage, 'the simplest, most normal human condition'.

'The simplest human condition': the organic body-mind

An unbiased reflection on Stanislavsky's 'system' inevitably results in a change of perspective. The point of departure cannot be the great Russian director's poetics or taste, as is usually the case. It must be the definition of what Stanislavsky calls 'the simplest, most normal human condition'. This is, in fact, the objective of the system, and such an objective has nothing to do with the director's aesthetic and operative choices.

Stanislavsky says later, in *Creating a Rôle*.[2]

Each director has his own way of working on the rôle and his own way of outlining his plan for the development of this work: there are no fixed rules. However, the initial stages of the work and the psycho-physiological procedures that originate in our own natures must be respected exactly'

The human condition of which Stanislavsky speaks, based on 'psycho-physiological procedures that originate in our own natures', can be defined as the 'organic body-mind'.

We can say that a body-mind is organic when the body responds to the demands made by the mind in a way that is neither 'redundant', 'defaulting' nor 'incoherent', that is, when:

9. Stanislavsky in the rôle of Astrov in Chekhov's *Uncle Vanya*.

- the body responds only to demands made by the mind;
- the body responds to all the demands made by the mind;
- reacting to all the demands made by the mind, and to those demands only, the body *adapts to them*, seeks to satisfy them.

The body-mind's organity is revealed in a body which does not act in vain, which does not avoid necessary action, which does not react in a self-contradictory and counter-productive way.

The organic body-mind actually is the 'simplest, most normal human condition', and it definitely is disconcerting that it 'disappears without a trace as soon as the actor sets foot on the stage'. Disconcerting but true, as we all know. As soon as it is on stage, the body tends to become redundant, defaulting and incoherent: it acts in vain, it refuses to act, it contradicts itself. It loses the organity that it had before it appeared on stage and that it will regain as soon as it leaves the stage. To recreate organity, the 'voice of human life, of reality', 'work, study and technique' are necessary. *This* is the 'system'.

The mind makes demands: perezhivanie[3]

Given that the body must react and adapt to all the demands made by the mind, and to those demands only, it is first of all necessary to train the actor's mind to construct demands. Mind, for Stanislavsky, means intellect, will and feeling in reciprocal relationship.

In daily life, this is not necessary: the demands that the mind makes of the body are real; on stage, however, demands that are not real must become so.

This is the purpose of *perezhivanie*: to train the actor's mind to make demands, that is, stimuli, to which the body can do nothing other than react appropriately.

Hence the necessity, and at the same time, the difficulty, of *perezhivanie* in Stanislavsky's 'system'. The actor's mind must not only create the reaction's logical, motivating and emotionalising context, but this context must also function *as if* it was a real demand; the actor must believe in the context he has created. If, and only if, the actor believes, will the spectator also believe, just as he believes when he sees someone reacting offstage.

Perezhivanie ends only when the context of rational, volitional and emotional justifications has become a real demand. At this point, reaction, while not yet developing in movement, is already active. For Stanislavsky, *perezhivanie* is already 'impulse to action' or, we would say, 'action in impulse', even though it is not yet in action.

10–11. The tiny theatre at Ljubimovka, the Stanislavsky family's summer home, where Stanislavsky, in his youth, practised theatre with his relatives and friends. 'It was summer and we were all living at Ljubimovka, so we could rehearse constantly, and performed every time we had a chance. And we took every advantage of this possibility. We would get up in the morning, have a swim, and then rehearse a comedy. Then we'd have lunch and rehearse another play, then go for a walk and rehearse the first play again. In the evening, if someone came for a visit, we would immediately ask, "Would you like us to perform something?" "Of course", the guest would say. The oil lamps were lit – the sets were never taken down – the curtain would be lowered, someone would put on a blouse, someone else an apron, a bonnet, a kepi . . . and the performance would begin, for just one spectator.' (Stanislavsky, *My Life in Art*, 1925).

The body responds appropriately: personification

The *personification* techniques are what make the transition from the 'action in impulse' to the 'action in action' possible.

There is an apparent incongruity here. The more that *perezhivanie* is necessary and basic to Stanislavsky's 'system', the more personification seems gratuitous. In fact, if the mind succeeds in creating a real demand, the body can do nothing other than react appropriately. What is the point, then, of training it?

One must not forget that *perezhivanie* is *not* a real demand but only functions as if it was so. This is the point. In order to function as a real demand, *perezhivanie* cannot be simple, linear: it *must* be complex and dynamic and include contrasts.

It must conform, that is, to those situations which in daily life are exceptional situations or, better, extreme situations.

In a famous passage, Stanislavsky urges the actor always to search for the good in the bad, the stupid in the wise, the sad in the happy. It is worthwhile restating Stanislavsky's conclusion: 'This is precisely one of the methods for dilating human passion' (*Creating a Rôle*, p. 62).

This is valid for the character in its entirety, just as it is valid for each element of *perezhivanie*. But it is not an expressive choice. On the contrary: on stage, in order to function as a springboard for action, passion must be 'dilated', amplified, vitalised by complexity.

One can therefore understand the necessity and importance of personification techniques in Stanislavsky's system. In fact, if, in order to function as if it was real, the demand created by the mind must be vitalised by complexity, then the body's appropriate reaction will also be 'amplified'.

The actor's body must be trained to respond to every minimal impulse of the mind, like a Stradivarius instrument responds to the lightest touch of the musician's hand. Stanislavsky in fact repeatedly makes an analogy between the actor's body and a precious musical instrument.

In daily life as well, of course, there are complex demands to which the body must automatically and appropriately respond. But this occurs in extreme, exceptional situations. In life on stage, on the contrary, *every* situation is extreme, since if this was not the case it could not be (could not function as) a 'real situation'. The body-mind's norm on stage is its exception in daily life.

Organity on stage is an amplification of daily organity. Therefore, it must be recreated by means of the 'system'. The internal scenic sensibility constructed by means of the *perezhivanie* technique and the external scenic sensibility constructed by means of personification technique must be joined and integrated in the general scenic sensibility which is the actor's 'normal, organic second nature' (*An Actor Prepares*, p. 607).

Organic body-mind, character, rôle

Organic body-mind is the actor's second nature. If this is the declared aim of Stanislavsky's system, analytically pursued step by step, one must ask oneself what the function of the organic body-mind is within the actor's overall strategy.

There is, in fact, an overall actor's strategy above and beyond the system: it is the interpretation of the rôle (that is, interpretation of the words and actions that the written text prescribes for the character).

What is the function of the organic body-mind in the interpretation of the rôle? As far as Stanislavsky is concerned, at least, we can answer this question in the following terms:

- the organic body-mind is the *condition for meaning* for the character, and
- the character is the *condition for meaning* for the rôle.

One must therefore begin with the character.

There are three stages in the Stanislavskyan interpretation of a rôle:

1. construction of the organic body-mind;
2. construction of the character starting from the (written) rôle;
3. construction of the (acted) rôle starting from the character.

These three stages are theoretically and methodologically distinct, but, in practice, they are interwoven.

What, for Stanislavsky, is the character? The character is the actor's organic body-mind in the 'given circumstances' of the (written) rôle.

What is the (acted) rôle? It is the character oriented towards the 'super-objective', channelled, one could say, into the 'through line of action'.

The character must also exist in the rôle's past and future, that is, even there where the rôle is not temporally present. The character must also exist in acts that are not foreseen by the rôle, that is, even where the rôle is not spatially present. Stanislavsky's recommendations in this regard are continuous and unequivocable.

The character is a person with an existence above and beyond the acts that it executes as part of the rôle. Even though it conforms to the 'given circumstances' of one rôle, the character could act other rôles. In the history of the theatre, there are numerous examples of the same actor-character acting different rôles, and our shared experience as spectators confirms that within the same (written) rôle, there can be different characters. There are a thousand Hamlets, one for each actor: this is a commonplace and conceals a profound truth. What is, then, the character with respect to the rôle? The character is not identified with the rôle, does not imply it, is not implied by it. The character is only the rôle's 'condition for meaning'.[4]

If the actor loses (or has not found) the character – these are Stanislavsky's reflections – the rôle loses meaning. If the actor has built *one* character, the rôle acquires *one* meaning; if the character built by the actor was *another*, the rôle would have *another* meaning, but it would still have meaning.

But just as the rôle can have no meaning without the character, the character can have no meaning without the organity of the actor's body-mind. If the actor's body-mind is inorganic, the character's actions, even though conforming to the rôle's 'given circumstances', cannot be appropriate reactions to the demands. They can only be mechanical executions of external orders.

If the organity of the body-mind disintegrates, the character also disintegrates: it is no longer a person and therefore cannot assure the rôle's meaning.

For Stanislavsky, the organic body-mind is the foundation of the rôle's meaning; it is the *first condition*, upon which that *final condition*, which is the character, can be built.

Conditions for meaning and the pre-expressive level

Construction of the organic body-mind, construction of the character starting from the (written) rôle: these two stages of the actor's overall work in the interpretation of the rôle occur *before* the manifestation of meaning. They establish the basic conditions for the manifestation of meaning in the construction of the (acted) rôle starting from the character.

In practice, it is difficult (if not impossible) to isolate the first two stages from the last; it is even more difficult to separate the first stage from the second.

This does not exclude the theoretical and methodological existence, in the Stanislavskyan actor's overall work, of a level that occurs before the manifestation of the meaning, a level that exists *before* expression and which is a condition for expression.

This level is the pre-expressive level with which theatre anthropology is concerned. Reciprocally: the pre-expressive level could be generally defined as the level at which the conditions for meaning are constructed.

In Stanislavsky's 'system', the actor's work is work at the pre-expressive level and is independent of the director's poetics and/or aesthetic choices.

Stanislavsky affirms this peremptorily. Stanislavsky the realist, the naturalist, the founder of a poetics, speaking about the 'system' says: 'It has nothing to do with "realism" or "naturalism", it is a question of a process indispensable to our creative nature' (*An Actor Prepares* p. 471). It is true that there are no fixed rules for the manifestation of the meaning, provided, of course, that the conditions for the manifestation of the meaning exist.

Equally, for the construction of the conditions for meaning, for work at the pre-expressive level, there are no fixed systems. Stanislavsky's 'system' is *one* system, not *the* system.

One can choose not to accept it, just as one can choose not to accept his poetics, provided that the actor's body-mind does, however, find its organity.

During the last part of his life, Stanislavsky isolated himself from the theatre and began an apparently senseless experiment with a group of actors. They worked together on Molière's *Tartuffe*, but they did not attempt to stage it. Their aim was to explore the theatre's 'natural laws' as deeply as possible. Toporkov, one of the students, has left us an unforgettable diary of those days of work and research.

Stanislavsky declared from the outset that the experiment was intended to provide the actor with a means to learn to work on all possible rôles while working on *one* rôle: 'Art begins when there is only the "I" in the given circumstances of the play.'[5]

Before the rôle, there is the character. And before the character? What is the basic condition for 'truth' on stage?

Stanislavsky, who did not use the term 'organic body-mind', answered the question with the following analogy:

No matter what kind of delicacy an artist brings to a painting, if the model's pose breaks physical laws, if there is no truth in the pose, if its representation of a sitting figure, say, is not really sitting, nothing will make it believable. Therefore, the painter, before he can think of embodying his painting with the most delicate and complicated psychological states, must make his model stand or lie down or sit in a way that makes us believe that the model really sits, stands or lies down.[6]

This was the aim of the 'system' in its infinite variations: to create a way for the actor, *before* performing and in order to *give meaning* to his performing, to be really and truly, seated or standing, organically present on the stage.

Notes

[1] In Italian, *Il lavoro dell'attore*, Laterza, Bari, 1968, 1975, pp. 607–608; in English, *An Actor Prepares, and Building a Character*, Eyre Methuen, London, 1980. The English editions are incomplete and revised versions of the original Russian edition. For this reason, the quotations have been taken from the Italian edition.

[2] *Creating a Rôle*, Eyre Methuen, London, 1981, the English edition of the third volume of Stanislavsky's works. This book corresponds to the Italian edition, *Il lavoro dell'attore sul personaggio*, Laterza, Bari, 1988, p. 106. The English edition is an incomplete and revised version of the original Russian edition. For this reason, the quotations have been taken from the Italian edition.

[3] The Russian term *perezhivanie* is translated into Italian as *reviviscenza*. It is sometimes translated into English as 'return to life', at other times it is more or less appropriately paraphrased. In order to avoid confusion, the Russian term is used here (cf. *Dilation*).

[4] 'Conditions for meaning' are all those physical and psychic elements which, on the whole and in their interrelation, give the actor the possibility to snake the character (and then the rôle) coherent and not meaningless.

[5] V. Toporkov, *Stanislavsky in Rehearsal*, Theatre Arts Books, New York, 1979.

[6] op. cit. p. 161.

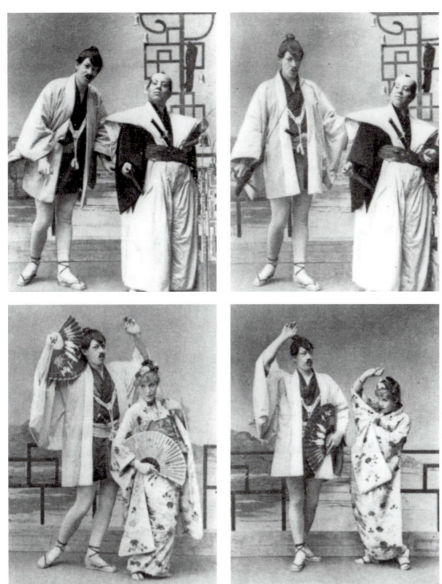

12–15. Stanislavsky with his 'amateur' actors in scenes from Gilbert and Sullivan's *Mikado* (1887). The body positions do not reflect the stereotyped image of realism which is generally associated with Stanislavsky. The composition of every position and every detail – notice the balance and the equivalences – is the result of the search for life on the stage, life which must flow, new and fresh, every night, for both the actor and the spectator. These images are also far from imitating the positions used by Japanese actors: at the time these pictures were taken, Stanislavsky had not yet seen Japanese actors, and what may be taken for 'Japanisms' are conventional (*uslovny*) elements on which Meyerhold in particular would later base his research.

Meyerhold: the grotesque; that is, biomechanics

Eugenio Barba

A plasticity that does not correspond to the words

Vsevolod E. Meyerhold begins to work with Nemirovich-Danchenko at the end of the nineteenth century. He is one of the pupils chosen to be a member of Stanislavsky's Moscow Art Theatre and remains there until 1902. Then he starts his own company and travels in the provinces, but comes back to Moscow in 1905, at Stanislavsky's invitation, to direct a theatre studio.

Here Meyerhold begins to practise and formulate his ideas about a 'new theatre' which he calls *uslovny*, meaning 'stylised' or 'conventional'. The 'old theatre' (Stanislavsky's naturalistic theatre) has formed actors who are skilled in the arts of metamorphosis and reincarnation, but plasticity (*plastika*) plays no part in their work.

The old theatre, too, regarded plasticity as an essential means of expression; one has only to consider Salvini in *Othello* or *Hamlet*. Plasticity itself is not new, but the form which I have in mind is new. Before, it corresponded closely to the spoken dialogue, but I am speaking of a plasticity which does not correspond to the words. What do I mean by this?

Two people are discussing the weather, art, apartments. A third – given, of course, that he is reasonably sensitive and observant – can tell exactly by listening to this conversation, which has no bearing on the relationship between the two, whether they are friends, enemies or lovers. He can tell this from the way they gesticulate, stand, move their eyes. This is because they move in a way unrelated to their words, a way which reveals their relationship.

(1907)[1]

For Meyerhold, plasticity – a key word – is the dynamic that characterises both immobility and movement. To make the spectator become perspicacious, a pattern of scenic movements is necessary.

The essence of human relationships is determined by gestures, poses, glances and silences. Words alone cannot say everything. Hence there must be a pattern of movement on the stage to transform the spectator into a vigilant observer. [. . .] Words catch the ear, plasticity the eye. Thus the spectator's imagination is exposed to two stimuli: the oral and the visual. The difference between the old theatre and the new is that in the new theatre, speech and plasticity are each subordinated to their own separate rhythms and the two do not necessarily coincide.

(1907)

This means that the actor does not allow his body to follow the rhythm of the words: synchronism between vocal and physical rhythms must be broken. Until Meyerhold made this distinction, the actor was considered a totality, at least in theatre theory. It was thought that the impulse for a specific task and the work done to materialise this task should involve the whole actor. Meyerhold proposes splitting this totality. During the work process, the actor can separate the different levels, work independently on each of them and reintegrate them in the result. The actor can proceed in this way. But why? The answer is in another text in which Meyerhold writes about:

a scenic rhythm that frees the actor from the arbitrary demands of his own temperament. The essence of stage rhythm is the antithesis of real, everyday life. [. . .] Where does the human body, possessing the suppleness of expression demanded by the stage, attain its highest development? In dance. Because dance is the movement of the human body in the sphere of rhythm. Dance is to the body what music is to thought: form artificially yet instinctively created.

(1910)[2]

The actors of the *uslovny* theatre give up an essential part of their personality, the organic synchronism between vocal and physical rhythms, and thus arrive at a scenic rhythm. They give up those habits that belong to their usual way of moving and reacting. It is as if their naturalness must be eliminated so that they can follow other laws that are specific for the stage, with the objective of attaining a plasticity, a scenic rhythm, which is dance.

16. Meyerhold in F. Shentan's *Acrobats* while he was director of the New Drama Association in Kherson from 1902 to 1905.

But which dance is Meyerhold speaking of? The ballet that one could see at the Marinsky, or something else?

Angelo Maria Ripellino, the scholar who has most poetically evoked Meyerhold's productions, describes his *Don Juan* (1910):

> He removed the footlights and manoeuvred the characters on a projecting semi-circular forestage where not a single gesture, not a single grimace, not a single wrinkle of the actor was lost. The forestage required an accurate *Nuancespiel* from the actor, a subtle micro-mimicry intensified by the bright lights on the stage and from the auditorium. The actors had an adroit way of continuously balancing their poses, weaving the web of their movements with the greatest attention to detail.[3]

This description is very similar to Meyerhold's own words on *Don Juan*. Only one expression is different: 'the web of movements'. Dance as a 'pattern', as a 'web' whose dynamic does not follow the laws of daily life.

The grotesque

What weaves a web? A spider. And it does not weave its web for aesthetic reasons, but to catch something. Meyerhold explicitly names what the actor wants to attract into his 'web' of movements through his dance: the spectator's senses.

> We can stimulate the spectator's brain and persuade him to reason and to argue. This is just one of the things the theatre can do. It also has another, quite different property: it can stimulate the spectator's sensibility (*chuvstvo*) and steer him through a complex labyrinth of emotions.

Meyerhold explains that it is not a question of an emotional sensibility, but of sensorial sensibility, as, for instance, when one says, 'I feel cold' or 'I feel hot'. And once again the actor stands as the main transmitter of energy (1929).[4]

Meyerhold wants to provoke an effective reflex in the spectator which is not necessarily conveyed through intellectual channels, but which relies on sensorial sensitivity, on kinaestheties.

The scenic procedure that leads to this effect is the grotesque, based on contrasts and making possible the continuous displacement of the spectator's perception. Refusing to accept this term as a synonym for the comic, he writes:

> The art of the grotesque is based on the struggle between content and form. The grotesque operates not only on the

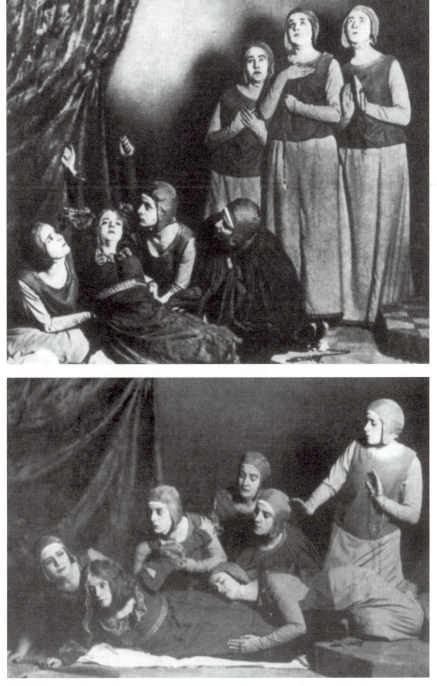

17–18. Two scenes from Maeterlinck's *Sister Beatrice*, performed by Vera Komissarzhevskaja and directed by Meyerhold, 1906. Even though the composition has the appearance of a tableau, the dynamism of the plasticity is obvious in the direction of the eyes, the position of the hands, and tension in the neck.

high and the low, but mingles the contrasts, deliberately creating sharp contradictions. [...] The grotesque deepens daily life until it ceases to represent only that which is usual. The grotesque unites the essence of opposites into a synthesis and induces the spectator to attempt to solve the enigma of the incomprehensible.

[...] By means of the grotesque, one constantly obliges the spectator to maintain a double attitude towards the scenic action, which undergoes sudden and abrupt turns. In the grotesque, one thing is essential: the constant tendency of the artist to transport the spectator from one newly reached plane to another, totally unexpected plane.

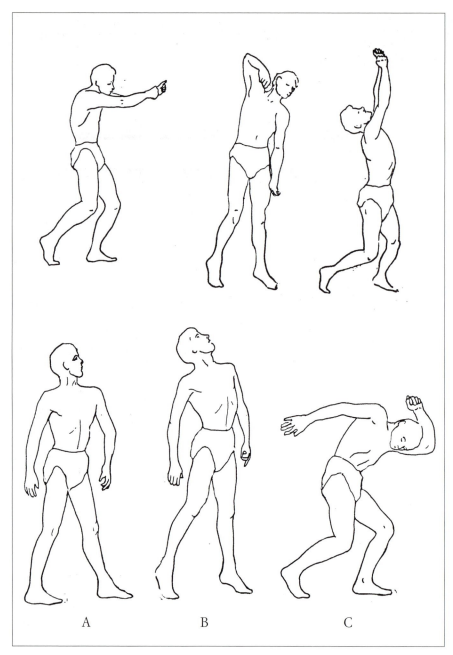

A   B   C

19–24. Example of *otkaz* (refusal) in the biomechanical exercise known as 'Shooting with a bow' (cf. ill.40 p.100 for the entire sequence of the exercise).

It is 1914. Meyerhold is a director at the Imperial Theatre, but he has also opened a studio, searching with his students for an answer to his old obsession: how should an actor move on the stage; how should he engrave the 'pattern of movements' that concretises the actor–spectator relationship on a sensorial level before the intellect and psychological interpretation become involved? The programme at his studio includes: dancing, music, athletics, fencing, throwing the discus, the basic principles of Italian improvised comedy, the traditional practices of seventeenth- and eighteenth-century European theatres, the conventions of Indian drama, stage and acting conventions from Japanese and Chinese theatres.

In 1922, after the revolution and the civil war, Meyerhold presents the latest results of his research: biomechanics.

Biomechanics

If we observe a skilled worker in action, we notice the following in his movements: (1) an absence of superfluous, unproductive movements; (2) rhythm; (3) the correct positioning of the body's centre of gravity; (4) stability. Movements based on these principles are distinguished by their dance-like quality; a skilled worker at work invariably reminds one of a dancer. [. . .] Every craftsman – the blacksmith, the foundry worker, the actor must have rhythm, must be familiar with the laws of balance. An actor ignorant of the laws of balance is less than an apprentice. [. . .] The fundamental deficiency of the modern actor is his absolute ignorance of the laws of biomechanics.

(1922)[6]

Faced with the enigma, the spectator is forced to mobilise himself to decipher it, to seize it, to orient himself. The spectator becomes, in a word, perspicacious, a 'vigilant observer'. And here, once again, dance reappears. 'Elements of dance are hidden in the grotesque, because the grotesque can be expressed only through dance' (1912).[5]

The actor must be able to create a synthesis which contains the essence of contrasts, and this synthesis must be materialised through plasticity, through the pattern of scenic movements which Meyerhold also calls dance.

But, once again, what sort of dance? In an attempt to define it, Meyerhold uses Loie Fuller and Charlie Chaplin as examples. He begins a voyage that is both transcultural and intracultural, towards 'exotic' theatre forms or towards epochs that have been neglected by his contemporaries. He cites Asian theatres he has never seen – kabuki, noh, Peking Opera – or he goes back to Western theatre's past, to the Spanish Siglo de Oro and, above all, to the commedia dell'arte.

Igor Ilinsky, at that time the main actor in Meyerhold's productions, participated in the development of biomechanics:

Meyerhold wanted our gestures and the bending of our bodies to follow a precise pattern. "If the form is right", he used to say, "then the tones and feelings will also be right, because they are determined by the physical postures" . . . The biomechanical exercises were not intended to be shown in performance. Their purpose was to give the sensation of conscious movement, of how to move in the scenic space.[7]

About a dozen biomechanical exercises were practised daily: an actor leaps onto another actor's chest, leaps down, throws a stone, shoots an arrow, slaps another actor in the face, stabs with a dagger, leaps onto another actor's back who then begins to run, lifts another actor onto the shoulder. Or

25. Meyerhold and Mei Lanfang. The great Chinese actor Mei Lanfang met many Russian artists in 1935 in Moscow. These historical meetings were 'immortal' as were the many photographs that were taken. When Meyerhold was taken prisoner and later shot in 1940, all his photographic archive disappeared including this photograph of Meyerhold with Mei Lanfang, which suddenly reappeared in a photographic album dedicated to Mei Lanfang recently published in China.

even simpler exercises: to take someone's hand, pull his or her arm, push them.

One can detect two lines of action in all these exercises. The first is the *otkaz*, the refusal. Each phase should begin with its opposite: to slap, one first moves the arm back, then forward. The exercises were therefore not a linear execution of an action, but a tortuous, zig-zagging procedure. The second line of action is the repetition of a three-phased dynamic sequence, a dactyl which progresses from (A) a neutral standing position to (B) an upward motion stretching the spine while standing on the balls of the feet to (C) bending the knees in a strong downward motion while throwing the arms back and transferring all the weight onto the front leg.

When we scrutinise the biomechanical exercises, we discover that none of them is executed in a straight line, but rather that all follow a series of transitions from one posture to another, with a continuous displacement of the centre of gravity, with a change from one perspective to another. It is as if the actor is embodying the *laws of motion*, not learning to be dexterous. The actor is weaving a dynamic web where theme and action do not always coincide. This contrast-rich swinging of the centre of gravity gives a dance-like quality to the actor's pattern of movements.

Bios means life; mechanics is the branch of physics concerned with the balance and motion of bodies. What Meyerhold calls biomechanics are the laws of the body-in-life. A decade before, he called them the grotesque.

'The fundamental rule of biomechanics is very simple: the whole body participates in every movement.' He says this in 1939, trying to defend himself against the accusation that

biomechanics is a formalistic device. But it was something that he had discovered and practised in Stanislavsky's studio in 1905.

The principles of dance, that is, of scenic life, which Meyerhold had searched for in the past and in the East were revealed to him by the contemporary West through the rules laid down by Frederick Taylor, the pioneer of scientific management and work productivity.

Meyerhold spoke of unstable postures, of precarious balance, of the dynamics of opposites, of the dance of energy. He merely used other terms. He used to say: 'In art, to guess is better than to know'. But the principles of the grotesque or biomechanics were not a fortuitous guess. They were a subtle insight into the same principles which today, in the light of theatre anthropology, we find at the base of the performer's pre-expressive level.

Notes

[1] V. Meyerhold, *First Attempts at a Stylised Theatre*, pp. 49–58, in *Meyerhold on Theatre* by Edward Braun, Methuen, London, 1969.

[2] V. Meyerhold, ibid. *Tristan and Isolde*, pp. 80–98.

[3] Angelo Maria Ripellino, *Il trucco e l'anima*, p. 151, Einaudi, Turin, 1965.

[4] V. Meyerhold, ibid. *The Reconstruction of the Theatre*, pp. 253–74.

[5] *Le Grotesque au théâtre*, pp. 104–9, in *Le Théâtre théâtral*, by Nina Gourfinkel, Gallimard, Paris, 1963.

[6] V. Meyerhold, ibid, *Biomechanics*, pp. 198–200.

[7] I. Ilinski, *Pamietnik Aktora*, p. 177, Widawnictwa Artystyczne i Filmowe Warsaw, 1962.

The performer's montage and the director's montage

Eugenio Barba

'Montage' is a word which today replaces the former term 'composition'. 'To compose' (to put with) also means 'to mount', 'to put together', 'to weave actions together', 'to create the play' (cf. *Dramaturgy*). Composition is a new synthesis of materials and fragments taken out of their original contexts. It is a synthesis that is equivalent to the phenomenon and to the real relationships which it suggests or represents.

It is also a dilation equivalent to the way in which a performer isolates and fixes certain physiological processes or certain behaviour patterns, as if putting them under a magnifying glass and making his body a dilated body. To dilate implies above all to isolate and to select:

'From afar, a city is a city and a landscape is a landscape, but little by little, as one approaches, there appear houses, trees, tiles, leaves, ants, ants' legs, *ad infinitum.*' The film director Robert Bresson quotes these words written by Pascal and deduces from them that in order to compose one must know how to see the reality that surrounds us and to subdivide it into its constituent parts. One must know how to isolate these parts, to make them independent, in order to give them a new dependence.

A performance is born out of a specific and dramatic relationship between elements and details which, considered in isolation, are neither dramatic nor appear to have anything in common. The concept of montage does not only imply a composition of words, images or relationships. Above all, it implies the montage of rhythm, but not in order to *represent* or *to reproduce* the movement. By means of the montage of rhythm, in fact, one aims at the very principle of motion, at tensions, at the dialectic process of nature or thought. Or better, at 'the thought which penetrates matter' (cf. *Energy*).

Eisenstein's comments on El Greco are particularly important with respect to montage because they demonstrate how montage is actually the construction of meaning. Eisenstein shows how El Greco, assembling the individual parts of his paintings (Eisenstein calls them 'frames'), succeeds not in *representing* ecstatic characters but rather in creating an *ecstatic construction* of the paintings, forcing the observer's eye, even his body, to follow the route designed by the creator.

Making use of art critic J. E. Willumsen's accurate analyses, Eisenstein examines El Greco's *View and Map of Toledo*: the proportions of the huge Don Juan Tavera hospital on the slopes of the hill have been so reduced that the building appears only slightly larger than a house, 'otherwise it would have hidden the view of the city'. What El Greco paints, therefore, is not the landscape as it appears from a particular perspective but an *equivalent* of a *view* which does not allow the great bulk of the hospital to become an obstacle.

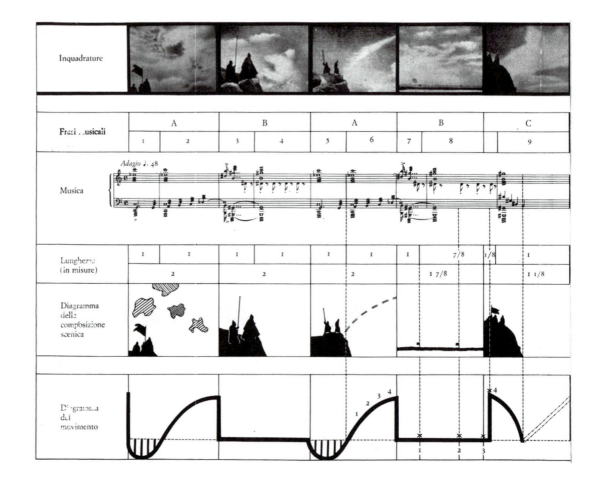

1–2. (**above**) *View and Map of Toledo*, painted by El Greco between 1608 and 1614 (El Greco Museum, Toledo); (**below**) Waiting for the battle on the frozen lake: sequence from Sergei Eisenstein's film, *Aleksandr Nevskij* (1938). The audiovisual diagram shows the relationship between the shots, the music (by Prokofiev), the scenic composition and the movement. Eisenstein used this example in order to show that the greatest degree of expressivity is attained through the synergy of the plastic element of the movement and the movement of the music: 'The art of plastic composition', he wrote, 'consists in guiding the spectator's attention along a precise trail, in exactly the order desired by the work's author. This is brought about by the movement of the eye on the surface of the canvas if the composition is in a painting, or on the surface of a screen if we are examining a film shot' (*Film Form*, New York, 1949).

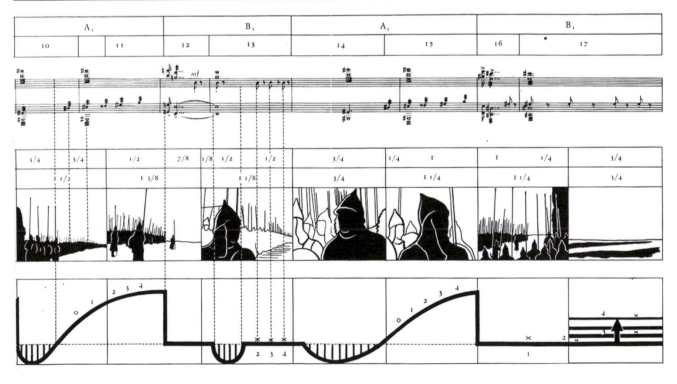

Moreover, the painter shows the hospital's principal and most beautiful façade, even though it is not actually visible from the angle from which the painting has been made.

Eisenstein writes: 'This view of Toledo is not possible from any real point of view. It is a mounted complex, a representation composed by means of a montage of objects, "photographed in isolation", which in nature mask each other or have their backs to the observer.' The painting, in short, is composed: 'of elements taken one by one and reunited in an arbitrary construction which is non-existent from a single point of view but which is fully consistent with respect to the internal logic of the composition.'

And again: 'El Greco did this painting at home, in his studio. That is to say, it is not based on a view, but on knowledge. Not on a single point of view, but on the assembling of isolated motifs collected while walking through the city and its surroundings.'

Montage is fundamental with regard to the effect the actions must have on the spectator. It guides the spectator's senses through the dramatic (*performance*) fabric (*text*), letting the spectator experience the *performance* text. The director guides, divides and reassembles the spectator's attention by means of the performer's actions, the words of the text, the relationships, the music, the sounds, the lights, the use of props.

The performer's montage

It is possible to differentiate two different spheres or directions of work: that of the performer who works inside a codified performance system and that of the performer who must invent and fix his way of being present every time he works in a new production, taking care not to repeat what he did in the previous production.

The performer who works in a codified performance system constructs the montage by altering his 'natural' and 'spontaneous' behaviour. Balance is modified and modelled, made precarious: new tensions are thus produced in the body, dilating it.

In the same way that particular physiological processes are dilated and codified, continuous eye movements (*saccades*), which in daily life occur two or three times a second and which alternate with phases of stillness (*nystagmes*), are also codified. These formalisations recreate, by means of very precise rules which dictate how the eyes should move, an equivalent to the continuous life of the eyes in daily reality.

The same applies to the hands. In daily life the fingers are continuously animated by tensions that individualise each finger. These tensions are reconstructed in theatre by means of *mudras*, which can have either a semantic or a purely dynamic value. They recreate the equivalence of the fingers' life, which move continuously from one codified position to another equally precise position.

Analogously, in positions of non-movement, regulated as action in time by means of tensions in the postural muscles, the equivalent of the life which regulates daily balance is recreated. In daily life, immobility does not exist and apparent immobility is based on continuous, miniscule movements of adjustment (cf. *Eyes, Hands, Balance*).

The result of all these procedures, which amplify behavioural and physiological processes, is a series of very precise 'scores'. Richard Schechner speaks of a 'restoration of behaviour' which is used in all performance forms from shamanism to aesthetic theatre (cf. *Restoration of Behaviour*):

A restored behaviour is a living behaviour treated the way a film director treats a strip of film. Each piece of film must be re-systemised, reconstructed. This is independent of the causal (social, psychological, technological) systems which have created it: it has its own behaviour. The original 'truth' or 'motivation' of that behaviour can be lost, ignored or covered, elaborated or distorted by myth. Originating a process – used in the course of rehearsals in order to obtain a new process, the performance – the strips of behaviour are themselves no longer processes but objects, *materials*.

What Schechner has written in order to explain how certain ritual dances (which today are considered classical) have been 'restored', applies perfectly well to the performer who works on the basis of a codification, or who fixes improvisations like 'strips of behaviour' on which montage work can be done. The restoration, that is, the work of selection and dilation, can only take place if there exists a process of fixing.

Thus, for example, when kabuki performers meet to perform, even if they have never before done the particular performance (or the variation of the performance) that they are about to present, they can make use of 'materials', already prepared for other scenic situations. These 'materials' are then re-edited in the new context. I have myself seen an *onnagata*, who had never performed a certain rôle, go on stage and perform it after only two rehearsals: he made a montage of materials available to him from rôles which he already knew.

The director's montage

If the performer's actions can be considered as analogous to strips of film which are already the result of a montage, it is possible to use this montage not as a final result but as material for a further montage. This is generally the task of the director, who can weave the actions of several performers into a succession in which one action seems to answer another, or into a simultaneous execution in which the meanings of both actions derive directly from the fact of their mutual presence.

Let us take an example, rough as all examples are, and even the more so here because we will use fixed images, photographs, to illustrate a process the meaning of which depends on the development of actions in space and in time and on their rhythm. But crude as it may be, this example can serve as a demonstration of the most elementary (grammatical) level of the director's montage.

Let us imagine having the following text as a point of departure: 'Then the woman saw that the tree was good to eat, pleasing to the eye, desirable for the gaining of knowledge. She took its fruit and ate of it. She gave some to her husband, who was with her, and he also ate of it' (Genesis, 3:6). We also have two performers' montages, two sequences of 'restored behaviour':

Sequence A: Kosuke Nomura, kyogen actor, shows how, in the tradition of his art, one picks a fruit (a plum) and eats it.

3–13. Actor's first montage: Kosuke Nomura in Sequence A: how one picks and eats a fruit in a kyogen scene.

We see the principle of selection and dilation at work: (ill.3) with one hand he grasps the branch, with the other, starting from the opposite side, he begins the movement to take the fruit; (ill.4) he grasps the fruit and then, in order to pluck it, he does not pull it, but . . . (ill.5) he turns it, showing its size; (ill.6) the fruit is brought to the mouth, not in a direct line, but with a circular movement; the fingers squeeze the fruit and are composed in a way that shows the fruit's size, its softness, its weight; (ill.7–10) with a movement that begins high up, the fruit is brought to the mouth; (ill.11) it is not the mouth that squeezes the fruit but the hand, executing an action *equivalent* to that which, in reality, would be done by the mouth; (ill.12) the fruit is swallowed (and again it is the hand which does the action): the performer does not show a man swallowing but his hand makes an otherwise invisible action – that of swallowing – visible; (ill.13) having savoured the fruit, the man smiles with satisfaction.

Sequence B: Etienne Decroux, the great mime master, shows how one picks a flower according to the principles of his art. He also begins from a position that is opposite to that towards which he will direct the action, first with the eyes and then with the action itself (ill.14–27).

The two sequences provided by the two performers, in spite of their different motivations and different original contexts, can be put together. We will thus obtain a new sequence whose meaning will depend on the new context into which it is inserted: the biblical text that we have chosen as the point of departure for our example. In this case, naturally, the sex of the two performers will not be taken into consideration: but there is no reason why the Japanese performer Kosuke Nomura cannot interpret the rôle of Eve.

Let's run through the two performers' sequences as if they now were a single sequence: Eve has just given in to the serpent's temptation, picks the fruit, tastes it. Her final reaction is a smile for the new world that has opened up in front of her eyes. Eve tempts Adam in her turn, puts the fruit of knowledge beside him on the ground, and now Adam glances sideways as if in fear of being watched by the angel of God. He begins the movement to take the fruit, starting in the extreme opposite direction: the principle of opposition now becomes legible as an initial reaction of refusal. Then Adam bends down, picks up the fruit and turns his back as if to leave, or as if to eat the fruit without being seen, or perhaps he is ashamed of what he has done or, having been left alone, he goes in search of Eve.

A montage of this type would be possible because the two performers are able to repeat each single action, each detail of each action, perfectly. And this is why the director can create a new relationship from the two sequences, can extrapolate them from their original contexts and create between them a new dependence, putting them in relationship with a text which is then faithfully followed. The biblical text does not in fact say *how* Eve gave Adam the fruit. At this point the director can fill the visual void in the text with the help of the sequences that have already been fixed by the performers. Some details of the actions can be amplified further, minimalised, accelerated.

Let us return to our example, to the 'material' furnished by the two performers, without adding anything new.

Since the two performers' sequences are already the result of a 'restoration of behaviour', since they are perfectly fixed and thus can be treated like two strips of film, the director can extract a few fragments from one performer's sequence and remount them, interweaving them with fragments from the other performer's sequence, taking care to ensure that, after the cuts and with the new montage, enough physical coherence remains so that the performers can go from one movement to another in an organic way.

Further montage by the director

Here is an example of a new montage which weaves together fragments from the original, autonomous and independent sequences furnished by the two performers (ill.28–37).

If we apply this montage to our theme, Adam and Eve, we have the meaning of the new situation: (ill.28) Adam looks incredulously . . . (ill.29) Eve has picked the forbidden fruit and is about to eat it. (ill.30) Adam: 'We have promised not to eat the fruit of this tree!' (ill.31) Eve persists, and brings the forbidden fruit up to her mouth. (ill.32) Adam: 'God's sword will punish us.' (ill.33) Eve is about to eat the fruit. (ill.34) Adam: 'Don't do it!'. (ill.35) Eve eats the forbidden fruit. (ill.36) Adam collapses on the floor. (ill.37) Eve is intoxicated with knowledge.

The same montage that we have applied to the biblical story (ill.28–37) can also be applied to Strindberg's *The Father*: the wife Laura (once again, Kosuke Nomura is cast as the female) makes the Captain (her husband) suspect that he is not the father of their daughter. The man is ridiculed and crushed. The director has used Kosuke Nomura's actions (originally a sequence based on picking a plum and eating it) to create a sign of adultery and especially the image of the *vagina dentata* which emasculates and crushes the male. At the end, Laura says, 'It's strange, but I've never been able to look at a man without feeling superior to him' (*The Father*, Act I, scene x).

Seen in the light of their new Strindberg context, the performers' interwoven actions would have to change, small details would have to be modified in order to make these actions consistent with the meaning they have now acquired. Above all, the rhythm and intensity with which the actions are interwoven will allow unexpected meanings to emerge from the materials furnished by the performers.

The level of this montage of photographs, which we have used as a rough example, is the elementary, grammatical level: the essential work, that is the process of elaboration and refinement, is yet to come. We are face to face with a body that has been coldly constructed, an 'artificial body' in which there is no life. But this artificial body already has within it all the circuits in which *scenic bios*, that is, life recreated as art, will flow. In order for this to occur, there must be something burning, no longer analysable or anatomisable, which fuses the performer's and the director's work into a single whole in which it is no longer possible to distinguish the actions of the former and the montage of the latter. In this phase of work no rules exist. The rules serve only to make the event possible, to provide the conditions in which the real artistic creation can occur without further respect for limits or principles.

In the director's montage, the actions, in order to become dramatic, must take on a new value, must transcend the meaning and the motivations for which they were originally composed by the performers.

It is this new value which causes the actions to go beyond the literal act that they represent on their own. If I walk, I walk and nothing more. If I sit, I sit and nothing more. If I eat, I do nothing more than eat. If I smoke, I do nothing more than smoke. These are self-referential acts that do nothing more than illustrate themselves.

The actions transcend their illustrative meaning because of the relationships created in the new context in which they are placed. Put in relationship with something else, they become dramatic. To dramatise an action means to introduce a leap of tensions that obliges the action to develop meanings which are different from its original ones.

Montage, in short, is the art of putting actions in a context that causes them to deviate from their implicit meaning.

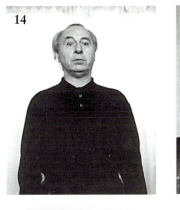

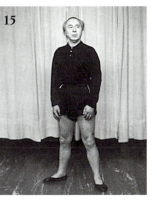

14–27. Actor's second montage: Etienne Decroux in Sequence B: how one picks a flower in mime.

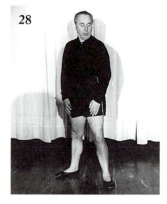

28–37. Director's montage: the new sequence obtained through the elaboration of the two actors' sequences, A and B, and the possible content variations: Genesis 3:6, and Strindberg's *The Father*, I, ix. If we apply this montage to our theme, Adam and Eve, the meaning of the new situation could be as follows: (28) Adam looks incredulously . . . (29) Eve has picked the forbidden fruit and is about to eat it. (30) Adam: 'We have promised not to eat the fruit of this tree!' (31) Eve persists, and brings the forbidden fruit up to her mouth. (32) Adam: 'God's sword will punish us.' (33) Eve is about to eat the fruit. (34) Adam: 'Don't do it!'. (35) Eve eats the forbidden fruit. (36) Adam collapses on the floor (37); Eve is intoxicated with knowledge.

The same montage which we have applied to the biblical story can also be applied to Strindberg's *The Father*: the wife Laura (once again, Kosuke Nomura cast as the female) makes the Captain (her husband) suspect that he is not the father of their daughter. The man is ridiculed and crushed. The director has used Kosuke Nomura's actions (originally a sequence based on picking a plum and eating it) to create a sign of adultery and especially the image of the *vagina dentata* which emasculates and crushes the male. At the end, Laura says, 'It's strange, but I've never been able to look at a man without feeling superior to him' (*The Father*, Act I, scene x).

Nostalgia or the passion for a return

Nicola Savarese

Ulysses, far from Ithaca, did not suffer from nostalgia. The word 'nostalgia', even though deriving from Greek (*nostos*, 'return', and *algos*, 'pain') was first used in the eighteenth century by a Dutch doctor. He coined the term to define that particular illness that afflicts people who are forced to live away from their homeland for long periods of time. The first to be diagnosed as suffering from nostalgia were Swiss immigrants who had left their mountain homes in search of work.

Until the end of the nineteenth century, the word 'nostalgia' was used exclusively in a medical context. It then was borrowed from the world of medicine and became part of the vocabulary of the aesthetes of European decadence, taking on the meaning of 'a vague desire', 'melancholy', which meaning it kept when it entered common speech.

We will use the word 'nostalgia' here in its original sense – a passion for a return – and will enrich it with a subtle nuance which the Italian poet Niccolò Tommaseo introduced in his famous dictionary of the Italian language, in which he defined the term as 'the noble privilege of poor nations'. In this sense, nostalgia is a characteristic of the artistic activity of the twentieth century and is particularly germane when used with respect to the theatre.

The study of performers of the past or of other cultures, the study of their scenic behaviour and their techniques, dates from the beginning of the twentieth century, when theatre practitioners, faced with the rise of mass communication media, began to search for new forms of theatrical language and a new identity for the theatre.

Actors, dancers and directors looked to heritages which were historically and geographically distant from the European tradition. These were heritages that could inspire a viable alternative to the theatre of the nineteenth century, provide arguments for a new cultural strategy and, above all, more diversified and richer means for the performer's language.

And thus the myths of commedia dell'arte, ancient Greek theatre and Asian theatres were born.

It was natural that these extremely diverse origins, far distant in time and space (whence their mythical and legendary character) inspired nostalgia in the artists' imaginations. In a time of change, they saw these distant sources as 'golden ages' of the theatre. It was less the eternal desire for a return to origins than technical research for a point of departure; less a vague nostalgia for the infinite than a search beyond the limits and borders of one's own culture.

Not only were the commedia dell'arte, ancient Greek theatres and Asian theatres rediscovered, studied and reinvented, but so too were more popular performance forms such as circus and cabaret. All these discoveries enriched the doctrines and practices of theatrical art and had a decisive influence on Western performance.

These theatre forms had certain characteristics in common which could be used both to oppose the bourgeois theatre of the nineteenth century and to revitalise the then current tradition of the performer's language. It was first of all a question of refusing a certain naturalism in favour of an aesthetic based not on mimesis but on a system of signs; second, the elimination of the barrier between performer and spectator – the famous 'fourth wall' – in order to discover new possible relationships between the performers and their audience; and finally, the rupture of the dramatic unities by means of a montage of symbolic spatial and temporal sequences.

Actors and directors, dancers and everyone involved in performance thus found themselves confronted with new examples of theatrical communication from which they could draw a certain freedom: they were culturally prestigious examples, technically perfect and yet so sufficiently foreign that they could be taken up and reversed, even *invented*, without the anxieties that more familiar models induce.

The commedia dell'arte and the Asian theatres in particular proposed a performer's art which seemed free of all psychological conditioning. In addition, they were based on a meticulous body technique that was the performer's only element and instrument, able moreover to represent emotions. The commedia dell'arte tradition was interrupted in the eighteenth century, but Asian performers were still incarnating their most ancient traditions, and one can readily understand how they could become the only models which were not only different but also *living* and therefore directly exportable.

Obviously, this nostalgia was not without its risks and pitfalls: fads, the temptation of the exotic and novel, and superficial interpretation were also facets of a utopia of total theatre which dreamed of a symbiosis with its audience. These phenomena were often the origins of more or less fertile misunderstandings, many of which have influenced recent theatre history. But we must not lose sight of the essential fact that direct contact with distant theatre cultures helped theatre artists to discover that the performer's art is the keystone of performance, and that the theatre exists only because performers exist. This was the beginning of a process which directed theatre research in the West towards performer pedagogy free of the demands of production and the market (cf. *Apprenticeship*).

The Western performer, who up until that time had been classified into different genres – mime, dancer, singer, actor – dreamed of unity and artistic dignity.

This was one of the first historical results of *nostalgia*: provided that the premise, or point of departure, is always accepted as being the actor, who beyond being someone who feels, is solely someone who appears on stage, a body in action. Then we can better explain the surprising analogies between position and gesture of actors, distant in space and time, which would never be corroborated were it not for what is contained within these pages. Nostalgia for integrity led the 'individual' actor to become known etymologically as the 'indivisible' actor.

The second possible result of nostalgia took longer to become apparent. It was the need to rediscover the origins of European theatre and the rough historiographical research to find out when the split between dancer and actor actually happened.

Recent studies confirm that the division occurred in the seventeenth century, when ballet and dance professionally separated the actor from the dancer. In the Renaissance period, and above all in the performances of the commedia dell'arte, the performers sang, danced, recited, as did the actors of the kabuki and the Peking Opera.

Commedia dell'arte was to a great extent based on the actor's dance, so it is rather surprising that this has been so little considered in dance specialists' investigations and even less by literary critics.

The process of making performance was based on collective devising of the story, the text and movement composition, and concentrated on the contribution and the particular conventions of each character, of each mask. However the essential ingredients were dance and acrobatics, and 'energetic language' of action and movement (cf. F. Taviani, *The Energetic Language* in *Historiography*). So the actor not only had to speak, sing and play at least one musical instrument, but also had to be a dancer and acrobat. They made death-defying leaps, and some walked the tightrope whilst reciting some exciting and mercurial text. They certainly executed feats of great difficulty which demanded great agility and their spectacular nature brought fame to many actors and groups of commedia dell'arte. And then, as if eight acts were not enough, the performance always ended with a musical set and dances.

The result of this specialisation in the commedia dell'arte can be summarised, after considering recent studies, as being the need of professional artists for competition, the need to perform before different audiences, different, that is, in terms of caste and language (many artists emigrated to Europe, particularly to France) and in the incidental necessity to compensate for dim lighting, and because of the mask, for the reduced expressivity of the face, by using the full potential of the body in action. Of course their dances were not conventional, like a minuet or a saraband, but personal, in a style closely linked to the character and above all to the actor.

From the professional standpoint, this way of composing particular actions for each character which transformed their ways of moving into a dance, can not have been so far removed from the methods used by the actors of kabuki and Peking Opera who create character according to their multi-secular traditions.

The dance of the actor came to France with the commedia dell'arte and entered the court in the ballet-comedies of Molière and Lulli. Molière had been a student of the Italian actors and was well acquainted with the technicalities as well as with the dramatic and spectacular importance of the dance element. This aspect of Molière's interest has not been sufficiently investigated. He was an actor, a mime, and he knew the songs and dances as well as the Italians that he was very familiar with. We could say that he served an apprenticeship on how to move on stage. We know that his company also danced short ballets in the intervals, whilst touring the provinces, and often his name appeared on the list of those dancing. This aspect of Molière's work culminated in the ballet-comedies which, with the collaboration of Lulli, became well known. This style, or better, genre, was considered of secondary importance to the so-called superior dramaturgical aspect of production. Both the historiographers and the literary critics have over-emphasised this second aspect. Théophile Gautier, however, back in the

1. Isadora Duncan (1878–1927) in a dance inspired by classical Greece. Duncan interpreted the myth of Greek dance in an anti-academic way, as a 'return to the origins', a means of giving dance a new orientation without offending the tradition of classical ballet, but rather by working with other dynamic principles.

nineteenth century, had complained that the works of Molière were not represented with the flavour they once had had; to him they had lost their artifice, their decorative and surprising 'side dishes', as for example in *Le Malade imaginaire*.

There is a close resemblance between the compositional methods of the commedia dell'arte and ballet. In the early stages of modern theatre, dance and theatre were not considered separately, the only distinction was based on the hierarchy of skill that an actor or group of actors had. This original unity bore some importance on the practice of Western theatre and can be summarised in two parts.

First: if it is true that there was originally no clear distinction between actor and dancer in Western theatre, then the idea that there is a resemblance (notwithstanding basic cultural differences) between the methods and practice of the Western actors and dancers and the Asian actors-dancers is consequently affirmed. Even the Western actors-dancers had to learn 'extra-daily' techniques in order to create a discipline and a way of scoring codified action, steps and movement.

The performance was in fact the fruit of all the previously investigated elements, combined and composed into a story that could, from time to time, change according to the demands of the actors, the audience, or the producer.

Second: this initial perspective on modern Western theatre was not a result of theatrical historiography. Its history had given priority not to an idea and conception of theatre that was based on the original creative and productive process of the actor, but to an image of theatre at the height of a moment in which its historical premises were being investigated. By dealing with the works of the nineteenth century, pride of place was given naturally to the dramaturgical and ideological quality of the work rather than to the art of the actor.

2–7. Parallel between Greek vase painting and Comédie Française actors. The juxtaposition is not ours but appeared in 1899 in the prestigious French magazine, *Le Théâtre*, in an article by D. B. Laflotte, *Théâtre antique, gestes modernes* (*Ancient Theatre, Modern Gestures*). The article drew attention to the origins of the archaeological style which was fashionable with French actors at the time and drew an analogy between Greek society and the socialist, populist aspirations of late nineteenth-century French theatre. The actors: Mounet-Soully (1841–1916), as Creon in Sophocles' *Antigone* (ill.2); and Sarah Bernhardt (1844–1923) in the title rôle of Medea in the play by Catulle Mendès (ill.3), and in the title rôle of Phaedra in the play by Racine (ill.4). As can be seen, the desire to take inspiration from the origins of theatre – that is, from Greek theatre – was first and foremost manifest in the copying of costume, qualified, however, by a hint of liberty, and with a generic tragic bearing, but there was no real connection made with the body behaviour of the Greek models, whose physicality seemed rather to be denied, almost contradicted, by the more clearly rhetorical physical attitudes of the two French actors.

Continuing on this line, theatre history has chosen to ignore the treatise of Domenico da Piacenza (*Sull'arte de ballare e danzare*, 1435), by for example relegating it to the history of ballet. For the first time in Europe this work considered the basis of dance as an autonomous art and affirmed the methods of composing scenic movement as forming the foundation of the actor-dancer profession.

Apart from these important assertions – the need for techniques, for set movements, for full extension of movement in the performance space – Domenico da Piacenza suggested two fundamentally different types of dance step: the 'natural' and the 'accidental'. The first grew from natural movements whilst the second was a product of artificial and artistic investigation.

From the point of view of theatre anthropology it is not difficult to recognise in these definitions the distinction between 'daily' and 'extra-daily' movements. In fact, Domenico da Piacenza, with his definition, tended to establish both the difference between the popular improvised dance and the more refined, noble dance of the courts, as well as the profession of the dancer, who by learning set steps – extra-daily – could place them in a sequence, in a personal and distinct choreography, thereby creating new interpretations.

His students Antonio Cornazano and Guglielmo Ebreo followed in his footsteps and were above all concerned with the 'fabricated' dance, which was constructed not on a simple reorganisation of the steps, but from the basis of a tale, a story.

So what were the basic characteristics of these first dance performances in the West? Music, actors, scenic movement and story; together these formed a unique whole, which could be repeated without loss of the original creation and with all the advantages of the actor-dancer's professionalism, the audience and the producer. In fact the set and learnt movements could change and be combined to make new stories and new performances, without having to go back to a clean page and find totally new steps each time. In all, it was a method, an economic and professional compositional technique, very similar to that adopted later by the commedia dell'arte players, and which was at the root of the theatre profession of the Asian actor-dancers.

8. (**top left**) Caricature of Nijinsky's choreography for the ballet *Le Sacre du printemps* (danced to music by Stravinsky), by Joel, in *Le Théâtre à Paris en 1913*. The text which accompanied the drawing remarked that the choreography seemed to have interchanged the parts of the body, in particular, the head with the extremities. Anti-academic attempts to reform the dance were not always accepted and understood by the public and the critics; *Le Sacre du printemps* was considered to be Nijinsky's most resounding failure as a choreographer.

9. (**above right**) Vaslav Nijinsky (1890–1950) in *L'Après-midi d'un faune* (London, 1912). Nijinsky, like Duncan, was inspired by classical Greece and made use of images that could help him break with classical ballet's academic approach. The culmination of this research was the choreography for *L'Après-midi d'un faune*, which created a scandal because of the realism of its physicality.

10. (**bottom left**) Ruth Saint-Denis in a Japanese inspired peacock dance.

11. (**bottom right**) Ted Shawn in *Shiva's Cosmic Dance* choreographed during Denis and Shawn's tour of India.

12. Scene from the production of Racine's *Phaedra* directed by Aleksandr Tairov (1885–1950) at the Moscow Chamber Theatre (1921). The tendency of early twentieth-century European directors towards the so-called modernisation of classical texts, which led to many combinations of ancient plays with modern art, is clearly recognisable in these images. Here, specifically, the Greek theme taken up by Racine is presented in a design which, while respecting Greek simplicity and geometry, is based on cubist futurism.

13. Final scene in Vakhtangov's production of Carlo Gozzi's *Turandot* at the Third Studio of the Moscow Art Theatre in 1922. The mythical world of commedia dell'arte was considered to be an element of pure theatricality: nostalgia for the past, introduced into a reconstruction which is neither superficial nor mimetic, tends to become a longing for the future.

14–15. The career of Ruth Saint-Denis (1877–1968) could be considered a classical example of the relationship of Western dancers with Asian dance-theatre. Interested in primitive and Asian dance, Ruth Saint-Denis in fact began her career by presenting extremely exotic performances. After travelling in Asia with Ted Shawn – her partner both in work and in life – she began to research the roots of various Asian dances, familiarising herself with the essential technical aspects which she had previously only intuited, and transforming her earlier primitive exoticism into technical and artistic skill. The influence of Denishawn, the dance company she directed with Ted Shawn, is unanimously considered to have had fundamental influence on the formation of modern dance; (**above left**) Ruth Saint-Denis and Ted Shawn in *Balinese Fantasy*; (**above right**) Ruth Saint-Denis in 1923 in a 'Burmese' dance.

16–17. (**above left**) Grotowski's production of Kalidasa's *Sakuntala* (1960). The deliberate search for 'Indian' gesture – notice the actor's hands in a kind of *mudra* (cf. *Hands*) – led Grotowski to the discovery of a specific and personal form of actor training; (**above right**) Jerzy Grotowski in Shanghai, China, in 1962 meeting Dr Ling, a specialist in vocal work at the Shanghai School of Traditional Opera. Through the travels of Grotowski in China in 1962 and Barba in India in 1963 a new phase of studying Asian theatre commenced and the tendencies of theatre practitioners were changed.

Paintings were once begun and finished in phases. Each day brought something new. A painting was a sum of additions. In my case, a painting is a sum of destructions. I first do the painting, then I destroy it. In the end, however, nothing is lost. The red I removed from one place is used somewhere else.
(Picasso)

Fragmentation and reconstruction

'Seen from afar, a city is a city and a landscape is a landscape; but, little by little, as one approaches, there appear houses, trees, tiles, leaves, blades of grass, ants, ants' legs, *ad infinitum*.' Commenting on this statement by Pascal, the film director Robert Bresson says: 'Fragmentation is indispensable if one does not wish to fall into description. One must see beings and things in their separate parts. Isolate these parts. Make them independent in order to give them a new dependence.'

The life of the performer's body on stage is the result of elimination: the work of isolating and accentuating certain actions or fragments of actions. Richard Schechner defines this process as the 'restoration of behaviour' (cf. *Restoration of Behaviour*). In exactly the same way that a film director makes a montage by cutting his film and reassembling the chosen sequences, a director or choreographer can work with the 'film-strip' of an actor's or dancer's actions. When this is done, the segments of the movements of actor's or dancer's actions seem much more complex than daily movements. An actor's score is the result of dramaturgy and montage, worked out first by the actor and then by the director, that is, it is the result of work based on dismantling and reconstruction. Every action is analysed according to its individual details and impulses and is then reconstructed into a sequence whose initial fragments may now have been amplified or moved into a new position, superimposed or simplified.

1–4. The transverse flute in four different cultures: (**top left**) the god Krishna (from a bas-relief in the Kesava Temple at Somnathpur, India); (**top right**) the god Hanxianzi, patron of musicians in China (from a popular Chinese print); (**bottom left**) the South African flute, the *naka ya lethlake*; (**bottom right**) and the flautist in a French military band in Edouard Manet's *The Regiment's Piper* (1866).

Omission is the principle which becomes immediately evident as soon as one begins to eliminate certain visual elements, such as props or instruments, from the performer's actions. The flute is an instrument which is so old and so popular that it is found in all human cultures (ill.1–4). To play the transverse flute, it is necessary to force the trunk to assume a particular slanted position with respect to the rest of the body; the head must also be slightly inclined so that the mouth and the fingers can rest comfortably on the pipe's openings. This position echoes the Indian *tribhangi* (cf. *Equivalence*).

The flute position is actually one of the most familiar positions in Indian dance: in fact, it represents the god Krishna himself. The position can also be held without the instrument: as soon as the instrument is taken away (ill.5), a completely different image appears. The play of tensions remains, but the action and the position, taken out of their necessary, original, historical, psychological and causal contexts, become a behaviour upon which both the performer and director or choreographer can subsequently work.

In this case, the omission of the visual element renders the action and the position independent: although they maintain all their organity, they can acquire a new dependence and therefore a new meaning. The act of playing the flute in kathakali theatre is no longer an action in and of itself, but indicates the arrival of Krishna, whose divine presence is announced by the sound of the flute (ill.6).

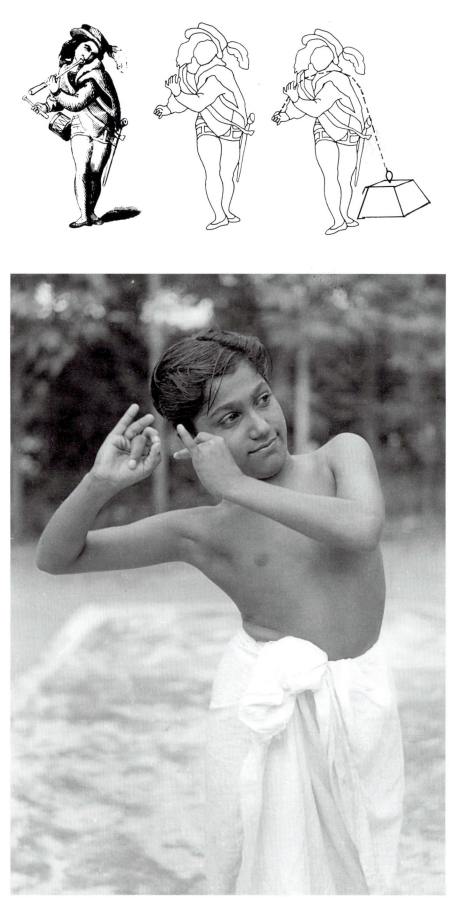

5. (**top**) Medieval public crier, fourteenth-century Germany. The omission of the flute gives the position a new value, a new availability, but the position remains intact and could be seen as a fragment in a completely different context.
6. (**bottom**) Young kathakali theatre student as Krishna playing the flute.

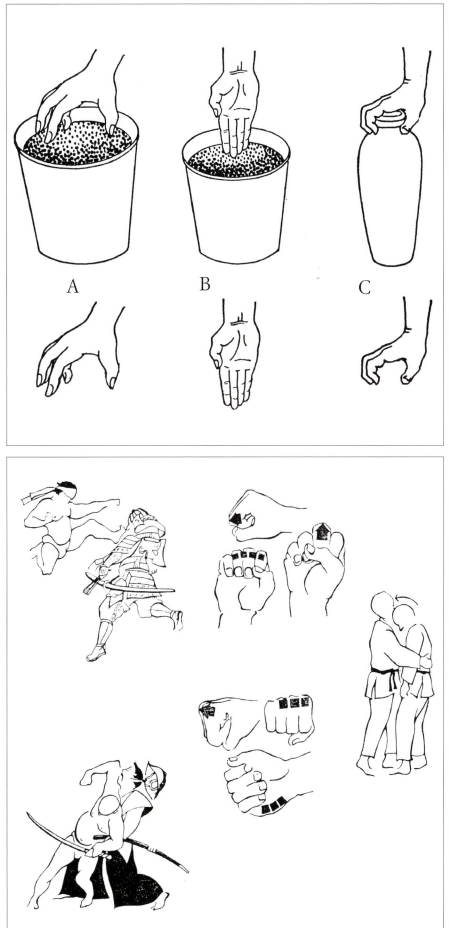

The virtue of necessity

The virtue of omission is not just a theatrical game. It is the logical rule of a synthesis. In Chinese and Japanese martial arts, the positions of the fingers – the characteristic articulation of the hand as a claw or stretched flat – are evidence of an omission and a synthesis used both in training and practice which help the practitioner control his muscles, even the less frequently used muscles of the hand. This is the technique known as *kanshu* or 'penetration with the hand'.

One of the origins of this technique lies in the Japanese occupation of Okinawa about 400 years ago. The inhabitants of the island were forbidden to carry any form of weapon and so, in order to be able to defend themselves against the invaders, they developed karate to such a high degree that they were able to break armour and deflect sword blows with their bare fists (ill.8).

Kanshu technique also originates in an ancient Chinese training method (ill.7A, 7B): a vase or jar is filled with light powder and the student trains plunging his hand into the powder in different positions. Gradually, the powder is replaced with rice, sand, hearts, and finally, stones. In the same simple and efficient way, the gesture of grasping firmly is trained: the student picks up a large terracotta jar by the rim and holds and carries it for a long time (ill.7C). At first the jar is empty; as the training progresses, it is filled with sand or water.

7. (**top**) *Kanshu* or hand-penetration technique in Chinese and Japanese martial arts.
8. (**bottom**) The omission of weapons in karate: the head, the arms, the fists and the feet as natural weapons.

To perform absence

We have already noticed, when dealing with the principle of equivalence, how in mime the arms are considered as non-essential with respect to the test of the body. Decroux often uses a process of concentration of energy in the trunk alone; the same is done in many Asian traditions. An action's superfluous elements are eliminated so that its necessary, essential aspect can become more clear. The opposition thus created between the force pushing towards the action and the force which holds a certain part of the action back produces that particular kind of energy which we have defined as *energy in time*. This is what happens when the performer eliminates a prop or a part of himself; but what happens when the performer eliminates himself entirely, yet without leaving the stage?

In Western theatre and dance, the use of the wings and a backstage area makes it possible for the performer to leave the stage to change costume or character out of the spectator's sight. Asian performances, which were originally presented outdoors, have made use of a great number of conventions which are commonly accepted by the spectators. In fact, the spectators accept the presence on stage of servants who assist and facilitate the performer's actions (ill.9) and also accept that the performer turns his back to them. This action was severely prohibited in Western theatre where frontality forced the actor to walk backwards in order not to offend the spectator.

Asian performers do not, however, abuse this convention. On the contrary, they are aware that they are seen even though they cannot see. We see here two examples: Katsuko Azuma (ill.10), bending backwards thus showing the *kimono*'s décolletage (considered erotic and elegant) and Sanjukta Panigrahi, seated in an uncomfortable position with her face hidden from view, displaying her long black braid (also considered erotic and elegant) and her hand, which gestures in an almost inviting way (ill.11).

9. Katsuko Azuma performing the dance of Shishi, a kind of lion-monkey in Japanese mythology. The butterflies, attracted by the flowers, flutter around Shishi and irritate him. They are attached to a flexible bamboo pole and are manipulated by a *kurogo* (or *kurombo*), literally, 'black man' or 'nothing'. A silent stage servant, the *kurogo* is a highly appreciated, essential element in the economy of classical Japanese theatres: his presence, indispensable for costume changes in full view of the public and for the placing of properties on the stage throughout the performance, eliminate the illusion of realism from the Japanese stage.

10. Performing absence: a stage servant (*kurogo*) adjusts Katsuko Azuma's costume in view of the public during a transition between two scenes.
11. Sanjukta Panigrahi absents herself from the performance: turning her back to the public in a theatrical way, she performs her own absence.

The virtue of omission

The virtue of omission in the theatre, but also in martial and figurative arts, is a necessary condition for achieving a synthesis: in the case of martial arts, it reinforces functionality; in the case of theatre, it reinforces scenic *bios*, the actor's presence.

Dario Fo, famous for his work as actor/playwright, composes his characters by carefully selecting certain physical actions and reactions, or even fragments of actions. He omits all the explicative passages and behaviour which would be necessary for the composition of a link between these actions and fragments: he has then created a dramaturgical synthesis of which he himself is the material, the instrument and the author (ill.12).

It is perhaps not a coincidence that comics are obviously the result of a choice made by the cartoonist: 'to strip' also means to tear to pieces, and a comic *strip* is therefore – also – the result of a series of cuts and omissions (ill.13).

12. Dario Fo in a series of physical actions and reactions which illustrate the synthesis in his performance, *The Story of a Tiger* (demonstration at the Volterra ISTA, 1981).

13. The richness and power of Dario Fo's score (ill.12) make it possible for him to isolate each single action and then to reassemble them into a new synthesis. In the new sequence, the four positions are used in a different story with its own new dramatic composition and its own new meaning, exactly as happens in a comic strip.

Manet is better than all of us: he creates light by using black.
(Camille Pissarro)

The dance of oppositions

If we really want to understand the nature of dialectics at the theatre's material level, we have to study Asian performers. The opposition principle is the base on which they construct and develop all their actions.

The Chinese performer always begins an action with its opposite. For example, in order to look at a person seated on their right, a Western performer would use a direct, linear movement of the neck. But the Chinese performer, and most other Asian performers, would begin as if they wanted to look in a different direction. They would then suddenly change course and turn their eyes to that person. According to the opposition principle, if one wants to go to the left, one begins by going to the right, then suddenly stops and turns left. If one wants to crouch down, one first rises up on tip-toe and then crouches down.

At first I thought that this was a scenic convention used by the Chinese performer to amplify actions, thus rendering them more perceptible, creating an effect of surprise and guiding the spectator's attention. And this is undoubtedly true. But I know now that this convention is not limited to Chinese theatre, but is a rule that can be found throughout the East.

If one watches a Balinese dancer, a noh actor (even when carrying out the simple gesture of holding a fan in front of the face), a kabuki actor in the *aragoto* or *wagoto* style (ill.15 p.36), a classical Indian or Thai khon dancer, one notices that the movements do not proceed in a straight projectory, but in sinuous lines. The trunk, the arms and the hands underline this roundness. In the West, one dances with the legs; in the East, one dances with the arms.

(Eugenio Barba, *Theatre Anthropology: First Hypothesis*)

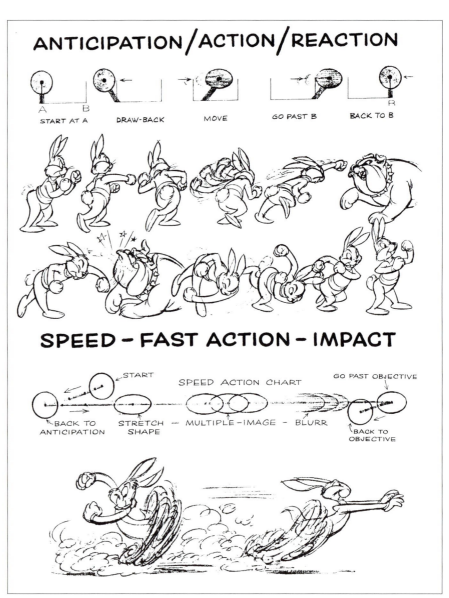

1. In order to move in a given direction it is necessary to start in the opposite direction; or rather, one accentuates the effect of a movement by anticipating it. From Preston Blair's manual on animation for cartoonists. According to Meyerhold, the *otkaz* ('refusal') technique, which was part of the training used in his school, was 'a movement opposite to that which one wanted to make and came immediately before the desired movement in order to accentuate expression'.

2. The principle of movement by means of opposition: from a manual for Peking Opera actors from the 1950s.

3–4. (**above left**) Pen sketches by Paulet Thevenaz which illustrate certain phases of Jaques-Dalcroze's eurythmic method: the 'anticipation' of the movements is clearly visible; the movements begin in a direction which is opposite to their final direction. The research done by Emile Jaques-Dalcroze (1865–1900) on rhythm and movement had considerable influence on the theatre, and especially on modern dance, at the end of the nineteenth century; (**above right**) exercises on the basic types of opposition from the book of Alfonse Giraudet (1895), a student of François Delsarte.

5. (**below**) A example of opposition being used by a European actor: notice the non-linear way of passing from a reaction of fear to one of disgust. From G. Austin's *Chironomia* (London, 1806).

6–8. Peking Opera actor Zhang Yunxi photogaphed by Czechoslovakian scholar Dana Kalvodova at the school for Peking actors. The sequence shows the movements used by the actor to make an entrance as a military hero (*wu-sheng*). Having made two steps on to the stage, the actor stops (ill.6) and picks up the sides of his costume-weapon (here, however, the actor is working without costume), bends the left leg towards the right, at knee level (ill.7), then bends the same leg towards the left, at pelvis level (ill.8), in order finally to move straight ahead towards stage centre. This entrance, based on a series of oppositions, is also typical of other Peking Opera rôles and is combined with a way of walking across the stage (cf. ill.9) which is also elaborated according to the principle of moving in directions that are opposite to the final destination.

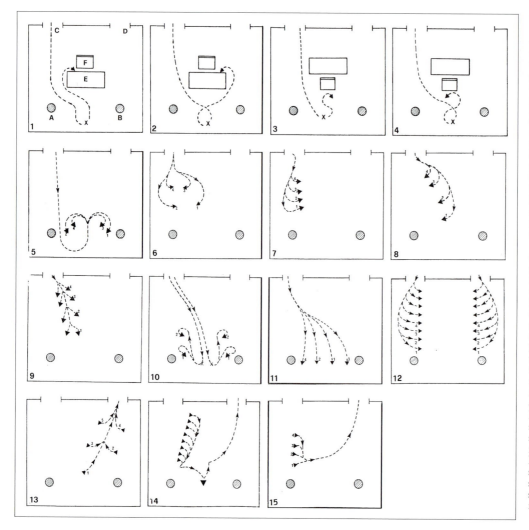

9. The traditional Peking Opera stage – at one time outdoors only, now also indoors – is made up of: a square playing area, usually very small, with two pillars (A and B) that support a ceiling; a bare rear wall with two doors – by convention, the left-hand door (C) was used for entrances, the right-hand door (D) for exits. There is no set and properties are few and very simple: a table (E) and one or more chairs (F) which can become 'a bed', for example, or 'a mountain'. The actors 'fill' the limited but completely empty space with their sumptuous costumes and complicated pattern of movements.

These diagrams show the entrances of various rôle types, or groups of actors, and the routes conventionally used by them to arrive at a pre-determined position, where they begin to speak, sing and dance (the 'X' indicates a pause): 1. Male rôle; 2. Female rôle; 3. Male rôle; 4. Female rôle; 5. Entrance of the retinue (servants, guards, followers): first style; 6. Entrance of the retinue: second style; 7. Entrance of the retinue: third style; 8. Entrance of the retinue: fourth style; 9. Entrance of the retinue: fifth style; 10. Entrance of the retinue: sixth style; 11. Entrance of the retinue: seventh style; 12. Entrance of the retinue: eighth style; 13. Exit of the retinue: first style; 14. Exit of the retinue: second style; 15. Exit of the retinue: third style.

10–13. (**left**) Balinese dancer Swasti Widjaja Bandem in a demonstration of gait at the Holstebro ISTA, 1986. The Balinese way of moving across the stage, which makes use of continuous variations of positions angled and cut according to series of oppositions, made a tremendous impression on Artaud when he saw Balinese theatre at the Paris Colonial Exposition in 1931: noticing how these movements and gestures impregnated the playing area, Artaud spoke of 'a new physical language' in the theatre, based on signs and not on words. He compared the Balinese actors to 'animated hieroglyphs'; (**above right**) Outline drawings of performers which are a leitmotiv in this book: a commedia dell'arte Zanni and an odissi dancer. Here they illlustrate the oppositions created inside the performer's body; (**bottom**) in dance, symmetrical positions result in balanced figures without oppositions; asymmetrical positions, on the contrary, tend to result in unbalanced figures and powerful oppositions. Dancers must be familiar with and use both possibilities while respecting the flow of lines. Diagrams from Doris Humphrey's *The Art of Making Dances* (New York, 1959).

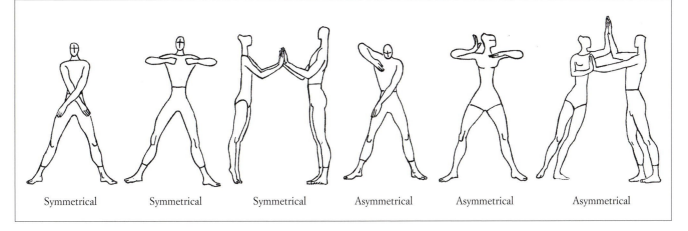

| Symmetrical | Symmetrical | Symmetrical | Asymmetrical | Asymmetrical | Asymmetrical |

The beauty line

In India, the opposition principle takes a characteristic form in both dance and the other figurative arts: it is called *tribhangi*, which means three arches. The dancer's body takes the form of the letter 'S' (head, trunk, legs): the result is a precarious balance, new resistances and tensions which create the body's extra-daily architecture (ill.14 and 19).

The serpentine line of *tribhangi* is also found in the most remote Western tradition.

It was the Greeks who discovered that a body's beauty is not only the result of correct proportions but also of a particular anatomical posture. The sculptor Polycletus was the first to establish a law for the sculptural representation of the nude body, determining the exact proportions which should be used, and, in particular, the relationship of 1 to 7 between the head and the rest of the body. The figures created by Michelangelo and Raphael bear witness to this law, which has remained unchanged for centuries.

What we wish to underline here, however, is less the body's proportions than the body posture common to all Greek and Hellenic statuary from Polycletus' *Ephebus* to the *Venus de Milo*. This posture is characterised by the lateral displacement of the hip caused by the body weight being supported on only one foot, and the lateral displacement of the head caused by the twisting of the torso.

This dynamic undulation of the body around an axis, which is the reason why the figures seem so animated, was taken up by Florentine sculptors in the fourteenth century as a reaction against the immobility of Byzantine and medieval figures. Naturally, it was refused by Renaissance artists, who took their inspiration directly from classical art. The artist's personal taste, as well as that of the epoch, certainly plays a decisive rôle. It was Dürer who affirmed that there is not just one type of beauty but many types. Nevertheless, the dynamic representation of the body by means of motion which winds around a central axis remains a fundamental principle of an artistic work's 'life'.

In the eighteenth century, this dynamic contour inspired William Hogarth to define what he called 'the beauty line', a sinuous line drawn on a pyramid (ill.18). A combination of movement and rest, balance and asymmetry, a dance of oppositions.

14. *Tribhangi* (three arches) in a statue of Vajravarahi, seventh to eighth century Tibetan silverwork (Newark Museum, USA).

15. Macuilxochitl (or Xochipilli) Aztec goddess of music, song, dance, love and spring (Borgian Cycle Codex). According to Mexican scholar Cayuqui Estage Noel, the goddess's black face is a mask.

16. Aphrodite, called the *Venus de Milo* (Louvre Museum, Paris) in a *tribhangi* position.

17. Early dynamic use of *hanchement* (displacement of the hips) in European sculpture: fifteenth-century statue of a prophet (Pistoia Cathedral, Italy), attributed to Florentine architect Filippo Brunelleschi (1377–1446).

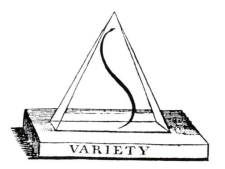

18. The 'line of beauty', or 'variety', in an engraving made in 1753 by English painter William Hogarth (1697–1764).

Tribhangi, *or the three arches*

The *tribhangi* formation, which is immediately identifiable in the dance and statuary of India, also manifests itself in the work of actors of other cultures. Here the 'dance of oppositions' is expressed more internally, or within the body. Look at the positions of Sanjukta Panigrahi, an odissi dancer and the classical ballet dancer, Natalia Makarova (ill.19–20).

The contrast can be perceived immediately: Natalia Makarova gives a sensation of grace, lightness, almost like the levitation of an ethereal being, whilst the Indian dancer has something earthy and sensual about her. Beyond these external appearances, both dancers are using their spines in the same way, and differ only in the manner in which they display the result. The classical dancer is using a dynamic which produces a long, streamlined – one could almost say upreared – body shape. The force of oppositions working in the odissi dancer are aiming at a paroxysm of sinuous movement. (For example, the series of angles which fracture the form of her arm are sublimated into a gentle fold in the wrist of the classical dancer.)

With Natalia Makarova, the oppositions are revealed through the enormous effort of precarious balance, the way she looks to one side, 'resting' her chin with a resistance and tension so great the left shoulder is lifted. The position of the chin breaks the symmetry of the vertical thrust and the balance is precarious by virtue of the position – but more so with this twist of the head which, by coming to rest on the shoulder, creates an asymmetrical opposition between the two shoulders.

19–23. (**top left**) Sanjukta Panigrahi in a classical odissi dance *tribhangi*; (**top right**) Classical ballet dancer Natalia Makarova in *Swan Lake* (choreography by Petipa, music by Tchaikovsky); (**centre left**) Igor Ilinsky as Shastlivtsev in A. N. Ostrovsky's *The Forest*, directed by Meyerhold in 1924. The actor's basic position is a *tribhangi*. Ilinsky, who worked in Meyerhold's theatre from 1920 until 1933, made fundamental contributions to the development of biomechanics; (**centre right**) it is interesting to see how the presence of this 'performer' is based on an alteration of balance and on a minimal *tribhangi*. She is a fashion model, not trying to express anything, merely 'presenting' a 1947 Dior design; (**right**) *tribhangi* posture in a fourteenth-century wooden statue of the Virgin Mary (Skellfteå Museum, Lövanger, Sweden).

24–26. Western performers' oppositions: (**left**) Franca Rame in one of her monologues, (**centre**) Henry Irving as Cardinal Wolsey in Shakespeare's *Henry VIII*, and (**right**) the German dancer, Mary Wigman in *Tanzgesänge* (1935).

27. (**above**) The same play of oppositions in a kabuki actor (eighteenth-century Japanese print).

29. (**above**) German actor Ludwig Devrient (1784–1832) as Franz Moor in Schiller's *The Highwaymen* (lithograph, 1830): the opposition is accentuated by the prop, a candelabrum used as a weapon.

28. (**above**) Action, reaction, opposition. English actors A. Youge and H. Nye as Stephano and Trinculo, respectively, in Shakespeare's *The Tempest* (daguerrotype from around 1840 by G. Greatbach).

30. Sequence of the 'small boats in the port of Odessa' from Eisenstein's *Battleship Potemkin* (1925). The entire sequence has been planned so as to create not only a montage based on the oppositions between the various shots but also oppositions between the lines of direction in the shots themselves. From Amangual's *Que Viva Eisenstein*! (Lausanne, 1980).

The shadow test

The performer develops resistance by creating oppositions: this resistance increases the density of each movement, gives the movement altered intensity and muscular tone. But the amplification also occurs in the space. By means of dilation in space, the spectator's attention is directed and focused; at the same time, the performer's dynamic action becomes comprehensible. The performer can verify if this dynamic is correctly present by putting it to *the shadow test*, a rule with which cartoon and comic-strip artists are very familiar. They use it to verify that their drawings are comprehensible and effective (ill.37).

Ingemar Lindh demonstrates here that a gesture designed to represent pointing (ill.33) and to illustrate the opposition principle is not very clear when seen from the front (ill.34). The front view does not pass the shadow test and is just as bad for the performer as for the cartoonist. Walter Benjamin quite correctly observed: 'The actor must space out his gestures like a typographer spaces out his words. He must work in such a way that his gestures can be quoted.'

31–37. (**top left** and **centre** and **centre left** and **centre**) Ingemar Lindh, in a demonstration of the various ways of 'showing' and 'pointing' in Decroux mime, at the Volterra ISTA, 1981: the opposition created by the body's oblique line makes the action dramatic; (**top right** and **centre right**) a dancer must find positions and directions that give the spectators a complete view. According to Doris Humphrey, a direction is 'wrong' when the dancer's body is oriented in a way that does not give the spectator the full impact of the action; the direction is 'right', on the other hand, when the dancer succeeds in showing all the sides of, say, the arms and legs; (**bottom**) the shadow test in Preston Blair's animation manual.

Here are some Decroux mime exercises. They are based on the principle according to which one creates *affirmation* and *confirmation* oppositions in the body. From the basic position (ill.38, 42, 46) to the first movement (ill.39, 43, 47), which are identical in all three exercises, one passes on to the third, decisive position. These exercises

clearly demonstrate the function of opposition and show the rôle of broken and oblique lines, which are more interesting than straight lines (ill.40 and 48).

These mime exercises, which recall Meyerhold's biomechanics, seem to be a simplification of the complex architecture of Indian *tribhangi*. In their

simplification, however, we rediscover the clarity and rigour of a work whose aim is to discover rules of movement for the performer in the light of what is perceived by the spectator. *Affirmation*, *confirmation* and *contradiction* are an explicit way of fixing the spectator's attention on the monosyllables 'yes' and 'no'.

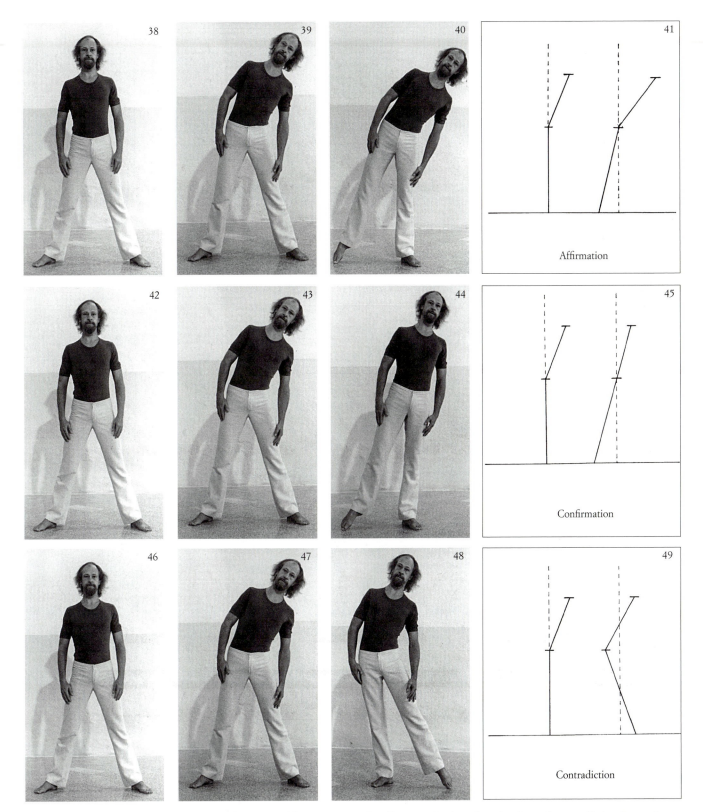

38-49. Three exercises from Decroux mime, demonstrated by Ingemar Lindh: affirmation (**top**) confirmation (**centre**); contradiction (**bottom**).

Organic effect

Eugenio Barba

Organicity: the quality or state of being organic.
Organic: of, pertaining to or derived from a living organism.
(New Shorter Oxford Dictionary)

Organicity, presence, scenic bios

In theatre and dance, the term 'organic' is used as a synonym of 'alive', 'credible'. Stanislavsky introduced it into the theatrical working language of the twentieth century. For the Russian reformer, *organichnost* (organicity) and *organicheskij* (organic) were an essential quality in the performer's actions, the premise for a spectator to react with an unconditioned 'I believe'.

Organicity is strictly connected to presence and scenic *bios*.

For European theatre artists, the need for a new way of *being present* on the stage as well as in society grew with the anthropological mutation which their craft underwent at the end of the nineteenth century. The first generation of great reformers – Stanislavsky, Appia, Craig, Meyerhold, Vakhtangov, Michael Chekhov, Copeau – felt, each in his own way, an urgency to oppose the loss of existence in the art of theatre. The word 'existence' must be taken literally: the capacity of *being and feeling alive* and of transmitting this awareness to the spectators.

Their search went in two complementary directions: on the one hand they strove for a new and meaningful presence of theatre in society, while on the other they made an effort to devise methods to develop a condition of life or an efficacious presence in the actor's art. Artaud affirmed that it was necessary to give life back to theatre. Before him, Stanislavsky spoke about organicity, and Meyerhold of bio-mechanics, or of the movement of life (*bios*=life, mechanics= the part of physics which studies motion).

The objective of their research was to let the actor embody 'authenticity', 'sincerity', 'cruelty', a rigorous *dynamis* that could give life to the poetic essence of Ibsen's, Strindberg's and Chekhov's plays. But which process should the actor follow in order to evoke this feeling of life, this organic effect in the spectator?

It is from this perspective that we have to see the introduction of a training based on exercises, a practice that was absent in the apprenticeship of the European actor.

That which is organic for the actor / that which is organic for the spectator

It sometimes happens that an actor experiences certain actions as organic, whereas the same is not true for the director and/or spectators.

On the other hand, it also happens that the director and/or spectators perceive as organic actions that the actor experiences as inorganic, tense and artificial.

This disparity of judgement or awareness contradicts the ingenuous belief in a direct correlation between what the actor feels and does, and what the spectator experiences. In fact, there is no such correlation, but there can be an encounter. The efficacy of this encounter determines the meaning and the value of the theatre.

The efficacy depends on the organic effect obtained by the actor in respect to the spectator. *Organic effect* means the capacity to make the spectator experience a performing body-in-life. The actor's main task is not to be organic, but to appear organic *to the eyes and senses of the spectator*. For the actors, the real problem concerns the directions and methods they choose in order to build a persuasive scenic presence. If they lose the point of reference constituted by the perception of someone looking on from the outside, and only use their own sensations as a measure of judgement, they will probably soon experience their own organic quality as illusory for themselves as well.

The shortest paths, whatever our illusions may tell us, are always tortuous. These paths can only arrive at their destination successfully if they first set out in the opposite direction.

For the actors, the search for the organic effect is often accompanied by a feeling of unease, by a sense of the inorganic character of their own body and actions. Only after a long and arduous process – and not always then – is a meeting possible between the new organic quality of the actor's actions and the perception of the spectator.

This new organic quality, which derives from a long apprenticeship – defined by Stanislavsky and Copeau as 'second nature' – is the consequence of the unease being overcome. It is the paradoxical use of a physiology and of a logic in the space-time in which actors and spectators meet. This extra-daily way of acting and thinking, remote from daily criteria, is an indispensable requirement for the efficacy and justification of the theatre craft.

(Eugenio Barba, *The Ripe Action*)

1–2. Ryszard Cieslak (1937–1990) (**left**) in *The Constant Prince* directed by Jerzy Grotowski (1965). The actor's position is inspired by the *frasobliwy* (sad) Christ, a well-known image in Polish religious iconography (**right**).

3–4. Ni Made Nugini and Ni Made Sarniani performing gambuh, a Balinese dance-drama. After the first impression of powerful suggestiveness, we become aware of the detailed artificial composition in the two dancers' posture. The organic effect which is experienced by the spectator, the impression of dilated life and vibrant immobility, are the consequence of tensions originating in a performer's two 'spines': the torso and the eyes. The head goes in one direction, the eyes in another, the spine is strongly arched, the shoulders slightly raised. The impression of diversity in the two postures is provided – as Decroux would say – by the 'anecdote' told by the arms (cf. *The action of seeing* in *Face and Eyes*). Peter Brook has also underlined the centrality of a performer's scenic presence: 'To me what matters is that one actor can stand motionless on the stage and rivet our attention while another does not interest us at all. What is the difference? Where chemically, physically, psychically does it lie? Star quality, personality? No. That's too easy and it's not an answer. I don't know what the answer is. But I do know that it is here; in this question we can find the starting point of our whole art' (Peter Brook, *The Shifting Point*, Methuen, London 1989, p. 232).

Natural and organic

Mirella Schino

The use of the word 'organic' designating a certain quality in the actor's performance is recent, dating from the twentieth century. Previously it was said that an actor was 'natural' if s/he was believable and effective. For centuries the appearance of a new 'great actor' with an original style was welcomed as the manifestation of Nature itself, in contrast to the artificiality of his/her predecessors. In this way an actor who was famous for his 'naturalness' was eclipsed in the taste of the spectators by one who at last seemed truly 'natural' and made the artificiality of his predecessor stand out. As soon as another new star appeared to shake up the spectator's emotions, then s/he in turn seemed 'artificial'. In the second half of the nineteenth century, that is to say in the period of the blossoming of the 'great actors', each new generation and each new style of acting was acclaimed as being 'natural at last'.

In this context, 'natural' has nothing to do with being faithful to the representation of daily life. The aim of all actors was to appear *verisimilar*, lifelike. Nevertheless, in one way or another, each one forged an individual scenic behaviour, camouflaged under the appearance of verisimilitude. 'Natural' does not imply realism: it has more to do with the *effect of coherence* provoked in the spectator. When spectators and connoisseurs spoke of an actor who seemed to be 'natural at last', they were witnesses to a composition so articulate in every detail that it made the spectators momentarily forget the artificiality of his/her scenic behaviour. It was as though no other way of moving or behaving existed or, as if the actor, through his/her art, had engendered a fragment of nature.

'Natural' should therefore be understood to mean the creation on the part of the actor of a complexity and coherence in his/her scenic behaviour, analogous and equivalent to the coherence and complexity characterising a living organism.

Organic and natural

'Natural' and 'naturalness' easily arouse confusion because on the one hand they bring to the fore the idea of imitation, whereas on the other they can be inappropriately associated with the artistic and literary current of 'naturalism'.

In the twentieth century, alongside 'verisimilar' acting, other explicitly artificial forms of acting are appreciated. These forms display deformed visions of the human figure and behaviour. The term 'organicity' is used to designate complexity and coherence in the actor's behaviour, sustaining the illusion of a style of acting which follows the rules of a diverse nature. The word 'organic' now indicates the effect produced on the spectator, as did previously the adjective 'natural'. It denotes the way in which the actor's composition is *perceived* rather than the process leading up to the result.

On the one hand the 'great actor' mingled with the other actors, while on the other s/he could be perceived as a separate world. Innumerable opposing forces met in clashes and dialogues in his/her body, transforming it into a field of contradictions whose power was able to fill the entire space. Structurally, the 'great actor' was a contradictory presence. As a *figure*, s/he was one individual amongst others; as a *field of energy* s/he was a complete world in him/herself, capable of monopolising the intelligence and the senses of the spectators. The whole performance, as well as the vibrant space of the stage, seemed to be concentrated within his/her body.

Performance as an organic unity

During the twentieth century, the inventors of the art of direction overturned the terms of this contradiction. They transformed the various figures of the actors into a joint *field of energy*. Previously the 'great actor' engendered multiplicity from his/her individual singularity. Now the reformers treated the multiplicity of individual actors as though they were parts of a single, paradoxical organic unity. The whole performance became a single living organism.

5–8. Four images of 'great actors': (**above left**) Sarah Bernhardt (1844–1923); (**above centre**) Tommaso Salvini (1829–1915); (**above right**) Elisabeth Rachel Félix known as Rachel (1821–58) and (**next page**) Adelaide Ristori (1822–1906). A 'great actor' is not just a good actor. It is an expression applied to specific and exceptional examples of the actor's art throughout Europe from the second half of the nineteenth until the beginning of the twentieth century. In the course of the performance, the 'great actor' had a paradoxical contrasting function in relation to the acting norms of the time, and therefore also to his/her fellow-actors. This contrasting function applied to the interpretation of the text, which diverged from the customary and known intellectual and emotional logic, thus opposing the spectators' habits and conditioning. The result was described by their contemporaries as 'interpretative complexity', 'naturalness stronger than nature itself ' or 'prodigious changefulness'. Another prominent characteristic of a 'great actor' was a singular capacity to impose himself/herself with vehemence on the attention of the audience. S/he filled the entire space not only with the authority of his/her presence but also through the voice, thus achieving an effect similar to the vocal impact of an opera singer. The consequence was not just seduction or fascination, but *powerfulness*. It is this particular effect that is lost in images, portraits or photos. Only a few traces are to be found in caricatures.

The invention of the performance as a 'unitary body', which could be contradictory, complex, shaken by many urges and tensions, rhythms and breathings, characterised all the reformers: Appia and Meyerhold, Stanislavsky and Copeau, Craig and Vakhtangov, Reinhardt and Dullin. It permeated Antonin Artaud's visions which, seemingly fanciful, were based on a wealth of precise details.

When the performance is seen as a single body, its basic cell is no longer the individual (whether actor or character), but consists of smaller units. Until the beginning of the twentieth century, the minimum unit of measurement for scenic composition coincided with the body and psychology of a human being (actor, *persona* or character). This unit could contain contradictions but was not divisible. Research into the principles of the actor's art, the scientific study of movement and the building up of organicity drive the reforming masters of the twentieth century to single out the actions of each part of the body and consider them as basic units. These actions-units may establish relationships with other parts of the same body. But they can also form connections with the actions-units of other bodies, creating an intricate and living web of dialogues, contrasts, assonance, dissonance and rhythms.

It is thus possible to work on the entire performance as though on a single body, starting out from basic cells (the actions-units) which are smaller than the individual seen as a unit. This perspective extends the perception of the organicity from the single actor to the whole performance. Previously, the spectators could see an entire performance in the body of a 'great actor'. Now, they are able to experience an organic unity behind a whole performance.

The 'great actor' enveloped the deep artificiality of his/her scenic nature in a veil of verisimilitude on the surface. The company-single body, on the contrary, structures and makes evident even on the surface its different nature, letting the spectator perceive its organic quality which is independent from the appearance of a natural organism.

Always nature, but a different nature

Thanks to the organic quality, invented by the 'fathers of direction' at the beginning of the twentieth century, the performance is transformed in an example of a *different* nature, thus becoming the privileged field for experiments on organicity.

Meyerhold, Copeau, Craig, Appia, Fuchs, Reinhardt as well as Stanislavsky are aware of a double problematic. On the one hand, the actor's body stands as a microcosm, that is, as a system of separable parts; on the other, the whole company is considered as an unitary body which must be steered in its totality. This dialectic implies a study in depth of the relationships between the different parts, independently from the story which is narrated, the skill of the individual actors and the features of the characters.

The consequence of the change generated by a barely visible transformation is evident in all the fields of scenic composition. From a dramaturgical point of view, for example, it hollows out the centrality of the text. The indivisible human body has been substituted with a subdivision of autonomous fragments to be connected with other ones. The director is able to work with a greater number of smaller and less complex, yet more malleable, units. The links between these smaller units of the human body open a wider field of work, radically different from the one made up by each individual considered as an indivisible unit. The many organic fragments can establish bonds and correlations according to criteria similar to those traditionally used to create relationships between individual actors or characters.

Steps, looks, movement directions, weight, torso, head, legs, arms, hands, feet, rhythm, speed, intensity, tension and relaxation can be treated as elements of relationships. They can be orchestrated in a dramaturgy of their own, which may be in accordance with or opposed to the dramaturgy of the plot.

The focal position of the text during the working process is shaken by two problematic aspects: the actors' body as a microcosm with diverse and autonomous organic cells, and the ensemble of all the actors as parts of a unitary organism. This double problem does not imply that the text is less important. It means that it is no longer the only steering instrument while creating a performance. Other factors have to be added to the logics of the text's depth and surface, to its contents, allusions and implicit meanings: the evident and hidden logics, principles, rhythms and the organicity of a different nature.

Both practically and theoretically, the question of the body-as-microcosm and the performance-as-entire-body had consequences similar to the ones engendered by the discovery of the life of a cell for the way of thinking and the practice of biologists, or by the discovery of the subatomic world for the physicists. The time through which the performance navigates changes. Present, past and future may intertwine, simultaneously weaving different actions and separate facets of the same story.

This procedure characterised the art of the 'great actor': the capacity to multiply the logics in shaping his/her own scenic presence, avoiding an unambiguous interpretation of the drama. Now, the multiplicity of perspectives becomes a usual way of working; it is, in fact, *the* way to work in theatre.

The possibility of operating with cells smaller than the human being allows the development of a scenic life – an organicity – which is not necessarily realistic. This may reproduce the complex web of relationships that denote organicity on a biological level. Mimesis with daily 'reality' becomes a secondary function, an accessory which does not concern the basic working principles for an actor and a director.

Directors with divergent tastes in their creations, such as Stanislavsky and Meyerhold, may share the same artistic foundations. The essential, in theatre, is the building of a parallel reality, whatever its stylistic feature. Style is not the most significant difference. Difference stems from scientific eagerness and tenacity against certainties in theatre, its way of being art and its function in society. Experiments on organicity are in themselves technical and existential revolt.

Working languages

Each performative tradition has its own working language, which is precise and easy to understand from inside, but difficult to explain to others. This applies to big as well as to small traditions, to traditions which are handed down from one generation to another, and to those that consist of a limited number of people sharing a common story and knowledge that will not survive their disappearance. An even more exclusive working language exists, the one that each of us uses while thinking and reflecting upon our own personal way of behaving professionally.

The multitude of these working languages – some codified and some personal, at times secret and at others so explicit that they sound like theories – generates a labyrinth of terms and shadows that conceals the concreteness of experience. Nevertheless, by scraping the surface of the words, of the images and the metaphors, we confront recurring principles and an awareness shared by theatre people of diverse and distant origins.

Presence

There are actors to whom we don't listen. They have handsome voices, an impeccable diction, are nice to look at and are entrusted with important rôles. When they enter on stage, you are attentive and say 'how beautiful he or she is', but after five minutes your attention is drawn by an unknown actor in a minor rôle who possesses this marvellous gift: presence.

Be there (whether liked or disliked). Awake interest even through irritation. Even when you want to be unobserved, *fill your own space, making yourself necessary*. Presence is a discrete quality emanating from the soul. It radiates and imposes itself. The actor, when aware of his/her presence, dares to express what s/he feels and will do so appropriately because effortless: the spectator follows and listens to him/her.

This necessary splitting occurs under the effect of a physical sensation which makes us say: 'How terribly I acted tonight, I didn't feel the audience'. For a reason which escaped our will, we were not there, we performed our part more or less well, but we didn't live it. The character's ghost had not followed us when we stepped onto the stage, and we searched for it in vain during the whole act.

9–11. In each theatre genre or tradition, the building up of scenic presence and of the organic effect begins with a rigorous alteration of the balance, according to principles of a pragmatic science which is incorporated: (**top**) Odin Teatret's 'tre-tre' chain with Julia Varley (Montemor ISTA, 1998); (**centre**) the *orixa's* dance with Augusto Omolú (Montemor ISTA, 1998); (**bottom**) I Wayan Bawa teaching the basic *agem* posture in Balinese theatre and dance (Seville ISTA, 2004).

The actor's art is something of a mystery. Its success does not depend only on study, preparation, intelligence and will. Even the person who is perfectly expert on the questions concerning our art, with an admirable body and a superb voice, can be an abominable actor. This idea is expressed in a thousand ways in our scenic jargon. The great Mounet-Sully said: 'This evening, the divinity has not descended'. An instinctive actor of melodrama said: 'The rôle was not in my shoes'. The vain actor will say: 'What a dull audience tonight!' Someone else, coming off the stage, will clear his/her throat, touching the vocal cords. The only certainty is that all of them need this presence which does not depend solely on them.

(Charles Dullin, *Souvenirs et notes de travail d'un acteur*)

Axé, shinmyong, taksu

The words 'organicity' and 'presence' are not to be found in the working languages of other traditions. But all have terms or metaphors to indicate this quality in the actor.

In cultures where trance is a common and recognisable event, it is usual to turn to the vocabulary of possession. Augusto Omolú, from the Afro-Brazilian dance originating from the candomblé, speaks of *axé*, a subtle energy which stems from the *orixás*, the divinities who embody different manifestations of the forces in nature.

Augusto Omolú says he is not sure whether in his dance that evening he will receive *axé*. The transformation does not depend on him, it is 'something' which arrives without him playing any part. *Axé* is bestowed. Then Augusto has the distinct sensation of manipulating something unknown, as though he had penetrated into an area within his body which encloses mysterious forces.

In Korea, where the shamanistic culture is still alive, the term *shinmyong* denotes the entering of the spirit into a human being. The same term is applied to the actor when s/he attracts the attention of the spectator.

Balinese performers speak of *taksu*, literally: 'the place which receives the light'. The actor is enlightened by 'another' energy which works on the spectator. A sort of divine inspiration takes possession of the performer escaping his/her control. As with *axé* and *shinmyong*, *taksu* too is not decided by

12–14. (**top**) Kathakali with M. P. Sankaran Namboodiri (Bielefeld ISTA, 2000); (**bottom left**) a demonstration by Jacques Lecoq, teacher of generations of actors (Odin Teatret, 1968); (**above right**) nihon buyo with Kanichi Hanayagi (Bielefeld ISTA, 2000).

the actor. S/he can only note: 'this evening there was *taksu*' or 'this evening there was no *taksu*' (cf. *Energy*).

Matah, mi-juku, kacha

In Bali, the feeling that the performer's change of energy constitutes a different quality of life is articulated in various ways. *Ngidupan* (or *menjivai*) means 'to give life'. *Hidup* is life. If *hidup* is absent, then the performer (or his/her performance) is *matah*, unripe, lacking the right taste. The term 'ripe' as opposed to *matah* does not exist. *Wayah*, old, is used, not in the sense of decrepit or weak, but of vigour and vital force. The sun is old at noon, young at sunset. *Wayah* is embodied knowledge. Sampun wayah is a dance that does not give the impression of being 'unripe' or 'undecided'. The Balinese master I Made Djimat affirms that a school can teach how to dance

correctly, and yet the performers will be unable to *ngidupan*, 'to give life' to their performance. An actor can dance in a correct way without being *wayah*. As Charles Dullin said: presence (or organic effect) does not depend on technical skill.

In Japan the term *mi-juku*, unripe, is used to indicate the performer who is not mature. Like the Balinese *matah*, the term *mi-juku* is applied to the performer who has not incorporated a dance to the point of giving it life. In Japan too they are aware that an actor may be technically perfect, and nevertheless miss *iki iki*, the quality of dazzling the spectator. *Iki iki* means 'vivid', 'brilliant', 'shining'.

Sanjukta Panigrahi, the great odissi dancer, recognised this recurring image in the working languages of different traditions. In Oriya, her own language, a performer is considered *kacha*, unripe or raw, as opposed to *pakka*, the ripe performer who rivets the spectator.

211

At work with physical actions: the double articulation

Marco De Marinis

The founders of the new theatre of the twentieth century have proved irrefutably that it is impossible to accomplish a real action – that is, to act in a real way on stage – through uncontrolled spontaneity or naturalism. To achieve such a goal, it is indispensable to follow the long path of discipline, technical training and the elaboration of form. On stage, a physical action can become real action only if it turns into artificial form, a score rooted on constraints of rigorous principles. Only in this way can it free itself from stereotyped, automatic and inorganic confusion: in other words, unfettered from false spontaneity. False spontaneity is the phase that comes before technical precision, and therefore before the voluntary control of the action. Consequently, false spontaneity is illusory and fictive freedom.

True spontaneity for the actor comes after technique and beyond its precision. It is effective freedom because based on the voluntary control of the action. Nevertheless, the necessary artificiality and technical constraints are not enough to achieve this quality of true spontaneity. A physical action, in order to be real – and thus efficacious – must be authentic, felt, sincere and experienced. It needs to be founded on an organic correspondence between the actor's inner and outer self. It must be accomplished by the whole body-mind.

We could resume in the following way the two required conditions that make an action real (conscious and voluntary) on stage:

1. precision, as formal external coherence (often supported by a score);
2. organicity, as inner coherence, assured by the actor's presence which, in turn, may be backed up by a subscore. Only organicity, understood as the action's psycho-physical entirety, guarantees the indispensable margin of freedom within precision and allows for improvisation within the score, acquiring the quality of true spontaneity.

The first articulation

There exists substantial agreement among the masters of the twentieth century concerning the conditions of the real scenic action. Let us see whether an analogous agreement may be traced in relation to how to shape these conditions, that is those technical procedures through which these masters have tried to realise these conditions. Such an agreement exists and I would call it double articulation. I could also speak of a double disarticulation since its primary purpose is to break (disarticulate) the mental and physical automatisms which bind the actor in his/her use of the body and during the montage of actions on stage. The first articulation (disarticulation) concerns the body, the second the movement and the scenic action.

I call 'first articulation' the process of segmentation in the actor's body. The body is disassembled in various pieces (like a puppet or a machine), then reassembled according to the combinatory rules of a different, artificial anatomy. The objective is to transform the living, biological and daily body into a 'body-in-life' (Barba), a fictive, extra-daily body ready to perform scenic actions.

The clever theoretician of scenic movement who clearly explained the first articulation was François Delsarte who segmented the body and each single limb according to three rules (introversion, extroversion and neutral). He laid down the fundamental principles of the artificial anatomy resulting from the first articulation:

1. the pre-eminence of the trunk which is elevated to the body's expressive centre by overturning the normal hierarchy of the organs;
2. the independence of the segments, that is, of the different parts of the body, each of which may accomplish autonomous actions even in contrast with the actions of the other parts.

Let's pause for a moment on the principle of the independence of the organs which both Meyerhold and Decroux investigated and enunciated in a very radical way, apparently in opposing terms: 'The entire biomechanics are based on the principle that if you move the tip of your nose, then the whole body moves. The entire body participates in the movement of the smallest organ' (Meyerhold).

One must mobilise only what one wants to mobilise: either one particular organ or several organs. The part which one does not want to mobilise must remain immobile. Everybody knows it, but it is necessary to repeat it. We believe that it is necessary not to want to move in order to remain immobile. In reality, since we move without wanting to do so, it is necessary to want not to move.

(Decroux)

These two formulations are opposite only in appearance since both presume:

1. the same idea of the scenic body as an ensemble of distinct and partially autonomous organs;
2. the necessity of the actor's total control on them and the constraint to a non-natural, non-daily use of these organs (that is, of the entire body) in order to break the automatisms and the mechanical reactions that condition its so-called natural and daily use.

Letting the whole body participate in the smallest movement as well as blocking a body part in order to act only with another, are clear examples of artificial behaviour. This non-natural, non-spontaneous, non-easy behaviour requires to be learnt and presupposes a technique, beginning precisely from a total blocking. In their different ways, both ways of behaving go against the principle of the least effort which regulates the daily conduct.

The first articulation, with its principle of the independence of the organs, is to be found in all fundamental experiences of the twentieth century concerning the actor's and the dancer's corporeal training: from Dalcroze, Laban, Stanislavsky, Meyerhold, and Decroux to Grotowski, Barba, Pina Bausch and many others. In the 1940s, Artaud gave the strongest and most poetic image by defining theatre as 'this crucible of fire and true flesh where anatomically, through the crushing of bones, limbs and syllables, the body is remade'.

Finally, let's not forget that the principle of the independence of the limbs is present in all Asian dance-theatres, as well as in modern dance where it is known by the term 'isolation'.

The second articulation

I call 'second articulation' the segmentation process which is applied to physical behaviour, that is, to sequences of gestures and movements during the actor's work of improvisation and montage.

This process may or may not transpose a concrete action from the daily life, just as it may or may not have an external reference. In the practice of the masters of the twentieth century we can discern a recurring tendency to disassemble the scenic behaviour in its minute articulations (atoms or cells of an action), and then to submit it to a process of reassemblage according to the horizontal axis of succession and more especially to the vertical axis of simultaneity. The procedures of reassemblage may be very different from one artist to another, but their logic is the same for all of them. In spite of appearances, it's never a question of a logic of verisimilitude and of realistic imitation, even in the case of Stanislavsky. It is a rather different logic aiming to preserve the scenic life of the action, that is, what makes the spectator experience it as real. Already in 1910 Meyerhold wrote: 'The essence of scenic rhythm is at the antipodes of the rhythm of reality and daily life'.

The first articulation deals with the breaking of the automatisms in the production of the single movements, gestures or postures. The second articulation deals with the

15–20. The search for a scenic presence, and therefore for an effect of organicity, has accompanied the mutation of the European theatre since the beginning of the twentieth century. One of the most conscious and persistent pioneers is Jacques Copeau (**top left**) and his 'small tradition': Charles Dullin (**above centre**), Antonin Artaud (**above right**), Etienne Decroux (**bottom left**) Marcel Marceau (**bottom centre**) and Jean-Louis Barrault (**bottom right**). In this genealogy of performers, prominent in text-centred theatre, corporeal mime and pantomime, it is possible to detect 'the recurring principles', from the opposition to the precarious balance.

breaking of the automatisms that condition the composition of more movements, gestures and postures, thus greatly limiting the dramaturgy of scenic action.

There is no doubt that Meyerhold and Decroux are the most outstanding examples within this field of research. But it is fair to remember Stanislavky (wrongly considered as the champion of psychological realism) and the importance he gave to the segmentation process. He demanded that both the student and the experienced actor dominate this process in each phase of the training and creative process. This applied in the work on oneself in order to achieve a flowing, uninterrupted 'plastic movement', supported by 'the inner sensation of the movement'; and in the work on the character through the progressive segmentation of each scene and its relative actions with their respective objectives and tasks.

General principles

I would like to stress, with no pretension to be exhaustive, some general principles which seem to regulate the disassembling/re-assembling process of scenic action.

The first principle was established by Stanislavsky in the pages describing the plastic movements that I have mentioned above: the uninterrupted flow of a scenic action constitutes an equivalent and not an imitation of the flow and the continuity of a physical action in real life. This flow can be achieved only through an opposite process, i.e., one of segmentation and discontinuity. The actor has to learn to think a continuum as a succession of well-defined minute phases.

The three main principles concerning the reassemblage/ montage of scenic actions are:

1. The play of contrasts (rhythmic, dynamic, etc.). After being disassembled, the different segments (atoms, cells) of an action are reassembled selectively according to a logic of continuous and sudden variation of speed, intensity, quality of energy, etc.
2. The non-linearity of an action. This principle, in its turn, implies three sub-principles:

a) The absence of a strict logical-causal concatenation: what comes before can be placed later and vice versa.
b) A different repetition: the same action (or part of an action) can be proposed several times from different perspectives. (This is one of the principles of cubist composition, and 'cubist acting' was a comment made on the behaviour of Meyerhold's actors.)
c) Vertical montage: the simultaneity of more actions (another cubist principle). Such a result could be achieved thanks to the preliminary process of the first articulation.
3. The non-predictability of an action: each action should be executed by the actor in such a way that the spectator is unable to foresee in which direction and according to which rhythmic and dynamic modalities the action will develop.

How to compose a scene with actions that the spectator is unable to foresee? For the time being I am able to give the following answers:

– variations should be created through a play of contrasts (principle no.1);
– the action should be segmented and punctuated over and over again through signs (or more exactly through signals) which 'negate' it.

These are micro-actions with opposing characteristics: to move forward before drawing back, to go to the left before moving to the right, to stoop down before getting up, and so on. We should keep in mind the biomechanical *otkaz* and the *toc* in the corporeal mime.

All this work can be taken to a level of refined and complex miniaturisation by blending the principle of opposition (as the non-predictability of an action can be called) with the principle of independence of the organs.

(Marco De Marinis, *In cerca dell'attore: un bilancio del Novecento teatrale*, Rome, Bulzoni, 2000).

21. Shamanistic ritual by the Korean Jindo Sitkim Kut in a demonstration at Odin Teatret (1999). In this regard, it is interesting to note that Grotowski spoke about 'the line of organic actions' in theatre and ritual in his last public appearance at Collège de France in Paris in 1998.

22–23. (**above**) Japanese noh Nobushige Kawamura teaches his son Kotaro a vocal score which is repeated in the performance (**right**). In the Asian classical genres, in contrast to what usually takes place in those of European origin, the building up of scenic presence occurs simultaneously to the assimilation of scores of actions and words belonging to a performance (cf. *Apprenticeship*, *Exercises* and *Training*).

As a person, the dancer has a body of flesh and blood, whose physical weight is controlled by physical forces. He has sensory experiences of what happens inside and outside of his body, and also feelings, wishes, goals. As an artistic instrument, however, the dancer consists – at least for his audience – of nothing but what can be seen of him. His properties and actions are implicitly defined by how he looks and what he does. One hundred and sixty pounds of weight on the scales will not exist if to the eye he has the winged lightness of a dragonfly. His yearnings are limited to what appears in posture and gesture. He has no more and no less of a soul than a painted figure in a picture.
(Rudolph Arnheim, *Art and Visual Perception*)

Totality and its levels of organisation

What did *Etruscan discipline* mean to the Romans?

The Romans understood Etruscan discipline or science as that doctrinaire system which had to do with the interpretation of divine will manifest as signs from Heaven and as singular and wondrous phenomena. It was also related to the rites of expiation that could possibly dispel the unfavourable effects of a negative omen.

Interpretation of natural phenomena also had to include the observation of their physical dynamics, but this did not lead the Etruscans to elaborate a rational science of natural phenomena. Seneca who, in his *Natural Questions*, has passed on to us the greatest amount of information we have on Etruscan discipline, disapproved of this mystic behaviour, since he believed that it went against every type of rationality that had governed science from the time of Aristotle.

'There is this difference', wrote Seneca, 'between we Romans and the Etruscans. We believe that lightning is caused by the collision of the clouds. They believe, however, that the clouds collide in order to create lightning. They give everything a divine justification and this leads them to believe that events do not have a meaning because they have occurred, but that they occur because they must have a meaning.'

1. Empress Maria Theresa of Austria in an eighteenth-century painting by an unknown master (Archbishop's Palace, Prague): even before one notices the sceptre and the crown, the figure's demeanour and the look in the eyes are a clear sign that this is a royal personage. The writer Henry James, searching for a narrative technique in which mystery and ambiguity were predominant, made the following remarks in his notebook about a plot for a story based on the recognition of a royal presence:

> Some painter (Pasolini) in Venice said, after painting the Empress Frederica [Victoria, Empress of Germany, and daughter of Queen Victoria]: "It is only Empresses who know how to sit – to pose. They have the habit of it, and of being looked at, and it is three times as easy to paint them as to paint others." – This gave me the idea for a short story. A woman comes to a painter as a paid model – she is poor, perfect for the purpose and very mysterious. He wonders how she comes to be so good. At last he discovers that she is a deposed princess! – reduced to mystery! as to earning her living.
>
> (Henry James, *Notebooks*)

On the same topic, Stanislavsky said to his actors:

> Without using the text, without a mise-en-scène, knowing only the content of each scene, if you play everything according to the line of physical action, your part will be at least thirty-five per cent ready. First of all, you must establish the logical sequence of your physical actions. No matter what kind of delicacy an artist brings to a painting, if the pose of the model breaks physical laws, if truth is not in the pose, if its representation of a sitting figure, say, is not really sitting, nothing will make it believable. Therefore, the painter, before he can think of embodying the most delicate and complicated psychological states in his painting, must make his model stand or lie down or sit in a way that makes us believe that the model really sits, stands or lies.
>
> The line of physical actions of a rôle has precisely the same significance in the art of the actor. The actor, like the painter, must make the character sit, stand or lie down. But this is more complicated for us in that we present ourselves as both the artist and the model. We must find, not a static pose, but the organic actions of a person in very diverse situations. Until these are found, until the actor justifies the truth by the correctness of his physical behaviour, he cannot think of anything else.
>
> (O. Toporkov, *Stanislavsky in Rehearsal*)

Many spectators believe that the performer's nature depends on his or her expressivity and often also believe that expressivity in turn derives from the performer's intentions. These spectators are like the Etruscans: clouds collide in order to create lightning, performers act in order to express themselves. In reality, above all in the traditions of codified theatre, the opposite occurs: the performers mould their body according to specific tensions and forms, and it is these very tensions and forms that create lightning in the spectator. Hence the paradox of the performer who, unmoved, is able to move the spectator.

216

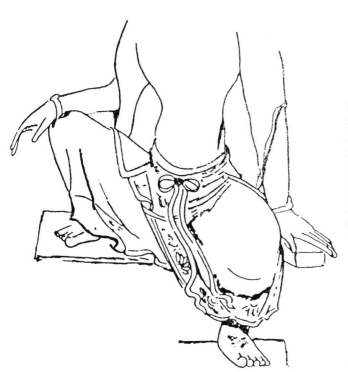

2. (left) Conventional position in Buddhist sculpture called *maharajalilsana*, literally 'the king's comfortable position', characterised by the feet being on two different levels. In Indian art of the classical period, and still today, particularly in theatre and dance, all actions and emotions are represented by means of a vast range of gestures (*mudra* and *hasta*) and codified poses. A conventionalised language, pre-determined gestures and poses, then, as now, understood only by initiates and specialists, was used for a simple reason: to portray the Buddha with a series of well-defined and universally recognisable gestures. These codified gestures made it possible for the devout to recognise immediately, in narrative, sculpted or painted scenes, the most memorable moments of Buddha's life and teachings.

3. (above) Kuan Yin, goddess of mercy, one of the most beloved of Chinese deities, often similar to the figure of the Christian Virgin Mary, is a Buddhist divinity of Indian origin. The particular way in which this version of Kuan Yin (a porcelain from the Qing dynasty, 1644–1911) is sitting reveals not only its Buddhist origins but also its nobility: portraying a seated figure with the feet on two different levels is in fact a convention of Buddhist art used only for superior, royal or divine characters.

4. (above) During a rehearsal of *Good-for-nothing and His Two Brothers*, taken from the story of the same name by Tolstoy, Vakhtangov shows his actors how to play an imp (drawing by B. Zakhava, 1919). Vakhtangov uses the staggered leg position to render the character's energy scenically alive in a way that will immediately catch the spectator's attention. In this phase of the work, Vakhtangov does not work on the character's psychology but on the quality of the actors' actions that create presence. This is the level of organisation which theatre anthropology defines as pre-expressive.

217

What name can be given to this level of the performer's tensions and forms?

When we see an organism alive in its totality, we know from anatomy, biology and physiology that this organism is organised on various levels. Just as there is a cellular level of organisation and a level of organisation of the organs, and of the various systems in the human body (nervous, arterial, etc.), so we must consider that the totality of a performer's performance is also made up of distinct levels of organisation.

Theatre anthropology postulates that there exists a basic level of organisation common to all performers and defines this level as *pre-expressive*.

The concept of pre-expressivity may appear absurd and paradoxical given that it does not take into consideration the performer's intentions, feelings, identification or non-identification with character, emotions . . . that is, psycho-technique. Psycho-technique has in fact dominated professional training and corresponding research into theatre and dance for at least the past two centuries.

Psycho-technique directs the performer towards the will to *express*: but the will to express does not determine what one must do. The performer's expression is in fact due – almost in spite of them – to their actions, to their use of their physical presence. It is the *doing* and *how the doing is done* that determine what one expresses.

According to 'result logic', the spectator sees a performer who is expressing feelings, ideas, thoughts, actions . . . that is, the spectator sees a manifestation of an intention and a meaning. This expression is presented to the spectators in its totality: they are thus led to identify *what* the actors are expressing with *how* they express it.

It is of course possible to analyse the performer's work according to this logic. This does, however, lead to a generalised evaluation which often does not offer an understanding of *how* that work has been done on the technical level.

The understanding of the *how* belongs to a logic which is complementary to 'result logic': 'process logic'. According to 'process logic', it is possible to distinguish between and to work separately on the levels of organisation that constitute the performer's expression.

The level that deals with how to render the actor's energy scenically alive, that is, with how the actor can become a presence that immediately

5. Cambodian dancer, costumed as a prince: example of acculturated technique.

attracts the spectator's attention, is the pre-expressive level and is theatre anthropology's field of study.

This pre-expressive substratum is included in the expression level, in the totality perceived by the spectator. However, by keeping this level separate during the work process, the performer can work on the pre-expressive level, *as if*, in this phase, the principal objective was the energy, the presence, the *bios* of his actions and not their meaning.

The pre-expressive level thought of in this way is therefore an operative level: not a level that can be separated from expression, but a pragmatic category, a praxis, the aim of which, during the process, is to strengthen the performer's scenic *bios*.

Theatre anthropology postulates that the pre-expressive level is at the root of the various performing techniques and that there exists, independently of traditional culture, a transcultural scenic 'physiology'. In fact, pre-expressivity utilises principles for the acquisition of presence and the performer's life. The results of these principles appear more evident in codified genres where the technique that *puts* the body *in form* is codified independently of the result/meaning.

Thus theatre anthropology confronts and compares the techniques of actors and dancers at the transcultural level, and, by means of the study of scenic behaviour, reveals that certain principles governing pre-expressivity are more common and universal than would first have been imagined.

Inculturation and acculturation technique

In order to be more effective in his context, in order to make his historico-biographical identity emerge, the performer uses forms, manners, behaviour, procedures, guile, distortions, appearances ... what we call 'technique'. This is characteristic of every performer and exists in all traditions. Making an analysis that goes beyond cultures (Western, Eastern, Northern, Southern), beyond genres (classical ballet, modern dance, opera, operetta, musical, text theatre, body theatre, classical theatre, contemporary theatre, etc.), going beyond all this, we arrive back at the first day, when the student begins to learn how to become effective relative to the spectator. And we find two points of departure, two paths. On the first path, the performers use their 'spontaneity', elaborating the behaviour which comes to them naturally, which they have absorbed since their birth in the culture and social milieu in which they have grown up. Anthropologists define as inculturation this process of passive sensory-motor absorption of the daily behaviour of a given culture. A child's organic adaptation to the conduct and life norms of his culture, the conditioning to a 'naturalness', permits a gradual and organic transformation which is also growth.

Stanislavsky made the most important methodological contribution to this path of elaborated spontaneity, or 'inculturation technique'. It consists of a mental process which enlivens and dilates the performer's inculturated naturalness. By means of the 'magic if', by means of a mental codification, the performers alter their daily behaviour, change their habitual way of being and materialise the character they are to portray. This is also the objective of Brecht's alienation technique or social gesture. It always refers to a

6–7. (top) Italian actor Ruggero Ruggeri (1871–1953) as Aligi in D'Annunzio's *Iorio's Daughter* (1904): example of inculturated technique; (left) a scene from the Pina Bausch performance *Two Cigarettes in the Dark* (1985). It is interesting to notice how dancers trained in the specific acculturation technique of classical ballet search for ways to free themselves of this technique by turning to models of inculturated technique.

performer who, during the work process, models his or her natural and daily behaviour into extra-daily scenic behaviour with a built-in social fabric or subtexts.

Acting technique which uses variations of inculturation is transcultural. The 'peasant' theatre of Oxolotlan, performed by indigenous people on an isolated mountain in Mexico, uses a technique which is based on inculturation. It is the same technique found in the Living Theatre of Khardaha on the outskirts of Calcutta, where the performers are farmers, workers and students. There are ways of being a performer in Europe and in America, in Asia and in Australia, which are manifest through inculturation techniques.

At the same time, in all cultures, it is possible to observe another path for the performer: the utilisation of specific body techniques that are separate from those used in daily life. Modern and classical ballet dancers, mimes and performers from traditional Asian theatres have denied their 'naturalness' and have adopted another means of scenic behaviour. They have undergone a process of 'acculturation' imposed from the outside, with ways of standing, walking, stopping, looking and sitting that are different from the daily ones.

The technique of acculturation artificialises (or stylises, as is often said), the performer's behaviour. But it also results in another quality of energy. We have all experienced this other quality of energy when watching a classical Indian or Japanese actor, a modern dancer or a mime. Such performers are fascinating to the degree that they have been successful in modifying their 'naturalness', transforming it into lightness, as in classical ballet, or into vigour, as in modern dance. Acculturation technique is the distortion of usual (natural) appearance in order to recreate it sensorially in a fresh and astonishing way.

The 'acculturated' performer manifests a quality and an energetic radiation that is presence ready to be transformed into dance or theatre according to convention or tradition. But the path of inculturation also

8–9. Demonstrations at Salento ISTA, 1987: improvisation by two performers with acculturated technique, Odin Teatret actress Roberta Carreri and Balinese dancer I Made Bandem in foreground; seen in background, Iben Nagel Rasmussen (**top**) and Ni Nyoman Candri (**bottom**) improvising vocally.

leads to rich variations and shades of daily behaviour, to an essential quality of the vocal action of language, to a flux of tensions, to sudden changes of rhythms and intensities that give life to a 'theatre that dances'. Both the inculturation path and the acculturation path activate the pre-expressive level: presence ready to re-present.

It is therefore useless to overemphasise the expressive differences between classical Asian theatres, with their accultured performers, and Western theatre, with its inculturated performers, given that they are analogous on the pre-expressive level.

(Eugenio Barba,
The Third Bank of the River)

220

Physiology and codification

Codification is the visible consequence of specific physiological processes in the performer in the attempt to dilate them and produce an equivalent of the dynamics which are active in life. Codification is formalization. Therefore it was acknowledged with a visual quality, and an aesthetic value was attributed to it.

Codification aims at a *dilated body* by means of a double path: by a dilation in space which amplifies the dynamics of the movements, or by a set of oppositions which the performer generates within his/her body, thus activating its muscular tonus. In the first case, the extension of the performer's actions in space, according to patterns which do not follow the daily ones, challenges the body's automatisms. In the second case, the performer holds back his/her own action, not allowing it to happen. This results in increased tensions and in an inner process necessary to sustain them, thus producing a particular quality of energy which is perceptible even in situations of immobility. In both cases, codification requires an extra-daily body technique.

10–14. (**top** and **centre left**) Chinese dancers: painted terracotta (Northern dynasty, AD 386–581) (Taipei Museum); (**top right**) Etruscan dancer, fragment of fifth-century BC bronze candelabrum (Karlsruhe Museum); (**centre right**) Etruscan dancer: early fifth-century BC bronze candelabrum base (British Museum, London); (**bottom**) the dilated body: Visvarupadarshanam, one of the many manifestations of Krishna (painting from Rajasthan, India, early nineteenth century).

Codification in the East and the West

The search for a codification that could give the performer a pre-expressive body has been carried out everywhere. In the West, however, because of the traditional categorisation of performers as exclusively either actors, dancers, mimes or singers, this search has led to only a few rare and sporadic results (with the exception, as already noted, of forms such as classical ballet or mime). In Asian theatres, because of the continuity of a living tradition represented by the master, codification has been transmitted without interruption, based on the process of imitation that is typical of all forms of direct theatrical pedagogy.

The respective histories of the various theatre cultures aside, however, one often finds surprising analogies, particularly with respect to the rules of conduct that define the basic attitudes of a performer on stage. For example, we know that all actors from the Paris Conservatory at the end of the nineteenth century obeyed certain fundamental rules: the hands had always to be kept above the waist; when pointing, the hand had to be kept above the level of the eyes. Kathakali actors and Balinese actor-dancers use the same principles: the hands, and therefore the arms, must never hang at the sides of the body, but must always be held above the waist, and the gesture of showing, like many others, must be carried out above the level of the eyes so as to be large and visible.

In the West, discontinuity in the tradition, the search for realism or, better, naturalism, and psychological rather than physical bases for action have gradually destroyed a heritage of rules fixing performer behaviour. Such rules certainly existed in European theatre at the height of the commedia dell'arte but the heritage has been lost because direct theatrical pedagogy, both in the West and the East, is never written down. Certain attempts have been made in European theatre to fix body movements into a particular form, to find laws for movement separate from all expressive motivation, just as rules for body proportion have been fixed in the figurative arts (ill.19–26). But since the originators of these essays lacked an a-priori codification or more or less objective classification criteria, they were often tempted to explain or rationalise, that is, 'scientificate' their

15–18. (**top row** and **second row**) Engravings from Johan Jacob Engel's *Ideen zu einer Mimik* (*Ideas on One's Mimicry*, Berlin, 1785–6) and drawings from Antonio Morrocchesi's *Lezioni di declamazione e d'arte teatrale* (*Lessons on Performing and Theatrical Art*, Florence, 1832). These two works are representative of two trends that dominated nineteenth-century theatrical culture. On one hand, codification of the actor by means of states of mind, proposed by Engel (1741–1838), a playwright and director who became a theorist and a proponent of Lessing's aesthetics; on the other hand, the personal research conducted by Italian actor Morrocchesi (1768–1838), which tended to imbue his art with a scientific value. (**third row**) Repose in Engel's work and in Henry Siddons' *Practical Illustrations of Rhetorical Gesture and Action* (London, 1807). Henry Siddons (1774–1815), the eldest son of famous English actress Sarah Siddons and himself an actor, translated part of Engel's treatise into English, adapting it and redrawing the illustrations according to English style and taste; (**bottom**) Geometric laws for the theatrical transformation of the human body (1925), according to Oscar Schlemmer (1888–1943), one of the main exponents of Bauhaus movement.

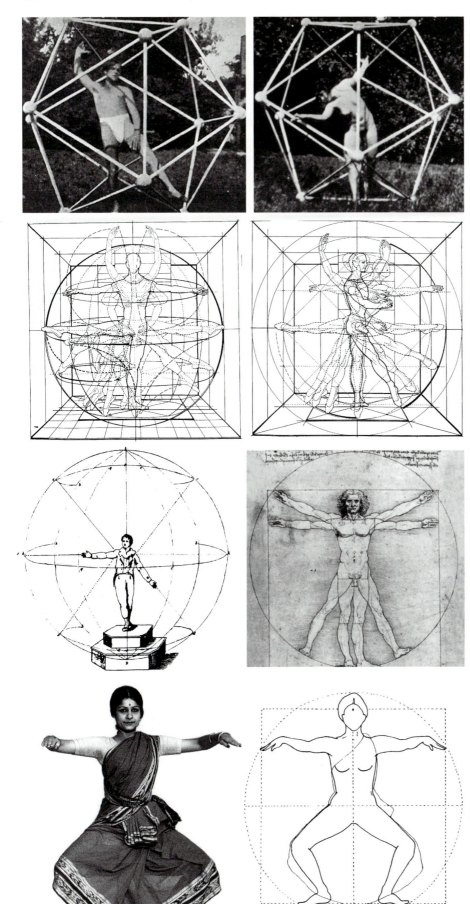

work in a totalitarian and obsessive way. One can also easily understand why these attempts, even though based on the physical body, had a tendency to connect the performer's expressivity with psychic criteria, since they were often made by men who had little contact with theatrical practice.

The tendency to connect expressivity with psychic criteria is one of the reasons why, in Western culture, the paradox of the performer who is able to elicit emotion without necessarily feeling the emotion himself is still misunderstood. At the same time, this misunderstanding has often been very fertile, precisely because of the inclination in European theatre to investigate the performer's emotions.

The proximity of the engraving from *Chironomia* (1806) by G. Austin (ill.23) and the diagram of the basic odissi dance position (ill.25–26) is not intended to establish a parallel between the two. Rather, we wish to draw attention to the need that has long existed in European theatre to find and fix all the performer's possibilities, to discover the aspects of scenic presence, of *bios*, on stage.

Looking at these two diagrams in the light of what has been said above, one has the impression that these two bodies are not yet expressing any feeling, any reaction; but at the same time, one perceives that they are ready, able to act, *on the lookout*. This is *scenic bios, pre-expressivity*, that is, a life ready to be transformed into precise motivations, actions and reactions.

19–26. (**top**) Rudolf von Laban's icosahedron (a solid figure with twenty equal faces), used to measure a dancer's actions in space (1920). The method of dance notation invented by Laban (1879–1938) is the only attempt made to date to transcribe codified movement graphically (cf. ill.38, p.226); (**second row**) spatial graphic diagrams by dance historian and theorist Lincoln Kirstein (1952) of two classical ballet movements executed by Carlus Dyer; (**third row left**) Spatial analysis of a gesture, in Gilbert Austin's *Chironomia* (London, 1806); (**third row right**) diagram of the proportions of the human body in a drawing by Leonardo da Vinci (1452–1519), (Louvre Museum, Paris); (**bottom row**) spatial analysis of the *asana*, a basic odissi dance position.

27–29. The dilated body: (**above left**) Tom Leabhart (Decroux's mime tradition, USA) and I Made Djimat (Bali) at Umeå ISTA, 1995; (**above right**) Augusto Omolú (dance of the *orixás*, Brazil); (**below**) Akira Matsui (Japanese noh) with participants at Seville ISTA, 2004.

30–32. The dilated body: (**above left**) Harlequin in a print by Italian painter Giuseppe Maria Mitelli (1634–1718); (**above right**) the fictive body: actor Motomasa Kanze in the noh play, *Hagoromo*; (**below**) Sanjukta Panigrahi and Augusto Omolú, Holstebro ISTA, 1994.

The fictive body

Western theatre, or, at least, modern Western theatre, is based on the identification of the individual daily body with the character's fictive body; it is thought, or, at least, it was thought, that these were the only levels that existed. In most traditional Japanese theatre forms, on the contrary, one can easily perceive an intermediate level, a level between the performer's daily body and what we could call the character's imaginary body. Let us consider a simple example. When a noh actor leaves the stage because to all extents and purposes the performance is over, he has a singular habit: he moves very slowly, as if his exit was an integral part of the performance. He is no longer in character, because the character's action is finished, but neither is he in his daily reality. He is in an intermediate state. In a certain way, he is performing his own absence. But this absence is performance and is therefore a present absence. Expressed in these terms, this technique would seem to be a paradox, but when practised it is very clear. The same thing occurs in kabuki: the actor must not fade away, he must show himself and keep himself in a fictive state. [. . .]

Rather arbitrarily, because I have not yet found a more fitting definition, I have called this phenomenon the fictive body: not a dramatic fiction but a body that commits itself to a certain 'fictive' zone which does not perform a fiction but which simulates a kind of transformation of the daily body at the pre-expressive level.'

(Moriaki Watanabe, *Between Orient and Occident*)

33. (**above left**) Scene from a performance by the Nyt Dansk Danseteater of Copenhagen. Classical dance, known as ballet, regulated by principles and techniques based on pre-determined movements and steps, is the only codified performance form in the West. While the first movements and first rules emerged from the work of Italian theorists in the fifteenth century – Domenico da Piacenza, Antonio Cornazano, Guglielmo Ebreo – the codification of classical dance was laid down by the Académie Royale de la Danse, founded in Paris in 1661, which also designed the terminology which is still in use in dance schools and academies. It is necessary to note, however (cf. *Nostalgia*) that when modern Western theatre began, between the end of the sixteenth and the beginning of the seventeenth centuries, the dancer's art was not separated from the actor's art, as is manifested by many examples: a prime example is that of Molière, playwright and actor but also author of and performer in many very well-known ballet-comedies, produced in collaboration with composer Giovan Battista Lulli.

34. (**above right**) Scene from a wayang wong (literally, 'a play with human beings) performance. Javanese dance-theatre began in the court of the sultan of Yogjakarta in the second half of the eigthteenth century and recounts the deeds of the heroes of the *Mahabharata*, the *Ramayana* and the *Panji* cycle. Although the wayang wong is a relatively new form, its performers move and dance according to an ancient codified system inspired, it is said, by the movements of the puppets and figures in the wayang kulit shadow theatre.

35–38. Four different dance notation systems: (**top far left**) first page of *L'Art et l'instruction de bien danser* (*The Art and Teaching of Dancing Well*), a small manual which is probably the first Western book on dance, printed in Paris by Michel Toulouze in the late fifteenth century: below the musical pentagram appears the title of the composition, the rhythm, and certain letters of the alphabet, which indicate the steps to be danced; (**top left**) *The Gavotte* by Vestris, according to the Theleur system (1831), one of the first systems to make use of abstract symbols; (**bottom far left**) choreographic notation of a musical score: the beginning of Debussy's *Après-midi d'un Faune*, drawn by Nijinsky (1912); (**bottom left**) Rudolf von Laban's system (Labanotation): diagram of the movements of the hands and the scarf in *bapang*, a movement used in Javanese wayang wong for strong, violent and proud male characters. With Laban's notation, which translates all the dancer's movements into abstract symbols, without however taking the music into consideration, it is possible, as in this case, to transcribe any codified movement whatsover, irrespective of the tradition to which it belongs.

39. (**left**) Thai khon dancer in a basic position inspired by martial arts.
40. (**right**) Dario Fo in a demonstration at the Volterra ISTA, 1981.

41. Various positions in the baris, the warrior-inspired Balinese dance. Drawings by Mexican painter Miguel Covarrubias, who spent considerable time in Bali in the 1930s.

Martial arts and theatricality in the East

Extra-daily body technique is found not only in performance situations but also in other situations in which non-daily behaviour is used.

Widely known and practised throughout Asia, martial arts use concrete physiological processes to destroy the automatisms of daily life and to create another quality of energy in the body. Martial arts are based on acculturation technique, that is, on a form of behaviour that does not respect the 'spontaneity' of daily life. It is this very aspect of martial arts, that is, their use of acculturation technique, which has inspired codified theatre forms.

The legs slightly bent, the arms contracted: the basic position of all Asiatic martial arts shows a *decided body* ready to leap and to act. This attitude, which could be compared to the *plié* in classical ballet, can be found in the basic positions of both Eastern and Western performers. It is nothing more than a codification, in the form of extra-daily technique, of the position of an animal ready to attack or to defend itself. When Japanese sculptor Wakafuji (responsible for many of the illustrations in this book) saw one of Dario Fo's mimed poses (ill.40), he remarked that the pose was very similar to the beginning of a karate move called *neko hashi daci*, 'to stand on cat's feet'. The drawing shows the Italian actor in a moment from his performance, *The Story of a Tiger*.

Studies have been made of the relationship between martial arts and personality and it has been found that the learning of a martial art by means of the repetition of physical actions leads the student to another awareness of themselves and to another use of their bodies. One objective of martial arts is to learn to be present at the very moment of an action. This type of presence is extremely important for performers who wish to be able to recreate, every night, that quality of energy which makes them alive in the spectator's eyes. It is perhaps this common objective, in spite of different results, that explains the influence that martial arts have had on most Asian theatre forms.

Because of historical contingencies, martial arts have generally lost their military value. To a large extent, this heritage has been transformed: some martial arts have turned into dances, and martial-art exercises have become the basis of various dances and other theatrical forms.

In Bali, one finds the baris dance (ill.41). Etymologically, baris means 'line, file, military formation' and was the name of an army of volunteers used by local princes in times of unrest. It has given rise to seven different dances which, little by little, have lost their military character and have become what are today known as the baris which is danced by both boys and girls. Pentjak-silat, the Indonesian national art of self-defence (called bersilat in Malaysia) is based on tiger movements and gave birth to the pentjak dance.

What is the Chinese doctor Hua To (ill.46, opposite page) doing? His different positions, which seem be a kind of dance, in fact illustrate a series of exercises based on five animals: stag, bird, tiger, monkey, bear. Today, these movements are the basis of a number of exercises in many schools of Chinese combat (ill.44, top right, opposite page). It is interesting to note that one finds the same movements in kathakali, in the south of India.

Kathakali has also been influenced by a martial art: *kalaripayattu*, 'the place where one trains' from the Sanskrit *khalorica*, the word for a field where military exercises are done (ill.42). Kathakali has taken from *kalaripayattu* (practised in the same state, Kerala) not only training exercises and massage, but also the very terminology used to describe certain poses: lion, elephant, horse, fish. In Manipur State, in the north of India, other martial arts such as takhousarol and mukna (a form of self-defence which is today a popular village sport) have influenced the traditional dances of the region, whose style is between that of Mongol dances and the classical Indian dances described in the treatise *Natyashastra*.

If, finally, one considers traditional theatre in China and Japan, such as Peking Opera and kabuki, one again becomes aware of the strong bond between martial arts and performance in Asia: duels, fights, even battles between armed troops are not only the basis of performer training, but are also performance elements blended with the original forms and presented with the most elevated and refined extra-daily body technique.

42–43. (**top**) Stick combat between two performers of kalaripayattu, the martial art of Kerala (India). The skill of the fighter on the right makes it possible for him to maintain a very stable position and yet be fully ready to throw himself into the fight; (**bottom**) Katsuko Azuma and Kanho Azuma during the ISTA session at Hostelbro in 1986 in a scene of nihon buyo requiring the use of traditional weapons, the sword (*katana*) and the halberd (*naginata*).

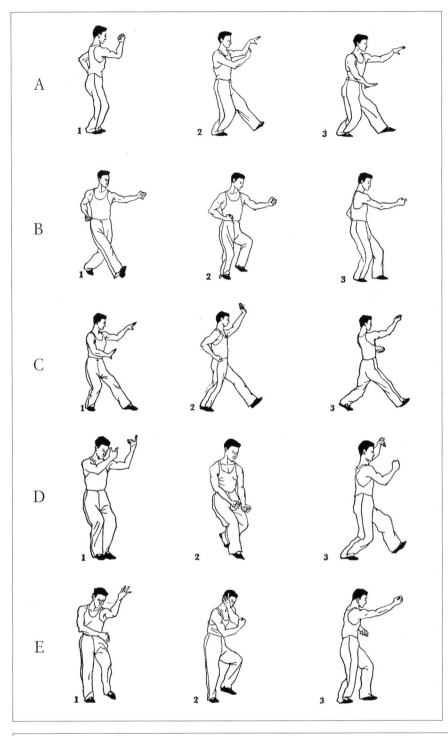

44–46. (**above right**) Scenic presence: demonstration of a basic bull-fighting posture at Seville ISTA, 2004. Garcia Lorca wrote: 'The toreador who scares the audience in the arena remains stuck in the ridiculous dimension which befalls everybody who risks his life. But the toreador who is bitten by the *duende*, gives a lesson of pythagoric music and lets the audience forget that he is constantly throwing his heart against the bull's horns'; (**left**) The five basic techniques of hsin-i, a particular form of Chinese gymnastics known as t'ai chi (literally, the summit of boxing): A. *P'i ch'uan* (dividing), elevation and descent, like when one chops with an axe; B. *Peng ch'uan* (compressing), simultaneous expansion and contraction; C. *Ts'uan ch'uan* (sowing), flowing curved currents; D. *P'ao ch'uan* (walking, slowing), sudden flames like gunshots; E. *Heng ch'uan* (crossing), blows struck forwards with a circular energy pattern. These blows are usually practised first with the left arm only and then with the right arm only; later, the arm actions are co-ordinated; (**bottom**) Chinese doctor and surgeon Hua To, who lived during the last Han dynasty (25 BC–220 AD), in a series of positions based on the combat strategy of five animals: from left to right, a stag, a bird, a tiger, a monkey and a bear. These positions are still in use in China today, as starting points for the various martial arts.

Martial arts and theatricality in the West

The relationship between theatricality and the arts linked to fight techniques has also been documented in Western culture since antiquity, especially with respect to the rôle these arts have played in the development of dance.

In ancient Greece, battle commanders were called 'principal dancers'; Socrates maintained that 'the man who dances best is the best soldier'. The *pyrrhic*, a Greek dance of Cretan origin, represented, according to Plato's description, the various phases of a battle. In Greece it was first danced in Sparta, by a single dancer, then later in Athens, where it became a group dance in which two rows of dancers 'confronted' each other. One of the most famous performances of the *pyrrhic* dance took place when *choreutes* (dancers) mimed protecting baby Zeus from the attacks of Chronos-Saturn.

In ancient Rome, during the annual festival in honour of Mars, the god of war, armed priests of the Sali caste made a procession through the streets. On a command from their leader, the *praesul*, they began a dance which consisted of three steps and a series of wave-like movements, during which they beat on their shields with their lances.

According to scholars of popular traditions, certain markedly mimetic medieval European dances also derived from armed and soldier dances. In certain cases these dances were also the basis of actual theatrical performances. In Italy, for example, *la danza della spada* (sword dance), very commonly found in both the north and the south, reproduced the armed conflict between Christians and Turks and was often transformed into popular performances in which the dancers also spoke dialogue.

First performed in the sixteenth century, the Italian *danza della spada* was based on the moresca, a medieval dance found throughout Europe (as the *morisca* in Spain, the *mauresque* in France, the morris dance in England, the *mohrentanz* in Germany), itself originally a representation of the conflict between Christians and Moors (Saracens) and a symbol of the conflict between civilisation and barbarity.

In the sixteenth century, the moresca developed away from its warlike origins

47–49. (**top**) Western etching from the nineteenth century showing the training in different martial arts taking place in a typical Japanese open-air training space called a *do-jo* ('*do*' means 'way', '*jo*' means 'place'; literally: 'the place where one studies the way'); (**centre** and **bottom**) training duel and performance duel in kabuki theatre, in two nineteenth-century Japanese engravings. Notice how the performance duel is more dramatic by the use of different weapons: a fragile paper umbrella against a steel sword. The reciprocal tension in the actors' bodies nevertheless remains identical.

50. Greek *pyrrhic* (war) dance on a cup by the painter known as Poseidon.

and became a court dance, although it did not lose its folk-dance character. In some cases the highly mimetic actions of the moresca were combined with dialogue between the dancers, resulting in actual dramatic performances; in other cases, it was danced in the interval between performances of comedies and tragedies.

The *danza della spada* in Italy, the *bal du sabre* in southern France, the moresca throughout all of Europe, all of these dances show that in the West as well as in the East there existed a close link between techniques of attack and defence and the origins of the actor's extra-daily art.

51. 'Fencing dance', performed only on the feast day of San Rocco in Torrepaduli (Lecce, Italia). This form of danced duel, which is extremely old, is found throughout southern Europe and is performed with precisely codified, fixed gestures: usually it is a duel with weapons (often knives). Here, the knife has been replaced with a hand, held with the palm straight.

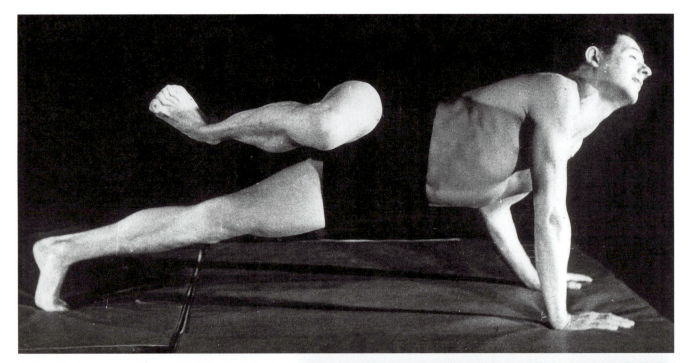

52–55. (**top**) Exercise called *danda* (in Sanskrit, *danda* means 'arm') or stretching as a cat, practised in Indian and Pakistani martial arts to develop the strength of the arms and the upper part of the body; (**centre**) in the early 1960s, Jerzy Grotowski's Polish Teatr Laboratorium (then called the Theatre of the Thirteen Rows and located in Opole), developed a series of exercises. In the photo, actor Antoni Jaholkowski doing the exercise called 'the cat', which was invented at the Teatr Laboratorium; (**bottom left**) duel with sticks which obliges the actor to react by jumping quickly: a training exercise developed by Odin Teatret actors, inspired by Peking Opera acrobatic exercises. Seen here are actors Torgeir Wethal and Iben Nagel Rasmussen, in 1966, just after the group had been founded; (**bottom right**) Augusto Omolú and Jairo da Purificaçao at Copenhagen ISTA, 1996, demonstrating capoera, a fighting dance of the African slaves in Brazil which has today become an artistic form.

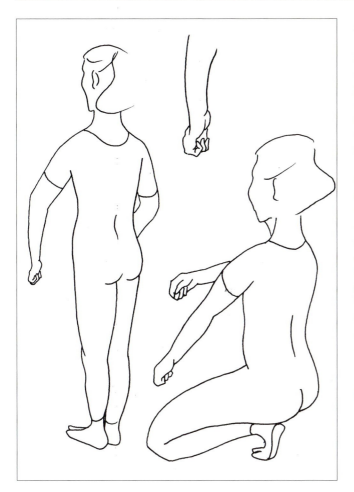

Body architecture

Kamae (ill.56–58), the basic body position in all forms of traditional Japanese theatre literally means 'attitude', 'body position' and thus the body's basic architecture. The ideograms with which the word is composed in Japanese are in fact used in other contexts to indicate 'structure', 'construction'. The term is also used to indicate the correct basic posture in Japanese martial arts.

In the theatrical terminology of Asian cultures, there are numerous terms that are connected to other art forms: painting, sculpture, architecture. One such example is the Indian word *sutradhara*, literally, 'holder of string', which is the word used for the head of a theatre company. First and foremost, the word means 'architect' (the one who has the string or tape used for measuring), and a theatre manager is in fact both architect and director, who 'holds the threads' of the play, like the puppeteer (who is also called a *sutradhara*) holds his puppet strings. *Sutra* ('string' or 'cord') also means the mnemonic text which serves as a conductor in science; the director of a theatre company is also a 'door string' in so far as it is he who holds the *sutra* of the dramatic art.

Investigating these various meanings, Gordon Craig, a great admirer of Indian theatre, succeeded in capturing an image of the director as the architect of both a performance and a super-marionette actor.

56–58. (**top**) Two variations (standing and kneeling) of the basic position for Japanese actors, called *kamae*, illustrated by buyo dancer Katsuko Azuma at Bonn ISTA, 1980 (**bottom left** and **right**). In the drawing (**top**), the details of the arms and hands clearly show the tension in the arms and the work done by the spinal column to maintain the position.

The spectator's pre-interpretation

The performer's pre-expressive state can correspond to a particular state of the spectator's way of seeing which, like a kind of immediate reaction, precedes all cultural and personal interpretation. This state could be defined as *pre-interpretation*. In the performer, pre-expressivity precedes the desire to express; similarly, in the spectator, one finds a 'physiological response' which is independent of culture, feelings or particular state of mind at the moment of seeing. While research on the performer's physiology is still young, considerable study has been made of the nature of seeing. Even if this research has not yet led to definitive theories, it has nevertheless made possible the proposition of certain interesting hypotheses applicable to the special way of seeing, characteristic of the theatre spectator.

To begin with, one must first consider the question of visual perception, that is, the interaction between biological and psychological phenomena which is produced between the eye and the brain. Studies of visual perception are today sufficiently advanced to make possible a considerable modification of former theories concerning the functioning of vision and the general processes that govern the brain. They have also led to contradictory and non-definitive hypotheses and deal for the most part with the way of seeing immobile forms, even if these forms are animated by a certain dynamic. The theatre spectator who reacts to the perception of forms in movement is a much more special and complex phenomenon.

Those studies whose results can be best applied to the theatre spectator are those concerning the way of looking at works of figurative art. *Art and Visual Perception* by Rudolf Arnheim is such a study. Professor of Art Psychology at Harvard University, Arnheim bases his hypotheses concerning the spectator of a work of art on the psychological principles of *gestalt* (which could be translated as pattern). He analyses art (painting, sculpture and architecture, as well as movement forms such as dance and film) on the basis of a series of principles, such as balance, form, development, space, dynamics. These principles, or better, these rules, are historically repeated in various latitudes and determine the *creation* of the work of art, but they also organise the way the work of art itself is seen.

There are surprising affinities between Arnheim's work and the criteria of our examination of pre-expressivity. We refer throughout this book to concepts such as balance and dynamics, or the opposition of forms. Aware of the similarities and differences between various phenomenologies of 'art', we quote here Arnheim's comments on that particular spectator reaction which precedes interpretation: that state of seeing which Arnheim defines as *inductive perception* and which precedes *logical inference*.

Visual experience is dynamic. What a person or animal perceives is not only an arrangement of objects, of colours and shapes, of movements and sizes. It is, perhaps first of all, an interplay of directed tensions. These tensions are not something the observer adds, for reasons of his own, to static images. Rather, these tensions are as inherent in any percept as size, shape, location, or colour. Because they have magnitude and direction, these tensions can be described as psychological 'forces'.

There are, then, more things in the field of vision than those that strike the retina of the eye. Examples of 'induced structure' abound. An incompletely drawn circle looks like a complete circle with a gap. In a picture done in central perspective the vanishing point may be established by the convergent lines even though no actual point of meeting can be seen. In a melody one may 'hear' by induction the regular beat from which a syncopated tone deviates, as our disk deviates from the centre.

Such perceptual inductions differ from logical inferences. Inferences are thought operations that add something to the given visual facts by interpreting them. Perceptual inductions are sometimes interpolations based on previously acquired knowledge. More typically, however, they are completions deriving spontaneously during perception from the given configuration of the pattern.

(Rudolf Arnheim, *Art and Visual Perception*)

59–60. Actress and singer Sonja Kehler in her performance of Brechtian texts and songs at Holstebro ISTA, 1986. Stage presence here is not the result of the interpretation of a character but of the use of inculturation technique which transforms daily positions and physical attitudes into a 'theatre which dances'.

We publish here an extract of the essay of the same title in which Richard Schechner compares the restoration of behaviour in various parts of the world: from traditional theatrical forms to ritual to historical situations such as the reconstruction of ancient villages. It is interesting to note that what Schechner calls the restoration of behaviour (with 'restoration' understood as both restitution and reconstruction) depends on a series of laws that are necessarily based on pre-expressivity. The definitive version appeared in Between Theater and Anthropology, (University of Pennsylvania, 1984).

Restoration of behaviour

Richard Schechner

Restored behaviour is living behaviour treated as a film director treats a strip of film. These strips of behaviour can be rearranged or reconstructed; they are independent of the causal systems (social, psychological, technological) that brought them into existence. They have a life of their own. The original 'truth' or 'source' of the behaviour may be lost, ignored or contradicted – even while this truth or source is apparently being honoured and observed. How the strip of behaviour was made, found or developed may be unknown or concealed, elaborated, distorted by myth and tradition. Originating as a process, used in the process of rehearsal to make a new process, a performance, the strips of behaviour are not themselves process but things, items, 'material'. Restored behaviour can be of long duration as in some dramas and rituals or of short duration as in some gestures, dances and mantras.

Restored behaviour is used in all kinds of performances from shamanism and exorcism to trance, from ritual to aesthetic dance and theatre, from initiation rites to social dramas, from psychoanalysis to psychodrama and transactional analysis. In fact, restored behaviour is the main characteristic of performance. The practitioners of all these arts, rites and healings assume that some behaviours – organised sequences of events, scripted actions, known texts, scored movements – exist separate from the performers who 'do' these behaviours. Because the behaviour is separate from those who are behaving, the behaviour can be stored, transmitted, manipulated, transformed. The performers get in touch with, recover, remember or even invent these strips of behaviour and then re-behave according to these strips, either by being absorbed into them (playing the rôle, going into trance) or by existing side by side with them (Brecht's *Verfremdungseffekt*). The work of restoration is carried on in rehearsals and/or in the transmission of behaviour from master to novice. Understanding what happens during training, rehearsals and workshops – investigating the subjunctive mood that is the medium of these operations – is the surest way to link aesthetic and ritual performance.

Restored behaviour is 'out there', distant from 'me'. It is separate and therefore can be 'worked on', changed, even though it has 'already happened'. Restored behaviour includes a vast range of actions. It can be 'me' at another time/psychological state as in the psychoanalytic abreaction; or it can exist in a non-ordinary sphere of socio-cultural reality as does the Passion of Christ or the re-enactment in Bali of the struggle between Rangda and Barong; or it can be marked off by aesthetic convention as in drama and dance; or it can be the special kind of behaviour 'expected' of someone participating in a traditional ritual – the bravery, for example of a Gahuku boy in Papua New Guinea during his initiation, shedding no tears when jagged leaves slice the inside of his nostrils; or the shyness of an American 'blushing bride' at her wedding, even though she and her groom have lived together for two years.

Restored behaviour is symbolic and reflexive, not empty but loaded behaviour multivocally broadcasting significances. These difficult terms express a single principle: the self can act in/as another; the social or trans-individual self is a rôle or set of rôles. Symbolic and reflexive behaviour is the hardening into theatre of social, religious, aesthetic, medical and educational process. Performance means: never for the first time. It means: for the second to the *n*th time. Performance is 'twice-behaved behaviour'.

1. Basic position in the Indian dance form known as bharatanatyam.

2. Indian dancer Rukmini Devi, founder of contemporary bharatanatyam.

Neither painting, sculpting, nor writing shows actual behaviour as it is being behaved. But, thousands of years before movies, rituals were made from strips of restored behaviour: action and stasis co-existed in the same event. What comfort flowed from ritual performances. People, ancestors and gods participated in simultaneously having been, being and becoming. These strips of behaviour were replayed many times. Mnemonic devices ensured that the performances were 'right' – transmitted across many generations with few accidental variations. Even now, the terror of the first night is not the presence of the public but knowing that mistakes are no longer forgiven.

This constancy of transmission is all the more astonishing because restored behaviour involves choices. Animals repeat themselves, and so do the cycles of the moon. But an actor can say 'no' to any action. This question of choice is not easy. Some ethologists and brain specialists argue that there is no significant difference – no difference of any kind – between animal and human behaviour. But at least there is an 'illusion of choice', a feeling that one has a choice. And this is enough. Even the shaman who is called, the trancer falling into trance, and the wholly trained performer whose performance text is second nature, give over or resist, and there is suspicion of the ones who too easily say 'yes' or prematurely say 'no'. There is a continuum from the not-much-choice of ritual to the lots-of-choice of aesthetic theatre. It is the function of rehearsals in aesthetic theatre to narrow the choices or at least to make clear the rules of improvisation. Rehearsals function to build a score, and this score is a 'ritual by contract': fixed behaviour that everyone participating agrees to do.

Restored behaviour can be put on the way a mask or costume is. Its shape can be seen from the outside, and changed. That's what theatre directors, councils of bishops, master performers and great shamans do: change performance scores. A score can change because it is not a 'natural event' but a model of individual and collective human choice. A score exists, as Victor Turner says, in the subjunctive mood, in what Stanislavsky called the 'as if'. Existing as 'second nature', restored behaviour is always subject to revision. This 'secondness' combines negativity and subjunctivity.

[. . .] Restorations need not be exploitations. Sometimes they are arranged with such care that after a while the restored behaviour heals into its presumptive past and its present cultural context like well-grafted skin. In these cases a 'tradition' is rapidly established and judgements about authenticity are hard to make. Let me give examples from India and Bali.

Bharatanatyam

Indian scholars trace bharatanatyam, the classical Indian dance, back not only to the ancient text on theatre, *Natyashastra* (c. second century BC–second century AD) which describes dance poses, but also to centuries-old temple sculptings that show these poses. The best-known of these sculptings is the group at the fourteenth-century temple of Nararaja (Shiva, the King of Dancers) at Cidambaram, south of Madras. Most writings assume a continuous tradition connecting *Natyashastra*, temple sculptings and today's dancing. According to Kapila Vatsyayan, India's leading dance theorist and historian:

Bharatanayam is perhaps the oldest among the contemporary classical dance forms of India ... Whether the dancer was the devadasi of the temple or the court-dancer of the Maratha kings of Tanjore, her technique followed strictly the patterns which had been used for ages.[1]

Whenever the contemporary forms of bharatanatyam, manipuri and odissi evolved, two things are clear:

first, that they were broadly following the tradition of the *Natyashastra* and were practising similar principles of technique from their inception, and, second, that the stylisation of movement began as far back as the eighth and ninth century ... Some contemporary styles preserve the characteristic features of this tradition more rigorously than others: bharatanatyam uses the basic *adhamandli* (postures) most rigorously.[2]

Vatsyayan's opinion is shared by virtually all Indian dance scholars. But in fact it's not known when the 'classical' bharatanatyam died out, or even if it ever existed. The old texts and sculptings surely show that there was some kind of dance, but nothing was remembered of this dance, not even its name, when moves were made in the first decades of the twentieth century to 'preserve', 'purify' and 'revive' it.

There was a temple dance called sadir nac danced by women of families hereditarily attached to certain temples. According to Milton Singer:

The dancing girls, their teachers, and musicians performed not only on the occasion of temple festivals and ceremonies, but also for private parties, particularly weddings, and at palace parties. Special troupes of dancing girls and musicians were sometimes permanently attached to the courts.[3]

3. Mrinalini Sarabhai, bharatanatyam dancer and Director of the Darpana Academy in Ahmedabad (India).

Many girls attached to temples were prostitutes. As dance scholar Mohan Khokar says [. . .]

the time-honoured tradition of the *devadasis*, or temple dancing girls, had fallen into such ignominy that the girls, considered sacred, continued to be considered sacred but in a different way – as prostitutes. And with this the dance that they professed – the avowedly divine bharatanatyam – too promptly got lost to shame.[4]

From 1912 on a strong campaign was waged by Indian and British reformers to ban the *devadasi* system. But a counter-movement, led by E. Krishna Iyer, wanted to 'eradicate the vice but have the art'. Opinions raged in the Madras press, especially during 1932 as Dr Muthulakshmi Reddi, the first woman legislator in British India, led the attack on the *devadasi* system while Iyer and 'lawyers, writers, artists, and even the *devadasis* themselves joined the fray'.

The upshot of the brouhaha was that Krishna Iyer and his confrères emerged triumphant. The anti-*nautch* (*devadasi*) movement, which is how Dr Reddi's crusade came to be called, was left in the lurch. The dance must survive, even if the *dasis* don't, boomed the slogan of the day.[5]

That's exactly what happened – in a way. At the January 1933 Conference of the Music Academy of Madras, Iyer, for the second time (the first was in 1931, but this earlier show stirred scant interest), presented *devadasi* dancing not as a temple art or as an advertisement for or adjunct to prostitution but as secular art.

The *dasis* . . . took the fullest advantage of the sudden, buoyant interest in their art: a number of them – Balasaraswait, Swarnasaraswati, Gauri, Muthuratnambal, Bhanumathi, Varalkasmi and Pattu, to name a few – readily quit the house of God for the footlights and in no time became public idols.[6]

Scholar and critic V. Raghavan coined the word 'bharatanatyam' to replace terms associated with temple prostitution. 'Bharatanatyam' stands for the basic elements of this old/new dance *bha = bhara* or feelings; *ra = rasa*, or the aesthetic flavour; *ta = tala*, or rhythm; *natyam* means dance.

Long before 1947 when Madras State finally outlawed the *devadasi* system, the dance moved out of the temples. People who were not *devadasi* families, even men, danced. Rukmini Devi, 'a singularly high-placed Brahmin and wife of the International President of the Theosophical Society . . . realised how great and lofty an art bharatanatyam was and how pressing the need was to rescue it from corrupt influences'. Not only did Devi dance, she and her associates codified bharatanatyam.

[. . .] Devi and her colleagues wanted to use sadir nac but be rid of its bad reputation. They cleaned up the *devadasi* dance, brought in gestures based on the *Natyashastra* and temple art, developed standard teaching methods. They claimed that bharatanatyam was very old. And, of course, a conformity to ancient texts and art could be demonstrated: every move in bharatanatyam was measured against the sources of which it presumed to be a living vestige. The differences between sadir nac and the old sources were attributed to degeneracy. The new dance, now legitimised by its heritage, not only absorbed sadir nac but attracted the daughters of the most respectable families to practise it. Today, many study bharatanatyam as a kind of finishing school. It is danced all over India by both amateurs and professionals. It is a major export item.

The 'history' and 'tradition' of bharatanatyam – its roots in the ancient texts and art – are actually a restoration of behaviour, a construction based on the research of Raghavan, Devi and others. They saw in sadir nac not a dance in its own right but a faded, distorted remnant of some ancient classical dance. That 'ancient classical dance' is a projection backwards in time: we know what it looks like because we have bharatanatyam. Soon people believed that the ancient dance led to bharatanatyam when, in fact, the bharatanatyam led to the ancient dance. A dance is created in the past in order to be restored for the present and future.

Purulia chhau

Purulia chhau, a masked dance of the arid region of West Bengal adjoining Bihar and Orissa, is an athletic dance-drama featuring many leaps, somersaults, struts, stamps and iconographic poses. Stories usually are drawn from the Indian epics and *puranas* and almost always depict duels and battles. Drummers of the Dom caste beat huge kettle-drums and long oblong drums, taunting the dancers into frenzied spinning jumps, screams and confrontations. Rivalries among villages competing at the annual festival at a hill station, Matha, are fierce. According to Asutosh Bhattacharyya, Professor of Folklore and Anthropology at Calcutta University, who has devoted himself entirely to chhau since 1961, the Purulia region is inhabited by many aboriginal tribes whose:

religious customs and social festivals show very little resemblance to those of Hinduism . . . But, it is also a fact that the Mura of Purulia are very ardent participants in chhau dance. With practically no education and social advancement the members of this community have been performing this art which is based on the episodes of the

Ramayana and the *Mahabharata* and the Indian classical literature most faithfully, in some cases, for generations . . . Sometimes an entire village, however poor, inhabited exclusively by the Mura, sacrifices its hard-earned resources for the cause of organising chhau dance parties.[7]

This presents a problem for Bhattacharyya. The system which is followed in chhau dance today could not have been developed by the aboriginal people who practise the dance. It is indeed a contribution of a higher culture keenly conscious of an aesthetic sense.[8]

He guesses that the drummers, the Dom, an outcaste group, originated chhau, for the Dom were at one time a 'highly sophisticated community, . . . brave soldiers in the infantry of the local feudal chiefs'. Thrown out of work when the British pacified the region in the eighteenth century, failing to farm because of what Bhattacharyya calls the 'vanity of their past tradition of warriors', they were reduced to their present untouchable status: workers of hides, drummers. But their war dance lives on as chhau. Revealing biases sparkle from Bhattacharyya's account. Aboriginal peoples have no developed aesthetic sense; high-caste dancers are transformed into low-caste drummers after passing on their war dance because they are too proud to farm. (Why didn't they use their swords to steal land and become landlords?)

The annual competition at Matha is not an ancient tradition but a festival initiated in 1967 by Bhattacharyya. It was discontinued in 1980 or 1981. Bhattacharyya recalls:

In April 1961 I visited an interior village in the Purulia District with a batch of students of the Calcutta University and for the first time observed a regular performance of the chhau dance . . . I found that there was a system of this dance and a definitely established method which was well preserved. But it was on the decline due to lack of patronage from any source whatsoever. I wanted to draw the attention of the world outside to this novel form of dance.[9]

And that he did. All-star parties of chhau dancers toured Europe in 1972, Australia and North America in 1975, and Iran. They have danced in New Delhi and, as Bhattacharyya delights:

I attracted the notice of Sangeet Natak Akademi, New Delhi (the government agency established to encourage and preserve traditional performing arts) to this form of dance. It took immediate interest and invited me to give performances of the dance in New Delhi. In June 1969, I visited New Delhi with a batch of forty village artists for the first time outside their native district. Performances were held there before very distinguished Indian and foreign invitees . . .

Performances were also shown on TV in Delhi. Only three years later it was also shown on BBC television in London and five years later on NBC in New York, USA. (Program used in 1975 at the University of Michigan, p.3)

Note how Bhattacharyya refers to the dances as his: 'invited me to give performances of the dance'. This is not bragging but an acknowledgement of the circumstances: without a patron the villagers would have gotten nowhere. And these days a patron needs more than money; he needs knowledge and a wish to devote himself to the form he's restoring. Government comes up with the cash.

Chhau, 1961 and after, is a creation of the mixture of what Bhattacharyya found and what he invented. As a folklorist-anthropologist he dug into the past and constructed a history of chhau and a technique, that he then proceeded faithfully to restore. His annual festival and Matha coincided with the Chaitra Parva celebrations common to the area and the occasion of the annual chhau festivals of Seraikella and Mayurbhanj (related forms of the dance). These festivals, once paid for by maharajas, are now sponsored, less lavishly, by the Government. In 1976 I went to Matha. The dances went on there all night for two nights. Villagers, arriving from towns as far away as two days' journey, set up camp. They roped together *charpois* (sleeping cots made of wood and twine) and jerry-built a theatre. Women and children watched, and slept, sitting and reclining on the *charpois* elevated to a height of 8 feet or more. Men and boys stood on the ground. A narrow passageway led from the area where performers put on costumes and masks to the roughly circular dancing ground. Parties enter down the passageway, stop, present themselves, then leap into their dancing. All dancing is done with bare feet on bare earth, swept clean of large rocks but still raw, pebbled, with turned-up clods and scrub grass. To me it felt like a rodeo in a backwater town. Torches and Petromax lanterns throw shadowy light, the drums bark and roar, the *shehanais* (clarinet-like) shriek, as party after party competes. Most parties consist of five to nine dancers. Some masks adorned with peacock feathers rise three feet over the dancers' heads. The mask of ten-headed Ravana is more than 4 feet long. Wearing these masks, dancers make full somersaults and twisting leaps. The dances are vigorous and it's very hot inside the papier-mâché masks, so each dance lasts less than ten minutes. Every village danced twice. There were no prizes but there was competition, and everyone knew who danced well, who poorly.

Just in case there were doubts, each afternoon following the night's dancing, Bhattacharyya critiqued the performances. During the dancing he sat behind a desk, where two Petromax lanterns made him the best-lit figure of the event; next to him were his university assistants. All night he watched and wrote. One by one the villages appeared before him on the morrow. I listened to what he said. He warned one party not to use story elements not found in the Hindu classics. He chided another for not wearing the standard basic costume of short skirt over leggings decorated in rings of white, red and black. Bhattacharyya selected this basic costume from one village and made it general. When I asked him about it he said that the costumes he chose were the most authentic, the least Westernised. In a word, Bhattacharyya oversaw every aspect of Purulia chhau: training, dance themes, music, costuming, steps. In January 1983 I attended a non-Bhattacharyya chhau performance in a town near Calcutta. There I saw energetic dancing of stories from the *Mahabharata*. This same group of village dancers, while performing for performers and scholars, assembled for a conference in Calcutta, sang at least one song that Bhattacharyya would have disapproved of. In English translation:

We will not stay in India,
We will go to England.
We will not eat what is here
But we will eat cookies and bread.
We will not sleep on torn rags
But on mattresses and pillows.
And when we go to England
We won't have to speak Bengali
But we will all speak Hindi.

4. Balinese dancer in trance in the *kris* dance.

The villagers assumed that in England the 'national language' was the same as it was in India: Hindi. The question: is this village's chhau, so full of contemporary longings, to be condemned for not being 'classical'? Or is the syncretic mixing of *Mahabharata* and England to be accepted as the 'natural development' of the dance?

Bhattacharyya selected individuals from different villages and composed them into all-star touring ensembles. He oversaw rehearsals and went with these 'foreign parties' on tour. Dancers and musicians who toured returned to their villages with enhanced reputations. Touring, in fact, has had deep effects on chhau. Three foreign parties have come into existence since the first tour in 1972: nineteen people went to Europe, sixteen to Iran, eleven to Australia and North America. Because foreigners won't sit through nine hours of dancing, Bhattacharyya made a programme of two hours' duration. And because he didn't think that bare chests looked good on the male dancers he designed a jacket based on an old pattern. Both these changes became a standard back in Purulia. Many of the people who went abroad formed their own groups at home. Each of these groups are called 'foreign parties' and bill themselves as such, this gives them status, drawing power and the ability to charge more. There is demand now for performances as performances, outside of the ritual calendar. A performance can be hired for about a thousand rupees, a lot cheaper than Jatra, the most popular entertainment in rural Bengal. But a thousand rupees is still a lot of money.

These changes can be traced back to Bhattacharyya. He is the big chhau man, and his authority is rarely questioned. He's a professor, a scholar from Calcutta. When he writes about chhau he emphasises its village base and ancient origins; he even suggests a possible link between chhau and the dances of Bali. (Around the third century BC the Kalinga empire of what is now Orissa and Bengal possibly traded across south-east Asia as far as Bali.) But he hardly mentions his own rôle in restoring the dance. Rather, he speaks of himself as 'discovering' it.

Trance and dance in Bali

Sometimes changes in traditional performances are made by insiders. One of the best-known films about non-Western performance is Margaret Mead's and Gregory Bateson's *Trance and Dance in Bali* (1938). At a showing of this movie shortly before her death, Mead said that the trance club of Pagutan decided that the visiting foreigners who were making the film would like to see young women go into trance and stab at their breasts with *kris*. In Bali at that time women often went around with their breasts bare – naked breasts did not mean the same thing in Bali as they do in New York (where, ironically, in a semantic double twist, clubs where dancers are bare-breasted are called 'topless' – perhaps a last-ditch puritanical revenge). But also – I suppose to please or at least not offend the foreign film-makers – the Balinese women covered their breasts for the filming and young women replaced older ones as dancers.

Without telling Mead or Bateson, the men of the trance club instructed the young women in proper techniques for entering trance and showed them how to handle the *kris*. Then the men of the club proudly announced to the film-makers the changes made for the special filming. The film itself makes no mention of these changes. In *Trance and Dance* there is one old woman who, as the narrator says, announced beforehand that 'she wouldn't go into trance' but who is nevertheless 'unexpectedly' possessed. The camera follows her; she is bare-breasted, deep in trance, her *kris* power fully turned against her own chest. Later, slowly, she is brought out of trance by an old priest who has her inhale smoke, sprinkles her with holy water and sacrifices a small chicken on her behalf. There is a period of time when, seated, after the drama is over, her hands continue to go through the motions of dancing.

It seems that members of the trance club were angry at this old woman because they felt that her trance disturbed the aesthetic refinements they had rehearsed for foreign eyes – and foreign lenses. As it turned out, the Mead–Bateson camera crew paid a lot of attention to this old lady: she appeared to be, and was, a very genuine trancer. But, speaking strictly from the Balinese point of view, which is 'authentic', the young women prepared by the Balinese themselves or the solitary old woman doing the traditional thing? Is there not, in Bali, a tradition of modifying things for foreigners? It's precisely when changes feed back into the traditional forms, actually becoming these forms, that a restoration of behaviour occurs.

Notes

[1] Kapila Vatsyayan, *Indian Classical Dance*, New Delhi, Publications Division, Ministry of Education and Broadcasting, 1974.

[2] Kapila Vatsyayan, *Classical Indian Dance in Literature and the Arts*, New Delhi, Sangeet Natak Akademi, 1968.

[3] Milton Singer, *When a Great Tradition Modernizes*, London, Pall Mall Press, 1977.

[4] Mohan Khokar, 'The Greatest Step in Bharatanatyam', *Sunday Statesman*, New Delhi, 16 January 1983.

[5] Ibid.

[6] Ibid.

[8] Ibid.

[9] Ibid.

5–8. Purulia chhau dancers (India): (**top left**) Ravana, the giant king of the demons, with his characteristic head mask and multiple arms; (**top right**) a female character. Notice the white-, black- and red-striped pants worn by the two dancers: this costume has been set by Professor Bhattacharyya as the basic Purulia chhau dance costume, the richness of the costumes and headdresses is also the result of a 'restoration of behaviour'.

I rhythm, therefore I am. (Marcel Jousse, *L'Antropologie du geste* [*The Anthropology of Gesture*]).
Rhythm is an emotion released in ordered movements. (Plato, *Timon*).

Carved time

The actor or dancer is s/he who knows how to carve time. Concretely: s/he carves time in rhythm, dilating or contracting her actions. The word 'rhythm' comes from the Greek verb *rheo*, meaning 'to run', 'to flow'. Rhythm literally means 'a particular way of flowing'.

During a performance, the actor or dancer sensorialises the flow of time, which in daily life is experienced subjectively (and measured by clocks and calendars). Rhythm materialises the duration of an action by means of a line of homogeneous or varied tensions. It creates a waiting, an expectation. The spectators sensorially experience a kind of pulsation, a projection towards something which they are often unaware of, a breath that is repeatedly varied, a continuity that denies itself. Carving time, rhythm renders it time-in-life.

Rhythm has its laws: just as we are not free to arrange the syllables of a word or the notes of a pentagram in any way we like, there similarly exist successions of duration that give rise to the sensation of rhythm and other even more numerous successions of duration that give no sensation of rhythm at all.

For example, the ear receives a rhythmic impression when, in certain languages, short and long syllables follow each other in a certain order (according to a metre), when strongly accented phrases alternate with unaccented phrases, when the inflections of the voice separate high notes from a deeper melodic base, or when the sonorous material is interrupted by more or less regular silences.

When one says rhythm, one therefore implies silences and pauses. Pauses and silences are actually the supporting fabric upon which rhythm develops. There is no rhythm if there is no awareness of silences and pauses and two rhythms are differentiated not by the sound or noise produced but by the way silences and pauses are organised.

One kind of fluidity is continuous alternation, variation, breath, which protects the individual tonic, melodic

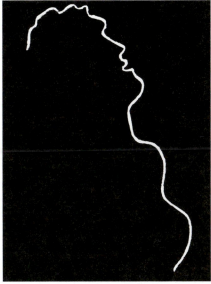

1–2. (**above**) *Musical Ideas* (1931): Mexican design by Eisenstein; (**left**) a straight line, negating itself, becomes tension: *Pasifae* (1944), engraved linoleum, Henri Matisse (1869–1954).

241

profile of every action. Another kind of fluidity becomes monotony and has the consistency of concentrated milk. This latter fluidity does not keep the spectator's attention alert, it puts it to sleep.

The secret of a rhythm-in-life, like the sea's waves, leaves in the wind or the flames of a fire, is found in the pauses. These pauses are not static stops but transitions, changes between one action and another. One action stops and is retained for a fraction of a second, creating a counter-impulse which is the impulse of the successive action. The way to avoid schematic patterns and stereotypes is to create dynamic silences: energy in time.

When the pause-transition loses its retained pulsation, a pulsation that struggles to continue, it coagulates and dies. The dynamic transition becomes a static pause.

One must learn to recognise the point up to which the pause-transitions can be dilated. They make concatenation possible for the performer. Concatenation models every detail/action in a sequence and also models and directs the spectator's perception. Playing with the dynamics of rhythm makes it possible to break the influence of both inculturation and acculturation technique and therefore the way in which our culture or a particular technique has taught us to use our organism's postural or kinaesthetic possibilities. We manifest our presence in time and in space by means of dynamic discharges or patterns which are induced by the practices and habits learned during our first biological and professional infancies.

In general, performers know what their next action will be. While they are carrying out one action, they are already thinking about the next. They mentally anticipate, and this automatically induces a physical process that influences their dynamics and that is perceived by the spectator's kinaesthetic sense. This is one of the reasons why a performance may not succeed in stimulating our attention: on the sensorial level, we have already perceived what the actor/dancer is about to do.

The problem is: how can the performer, who knows the succession of the actions that must be carried out, be present in each action and make the successive action appear like a surprise for herself and for the spectator?

The performer must carry out the action by negating it.

There are many ways of negating an action. Instead of continuing in the

3. The rhythm in this scene results from a fixed line. Buyo dancer Katsuko Azuma performing a male rôle, being in contrast with a fluctuating line, the *onnagata* (performer of female rôles) Kanichi Hanayagi. Together they create an image of simultaneous rest and movement in a scene about the meeting of two lovers.

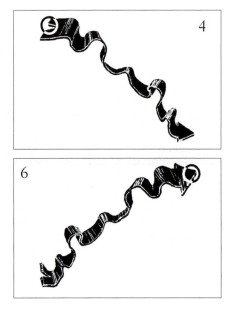

4–6. The performer becomes 'rhythm' not by means of movement alone but by means of an alternation of movements and rests, by means of a proportioning of body impulses, retentions and supports, in time and in space. In these drawings, Doris Humphrey indicates three possible developments of a dance phrase. A climax at the beginning of the phrase, which then descends (ill.4); a phrase which begins slowly, climaxes in the middle and descends to the end (ill.5); a phrase which slowly builds to a climax and then abruptly ends (ill.6).

foreseen direction, one can change course. One can begin in the opposite direction. One can slow the action down, always nevertheless respecting the precision of its pattern. One can dilate the pause-transitions. To execute an action while negating it means inventing an infinity of micro-rhythms within it. And this obliges one to be 100 per cent in the action one is carrying out. The successive action will then be born as a surprise for the spectator and for oneself.

This effect is due to kinaesthesis: our awareness of our bodies and their tensions. Kinaesthesis also helps us perceive the quality of tensions in another person. It helps us guess another's intentions: whether they are approaching us to caress us or to hit us. Kinaesthesis helps us avoid bumping into other people when we walk down the street. It is a kind of physiological radar that makes us aware of impulses and intentions and that motivates us to react before thought intervenes. Kinaesthetic

sense is essential in every kind of performance. It helps the spectator follow, perceive and often even foresee the actor/dancer's intentions, yet without the spectator being completely aware that this is happening. Kinaesthetic sense often makes the spectator discover what an actor's intention is before she herself realises it, thus destroying the surprise effect that the action ought to have had.

(Eugenio Barba, *Silver Horse*)

Jo-ha-kyu

In Japanese, the expression *jo-ha-kyu* describes the three phases into which every action performed by an actor or dancer is divided. The first phase is determined by the opposition between one force which is increasing and another force which is resisting the development of the first (*jo*, 'to restrain'); the second phase (*ha*, 'to break', 'to interrupt') is the moment when the resisting force is overcome until one arrives at the third phase (*kyu*, 'speed'), when the action culminates, releases all its power and suddenly stops as if meeting an obstacle, a new resistance.

In classical Japanese theatre, the *jo-ha-kyu* rhythmic phrase has not only to do with the actor's or dancer's actions, but is also part of all the various levels

7–8. (**top**) The set transforms itself in rhythm, opening out to become like a piano keyboard in *Bubus, the Teacher* by Meyerhold, 1925; (**bottom**) the pause as dynamic transition: what will the next action be? Spanish actor Toni Cots and Indian dancer Sanjukta Panigrahi in a demonstration at the Blois-Malakoff ISTA, 1985.

of organisation of the performance: it is applied to gesture, to the music, to each version of each play performed, and ultimately determines the rhythm of the entire performance day. In any case, it is essential that student actors and dancers be familiar with *jo-ha-kyu* since it teaches them to incorporate rhythm in their work from the very beginning of their apprenticeship.

Katsuko Azuma teaches her student to move according to the dynamic principles of *jo-ha-kyu* by setting up resistances and new tensions. In the first photo (ill.9), the master stands behind the student and holds her by the belt. The student, restrained, must make an effort in order to take her first step: she bends her knees, presses her feet to the floor and leans her torso slightly forwards. Suddenly released by the master, she moves quickly forward until she reaches the movement's pre-determined limit, then suddenly stops. In the second photo (ill.10), the procedure is similar, but done facing the student. The master creates a resistance by pushing against the umbrella. She then gradually diminishes the resistance, allowing the student to move quickly forward to the point where she is suddenly stopped with a new resistance against the umbrella.

Also the Western performer is aware of the importance of executing actions according to varying rhythms. Here are Toporkov's comments on Stanislavsky's work in this regard:

Stanislavsky admirably demonstrated his own skill in using different rhythms. He would take the simplest episode from everyday life – for example, buying a newspaper at a stand in the station – and play it in completely different rhythms. He would buy a paper when there is a whole hour before the departure of the train and he doesn't know how to kill the time, or when the first or second bell has rung, or when the train has already started. The actions are all the same but in completely different rhythms, and Konstantin Sergeyevich was able to carry out these exercises in any order: by increasing the rhythm, by diminishing the rhythm, by sudden change. I saw the mastery, I saw the technique, the tangible technique of our art. He had mastered all this thanks to persistent work on himself.

(V. O. Toporkov, *Stanislavsky in Rehearsal*).

9–10. The transmission of experience in Japan: various ways used by a Japanese master (Katsuko Azuma) to teach a student (Mari Azuma) to 'kill rhythm' (Volterra ISTA, 1981).

Biological motions and the body's micro-rhythms

Human beings share with the other animal species the ability to perceive the presence of life. Numerous observations made during experiments with men and animals show that the perception of a congener, or of an individual of another species, induces tonic, motor, humoural and behavioural variations. Many experiments have proved the fact that certain types of movements can be associated with the characteristics of living organisms.

When a number of small luminescent pellets are placed on the limbs and joints of a human being in movement, the displacement of these points of light, which Johansson called biological motions, are immediately recognisable to adult observers as human activity.

Complex combinations of mobile visual signals can also be deciphered as being related to specific human activities. Researchers believe that this is an innate perceptual behaviour of the vision system rather than knowledge acquired through experience.

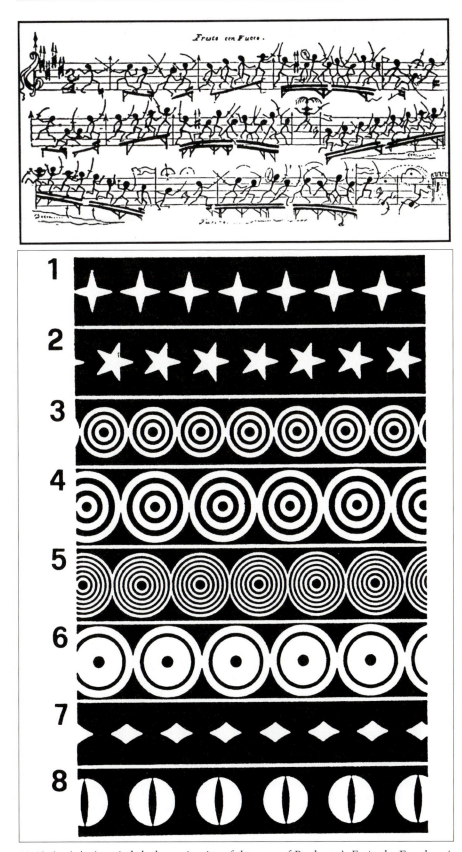

Performance arts and performance sports are partly based on the organisation and evaluation of biological motions. The codes that sustain the actor's, dancer's or athlete's activity seem to restore the organisation of corporal micro-rhythms of efficient behaviour as it occurs in the animal world, although in man this behaviour is moderated by the effects of cultural experience and the principle of economy. In fact, cultural development renders the efficiency of the primitive body secondary: today there is no longer any need to hunt down wild prey in order to have something to eat. On the other hand, the pleasure of seeing trained bodies in action endures.

It is likely that the success of various publicity films, which make use of dancers and athletes, is due to this visual impulse generated by living beings. The perception of bodies in movement induces a kind of echo of subtle tonic variations in the observers, who respond to the perceived movements with their own body. This motor response to transmitted stimuli – during a religious ceremony, a political demonstration or a performance, for example – results in the setting up of particular bonds between spectators and performers. This also occurs during film projections and television transmissions of sports events – especially athletics and tennis – when it is manifest as reflex leg movements.

(Jean-Marie Pradier, *Eléments d'une physiologie de la seduction*, [*Elements of a Physiology of Seduction*], in *L'oeil, l'oreille, le cerveau* Paris, 1989)

11–12. (**top**) Anti-musical rhythm: animation of the notes of Beethoven's *Eroica*, by French caricaturist Jean Grandville (1803–47); (**bottom**) synthetic rhythm: Fischinger's 'band drawings'. The research on animation conducted by German artist Oskar Fischinger led him to the creation of a very particular musical world. He was attracted by the hypothesis that a drawing laid out according to a 'decorative' rhythm ought to be able to produce sounds. And in fact the 'reading' of his drawn compositions produced surprising effects: many of the new sounds, obtained by the repetition of geometric motifs, did not resemble any sounds he had ever heard before, and moreover, the drawing of the 'row of cobras', based on Egyptian stylisation, produced sounds similar to that made by the snakes themselves. Concentric rings produced ringing sounds of many kinds, and a chain of pearls produced a bassoon-like sound. These experiments were the beginnings of synthetic music: positioned in front of photo-electric cells, Fischinger's drawings could produce a vast range of synthetic sounds. For example: 1. a steam whistle; 2. a bus horn; 3. an electric bell; 4. an alarm clock; 5. a telephone bell; 6. an alarm siren; 7. Morse code; 8. a ship's whistle.

Meyerhold: rhythm is essential

From the very beginning of his theatrical activity, Meyerhold was obsessed with the problem of scenic movement and its interweavings with rhythm. He began to use music to induce an extra-daily technique in his actors.

Music, which determines the tempo of every occurrence on the stage, dictates a rhythm which has nothing in common with everyday existence. [...]

The essence of stage rhythm is the antithesis of real, everyday life. In most cases the art of the naturalistic actor lies in surrendering to the dictates of his temperament. By prescribing a strict tempo, the musical score frees the actor in music drama from the demands of his own temperament.

The actor in the music drama must absorb the essence of the score and translate every subtlety of the musical picture into plastic terms. For this reason he must strive for complete control over his body. [...]

Where does the human body, possessing the suppleness of expression demanded by the stage, attain its highest development? In the dance. Because the dance is the movement of the human body in the sphere of rhythm. The dance is to the body what music is to thought: form artificially yet instinctively created.

Thus 'visible and comprehensible action' embodied by the actor implies choreographic action. [...]

It is principally through the actor that the music translates the dimension of time into spatial terms. Before music was dramatised, it could create an illusory picture only in time; once dramatised, it was able to conquer space. The illusory became real through the mime and movement of the actor subordinated to the musical design; that which before had dwelt only in time was now manifested in space.

(Meyerhold, *Tristan and Isolde*)

The most fascinating aspect of Meyerhold's research was the period of work on biomechanics. Mechanics is that branch of physics which studies the motion and balance of bodies. *Bios* means life. Hence *biomechanics*: the study of the motion and balance of the body-in-life.

A series of exercises based essentially on a continual 'dance of balance' (cf. *Balance*) made it possible for the actor to create 'that scenic rhythm whose essence is the antithesis of real, everyday, life'. One of the basic devices was *otkaz*, refusal, which was composed of three phases, involving the whole body and radically varying body posture. Another exercise was called the dactyl, a term borrowed from poetic metre.

Meyerhold described how the three-phase action was to be executed:

An actor must possess the capacity for Reflex Excitability. Nobody can become an actor without it.

Excitability is the ability to realise in feelings, movements and words a task which is prescribed externally.

The co-ordinated manifestations of excitability together constitute the actor's performance. Each separate manifestation comprises an element of acting. Each element of acting comprises three invariable stages:

1. intention
2. realisation
3. reaction.

The intention is the intellectual assimilation of a task prescribed externally by the dramatist, the director, or the initiative of the performer.

The realisation is the cycle of volitional, mimetic and vocal reflexes.

The reaction is the attentuation of the volitional reflex as it is realised mimetically and vocally in preparation for the reception of a new intention (the transition to a new element of acting).

The term 'feeling' is used in the strictly technical sense with no loose, emotional connotation.

(Meyerhold, *The Actor's Emploi*, London, E. Braun, 1969).

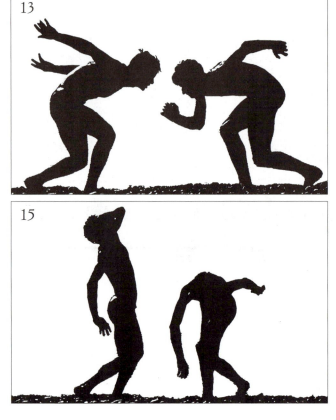

13–15. A basic biomechanical exercise, the slap in the face, an example of the rhythm of an action divided into three phases: (ill.13) beginning with a preparation, then (ill.14) going in the opposite direction, and finally (ill.15) the slap itself. The change in the position of the torso influences balance and the result is a new posture and new muscular tonus. Notice how this action is developed by means of the biomechanical principle called *otkaz* (refusal): to act in such a way that an action begins with its opposite (cf. *Balance* and *Oppositions*).

16–17. (**top**) The actor Garin in the rôle of Klestakov, the protagonist of *The Government Inspector* by Gogol/Meyerhold. The drawings by Ivan Biezin show how Meyerhold's actors danced continuously. As Grozdiev wrote: 'All the body has a tendency to go down towards the position of the comfortable sofa, but the body fights against the gravitational pull and meeting this resistance transforms itself into a sort of dance'; (**bottom**) the passing on of tradition, Umeå ISTA, 1995: Chris Torch (former actor of the Living Theatre, USA), and Ralf Raüker (Germany) demonstrate a study in biomechanics as it was reconstructed by Julian Beck and Judith Malina, and as it is taught by Gennadi Bogdanov who learnt it from Nikolai Kustov, one of Meyerhold's actors.

It is not a question of painting life, but of making painting live.
(Pierre Bonnard)

The costume is the set

It is well known that, in general, Asian theatres do not use any form of set, in so far as a set is a device which represents, in a more or less realistic way, the locations where dramatic actions take place. With the exception of kabuki's complex set (to which Western theatre is indebted for the idea of the revolving stage, among other things), one can say that the scenic space used by Asian actors has a fixed background, whether it be part of the closed space of noh or Peking Opera, or the natural, open-air décor provided by temple walls or the houses of a village in kathakali, Balinese dance or any of the other dance forms of southeast Asia.

It is precisely thanks to the absence of a realistic setting that a few simple props (a table and two chairs in Peking Opera, for example) are all that the performer needs to be able to unfold the most incredible phantasmagoria of places and situations for the spectator. It is thanks to the *omission* of the setting, of the locations, but especially thanks to the craftsmanship of the performers, who are able to bring these places alive by means of their bodies' reactions. They use conventional gestures understood and accepted by the spectators and execute them with skill and dexterity, as, for example, in the famous scenes 'in the dark' in Peking Opera. These scenes are in fact performed in full light: the actors feign obstacles and engage in duels without seeing each other.

Similar techniques are used in Western pantomime and were also found in the traditions of the past. They remind one of commedia dell'arte performances, of the rudimentary mise-en-scène of the mystery plays of the Middle Ages and of Elizabethan drama. But

1–5. The costume as moving set: a Peking Opera actor as a general (**top left**); a Balinese topeng actor (**top right**); a traditional Indian *sari*, worn by odissi dancer Sanjukta Panigrahi (**centre left**); a *geisha kimono*, worn by buyo dancer Katsuko Azuma (**centre right**); (**bottom**) the costume which dilates the performer: Indian yakshagana costume.

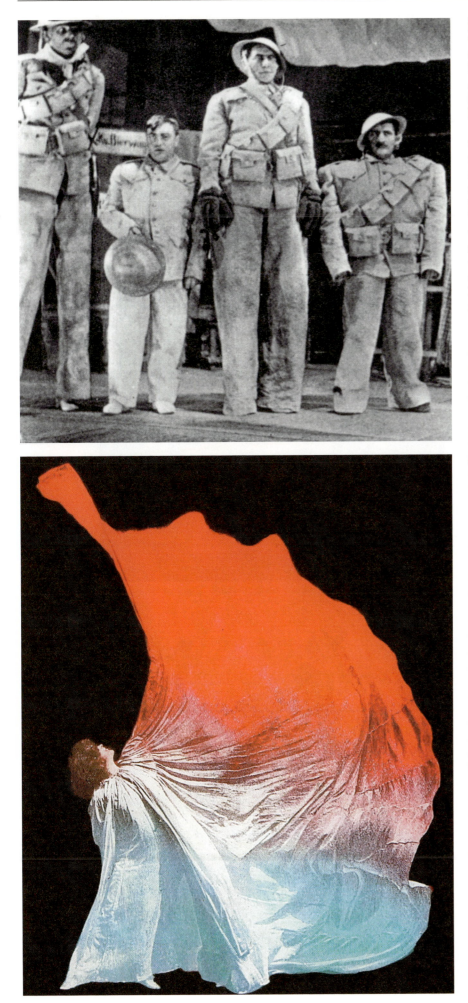

just as Shakespeare's ability to use words to evoke places and to make the atmosphere of his plays come alive has been defined as 'verbal design', so in Asian theatre we find the 'setting in movement', represented in this case by the performers' costumes.

Proportions, colours, scintillating costumes, masks and other props transform the Asian performer into a 'miniature set' in constant movement on the stage, and presents an infinite succession of perspectives, dimensions and sensations. The origins of these costumes are unknown and possibly date back to military practices which doubled the size of the warrior's armour and clothing in order to impress and terrify the enemy. Peking Opera costumes (ill. 1) have inherited some of this armour: the shoulder flags indicate, like our pips and stripes, the officer's military rank and the number of battalions under his command. Similarly, the long strips of costly fabric on Balinese costumes recall the glory of ancient warriors.

But whatever their origins, and even when they were borrowed from daily life, such as the Indian *sari* and the Japanese *kimono* (ill.3 and 4), Asian performers' costumes are not just an embellishment, not just a gilded covering for the body. In the East, and sometimes also in the West, the principle is that one uses the costume like a *living partner*. The spectator is then able to visualise the dance of oppositions, the precarious balances and the dynamic web created by the performer.

A great deal of care and attention is given to these costumes and the effects which they can create: the costume then becomes a *prothesis* (this is the term that was used by Grotowski in the first years of his Teatr Laboratorium) which assists the performer's body, dilates it and conceals it while continuously transforming it. Hence the effect of power and energy which the performer is able to manifest is reinforced and heightened by the metamorphosis of the costume itself in a reciprocal relationship of exchange: performer-body, performer-costume, performer-in-the-costume.

6–7. (**top**) Costumes which dilate the performer: Berlin Staatstheater production of Bertold Brecht's *Man is Man* (1931), with Peter Lorre (1904–64); (**bottom**) Loie Fuller (1862–1928), the famous American dancer, considered a precursor of modern dance, seen here in a performance in which, thanks to the skilful use of bands of coloured light, she succeeded in bringing a long cape of white cloth to life. Loie Fuller was one of the first dancers to abandon the nineteenth-century perspective stage, turning instead to the use of costume as set piece and to innovative use of light.

8–11. (**top**) English actor David Garrick (1717–79) as Sir John Brute in John Vanbrugh's *The Provok'd Wife*. This painting by Johan Zoffany, kept in the National Theatre Collection in London, shows a male character dressed as a woman for comic and satiric effect. In this scene, in which the character is drunk, the actor makes a brusque movement which causes the front of the dress to swing up so that the spectators can glimpse the man's costume he is wearing underneath; (**bottom right**) costume for a shepherd-dancer drawn by P. Lior, who worked in England from 1725 to 1750. Until the end of the nineteenth century, stage costumes in Europe reflected contemporary fashion and in most cases were therefore far removed from the historical reality of the characters represented. Before the theatre of the Romantic period brought the taste for historical accuracy onto the stage, which influenced costuming and sometimes also stage behaviour and actions, theatrical costumes were simply more beautiful and more sumptuous clothes than those worn in daily life. The extraordinary elegance of the costume shown here, with its peacock plume and with its skirt supported by a framework of iron wire, was intended for use in a 'pastoral ballet' and is typical apparel for a dancer from the nobility. This particular skirt is a male garment, a carry-over from the tunic which in earlier times was worn under armour. The skirt was wider than the actor's armspan; (**centre**) eighteenth-century print of a Harlequin: he is not sure which costume, the large skirt or the pair of pants, suits him best; (**bottom left**) the *maulavi*, the large skirt worn by dervishes, spreads out into a cone during the dancer's frenetic whirling.

12–16 (**top left**) Scene from kathakali theatre with actors M. P. Sankaran Namboodiri and K. N. Vijayakumar, playing male and female rôles respectively. The width of the skirt, which is not supported by a framework but by multiple layers of underskirts, can be varied with the help of the knees and legs. Costume and actor continuously conspire against monotony and boredom; (**top right**) the use of particular costumes and props such as stilts help the performer change the daily nature of an open and not specifically theatrical space: Julia Varley in an Odin Teatret street performance in New York; (**bottom left**) Harlequin on stilts: detail from an engraving in the *Recueil Fossard* (Stockholm Museum); (**bottom centre**) Mayan actors on stilts; (**bottom right**) Actor on stilts: detail from a Wei dynasty (220–265 BC) wall painting in Dunhuang, China.

251

17–22. The *Shishi* is a mythical lion of Chinese origin. Here Katsuko Azuma is seen swinging the lion's mane. Balinese, Indian and Japanese costumes often involve extra weight, sometimes as much as 20 or 30 kilos, and oblige the performer to create counter-impulses that continously engage the spinal column. The costume accessories must also be brought alive through the action of the entire body. The *Shishi*, an amazing sight even when immobile, suddenly begins to move: it swings its long mane to rid itself of the butterflies that are fluttering around its head. The effect of the costume is greatly enhanced by the precision of the performer's action, her steadily increasing size and by the mane-wig which is whipped around and up, intensely, energetically.

23. The alteration of this Mayan dancer's balance, caused by the position of the head is now more clearly understandable: the dancer is probably shown in the act of swinging the ornament on his headdress, in much the same manner as the Japanese *Shishi* swings its mane.

24–26. (**top**) Else Marie Laukvik, Odin Teatret actress, working with props during *The Book of Dances*. The props, two flags, continuously change function: at one moment they are weapons, at another moment a cloak, then a curtain which can be raised to hide the face. A continuous and elegant play of metamorphoses in black and white; (**bottom left and right**) Lin Chun-Hui as Yu-chi, a female warrior in Peking Opera. The actress uses the same costume with two different props, creating two very different effects: a cloak, whose large volume focuses attention on the performer's face, and two swords, held in a guard position, which also frame the face. In both cases, the eyes look in the same direction, the legs are bent in the same way, the arms are held above the waist: but in the first case the effect is extremely soft (notice the delicacy of the raised little fingers), while in the second case, the effect is one of vigour.

Daily clothing, extra-daily costume

The *kimono*, the daily and traditional Japanese national dress, becomes an extra-daily theatre costume: performing while wearing a *kimono* results in changes in the position of the legs, which sets up tensions and oppositions of precarious balance (ill.27–28); as well, the *kimono* has a volume effect that considerably modifies the spectator's perception.

The *kimono* transforms the proportions of the performer's body, thanks to the belt (*obi*), placed well above the waist. It also conceals the bending of the legs (ill.28). The wide sleeves create contrasting proportions between the solemnity of the pyramidal form and the narrowness of the wrist (ill.29, 31). When kyogen actor Kosuke Nomura demonstrates the same positions without the *kimono*, one has a completely different perception of his body (ill. 30, 32).

Clearly, one cannot say that the costume itself is pre-expressive, since it is the performer who is giving the costume life. However, in the case of the *kimono*, with its severe and geometric lines, which respect the original dimensions of the roll of silk from which it was cut (no waste of fabric), the costume has a considerable influence on the way the performer is perceived. Japanese performers are well aware of this and consciously exploit it.

27–32. (**top**) The change in the position of the leg modifies the spectator's perception of the volume of the dancer's costume: Katsuko Azuma in a demonstration at Bonn ISTA, 1980; (**centre** and **bottom**) kyogen actor Kosuke Nomura in a demonstration at Volterra ISTA, 1981: the same actions with and without the *kimono* costume.

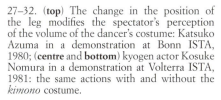

The water sleeves

Nothing gives performers more trouble than their hands and arms. All the positions they invent for them – hiding them in their pockets, smoking a cigarette to give them something to do, clasping and folding them – disturb the spectator even more. Peking Opera performers, or rather, their traditional costumes, have 'water sleeves': an artificial extension of the costumes' sleeves made of another piece of silk, most often white and shiny (ill.33). The 'water sleeves' are in continuous movement during the long moments of dialogue or song when the performers must remain in quasi-immobility so that their high-pitched voices can be heard. The sleeves slide, flow and plunge like the waters of a mountain torrent. The performer uses his/her arms to control the fluidity of the extremely slippery silk, following or countering the rhythm of the music, while the whiteness of the moving cloth underlines the cadences of the speeches or songs with an almost natural grace. The 'water sleeves' are an invaluable tool for the Chinese performer, but Western performers are also familiar with their use, as is shown by a number of old engravings (ill.34).

This costume detail, the arm's faithful partner, acts as a counterweight. Actual sculptural elements, these sleeves seem to have a life of their own and can adapt to the movements and oppositions created by the performer. The energy needed to master their bulky and cumbersome volume dispels and subliminates the unease which the performer often feels vis-à-vis arms and hands.

33–38. (top) Peking Opera actor in a typical position, working with the long white silk sleeves called *shui xiu* (water sleeves); (below) 'Water sleeves' in various traditions. From left to right: female rôle in Peking Opera; Pulcinella in a seventeenth-century print; Pierrot in a nineteenth-century French print; Pulcinella in an eighteenth-century print.

39. The costume as moving set: the actors of Théâtre du Soleil, directed by Ariane Mnouchkine, in *Iphigenie in Aulis* from the tetralogy of *Les Atrides* (1990).

Hana is the mind, Technique is the seed.
(Zeami, *Fushikaden*)

The ways we use our bodies in daily life are substantially different from the ways the body is used in performance situations. In everyday life, we use a body technique which has been conditioned by our culture, our social status, and our profession. But in a performance situation, the use of the body is completely different. It is therefore possible to differentiate between daily technique and extra-daily technique.

The French anthropologist Marcel Mauss was the first to speak of 'body techniques', in a conference given at the Paris Psychology Society in 1914. We quote here excerpts from Mauss's text, which was published in 1936 in the *Journal of Psychology* (23: 3/4).

The notion of body techniques

I deliberately say body techniques in the plural because it is possible to produce a theory of *the* technique of the body, in the singular, on the basis of a study, an exposition, a description pure and simple of techniques of the body in the plural. By this expression I mean the ways in which from society to society men know how to use their bodies. It is essential to move from the concrete to the abstract and not the other way round.

The body is man's first and most natural instrument. Or more accurately, not to speak of instruments, man's first and most natural technical object, and at the same time technical means, is his body.

Biographical list of body techniques

Marcel Mauss

I shall simply follow more or less the ages of man, the normal biography of an individual, as an arrangement of the body techniques that concern him or that he is taught.

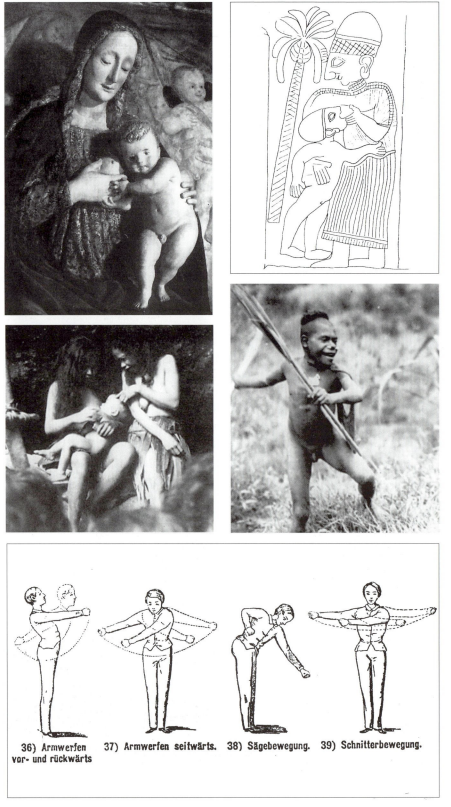

36) Armwerfen vor- und rückwärts   37) Armwerfen seitwärts.   38) Sägebewegung.   39) Schnitterbewegung.

1–5. Childhood techniques: feeding a new-born child: (**top left**) sixteenth-century Italian madonna; (**top right**) eighth-century BC Ithacan divinity; (**centre left**) Tasaday woman (The Philippines). Adolescence techniques: (**centre right**) Eipo boy (New Guinea) at play, training combat techniques; (**bottom**) European boy doing gymnastics (from a late nineteenth-century German manual).

1. Techniques of birth and obstetrics

The forms of obstetrics are very variable. The infant Buddha was born with his mother Mâya upright and clinging to the branch of a tree. She gave birth standing up. Indian women in the main still give birth in this position. Something we think of as normal, such as giving birth lying on one's back, is no more normal than doing so in other positions, e.g., on all fours. There are techniques of giving birth, both on the mother's part and on that of her helpers, of holding the baby, cutting and tying the umbilical cord, caring for the mother, caring for the child.

2. Techniques of infancy: rearing and feeding the child

Attitudes of the two inter-related beings: mother and child. Take the child – suckling, etc., carrying, etc. The history of carrying is very important. A child carried next to its mother's skin for two or three years has a quite different attitude to its mother from that of a child not so carried; it has a contact with its mother utterly unlike our children's. It clings to her neck, her shoulder, it sits astride her hip. This remarkable gymnastics is essential throughout its life. And there is another gymnastics for the mother carrying it. It even seems that psychical states arise here that have disappeared from infancy with us. There are sexual contacts, skin contacts, etc.

Weaning – Takes a long time, usually two or three years. The obligation to suckle, sometimes even to suckle animals. It takes a long time for the mother's milk to run dry. Besides this there are relations between weaning and reproduction, suspension of reproduction during weaning. Mankind can more or less be divided into people with cradles and people without.

The weaned child – It can eat and drink; it is taught to walk; it is trained in vision, hearing, in a sense of rhythm and form and movement, often for dancing and music.

It acquires the notions and practices of physical exercise and breathing. It takes certain postures that are often imposed on it.

3. Techniques of adolescence

The big moment in the education of the body is, in fact, the moment of

6–11. Adulthood techniques: to sit. (**top left**) Indian craftsman; (**top right**) Egyptian potter and (**centre left**) scribe; (**centre right**) French draftsman. Climbing techniques: (**bottom left**) telegraph worker in the USA; (**bottom right**) date picker in India.

initiation. Because of the way our boys and girls are brought up, we imagine that both acquire the same manners and postures and receive the same training everywhere. The idea is already erroneous about ourselves – and it is totally false in so-called primitive countries. Moreover, we describe the facts as if something like our own school, beginning straight away and intended to protect the child and train it for life, had always and everywhere existed. The opposite is the rule. For example: in all black societies the education of the boy intensifies around the age of puberty, while that of women remains traditional, so to speak. There is no school for women. They are at school with their mothers and are trained there continuously, moving directly, with few exceptions, to the married state. The male child enters the society of men, where he learns his profession, especially the profession of arms. However, for men as well as women, the decisive moment is that of adolescence. It is at this moment that they learn definitively the techniques of the body that they will retain for the whole of their adult lives.

4. Techniques of adult life

To list these we can run through the various moments of the day among which co-ordinated movements and suspensions of movement are distributed.

We can distinguish sleep and waking, and, in waking, rest and activity.

Techniques of sleep – The notion that going to bed is something natural is totally inaccurate. It is possible to distinguish between those societies that have nothing to sleep on except the 'floor', and those that have instrumental assistance. [. . .] There are people with pillows and people without. There are populations that lie very close together in a ring to sleep, round a fire, or even without a fire. There are primitive ways of getting warm and keeping the feet warm. [. . .]

Finally there is sleep standing up. The Masai can sleep on their feet. I have slept standing up in the mountains. I have often slept on a horse, even sometimes a moving horse; the horse was more intelligent than I was. The old chroniclers of the invasions picture the Huns and Mongols sleeping on horseback. This is still true, and their riders' sleeping does not stop the horses' progress.

There is the use of coverings. People who sleep covered and uncovered. There is the hammock and the way of sleeping hanging up.

12–17. Body-care techniques: (**top left**) Japanese woman at her toilet; (**top right**) Italian labourers after work. Eating techniques: (**centre left**) eighteenth-century Japanese eating noodles; (**centre right**) customer at the bar of an American saloon at the end of the nineteenth century. Movement techniques: (**bottom left**) German soldier's goose step; (**bottom right**) English athlete in a race at the beginning of the century.

18–25. Relaxation techniques: (**top row left**) Chinese opium smokers in the middle of the nineteenth century; (**top row right**) Etruscan couple at the banquet table (first century AD); (**second row left**) old Dutch seaman; (**second row right**) Polynesian man; (**third row left**) Javanese woman; (**third row right**) Indian musician; (**bottom left**) Arab at prayer; (**bottom right**) techniques of reproduction: tantric union in India (tenth century).

Waking: techniques of rest – Rest can be perfect rest or a mere suspension of activity: lying down, sitting, squatting, etc. The way of sitting down is fundamental. You can distinguish squatting mankind and sitting mankind. And, among the latter, people with benches and people without benches and daises; people with chairs and people without chairs. [. . .]

There are people who have tables and people who do not. The table is far from universal. Normally it is still a carpet, a mat, throughout the East. Certain societies take their rest in very peculiar positions. Thus, the whole of Nilotic Africa and part of the Chad region, all the way to Tanganyika, is populated by men who rest in the fields like storks. Some manage to rest on one foot without a pole, others lean on a stick.

Techniques of activity, of movement – By definition, rest is the absence of movement, movement the absence of rest. Here is a straightforward list: movements of the whole body: climbing; trampling; walking.

Walking – The *habitus* of the body being upright while walking, breathing, rhythm of the walk, swinging the fists, the elbows, progression with the trunk in advance of the body or by advancing either side of the body alternately (we have got accustomed to moving all the body forward at once). Feet turned in or out. Extension of the leg. We laugh at the 'goose-step'. It is the way the German army can obtain the maximum extension of the leg, given in particular that all northerners, high on their legs, like to take as long steps as possible.

Running – Position of the feet, position of the arms, breathing, running magic, endurance.

Finally we reach techniques of active rest that are not simply a matter of aesthetics, but also of bodily games.

Dancing – You have perhaps attended the lectures of (Erich Maria) von Hornbostel and Curt Sachs. I accept their division into dances at rest and dances in action. I am less prepared to accept their hypothesis about the distribution of these dances. They are victims of the fundamental error which is the mainstay of a whole section of sociology. There are supposed to be societies with exclusively masculine descent and others with exclusively uterine descent. The uterine ones, being feminised, tend to dance on the spot; the others, with descent through the male, take their pleasure in moving about. Curt Sachs has better classified these dances into extravert and introvert dances. [. . .]

Lastly we should realise that dancing in a partner's arms is a product of modern European civilisation, which demonstrates that things we find natural have a historical origin. Moreover, they horrify everyone in the world but ourselves.

I move on to the techniques of the body that are also a function of vocations and part of vocations or more complex techniques.

Jumping – We have witnessed a transformation of jumping techniques. We all jumped from a springboard and, once again, full-face. I am glad to say this has stopped. Now people jump, fortunately, from one side. Jumping lengthways, sideways, up and down. Standing jump, pole jump.

Climbing – I can tell you that I'm very bad at climbing trees, though reasonable on mountains and rocks. A difference of education and hence of method.

A method of getting up trees is by using a belt encircling the tree and the body is of prime importance among all so-called primitives. But we do not even have the use of this belt. We see telephone workers climbing with crampons, but no belt.

The history of mountaineering methods is very noteworthy. It has made fabulous progress in my lifetime.

Descent – Nothing makes me so dizzy as watching a Kabyle going downstairs in Turkish slippers (*babouches*). How can he keep his footing without the slippers coming off? I have tried to see, to do it, but I can't understand.

Nor can I understand how women can walk in high heels. Thus there is a lot even to be observed, let alone compared.

Swimming – Diving, swimming; use of supplementary means; air-floats, planks, etc. We are on the way to the invention of navigation. [. . .]

Consumption techniques

Eating – You will remember the story Höffding repeats about the Shah of Persia. The Shah was the guest of

26–30. Extra-daily techniques in dance: (**top left**) American duo in the 1930s; (**top right**) Cossack dancers; (**second row**) dervish dancers in Turkey. Techniques of control of body and mind: (**third row**) two hatha yoga positions. Techniques of control and retention of energy (**bottom**) Taoist gymnastics (nei-kong) in a nineteenth-century Chinese treatise. Each exercise builds breath control.

31–32. Extra-daily body technique: (**top**) Peking Opera pupil during training; (**bottom**) kabuki actor, commedia dell'arte zanni, Balinese performer, odissi dancer.

Napoleon and insisted on eating with his fingers. The Emperor urged him to use a golden fork. 'You don't know what a pleasure you are missing,' the Shah replied. Absence and use of knives.

Drinking – It would be very useful to teach children to drink straight from the source, the fountain, etc., or from puddles of water, etc., to pour their drinks straight down their throats, etc.

Techniques of Reproduction – Nothing is more technical than sexual positions. Very few writers have had the courage to discuss this question.

General considerations

I believe that this whole notion of the education of races that are selected on the basis of determinate efficiency is one of the fundamental moments of history itself: education of the vision, education in walking – ascending, descending, running. It consists especially of education in composure. And the latter is above all a retarding mechanism, a mechanism inhibiting disorderly movements; this retardation subsequently allows a co-ordinated response of co-ordinated movements setting off in the direction of a chosen goal. This resistance to emotional seizure is something fundamental in social and mental life. It separates out, it even classifies the so-called primitive societies according to whether they display more brutal, unreflected, unconscious reactions or, on the contrary, more isolated, precise actions governed by a clear consciousness.

It is thanks to society that there is an intervention of consciousness. It is not thanks to unconsciousness that there is an intervention of society. It is thanks to society that there is the certainty of pre-prepared movements, domination of the conscious over emotion and unconsciousness.

My friend Granet has already pointed out his great investigations into the techniques of Taoism, its body techniques, and breathing techniques in particular. I have studied the Sanskrit texts of yoga enough to know that the same things occur in India. I believe precisely that at the bottom of all our mystical states there are body techniques that we have not studied, but that were studied fully in China and India, even in very remote periods. This socio-psycho-biological study should be made. I think that there are necessarily biological means of entering into 'communication with God'.

The spine: energy's helm

The quality of muscular tone which determines pre-expressivity is directly linked to the position of the spinal column.

The spinal column can sag, emphasising weight and the power of inertia, but it can also be held erect or bent in particular ways, thus creating an architecture of tensions that dilate the performer's presence.

All extra-daily body techniques, part of or connected to codified theatrical forms, are based on the mastery of a particular posture, that is, a particular placement of the spinal column and the parts of the body connected to it: the neck, the back, the shoulders, the abdomen and the hips.

The various theatrical forms are distinguished by the different ways the spinal column is used to affect muscular tonus.

Attentive observation reveals that a performer from the Peking Opera has his spinal column extended upwards and that a Japanese noh performer maintains a slight curve in the upper part of the spinal column while holding the pelvis back.

In India's bharatanatyam, the spinal column is perfectly vertical. In relation to this vertical line, the shoulders and the neck are used as dynamic elements that discipline and channel the performer's temperament. Still in India, in another classical dance form, odissi, the spinal column is held in a curved 'S' form caused by the lateral displacement of the hips and by a slight movement

of the neck in the opposite direction in order to balance the shoulders (cf. *Tribhangi* in *Opposition*).

In Java, the origin of wayang wong lies in puppet theatre. This perhaps explains why the spinal column is upright and uplifted. Imperceptible movements forwards create an effect of new energy with each new step.

On the neighbouring island of Bali, the spinal column is bent in the same way as occurs in Indian kathakali, and the head-dress trembles due to the rapid movements of the neck.

Every extra-daily technique is the consequence of a change of a point of balance in daily technique. This change affects the spine and therefore the way the upper part of the body is extended, and the way the pelvis is held: that is, the way of moving in space.

33–42. Position of the spinal column in various dance cultures, selected by American dancer Russel Meriwether Hughes, known as La Meri (1899–1988), an avid student of ethnic dance; she practised and taught the techniques throughout Europe and America.

43–46. (**top**) Japanese salutation in the kneeling position, demonstrated by Kosuke Nomura at the Volterra ISTA, 1981: a daily technique which has been transferred intact to the theatre. The spinal column is curved opposite to its natural position, giving the action a great dignity. In European actors who imitate the action in a superficial way, without physical awareness, this dignity becomes servility. (**bottom**) The actors of the Paris Vaudeville Theatre in Judith Gautier's *The Princess of Love* (1907).

The silent scream

At the end of the third scene in Brecht's *Mother Courage*, the soldiers carry Schweizerkas's body onstage. They suspect that he is the son of Mother Courage and want her to identify the body. According to Brecht's text, when her son's body is laid before her, Mother Courage shakes her head twice, indicating that she doesn't recognise him. The soldiers then carry the body away to bury it in a common grave.

When Helene Weigel, the greatest performer of female Brechtian characters, played this scene, she remained immobile: she moved only her head, signalling to the soldiers that the body was not that of her son. When they forced her to look at the body one more time, she again refused to recognise it, maintaining a fixed and absent expression. But when the body was carried away, Weigel turned her head in the opposite direction and opened her mouth wide, in a 'silent scream'.

George Steiner, who saw Weigel at the Berliner Ensemble, relates:

> She turned her head the other way and stretched her mouth wide open, just like the screaming horse in Picasso's *Guernica*. A harsh and terrifying, indescribable sound issued from her mouth. But, in fact, there was no sound. Nothing. It was the sound of absolute silence. A silence which screamed and screamed throughout the theatre, making the audience bow their heads as if they had been hit by a blast of wind.
>
> (G. Steiner, *Death of Tragedy*, 1961)

This was a spectator's impression. Now here is how the same work is described by a theatre historian:

> Weigel found that she was to perform in the midst of symbols, onstage with a cart that was partly a war-machine, partly a bazaar, mounted on a revolve which represented Mother Courage's world and which carried her around the stage in her various scenes. She managed to avoid being overwhelmed by all of this because, as an actress who had worked with Piscator, she knew that she could combat the abstract by exploiting her character's physicality and the creativity of her own body in the situation.
>
> She began to rehearse, using a criterion which Brecht had established in the Berliner Ensemble: she worked through the whole part over and over again, concentrating only on approximated interpretative

47–49. The 'silent scream': Helene Weigel (1900–73) in Bertold Brecht's *Mother Courage* at the Berliner Ensemble (1949). The intensity of the scream is sustained by the various tensions in the spinal column.

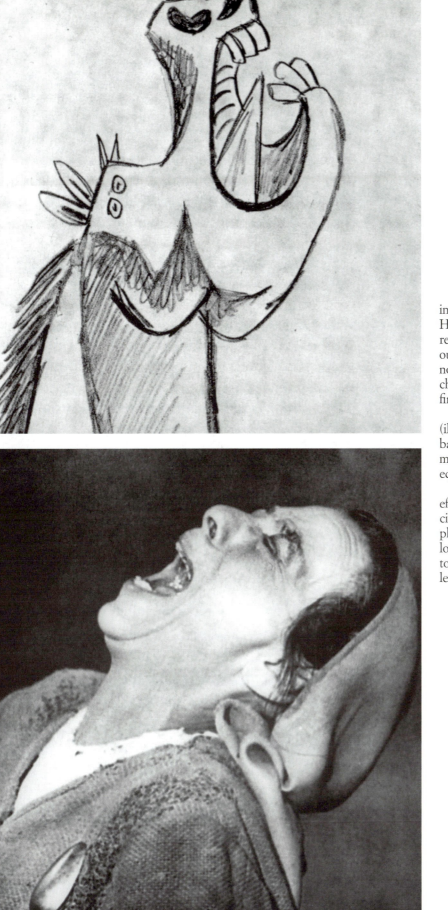

sketches. By the time of the opening, Weigel had at her disposal about a hundred different details and narrative poses that she could use to reveal the relationship between Mother Courage and the other characters; and she developed other details and poses in subsequent performances. The pose of tremendous suffering, the unforgettable image of Weigel standing with her mouth stretched wide open but emitting no sound, first appeared after many performances, when out of her subconscious came an image she had once seen in a newspaper photo, that of an Indian woman crying over the murder of her son.

(Claudio Meldolesi, *Brecht in Rehearsal* in C. Meldolesi, L. Olivi, *Brecht Regista*, *Brecht the Director*).

A propos of the same performance – in the same book, in the diary kept by Hans Bunge, Brecht's assistant – one reads: 'Weigel, for example, had worked out Mother Courage's way of walking not by theorising, but by wearing the character's dress and shoes from the very first rehearsal'.

As can be clearly seen in the photo (ill.47–49), Weigel's 'silent scream' is based on tension in the spinal column by means of which she conveys an energy equivalent to that of a scream.

The understanding of the emotive effect of the spinal column, and especially the attention given to concrete physical details, is also clear in the following episode, told by Helene Weigel to Ekkehard Schall, one of her colleagues at the Berliner Ensemble:

Helene Weigel once told me the following story. As a young actress she once played at the side of the great Albert Bassermann, in one of Ibsen's plays, I think. In one scene in which she was on the stage with him, he received one piece of catastrophic news after another: father dead, mother dead, children dead. (Laughter) To take in these catastrophic bits of news, Bassermann chose to stand with his back to the audience. One day Helene complained to him that his face, turned away from the audience, did not show any emotion, and what was worse, took on some private expressions. And she quoted him as having replied: "So what, the audience doesn't see my face." He played everything with his back: he played every shock he received with his back.

(Interview with Ekkehard Schall in *New Theatre Quarterly*, no. 6, May, 1986)

50–51. (**top**) Picasso: third rendering of *Head of a Neighing Horse* (1937), study for *Guernica* (Picasso Museum, Madrid); (**bottom**) the 'silent scream' of Helene Weigel.

From 24–6 October, 1980, an international symposium was held as part of the first public session of ISTA in Bonn. Among the participants was Jerzy Grotowski, who, in an interview with Franco Ruffini, commented on Barba's investigation of the principles for the performer's technical work.

Pragmatic laws

Jerzy Grotowski

Barba has formulated three essential principles in the field of work we call performer's technique. Generally speaking, he has stated that the performer's technique is an extra-daily body technique. Daily body technique, such as has been defined by the French anthropologist Marcel Mauss, and extra-daily body technique, which I would call a technique of amplification, exist and have always existed in every culture. There are integration techniques, such as yoga for example, and there are others, also extra-daily, which are the amplification of a socio-biological phenomenon.

When we watch a noh performer walk by dragging his feet without lifting them from the ground, we are in fact seeing an amplification of something that is found in the normal way of walking in his particular culture. This appears to me to be very important. In his work on the clear, practical differentiation of the difference between daily technique and extra-daily technique, Barba is dealing with extra-daily technique as amplification. Therefore, when he compares daily techniques from certain Asian cultures and the extra-daily techniques of the performer, he is discovering certain laws, or objectives, which deserve to be pointed out.

This could give rise to endless polemics from the scientific point of view but to give in to such discussion would be an error or would in any case not be very useful, since in reality the laws of which Barba is speaking are pragmatic laws. Pragmatic laws are those that tell us how to behave in order to reach particular states or particular results or particular necessary connections. They do not tell us that something works in a specific way; they tell us: you must behave in a certain way. Barba has established three pragmatic laws. Something happens in a certain way if one behaves in a certain way. It is not a question of analysing how this happens, but of knowing what one must do so that it happens.

The first law of which Barba speaks has to do with the body's balance, which, in extra-daily techniques, operates on a completely different level than in daily life. In daily life, we use a kind of balance which we might call 'easy', easy because it has been incorporated since childhood. In extra-daily technique, this balance is given up in order to reach another level of balance which – this is my observation – amplifies normal balance.

One could say that this is an extra-daily balance, a 'luxury balance', as Barba calls it.

The second law is the law of the opposition of the direction of movements or impulses. When one part of the body executes an impulse in a given direction, another part of the body executes an impulse in the opposite direction. This has important consequences on the muscular level, especially with respect to contraction and relaxation. In certain acting schools it is said that the key to everything is relaxation. But the key is not relaxation, it is the relationship between contraction and relaxation. In a performer who is completely relaxed, nothing happens; on the other hand, completely blind contractions, which are neurotic contractions, are, as we know, impediments.

But there is a particular interplay of contractions and relaxations which, although it also occurs in daily life, is amplified in the performance situation, which Barba calls a luxury situation. This is, certainly, a question of opposite directions at the same time. But it takes place inside the body: if one executes an impulse towards the left, there is something that executes a counter-impulse towards the right. And so on, up and down, forward and backward. This happens in normal life, in daily techniques, but in the performance situation there is an extreme amplification, which results in something that already possesses another quality.

This interplay of contradictions, of contractions and relaxations, of the opposite directions of impulses, is carried to such an extreme that one can say that man is converted, physiologically, into a sign. It is important to understand that this state is reached through training and conscious effort, in accordance with the laws of physiology. The sign is the result of the amplification of both biological laws and social conditions: the amplification takes place on two levels.

The third pragmatic law is that the process of action taken to the extreme by the performer can be executed and observed from the point of view of energy in space or from the point of view of energy in time. Obviously, we could begin a new terminological discussion concerning what energy is and what the terms energy in space and energy in time mean. In any case, the difference is very clear. It has to do either with causing the process to result in movement as a kinetic quality which is produced in space, or to compress that which is essential to a potential movement in space, to conceal it beneath the skin. The movement's impulses are begun, but then held back. One then sees that the body is alive and that something is happening in the space, but as if retained under the skin. The body is alive, it is doing something which is extremely precise, but the river is flowing in the realm of time: kinetics in space passes to a second level. This is energy in time.

There are also sub-laws. For example, what one could call anti-impulse, anti-movement, which Barba describes with the Scandinavian term *sats*. And it is very concrete, it exists. It can occur at different levels, as a kind of silence before a movement, a silence filled with potential, or it can occur as the suspension of an action at a given moment.

Sats

The result of the *sats* is that what is seen, what happens, has the time to be absorbed. Because of the *sats*, one also understands that the process has had the time to be absorbed as form, form understood as *shape*. But how can this be studied in the various extra-daily techniques, in the performance situation? Differences can be observed between Japanese performers, Balinese performers and the different forms of

Indian theatre. Barba has taken the specialisations of Asian performers as a point of departure for pragmatic analysis. One could say that each of these types of classical Asian theatre relates to a specific daily body technique but has a physiological base which causes what is observed to be valid for everyone.

If the body technique changes, then it changes from the social point of view, but remains rooted in the same biological reality. Every form of Asian theatre has a very conscious, extremely formalised specialisation which is an extra-daily technique of amplification, and this particular technique has a very defined field of possibilities. If different extra-daily techniques work in a similar way in the performance situation, in spite of different specialisations, one can obviously deduce that the laws which are in operation are, *tout court*, universal.

There is no codification of the performer's art in European theatre. The performer improvises, but according to stereotypes of daily life, or according to a misunderstood spontaneity, where to be spontaneous means to be wild, to move violently, to shout, to act violently towards others or to embrace. In fact, improvisation really begins when the performer chooses certain very concrete and precise limits. For example, for the character of Kattrin, the mute daughter of Mother Courage, Iben concentrated only on her way of walking [Grotowski is referring here to *Moon and Darkness*, the performance presented by Odin Teatret actress Iben Nagel Rasmussen during the International Symposium]. Only then can the performer go beyond his or her own sociological and biological objectivity and reach personal subjectivity. And at the moment when objectivity and subjectivity meet, the performer comes alive. One could say that there is no freedom that does not pay the price of asceticism. But here asceticism is not mysticism or religiosity but rather something concrete, a limitation of the self.

In the theatre, this is the task for directors. On the one hand, they must follow what I have called the *via negativa*, that is, they must eliminate any obstacles that stand in the performer's way, and on the other hand, they must also represent the positive pole, they must give the performers precise, definite themes. The performers then have a point of departure for their improvisation.

Logos *and* bios

When I speak about socio-biological objectivity and about subjectivity, I am also speaking about the problem of *logos* and *bios*. There is *logos* and there is *bios*. *Logos* is linked to descriptive, analytical reasoning. In a different way, it also relates to the Asian performer. The Asian performer, rooted in his tradition, uses his body to express words, sentences, speeches . . . and is therefore *logos*. But it is as if, due to the strength of his tradition, his *logos* has preserved certain principles of *bios*. And this is why the Asian performer appears to us to be alive. *Logos* and *bios* represent division, and therefore it is very dangerous to talk about the performer's expressivity. Barba rightly talks only about the performer's pre-expressive level. If the performer expresses, it is because he *wants* to express. And so, division once again arises. There is a part of the performer which orders, and a part which executes the orders. True expression, one could say, is that of a tree.

There exists a profound relationship between what Barba is doing in ISTA and what I am doing in the Theatre of Sources: we are both concerned with transcultural phenomena. Culture, any specific culture, determines the objective bio-sociological base because every culture is linked to daily body techniques. It is therefore important to observe what remains constant when these cultures vary, what transcultural elements are discernible.

52. Dario Fo, Eugenio Barba and Jerzy Grotowski at the Volterra ISTA, 1981.

The culture of the text and the culture of the stage

Franco Ruffini

Text, mise-en-scène, performance, theatre . . . these are terms that need to be reviewed so that we can clearly distinguish one from the other. The best way to do this is to approach the question from a distance.

The sound of two hands clapping

One of the techniques used in zen to reach enlightenment is the *koan*, a paradoxical question on which the master invites the student to meditate. One of the most well-known *koans* is the following: the master asks the student to make the sound of two hands clapping, which the student has no difficulty in doing. Then the master asks to hear the sound of one hand clapping. And so the process of enlightenment begins.

But what is the paradox in this *koan*? Upon reflection, one realises that the paradox arises out of the logical and rigorous application of a premise which is so spontaneous that it does not even need to be verbalised. The premise is the following: if the sound of two hands clapping exists (and it does exist), then it cannot be other than the sum of the sounds of each individual hand clapping.

Analogously, one could say: if the 'two-handed theatre' exists (and it does exist), then it cannot be anything other than the sum of two 'one-handed theatres', the 'text' and the 'stage', the latter being understood as the collection of human, technical, material, aesthetic and other values that make possible the representation of the text itself.

However, the sound of two hands clapping is obviously not the sum of the sounds of each individual hand clapping, but the result of a particular kind of relationship in which the two hands collaborate as partners.

I therefore propose to call *theatre* the product of the collaborative relationship between the *text* and the *stage*, with stage understood as defined above. And also propose to say immediately that according to this definition there has not existed and does not exist a *single* theatre but *as many* theatres as there have been and are particular types of relationships contracted between the text and the stage.

1–2. The text–stage relationship understood as a poor/rich, hard/soft, programmable/non-programmable, univocal/varied relationship: Shakespeare's *Hamlet* through the ages. As Hamlet: (**left**) English actor David Garrick; (right) American actor Edwin Thomas Booth. Garrick (1717–79) was one of the first actors to restore the Shakespearian text, reinstating much of the text that had not been performed since Shakespeare's time. Edwin Booth (1833–93), endowed with a beautiful voice and fine presence, played Hamlet for 100 consecutive nights in the 1864–5 season, a record which helped establish him the first American actor to become famous in Europe.

One can deal with the text or with the stage in isolation or one can speak of them as the respective partners of other collaborators but in both these cases one could no longer presume to be speaking of theatre.

Only when the text and the stage collaborate are *theatres* born. And it is this particular relationship that determines the varied typology of theatres throughout history. This does not, however, jeopardise the extra-theatrical motivations (political, social or of any other kind) which, on the contrary, often contribute to the orientation and definition of the relationship itself.

In the light of all that has been said up to this point, a short introduction to the history of theatres could be put as follows: there exist, and there have existed, a text civilisation and a stage civilisation. These two civilisations have lived and live according to different *tempi* and in different ways, proceeding along parallel lines or diverging. One is often ignorant of the existence of the other. Each of them has established individual relationships with other civilisations and sometimes, under particular historical circumstances, they have established specific relationships between themselves, giving birth to theatres. Among the many relationships, there is one that has played an important rôle in historiographic reflection: the relationship between *repertory-text* and the *academic stage*, whose statutes became hegemonies in Europe's great capitals from the 1600s to the 1800s. The result of this relationship is the rather homogenous grouping which we could call the *traditional theatres*, whose ideological hypostasis is THE THEATRE, or the *theatre-institution* of generic speeches.

Obviously, there are many different forms of relationship and cultural relativism that prevent us from saying that one form is a priori better or healthier than other forms. The form we have called the theatre-institution gives us the opportunity to extend our investigation a little further, even if only in a negative way. What is the 'impelling reason' for its hegemony? It is the presumed functioning of its two partners, which in turn is based on 'adherence to reality'.

But are repertory-text and the academic stage really so healthy? Let us consider the former for a moment, already accepting that each of the following affirmations will have at least one exception, a fact which merely confirms their validity as rules.

In repertory-text there are no silent characters who are important in the overall plot, no characters that, while not being prevented from speaking, choose to be silent. There are, on the contrary, characters who declare their silence, that is, characters who speak of their desire not to speak.

In repertory-text there are no disassociated, schizophrenic characters who concretely manifest a contradiction between thinking and doing. There are, however, characters who, speaking, expose the often painful contradictions of their thoughts and who from time to time act according to a specific intention.

In repertory-text there is no simultaneity of actions, that is, there are no differing (but equally important) actions occurring at different places at the same time. Neither is there temporal displacement: the before and after, with respect to the now of the action, only occur as memories and dreams related in the present.

One could continue in the same vein, analysing, for example, the barely realistic state of the monologue, but this would not be particularly helpful to us. It is useful, however, to point out how all the above mentioned 'pathologies' (which are, I repeat, only true as statistics or maxims) are explicable and necessary if one observes with a less than normally pious eye the state of health of the other partner, the academic stage.

The absence of silent characters in repertory-text compensates for the pathology of the academic stage, where an actor regularly and for consistent periods of time can be on stage and in a scene only when he is speaking. Another characteristic of the academic stage is equivalent to the incoherent coherence of schizophrenics: the academic stage is a gesture tradition which favours macro-movements, those which have a clear and codifiable semantic co-respective, rather than micro-movements, considered either too subtle to be significant, or, even worse, deleterious to the general action, like a noise in the background.

Are the 'to oneself' and 'aside' speeches, which are declaimed in such a way that they reach the last row of the theatre, consistent with reality? And what can be said of the curtain between one act and another? It was not by accident that the curtain was adopted in the second half of the 1700s just when the statutes of the theatre-institution were being established. It is obvious that each of these pathologies, and others, are equivalent to and compensate for, with respect to an adherence to reality, a symmetrical pathology in the text. The fact that they can be legitimately called conventions takes nothing away from the fact that they are, however, conventions motivated by the specific collaborative relationship between the text and the stage.

'Poor' text and 'rich' stage

Etienne Decroux, discussing the relationship between mime and words, wondered about the chances for a successful meeting between the two, and generalising, concluded that the two could contract a profitable relationship only if one of them is 'rich' compared to the 'poverty' of the other: two richnesses are not complementary. Let us try to explore this idea a little further.

Poverty is not destitution. One associates poverty with sobriety, rigour, severity. Austerity, perhaps, is the word that comes closest. Austerity, understood here as poverty, rather than evoking the desperate and unprogammable disorder of destitution, has more in common with the proper balancing of a budget. It is a line of conduct that is primarily attentive to what is essential. A person living in 'dignified poverty' is spoken most highly of, precisely because he is able to ensure that his family does not lack the essentials. Poverty, then, as austerity, as precise direction, or, also, as toughness, rigidity, programmability: almost exclusive attention to the essential.

Richness is not only opulence. The term 'rich' can be used to refer to a drapery, a pattern-book. In both cases the term has nothing to do with value or with price, but rather with variety, configuration, and unprogrammability. A rich drapery can also be made with a poor fabric. A rich assortment can also be an assortment of knick-knacks. Richness, then, as flexibility, as variety, ordered and living disorder.

In the context of the definitions that we have tried to delineate here, Decroux's affirmation appears to be something more than a tempting metaphor. It is perhaps a general principle which, upon reflection, can be seen to define the internal dialectic of every vital and artistic process in its state of being and becoming. The foregoing will be considered here as a regulatory hypothesis.

3–7. *Hamlet* through the ages: interpretations of the play by Gordon Craig (**top left**); André Antoine (**below left**); John Barrymore (**right**); Sarah Bernhardt (p.273, **left**). Gordon Craig's directorial inventions – we see here his design for the Hamlet produced at the Moscow Art Theatre in 1911 – revealed new possibilities for the use of light and space in modern directing. The 1908 mise-en-scène at the Théâtre Antoine in Paris had actress Suzanne Desprès in the lead rôle, an attempt to reverse the traditional interpretation of the character which had prevailed during the nineteenth century. The desire for change and the phenomenon of star-worship went hand in hand when it came to Sarah Bernhardt (1844–1923) and John Barrymore (1882–1942), seen here in a photo from 1923. With director-oriented theatre came the taste for a modern and expressionistic mise-en-scène of Shakespeare's tragedy, a tendency represented here by a project of Meyerhold. According to Alex Gladkov, Meyerhold was to have inaugurated his new theatre with a *Hamlet* designed by Picasso and played by actress Zinaida Rajkh (1894–1939), seen in a photo from a rehearsal (1937) (p. 273, **right**).

Seen in the light of this hypothesis, the text/stage relationship must be considered as a poor/rich relationship, that is, rigid/flexible, programmable/unprogrammable, specific/varied, and so on. Given the relation between the terms in the original pair (text/stage) and the terms in the following pairs, it will be necessary to consider, even if it may seem paradoxical, that text = poor and stage = rich.

In what way can the text be defined as 'poor' in relation to the stage, which in turn is defined as 'rich'? In its dialectic with the stage, the text is the direction factor, the element of programmability, the barrier which (because of friction or resistance) allows the scenic factors of variety, of non-programmability, of disorder, to express their own energy as richness. Paradoxically, for those theatres throughout history in which the text has totally dominated the stage, what is expressed is not a richness of the text but actually its austerity, its intransigence, the predomination of a programming which submits the entire life of the performance to the textual narrative. Even more paradoxically, when the stage has tried to express its richness without the resistance of text, this very richness has been transformed into its parody, opulence: not ordered disorder, but chaos; not variety, but indiscriminate proteanism; not elastic flexibility, but flaccid inelasticity.

One must ask oneself if the same dialectic might also be found at the synchronic level and at the very core of the terms 'poor' and 'rich' that define it: if perhaps the 'life' of the text and the stage is also the result of a text/stage, poor/rich, rigid/variable relationship. This leads us immediately to a re-examination of the notion of dramaturgy.

Dramaturgy

Dramaturgy has always been understood as something which has to do only with text. The actor's or director's dramaturgy have until now, been only metaphorically discussed. Eugenio Barba has written:

The word 'text', before meaning spoken or written, printed or manuscripted text, meant 'weaving'. In this sense, there is no performance without text. That which concerns the 'text' (the 'weaving' or 'thread') of the performance can be defined as 'dramaturgy', that is, *drama-ergon*, the work of the actions. The way in which the actions work is the plot. (c.f. *Dramaturgy*)

Leaving aside for the moment this interesting definition of text, let us try to develop the considerations more specifically with respect to dramaturgy.

Dramaturgy is seen as 'work' in a way that seems to me to be totally consistent with the meaning of the word as it is used in physics. In physics, work is not synonymous with energy. Energy expresses the capacity to carry out work and this only occurs when a force is manifest in movement. In a certain sense, work is the intermediate phase between energy and the movement determined by a force, and it is the phase which makes it possible for energy to be explicitly modulated. Dramaturgy understood in this way thus appears as the filter, the channel, by means of which energy takes form in movement. Actions carry out the work, whether they be actions understood in the Aristotelian sense, and therefore part of the text, or whether they are actions in the more direct sense: the actions of the actors, the props, the lights, etc., that is, actions that belong to the stage.

One can therefore affirm that there is a text dramaturgy, and a dramaturgy of all the stage's components. And that there is also a comprehensive dramaturgy, of the performance, in which both the actions of the text and the actions of the stage are interwoven. Dramaturgy seen from this perspective can be considered as the concept which unifies the text and the stage as well as the concept which makes it possible to formulate in less vague and elusive terms that which has often been called 'life' whether it be the life of the text, the stage or the performance.

But let us return to the principal argument. Both the actions of the text and the actions of the stage carry out 'work': but where does the energy come from that makes this work possible? The answer to this question lies in what was discussed previously with respect to the text/stage (poor/rich) dialectic. Both the energy of the text and the energy of the stage are determined by the friction or resistance between the opposed and complementary poles of the dialectic. Barba defines the two types of 'plot' as:

'concatenation' and 'simultaneity'. We can add a further refinement to this proposal, synthesised as follows.

Theatre is the result of the collaborative relationship between the text and the stage: this was the initial hypothesis. We then questioned the nature and dynamics of this relationship, proposing to consider it both diachronically and synchronically as a relationship between a poor pole (rigid, programmable) and a rich pole (flexible, non-programmable). We then proposed the hypothesis that the poor/rich dialectic is not established only *between* text and stage but also *within* both the text and the stage. The definition of dramaturgy proposed by Eugenio Barba has permitted us to see this dialectic (the dialectic of the text, of the stage, of the entire performance) as the work of actions, work made possible, in terms of necessary energy, by the friction, resistance, or opposition between the poor element and the rich element of the relationship. The concatenation and simultaneity poles thus make it possible for us now to name and operatively define the two terms of the dialectic.

Concatenation = poverty, rigidity, the essential, programmability = the text.
Simultaneity = richness, flexibility, variety, non-programmability = the stage.

Seen from this point of view, the 'text' of the text, the rigid, directed, programmed element, is the conflict (as defined by Szondi) and the narrative. The 'stage' of the text, the flexible, non-directed, non-programmable element, is the character and all that has to do with the character (dialogue, micro-situations), above and beyond the direction imposed by the conflict and the story. The 'text' of the text is its concatenation component, and the 'stage' of the text is its simultaneity component, the diverse and often contrasting but co-present aspects that emerge in the character and, literally, enrich it. The friction between concatenation and simultaneity gives rise to the energy by means of which the work of both macro- and micro-actions is revealed in movement, logical even if non-programmable, varied although directed: that is, in the life of the text.

As far as the stage is concerned, the 'text' has to do with meanings, or, as Ferdinando Taviani proposes, with the 'accorded meanings' (c.f. *Views*), while the stage has to do with the 'non-accorded meanings'.

Briefly outlining the dramaturgy of the performance, we could suggest that the textual term (deriving from both the text and the stage), performs the function of guaranteeing a semantic anchor for the spectator and that the stage term (it also deriving both from the text and the stage) performs the function of guaranteeing an opening, a zone of profound fruition, or at least, a more personalised zone.

Rôle type and character

The text/stage dialectic between the respective terms of the primary relationship can be clarified by briefly delving into some of the questions relative to the actor.

Actor and character are the two poles of a duality which have been the subject of considerable historical and theoretical investigation. The actor who enters the character; the character which, adapting itself, enters the actor; the actor and the character which meet at a point halfway between them; the actor who fixes and maintains a critical distance from his character . . . these are only a few of the more familiar formulations regarding this issue. Then there is sensitivity and insensitivity, hot and cold, technique and talent, possession and division, the 'absurd profession' . . . one could continue at length with these references which are evidence of a metaphorical attention to the myth of the actor more than of a real attention to his person.

But how, concretely, does the actor's work, as it is understood in relation both to Stanislavsky and to physics, develop? What does it feed on, where does it draw its energy from? As a heuristic hypothesis, one can assert that the actor's work is nourished by the friction or resistance between a rigid and directed pole, the text, and one which is on the other hand variable and non-directed; again, the text and the stage. The work method consisting of parts and rôles illustrates exemplarily what we have been discussing here. It is a method that actors have used until recently in an explicit way and that they still perhaps use, indirectly and incompletely, even today.

From the end of the sixteenth century until the beginning of the twentieth century, each theatre company was organised on the basis of rôles (lead actor, young actor, lover, noble father . . . to name but a few) each of which was given to a particular actor. The actor took on a certain rôle because of his physical appearance, voice type, etc., that is, on the basis of extra-theatrical characteristics and also on the basis of other acting parts he had previously played. The rôle, then, was not only the sum of individual parts, but also something which, while deriving from the parts, determined them, both in the process of their being undertaken and in their treatment. In any case, it is possible to say that in the actor's work, the rôle constituted the rigid element (the text) while the individual parts were the variable element (the stage).

With respect to his rôle, the actor could 'work' on his particular character, causing it to interact with the rôle by means of friction or resistance, both in relationship to the specific part and in relationship to other analagous parts which could be played by the same rôle. The parts of the rôle, as an aspect of the phase of work, constituted the 'pattern-book' of variability which has often been referred to: a variability, then, which was not indiscriminate but controlled by the relative rigidity of the rôle. Perhaps the relationship between part and sub-text in Stanislavsky's 'method' could be considered in the same terms; training, practised by many group theatre actors and imposing the continuity of exercise, could be seen to have an analagous function, providing these actors with a rigid barrier, a 'poor' reference point, in short, a kind of rôle on which (and against which) the actor causes the part to interact.

During the process of building the character it is possible to actually see the rôle and the part, the text and the stage, the term poor and the term rich of the relationship at work. This visibility usually ends at the moment of the performance, that is, when the process of construction is completed, when the spectator and the scholar are induced to infer that such an interaction is not present and was not present before and behind the curtain. But in this case something occurs which is similar to what occurs at dusk when one looks out to where the sky and the sea meet. It seems that there the sea and the sky blend, that they literally melt into each other and are a single thing. Naturally, we know that this is just an optical illusion and to convince ourselves that this is so, it is enough to look first at the horizon and then at the sea before it meets the horizon, and we see that the sea and the sky are visibly separate.

What produces this optical illusion? Not the elimination of *difference*, but only the elimination of *distance*. And so it is with the actor's work. In the moment of performance (and only in the best cases), while maintaining the substantial and vital difference between rôle and part (between the text and the stage, between rigid and variable), distance is eliminated. The two terms, come together, adhere, making the spectator see the optical illusion of an identity. But to become aware that this is not the case, it is necessary to go behind the footlight and the curtain, into a space that spectators, because of convention, and scholars, because of laziness and prejudice, are wary of entering.

8–11. *Hamlet* through the ages: Karel Ilar (**top left**); Alec Guinness (**top right**); Laurence Olivier (**bottom left**); Ingmar Bergman (**bottom right**). The Czechoslovakian director Karel Ilar (1885–1915) belongs to the generation and milieu of the great theatrical experimenters of the 1920s (National Theatre of Prague, 1926). The modern dress production of *Hamlet* mounted by Tyrone Guthrie (1901–71) at London's Old Vic Theatre in 1938 featured Alec Guinness (first on the left) as a popular Hamlet. But it was the famous film version of the play produced by Laurence Olivier (1907–89) in 1948, with himself in the title rôle (**bottom left**), that brought *Hamlet* to the attention of the large cinema-going public. Ingmar Bergman's version is an interpretation of the Shakespearian tragedy filtered through Strindberg, French existentialism and film. In the photo (**bottom right**) the actors are: Peter Stormare (Hamlet), Gunnel Lindblom (Gertrude) and Borge Ahlstedt (Claudio).

From 'learning' to 'learning to learn'

Eugenio Barba

When it comes to observing the noh, those who truly under-stand the art watch it with the spirit, while those who do not, merely watch it with their eyes. To see with the spirit is to grasp the substance; to see with the eyes is merely to observe the effect. Thus it is that beginning actors merely grasp the effect and try to imitate that.

(Zeami, *Shikadensho*)

The myth of technique

During our first years of work, we too believed in the 'myth of technique', something which it was possible to acquire, possess, and which would give the actor conscious mastery of his body. So, at this stage, we practised exercises to develop the dilation of the eyes, for example, in order to increase their expressiveness. They were exercises I had observed in India in 1963 while studying kathakali actor training.

Like in a melting pot, where the most disparate metals fuse, I began by trying to blend together, inside myself, the most diverse influences, the impressions which for me had been the most fertile: Asian theatre, the experiments of the Great Reform, my personal experience in Poland and with Grotowski. I wanted to adapt all this to my ideal of techni-cal perfection, even in the part of the artistic work which we called composition, a word which had arrived at Odin Teatret via the Russian and French terminology and Grotowski's interpretation of the same. I believed that com-position was the actor's ability to create signs, to mould his body consciously into a deformation that was rich in sug-gestiveness and power of association: the body of the actor as a Rosetta stone and the spectator in the rôle of Champollion. The aim was to attain consciously, by cold cal-culation, something that is warm and that obliges the spectator to believe with all their senses.

In the first stage of our work, all the actors did the same exercises together, following a common collective rhythm. Then we realised that rhythm varied for each individual. Some people have a fast vital rhythm, others a slower one. We began to talk about organic rhythm, not in the sense of a regular beat but of variation, pulsation, like the rhythm of the heart. This perpetual variation, however minute, revealed the existence of a wave of organic reactions that engaged the entire body. Training could only be individual.

This faith in technique as a sort of magic power that could render the actor invulnerable also guided us in the field of voice work. At first, we followed the practices of Asian theatre: straightforward imitations of certain timbres of the voice. Using Grotowski's terminology, we called the differ-ent voice tones 'resonators'. In Asian theatre training, the student learns entire rôles mechanically, with all the vocal nuances, timbres, intonations, exclamations – a complete

1. Iben Nagel Rasmussen in a demonstration of her early training at Odin Teatret (Holstebro ISTA, 1986).

fabric of sounds perfected through tradition that the actor must repeat precisely in order to gain the approbation of a critical audience. We too began coldy to find a series of timbres, tones and intonations, and exercised them daily.

This period of calculated work, of pure 'technicity', seemed to confirm that the hypothesis of the actor-virtuoso was correct. The effects produced were interesting.

(Eugenio Barba, 'Words or Presence', in
Theatre: Solitude, Craft, Revolt, Black Mountain Press,
Aberystwyth, 1999)

A decisive phase

Our experience entered a decisive phase when I said to each of my actors: 'Go your own way, there is no common method.' What happened? With the loss of an external reference point, each actor's work became more difficult, but also more per-sonalised. After more than twenty years, some of my actors still train regularly. The meaning of this work belongs to them alone. And yet they know that training does not guarantee artistic results. It is a way of making one's intentions coher-ent. If one has chosen to do theatre, one must do it. But one must also shatter the theatre's framework with all the power of one's energies and intelligence.

(Eugenio Barba, 'Seminar on Training
at the University of Lecce', in
F. Taviani, *Il libro del'Odin*, Feltrinelli, Milan, 1975)

2. (**left**) Roberta Carreri and Julia Varley during training at Odin Teatret, 1982–4.
3. (**right**) Toni Cots during training at Odin Teatret, 1982–4.

Total presence

The way performers exploit and compose the weight/ balance relationship and the opposition between different movements, their duration and their rhythms, enables them to give the spectator not only a different perception of their (the performers') presence, but also a different perception of time and space: not a time in space, but a 'space-time'.

It is only by mastering the material opposition between their weight and their spinal column that the performers acquire a yardstick with which they can measure their work. They can apply this yardstick to all other physical, psychological and social oppositions in the situations which they analyse and articulate in their creative process.

The process of mastering one's own energies is extremely long: it is a veritable new conditioning. At first the performer is like a child learning to walk and move and must repeat the simplest gestures *ad infinitum* in order to transform his inert movements into action.

Our social use of the body is necessarily a product of a culture: the body has been incultured and colonised. It knows only the uses and perspectives for which it has been educated. In order to find others, it must be detached from its models. It must inevitably be directed towards a new form of 'culture' and undergo a new 'colonisation'. It is precisely this path that makes performers discover their own life, their own independence and their own physical eloquence.

The training exercises are this 'second colonisation'. [. . .]

An exercise is an action that one learns and repeats after having chosen it with very precise objectives in mind.

For example: an actor wants to be able to go down onto his knees while bending both legs at the same time. At a certain moment, as he moves his body downwards, he loses control, his weight takes over, and he bangs his knees on the floor. The problem is therefore to find a counter-impulse that will permit him to go down to the floor, even rapidly, yet without hitting his knees and hurting himself. In order to solve this problem, he must find an exercise and repeat it.

Another exercise might be the result of trying to solve the problem of how to shift one's weight forward to the point where one no longer has control over the body. At this moment, the body, pulled by the force of gravity only, falls forward. It is therefore necessary to find a counter-impulse in mid-fall that enables one to avoid falling forward and to lower oneself to the side so as to absorb the shock of meeting the ground, gradually, along the side of the body.

The meaning of an exercise resides, finally, in:

1. beginning with a precise action that projects all energies in a determined direction;
2. giving a counter-impulse in mid-process that produces a deviation of direction and a change of dynamics and
3. managing to conclude in a precise position that contains the impulse (the *sats*) of the next action.

In this way, one builds up a whole series of exercises that one can learn and repeat, just as one repeats the words of a language. At first, the exercises are repeated like the words of a foreign language one wants to learn, in a mechanical fashion, but later they will become absorbed, will begin to come on their own. Then the performer can choose. It is possible to make a long training with even a very small number of exercises. The exercises can not only be repeated in a different order, they can also be done with different rhythms, in different directions, in an extroverted or introverted manner, by putting the accent on one or another of its phases. It is like the meaning of a sentence which, in spoken language, is not only the result of syntax but also of the stress and the tone that underline certain words. So it is in training, where the same chain of exercises takes on various logics, depending on the accents used.

It is the rhythm that is important, the linking of one exercise to another, and the organic way in which the performer directs the resulting chain. It is the same process that occurs in spoken language, where one doesn't pronounce words in a staccato fashion, but makes the end of each word coincide with the beginning of the next, in a series of waves that reflect emotional and rational rhythms, the moments of slowing down and of suspension, the moments of force and incisiveness.

Total presence has nothing to do with violence, with pressure or with the search for speed at any price. The performer can be extremely concentrated, motionless, but in this immobility keep all energies in hand, just like a drawn bow, ready to let the arrow fly.

What then is the value of an exercise once the performer has mastered it? It will no longer be of any use to repeat it, since from now on there will be no resistance to overcome. It is at this point that the other meaning of the word 'exercise' comes into play: to put to the test. One puts one's energies to the test. During his or her training, the performer can model, measure, explode and control their energies, let them go, and play with them, like something incandescent which is nevertheless controlled with cold precision. Using the training exercises, the performer tests his or her ability to achieve a condition of total presence, a condition that he or she will have to find again in the creative moment of improvisation and performance.

In fact, all physical exercises are spiritual exercises that are part of the person's overall development, his or her way of making their physical and mental energies burst forth and be controlled: those energies of which one is aware, which can be described with words, as well as those of which one is unable to speak. [. . .]

It is essential to transmit one's experiences to others, even at the risk of creating epigones who, out of excessive respect, will only repeat what they have learned. It is natural for someone to begin by repeating something that one does not own, which neither belongs to one's history nor arises from one's own research. This repetition is a point of departure that will permit the performer to make his or her own voyage.

Pierre Boulez once wrote that 'it is the relationship between *bad* fathers and *bad* sons' which makes cultural and aesthetic evolution possible. The risk one runs is of being a good father or a respectful son.

The worst thing is the lack of any relationship between father and son. Influencing a student is, according to common opinion, negative. The mark of influence is thought to reveal an unhealthy relationship. But one gets nowhere with this way of thinking: we are all influenced by someone.

The essential issue is the nature of the charge of energy that is released by the relationship: whether the influence is strong enough to make it possible to go a long way or whether it is so weak that it results only in a step on the same spot.

(Eugenio Barba, 'The Way of Opposites' in
Beyond the Floating Islands, Performing Arts Journal,
New York, 1986)

The period of vulnerability

The first days of work leave an indelible imprint. In the first days of his/her apprenticeship, the performer has all his/her potentialities intact: S/he then begins to make choices, to eliminate some potentialities in order to develop others. S/he can enrich their work only by narrowing the territory of his/her experiences, in order to be able to penetrate more deeply.

This is the period of vulnerability.

Every apprenticeship, every performer who begins to work, is characterised by the acquisition of an *ethos*. *Ethos* as scenic behaviour, that is, physical and mental technique, and ethos as a work ethic, that is, a mentality modelled by the environment, the human setting in which the apprenticeship develops.

The nature of the relationship between master and student, between student and student, between men and women, between old and young, the degree of fixity or elasticity in the hierarchy, norms, demands and limits that the student is placed under – all these factors impregnate his/her artistic future.

In other words: one must select without suffocating.

This apprenticeship dialectic is constant, whether it takes place in theatre schools or in the more direct relationship between master and student, in the performer's practical initiation, from when s/he first starts to 'rise from the ranks', or in autodidactic situations.

Serious impediments, which can suffocate the performer's future development, sometimes arise for unnoticed reasons.

In the period of apprenticeship, with unconscious violence or in order to be expedient, the student often arbitrarily limits the territory in which s/he explores the individual propensities of his or her energy. The range of the orbit whose poles are the vigorous *animus* energy and the soft *anima* energy are thus reduced. Some choices, apparently 'natural', become a prison.

If, in the period of apprenticeship, a male student adapts himself exclusively to male rôles, or a female student adapts herself exclusively to female rôles, then s/he is already undermining the exploration of his or her own energies on the pre-expressive level.

Instead, during apprenticeship, individual differentiation can undergo the negation of the differentiation of the sexes. The field of complementarity dilates. This is seen in the West (in modern dance, in mime or in certain theatre groups) when in training – work on the pre-expressive level – no account is taken of what is masculine or what is feminine; or in the East, when a performer takes on masculine or feminine rôles indiscriminately. The double-edged nature of the performer's particular energy becomes tangibly evident. The balance between the two energy poles, vigorous and soft, *animus* and *anima*, is preserved.

(Eugenio Barba, 'The Actor's Energy: Male/Female versus
Animus/Anima' in *New Theatre Quarterly*, 3:11,
Cambridge University Press, Cambridge, 1987)

Training interculturally

Richard Schechner

What is training for? I think of five functions that do not always exist separately. They overlap. In North America we train performers so they can interpret dramatic texts. That is a Euro-American cultural need. For this job of interpreting of a variety of texts from many periods in different styles you want flexible performers, people who can play Hamlet one day, Gogo the next, and Willie Loman the day after. Training to do this means that the performer is not the primary author or guardian of the text. He is the transmitter. And you want a transmitter to be transparent, as clear as possible.

The second function of training is to make the performer into one who transmits a 'performance text'. The performance text is the whole multi-channel process of communication that makes up a performative act. In some cultures, in Bali and Japan, for example, the notion of a performance text is very clear. Noh drama does not exist as a set of words which are then interpreted by actors. Noh drama exists as a set of words inextricably woven into music, gesture, dance, methods of recitation and costuming. We must look at noh not as the realisation of a written text but as a total performance text, where during portions of the performance non-verbal components are dominant.

These performance texts – noh, kathakali in India, classical ballet – exist as networks of behaviour rather than as verbal communications. It is not possible to translate performance texts into written texts. All attempts at 'notation' can be only partly successful. Training for the transmission of performance texts is fundamentally different than training for the interpretation of dramatic texts.

The third function of training – not too well known in Euro-American culture but very well known in Native America, Japan and elsewhere – is the preservation of secret knowledge. Methods of performing are valuable and they belong to specific families or groups who guard their secrets carefully. To be selected for training is to gain access to esoteric, powerful, closely guarded knowledge. This gives performance a power. Training is knowledge, knowledge is power. Training is the link to the past, to the other worlds of reality, to the future. And for a person to have access to performance knowledge is both a special privilege and a dangerous risk. It's not advertised, offered for sale at schools or freely written up in books.

This is the way shamans work. To shamans, performance knowledge is not simply about how to entertain, although it does not disparage entertainment, but goes beyond entertainment to getting at the core of the culture. The shaman is a performer whose personality and tasks put him or her at the fringe or the margin, but whose knowledge locates him or her at the centre. There is always that terrible tension between the centrifugal and the centripetal. Sophocles' Philoctetes is a kind of shaman – to get use of his bow, society must put up with his stinking wound.

The first two functions of training – the interpretation of dramatic texts and the transmission of performance texts can be abstracted and encoded. But this third – the learning of secrets – can only be acquired person to person. It is a most intimate process.

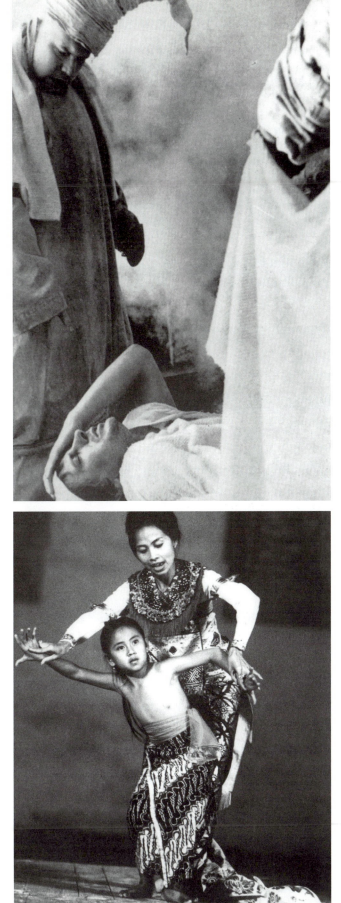

4–5. (**top**) Interpretation of a dramatic text: Peter Brook's production of *Marat-Sade* by Peter Weiss (1964). Transmission of a performance text: (**below**) Balinese dancer Swasti Widjaja Bandem teaching her daughter Ari.

279

The fourth function of training is to help performers achieve self-expression. This is an outgrowth of individualism. This kind of training specialises in getting the inside out – it is more concerned with psychology than behaviour. This kind of training is manifest in Grotowski's work, Stanislavsky's, and the Actor's Studio. Personal expression is closely woven into the interpretation of dramatic texts. So that we have Olivier's, Burton's, Brando's, Langella's Hamlet, but not England's or America's or Canada's Hamlet. The performer comes through the rôle. This kind of performer does not add to or vary a set rôle but shows himself in and through the rôle. The performer has a fuller claim on reality than the rôle. The rôle exists as a dramatic rather than a performance text. The personal expression of the performer is somehow twisted and kneaded into the interpretation of the written text. The text takes on a distinct personal flavour. And thereby, audiences enjoy both the sense of a collective act and the participation in a private revelation.

The fifth function of training is the formation of groups. In a culture as individualistic as the Euro-American, training is needed to overcome individualism. Even to work together as a group takes extensive training. Group expression with individual variation is the norm in Japan and India. It must be learned in Euro-America. Interculturally, there are two kinds of group training. In individualistic cultures, groups are formed to stand against the mainstream. In cultures with traditions of collective performances, the group is the mainstream. The group is either biological or sociological. Its bonds are very strong. And its leader is a 'father' or 'mother' who teaches the 'children'. Groups draw on the strongest allegiances a culture can offer. That's why Euro-American groups sometimes resemble families, religions, or political cells.

Let me now summarise these five functions of training:

1. interpretation of a dramatic text
2. transmission of a performance text
3. transmission of secrets
4. self-expression
5. group formation.

This text by Richard Schechner is an excerpt from a talk given by him at the University of Toronto, Canada, in 1981. Subsequently expanded, it was published as *The Performer: Training Interculturally*, in *Between Theatre and Anthropology* (Philadelphia, Pa. University of Pennsylvania Press, 1985).

6–8. (**top**) Transmission of the secret: page from the manuscript by Zeami, the founder of noh theatre, on the interpretation of female rôles. Zeami's treatises, written in the fifteenth century, remained a secret kept by noh actor-families until the beginning of this century; (**centre**) self-expression: 'plastic' training by Ryszard Cieslak (1971) one of the actors most representative of Grotowski's Teatr Laboratorium. Beside him stands Tage Larsen, at that time just beginning his work with Odin Teatret; (**bottom**) group formation: Roberta Carreri training at Odin Teatret (1974).

Training and the point of departure

Nicola Savarese

It is the first day of work which determines the meaning of one's journey in the theatre.
(Eugenio Barba, *Beyond the Floating Islands*)

Preliminary considerations

Contrary to what one might think, Asian performers do not, strictly speaking, undergo training: starting in early childhood, they often learn a performance score by imitating a master and repeat it until they have mastered it perfectly and can both perform it on its own or can link it to another score without becoming confused. The learning thus takes place during the accumulation of the part and usually ends up by determining the rôles best suited to the performer's physical and aesthetic qualities. The time taken for this learning assures the quality of the result; because the performances have been repeated for centuries, the scores have become very sophisticated and their exact execution is guaranteed by the transmission of a living tradition from father to son.

The same must have been true for European actors' so-called 'art families', but the pedagogy was undoubtedly very different, being based primarily on text, although not to the exclusion of movement and mime. The young apprentices began with a small rôle and took on larger and more important rôles as they gradually became more experienced. The actors would perform one play and rehearse the following play at the same time, until they had built up a more or less extensive repertoire. Their physical attributes and natural gifts were just as important as time in determining the quality of the performances. We should note that for both Asian and Western performers, we are referring here to standard situations; the exceptions were a completely different story.

In the West, it was not until the beginning of the twentieth century that the necessity for performer preparation independent of production was affirmed. This was in reaction to the conservatories and schools of the nineteenth century which had institutionalised the performer training described above based on the learning of texts and the elaboration of rôles. Professional preparation, study and training, and the invention of performer pedagogy are revolutionary innovations initiated by the schools and ateliers which prioritised the education of the performer rather than performance production (cf. *Apprenticeship: Western examples*).

The concept and practice of performer training was considerably developed by Grotowski and his Wroclaw theatre laboratory in the 1960s. From Grotowski on, the word 'training' became an integral part of Western theatre vocabulary and does not refer only to physical or professional preparation. The purpose of training is both the physical preparation of the performer and his personal growth above and beyond the professional level. It gives him a way of controlling his body and directing it with confidence in order to acquire, in a word, *physical intelligence*.

The profound commitment that such a process implies, as well as the results obtained by the actors in Grotowski's laboratory, had tremendous repercussions on the way of thinking about performer training and technique. However, conditioned by the phenomenon of indirect knowledge and by the way knowledge is disseminated, more attention ended up being given to the form of training and less to its content. And thus the myth of training and physical exercises was born. In auto-didactic and autonomous theatre groups, training became the indispensable key to the performer's art. But training can only serve this function if its more complex and deeper aspects are understood. The problem of training today is that many people think that it is the exercises which develop the performer, when in fact the exercises are only the tangible and visible part of a larger, unitary and indivisible process. The quality of training depends on the work atmosphere, the relationships between individuals, the intensity of the situations, the modalities of group life. As Eugenio Barba puts it, 'it is less the exercise itself than the temperature of the process which is decisive'.

These were among the first discoveries made by Odin Teatret from 1964 to 1966, the years in which research on physical training was carried out in Grotowski's Teatr Laboratorium in Poland and in Odin Teatret in Denmark. From there, it slowly spread to the USA via Grotowski and the rest of Europe and South America via Eugenio Barba and his actors.

Exercise models

Training as elaborated in the West by Grotowski and Barba underwent a process of development. At first, the actor had to learn and master fragments of exercises, or patterns, until he was able to use them to model his energies. At the end of a certain period of time, depending on the actor's individual abilities and the 'temperature of the process', the actor was no longer executing learned exercises but controlling something more complete and deeper: the principles that make his body live on the stage.

Once again, these are the principles of balance, of opposition, of variations of rhythm and intensity (as Decroux would say, 'dynamo-rhythm') that become a kind of second conditioned reflex, the base on which the actor can build his power and his ability to attract the spectator's attention. It is also for this reason that any exercise can be used, as long as it respects certain elementary rules.

It is therefore interesting to note that one of the first exercises used by Grotowski and Barba, the 'bridge', is also one of the first, preliminary exercises learned by Asian performers (ill.11–15), in kathakali, in odissi dance, and in the Peking Opera. One must learn how to mould the spinal column, how to make it work against its natural inclination to lean forward, so that it can become the helm that directs and orients the rest of the body. This is done coldly by means of exercises, without excluding the possibility of giving these exercises a performance dimension, of using them in a performance, as is shown by a stone engraving of an ancient Egyptian dancer (ill.14). But, as we have said, the objective of training is not utilitarian, at least not directly. The 'bridge', handstands, etc., are the basis for the development of any form of training, especially in an acrobatic context.

9–10. Actors walking on their hands: (**top**) Japanese acrobats in a late nineteenth-century print; (**bottom**) Harlequin in an engraving from the *Recueil Fossard* (cf. *Set and Costume Design*).
11–15. (opposite page, **top**) The 'bridge' in the training exercises at Grotowski's Teatr Laboratorium. The actor on the right is Ryszard Cieslak; (**centre left**) kathakali students at the Kalamandalam School (Kerala, India) in the 'bridge' exercise; (**centre right**) Egyptian dancer: drawing on stone found in Saqqara; (**bottom left**) Peking Opera actor Tsao Chun-Lin helping a participant at the Bonn ISTA, 1980 find the correct position for the 'bridge'; (**bottom right**) odissi dancer Sanjukta Panigrahi doing the 'bridge' during her apprenticeship.

Acrobatics

When one attends a kabuki or Peking Opera performance, one is struck by the performers' physical virtuosity. Actual acrobatics lift the bodies and make them fly above the ground with an extreme lightness. The music, the costumes and the props make these actions even more spectacular, but what most attracts one's attention is the exaggerated and unexpected repetition of these acrobatic exercises. Then, to our great surprise, the performer stands up and in the most natural way imaginable, speaks without giving the least sign of being out of breath. Often there are perfectly co-ordinated duels or battle scenes, or exits and entrances in which acrobatics are used by a character to announce his physical presence. Other times, acrobatics underline passages in the dialogue or interrupt the action of a slow-paced scene with a surprise effect.

Examining this phenomenon more closely, one realises that it is actually a process of an *action rhetoric*. In Chinese theatre, the heroine is often attacked by enemies who threaten her from all sides. But since it is impractical to bring whole armies on to the stage, she repels the attack *alone*. And

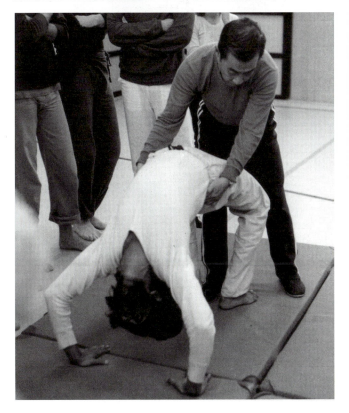

so we see her fend off the arrows and lances hurled by innumerable assailants, literally using her hands and feet, her elbows and shoulders and back.

In kabuki theatre, the heroic samurai would not stoop so low as to fight with attackers of inferior standing. A single gesture from the samurai starts a chain reaction of fatal falls among the ranks of his enemies. Here again, an *action rhetoric* is physically respected. It is as if Hamlet was expressing his famous doubt with a series of perilous leaps. Such an interpretation would perhaps be out of place in the Western tradition, but it would give the spectator, without boring him, an appreciation of the physical dimension of Hamlet's dilemma. Is such a way of performing conceivable in the West? The history of Russian theatre at the beginning of the century shows that it has already been done.

Many sources of inspiration converge in training: Asian theatres has contributed both its dynamics and, more directly, the acrobatic exercises from Chinese and Indian theatre. The influence of these elements is obvious in Grotowski's and Barba's theatres but these familiar achievements should not make us forget an essential aspect of these virtuosity techniques: it is not only a question of learning to do perilous leaps, but of confronting a potentially even more dangerous enemy. The acrobatic exercise gives the performer the opportunity to test his power. At first, the exercise is used to help him overcome fear and resistance, to help him overcome his limits; later, it becomes a way of controlling apparently uncontrollable energies, of finding, for example, the counter-impulses necessary to fall without hurting oneself or of gliding through the air in defiance of the law of gravity. Above and beyond the exercise, these victories reassure the performer: 'even if I don't do it, I am *able* to do it'. And on stage, because of this knowledge, the body becomes a *decided* body (cf. *Theatre Anthropology*).

16–18. (**top right**) Acrobat: sculpture from Tlatilco (National Museum of Anthropology, Mexico City); (**bottom left**) kabuki actor acrobatic exercises in an eighteenth-century print; (**bottom right**) actors and directors at the Bonn ISTA, 1980 during a practical session of acrobatic exercises.

19–21. (**top** and **bottom left**) Acrobatic training in the early years of Grotowski's Teatr Laboratorium (1963); (**below right**) Odin Teatret actor Torgeir Wethal doing an acrobatic exercise during his apprenticeship (1965).

Training with the master

One does not usually see a director working on training; it is equally rare for Eugenio Barba to do so. In this case (ill.22–41), the director is not teaching any kind of exercise but is trying to make the actor understand that he must react with his whole body: he must not limit himself to the exercise per se, but must find resistances or be ready to face resistances (ill.22–29). A relationship is set up, in which the director holds the actor or lets him go (ill.30–32), or vice versa, the actor supports himself but at the same time must be ready to avoid falling (ill.33). Or, when the director tries to tempt him into action obliging him to lift him (the director) up (ill. 36–37) or helps him into the 'bridge' and then raises him up to a standing position (ill.38–39). This is the dynamic that underlies the relationship: to vary the rhythm through real actions, to create obstacles with which the actor must continually confront himself physically, letting himself go.

22–41. Eugenio Barba guides the training of Colombian actor Juan Monsalve, making him react and develop a rhythm through precise actions (Bonn ISTA, 1980).

The view of the performer and the view of the spectator

Ferdinando Taviani

I

Historical and theoretical investigation of the theatre is made particularly useful and fascinating by the fact that, in this field more than in others, we are continually confronted with the interplay between reality and appearances. Many of the diffuse and seemingly obvious opinions about theatre and its history are in fact due to an optical inversion.

One of these opinions could be summarized as follows: the best theatre occurs when an intimate union is created between the performer and the spectator, when both come to feel the same way, or when one of them succeeds in transmitting thoroughly to the other what he or she is thinking and experiencing. A corollary: to make 'good' theatre one must have interesting things to say and must know how to make them understood by the spectator. Or: one must know how to feel deeply and be able to transmit one's emotion to the spectator.

These opinions are neither transformed nor amended by that other opinion stating that the power of the theatre is due to its fiction and to our awareness of the fiction. The fiction which is accepted, and of which one is aware, is held to be the means to realise the union of performer and spectator, that perfect emotional, rational and artistic communication which, according to common sense, is fundamental to all 'great' theatre.

Common sense, however, demonstrates exactly the opposite: it is the divergence, the non-coincidence or even the mutual lack of awareness between the spectators' view of the performance and the performers' view of the same which makes theatre an art, and not just an imitation or a replica of the known.

It would be possible to demonstrate that those exalted moments which have become legendary instances of communion between performer and spectator are moments in which, within the strong bond between them, there is an enormous gap between the spectator's view and the performer's view. In 'good' theatre – or simply, in theatre which works – performers and spectators are gathered at a unique performance which has this characteristic: the more the performance links them together without obliging them to agree, the richer is the performance.

In short, simple common sense obliges us to recognise that to understand a performance does not only mean to see what its authors (performers, director, playwright . . .) have put into it, or to find out what has been hidden deep within it, but rather to make discoveries during a carefully studied journey.

This is equivalent to saying that 'to make a performance understood' does not mean to plan discoveries but to design and construct embankments along which the spectators'

attention will navigate, and then let a minute, multiform and unforeseen life grow on these embankments. Spectators should be able to immerse their gaze into this life and make their own discoveries.

II

In a collection of stories published in 1887, H.G. Wells tells *The Sad Story of a Drama Critic*: a journalist who had never been to the theatre is appointed drama critic by his superior. 'Precisely because you have never been interested in theatre and have no preconceptions', his superior explains to him. The journalist goes to the theatre for the first time and commits the natural error of supposing that it is the actors' intention to represent human beings. The journalist is first shocked and then becomes indignant because of the way in which daily behaviour is reproduced and exaggerated. He sees everyday gestures – the etiquette instilled by a good education – readapted for the stage and reproduced gracefully. The educated norms which the actors imitate with their scenic behaviour are those of the social class to which the spectators belong. Each spectator understands perfectly well the meaning of every gesture an actor makes. Each actor knows how to be perfectly transparent for the spectators.

Wells treats all this as a singular example of degradation. In spite of his indignation, the poor drama critic experiences how infectious the actors' gestures are, he recognises them in himself, realises that 'they' (the actors) breathe as he breathes, and he even begins to breathe as 'they' breathe. Little by little he begins to exaggerate his daily way of behaving. He pronounces certain phrases as 'they' pronounce them. He moves as 'they' do. Even though the story has a realistic setting, its plot is typical of many science fiction stories: a man captured by 'androids'.

Joseph Conrad, one of Wells' best friends, wrote to Edward Garnett in 1908: 'I have a morbid horror of the theatre, and it's getting worse. I can't make myself enter that place of infamy. It's not a horror of drama, it's horror of the acting'.

Both Wells' story and Conrad's assertions seem paradoxical. They reflect, however, in an almost pure state and in an incisive way, an opinion that is found throughout the history of the theatre, whether in a negative form (hence the idea of the actors' infamy) or in a positive form, as aesthetics. Does not every aesthetic reflection on theatre express, implicitly or explicitly, an anxiety concerning the horror that the theatre can be when a man is nothing but the copy of a man?

III

The images of the performer that we find in Diderot and Artaud, the visions of the actor created by Stanislavsky, Craig or Brecht, Meyerhold or Grotowski, and above all, what great actors and dancers have achieved, prove that the art of the theatre is always a mimesis that surpasses itself. Is this a particular case of the more general divergence between the performer's view and that of the spectator?

1. (**above**) Noh actor weeping. Referring to this action, the French writer Paul Claudel and the renowned noh actor Hideo Kanze present two different views. Claudel writes:

'The slowness of the gesture makes all interpretations possible: for example, the woman wants to cry and so moves her hands up to her eyes, but this action can also be the image of her grief, which she brings closer so as to see it better. She seems to draw up the water of her tears, the weight of the pain, then comes the withdrawal from the cup of bitterness which she has drunk, the abdication from life.'

(Paul Claudel, *Journal*, February, 1923)

Hideo Kanze states:

'When you cry in noh, you put your hand in front of your face, but this is not to show that you are crying, it is to dry the tears. The action is completely neutral and consists of drying tears, nothing more. It doesn't matter how you do it, some actors lower their eyes, other actors look up. The simple action of drying tears has been chosen as a paradigm for the act of crying. All other unnecessary gestures have been eliminated.'

(from an interview with Hideo Kanze, 1971)

2. (**below**) A paradoxical example of the double projection of meaning: the Latin inscription on the Roman arch in Orange (France). According to the opinion commonly held by epigraphists from 1866 to 1957, this inscription meant 'AUGUSTI F DIVI IVLI NEPOTI AUGUST', but recently many scholars have decided that the 'inscription' is nothing more than a series of holes, made by the supports holding garlands and lights.

3. (**left**) The ancient spectator: an audience of courtesans watching jugglers perform 1700 years ago. Drawing taken from a relief on a tomb in the province of Szechwan, China.
4. (**right**) The elegant spectator: *The Loge*, anonymous English engraving from 1781 (Theatre Museum, London).

If one accepts the idea that there is a distance between the spectator's view and that of those who have built the performance, then the meaning of the performance will be jeopardised. And there are many ambiguities concerning the meaning of a performance. These ambiguities are not serious when one examines the theatrical phenomenon a posteriori. They become more serious, however, when they are examined a priori, from the point of view of the makers of theatre and of the artistic process.

IV

The problem of the 'meaning' of a performance is a pitfall: it conceals a more complex reality. The common expression 'to have a meaning' adapts well to situations in which a thing or a sign have the same meaning for everyone. When this does not happen, as is the case in the less superficial strata of artistic expression, one can no longer maintain that a work *has* or *does not have* a meaning. One must be aware that things or signs do not have a single meaning but they can refer to a gamut of meanings. The problem then is to determine up to what point one should attempt to force an accord between the meanings that something *can have* for those who have constructed it, and the meanings that it *can have* for those who are its spectators.

Accustomed to considering all communication in terms of the model of linguistic communication, we do not usually give too much importance to the fact that a sign can only be a sign for those who see it as such. Some will see it as a sign, while others will not. In language, a word is understood to be a word by all those who speak the same language. Moreover: with a certain approximation, the fact of a word being a word – a sign – is understood even by those who do not understand the language but are aware that that particular sound must *mean* something, even if they don't know *what* it means. It is not necessary to stress here that a word is a sign for *somebody*: it is a sign, in fact, for practically everyone.

The case is very different when we are dealing with situations that are not, strictly speaking, linguistic. It is true that a theatre performance communicates something to the spectators by means of diverse and complex sign systems, but a sign in this case is not a sign in itself: it is something that *can become* one. It is not only something that 'takes the place of something else' and that thus gives it a meaning. It is something – according to Charles S. Peirce, the founder of modern semiology – which *in somebody's eyes* stands for something else.

'Everything can be considered as a thing or as a sign'. This assertion was made by Bonaventura da Bagnoregio in the thirteenth century.

It is common knowledge that under certain conditions, in the case of powerful spiritual tension, for example, or anxiety, or exaltation, we begin to consider the things around us, or events which occur, as 'signs'. But we do not believe that they are signs in everyone's eyes. If one stops being aware that a particular thing is a sign *for oneself* and begins to think that it is a sign *in itself*, one stops being attentive and becomes superstitious or delirious.

In the performance field, it is an illusion to think that those things which can become 'signs' for the spectator – and which therefore can refer to specific meanings – correspond to the same meanings for the performers and other authors of the performance. It is sheer superstition, therefore, to think that the various elements of a performance which can become 'signs' must be developed in a way which takes into consideration an accord between the meanings they have for the spectators and the meanings they have for the authors of the performance.

This foreseeable and programmed accord is certainly necessary for everything that has to do with the shell, the skin of the performance: the surface of the basic meanings and the zones of the fundamental conventions. But it is not true or valid for what is essential: the multiform life of details, of *things*, that transform the performance into art. At this level the spectators' reactions, the choices they make considering a thing as *thing* or *sign* are perhaps imaginable but not foreseeable. For this reason, the process undertaken by those who create the performance cannot be oriented too much with respect to the spectator's view and must therefore have its own independent views.

V

When semiologists analyse a performance as a varied, stratified complex of signs, they examine the theatrical phenomenon from the end: the result. There is nothing to show, however, that their process is in any way useful for those who must begin at the beginning, that is, for the authors of the performance, whose final goal is what the performance will be in the eyes of the spectators.

The same condition applies in the case of a drama critic who analyses the contents of the performance and judges the value of its 'interpretation'. Even a less traditional critic who pays careful attention to how a performance is constructed by means of the combination of its diverse parts, even such a critic always has the *performance* as the object of his analysis. What s/he analyses is the work's final phase (from the point of view of those who have made it) which is also the point of departure for the spectators' process.

It is a feeble logic which leads one to think that knowing how the performance functions (or having opinions in this regard) also means possessing the basics necessary to make it function.

Let us examine for a moment the verb we have just used: 'to function'. We associate this verb with the idea of a machine, and this implicit and at times unconscious metaphor gives an appearance of veracity to the idea according to which knowledge of the way a performance is interpreted and enjoyed by the spectators can guide the way of building it. This deceptive idea is reinforced by other metaphors, such as when one speaks of the 'mechanism' of the performance and of its 'driving force'.

But what happens if we change the verb and instead of 'to function' we use 'to live'? Knowing *when* and *why* a performance 'lives' does not presuppose knowing *how* to make it live. The verb 'to live' is used, for example, when speaking of a plant, and it is obvious that the processes which form a plant are not merely the assembling of its vital parts.

A plant *can* be analysed scientifically as if it were a machine, but it *cannot* be created like a machine. To enable it to live, one must create an environment that is adapted to it and remove the obstacles to its development. One must have a seed or a cutting. This has very little to do with the effort necessary to understand how it 'functions'.

The question, therefore, could be put in these terms: do those who make a performance think of it as a machine or as a plant? In the first case, the sought-for result can direct and guide the composition process. In addition, the result will coincide with the totality of the instructions for the use of theatrical means. In the second case, the process, the use of the theatrical means, cannot be deduced from the desired result, but must be developed independently of the theatrical means, each one dealt with according to its own principles.

The first case implies a centripetal procedure: the various parts are collected and unified in the context of a plan. In the second case, the process is centrifugal, it develops and ramifies starting from one or more nuclei.

The final state of a machine is 'good' and 'functions' if it corresponds exactly to the original plan and if each part works correctly at the right place at the right time. The final form of a plant never corresponds to a plan, it is the result – imaginable but unforeseeable – of an organic process.

I believe that it is more fitting to compare the work on a performance to organic growth rather than to the construction of a machine. The results of the analyses made by those who seek to understand how a performance is seen by the spectators are not very helpful to those who must make the performance live. This is another way of putting the question concerning the divergence between the views of the creators of the performance and those of its spectators. It is a block to the creative process to examine a performance starting from the end of the process. This reinforces the risk of becoming superstitious, of believing that what can be a

5–6. The sensitive spectator: audience at a Parisian melodrama, drawings by Damourette.

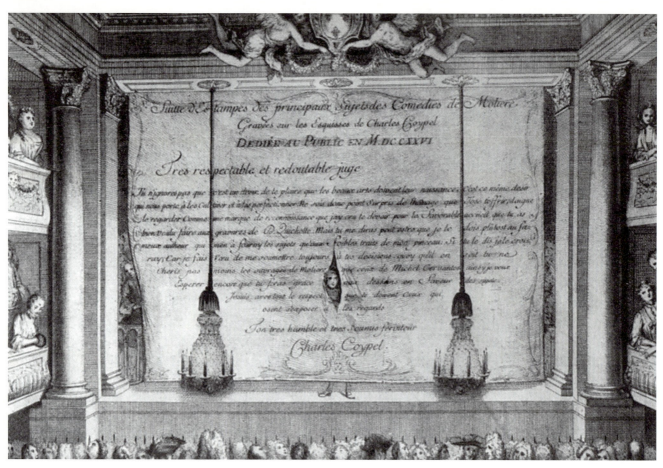

7–8. The spectators seen by the actors: (**above**) the peephole in the curtain in a French theatre at the beginning of the eighteenth century (engraving by Charles Coypel, 1726) and (**opposite**) in a kabuki theatre from the same period (print by Ippitsusai Buncho, 1770).

sign in the spectator's eyes is not only a sign *in his eyes* but a sign *in itself*.

VI

This entire discussion would be banal if it had to do with other forms of art, but it is not so when it has to do with theatre. In other forms of artistic expression, the distance between the forces that govern them and the commonplaces based on the impressions of those who – in a critical way or otherwise – enjoy them, is an obvious distance and an uninteresting one, given that it does not have important consequences (the artist nearly always works alone and uses materials that impose their own precise rules). In theatre, commonplaces about scenic art have tremendous influence on the work of those who make the performance.

The solitary artist can have many preconceived ideas and many superstitions, but s/he will be saved by his/her instinct (that is, by an experience that operates without needing to be formulated in clear and theoretical terms). But in theatre different artists must work together: their techniques are nearly always less specific and the experience of each individual is not free to operate through trial and error, but must co-exist with the experience and the willingness of all those involved. Under these conditions, theories and ideas about scenic art become instruments for orientation.

The possible autonomy of the performer's view relative to that of the spectator (and in specific cases, as we will see, relative to that of the director) is not as interesting from the theoretical point of view as it is from the practical point of view. It is one of the cardinal points around which one can orient oneself in order to escape many of the blocks that threaten creative work. This is particularly relevant with respect to the ambiguous concept of 'interpretation' which often introduces rigidity into the artistic process because of nebulous and preconceived ideas about the meaning of theatrical actions.

Since it seems that theatre must interpret, it appears that its *meaning* must be given, known beforehand, right from the beginning, and that the entire problem consists of making this meaning explicit. Thus it seems strange to consider theatre work in the same way as one normally considers that of a poet or a novelist, a painter or a musician. These artists often proceed with secret intentions by means of signs *that remain signs* in their eyes only, while for other people they are often just interesting details, living and bizarre *things*. For these artists, it is normal that the meaning of the work is the last thing to appear from among its various connotations.

VII

Some people think that in order to make a performance that says interesting things it is necessary to have something interesting to say. Therefore, instead of concerning themselves with 'material' things – which could, for the performer, be pre-expressive work on extra-daily behaviour – they devote themselves to profound and spiritual research in order to immerse themselves in a creative situation. This is a bit like the following story. A group of people are living in an arid

area. Some of the people turn their attention to the earth, to rocks and cement, in order to make dikes and cisterns. Others can think of nothing but water and perform rain dances.

The interesting things, the 'difficult thoughts', which theatre sometimes offers to its spectators, are not there from the beginning, but *allow themselves to be thought*, and arrive at the end rather than the beginning of the work process which one prepares in order to receive them. They respond to an ecology of thought which programmed thought cannot manage.

In theatre, as has already been said, the situation is more delicate, more fragile. Awareness must be more acute because the ecology of thought has to do with the minds of several individuals who are gathered together.

The problem, then, is the process of work, not the planning of the way it will end. In other words, the solution to the problem of having interesting things to say, of 'difficult thoughts', is not found in the search for interesting things and interesting thoughts.

The clearer it is that everything happening in a theatrical context is ready to be transformed into signs in the spectators' eyes, the less rational is the blocking of the artistic process caused by the illusion that this process can be regulated by the final meaning.

Many anecdotes have to do with what the person entering a theatre experiences when no spectators are present: if certain people appear by accident on the bare stage, if they then look around or speak, it seems as if they are in a performance. It is as if their actions have a presence that transforms them into extra-ordinary, spectacular actions. Max Frisch (in *The Pre-Peace Diary*, 1950), telling the story of an episode of this kind that he experienced just after the war in a theatre where one of his plays was being rehearsed, says that this impression is caused by the apron and the proscenium. He claims that they function like a frame and seem to suggest: 'Look here, and you will see something worth looking at, something which neither chance nor time will be able to change. Here you will find the *lasting meaning*, not fading flowers but the image of flowers, their tangible symbol'.

The apron and the proscenium are the simplest examples of those theatrical artifices that determine the ability of the spectators to find *lasting meanings* in what they see, transforming *things* into *signs*. The apron and the proscenium arch are, moreover, definitely weak artifices: their effect doesn't last long. So temporary is their effect that when they seem to function almost because of their own power, transforming a casual fragment of daily life into performance, they become the object of oft-repeated anecdotes, jokes, or – as in Max Frisch's writings – almost philosophical apologies.

Many other artifices, and above all the performer's extra-daily techniques, help the spectators to project meanings onto the things the performers do without a preliminary accord with respect to conventional or traditional signs.

All this could lead one to deduce certain guiding principles, such as the fact that representation of the known – which is the degraded condition of theatre – is in the final analysis the result of a scenic composition intended to be recognised by the spectators and which is adapted to the spectators' expectations like a mould. Similarly, a performer's view which is homogenised to that of the spectator results in a lack of depth, a view seen by one eye only, an alliance between two failed autonomies.

That which in fact determines, on the one hand the *comprehensibility* of a performance and, on the other, its *life* is the degree of relationship between two zones: the zone of accordance between the view of those who make the performance and the view of those who see it, and that other zone in which such accordance is not necessary, or is even accurately and skilfully avoided.

VIII

The 'spectator's view' is to be understood here as the meaning acquired by what the spectators see with 'their eyes', both the general picture and the details.

The 'performer's view', on the other hand, is to be understood as something more varied and complex: not only the meanings in the eyes of those who are acting, but also the purpose for which they do it and the logic which guides them in the doing. For example, the subtext that the performer uses to find personal motivation for a character's speeches, as well as the sequence of actions created in one context and used in another (cf. *Montage*) also belong to the performer's view. Another part of the performer's view is the use of an extra-daily behaviour technique which is independent of the semantic and expressive values that characterise the performer's work in the performance.

We could try to add more precise nuances for the spectator's view, but in this case they would be useless. It is easy to intuit what is implicit in the expression 'spectator's view': it has to do with a complex of mental activity – emotional and conceptual – which everyone has experienced and which does not refer to a relatively unknown area such as the profession or the performers' culture, but to the vast area of the conventions that characterise our civilisation, or to the restricted area of personal mentality and mythology.

It seems that here we are not taking the director's view into account, not because it is not important but above all because the director is not always present (even if the function, if not the person, is always present) and because, from our point of view, the director has a double position. On the one hand, it can be similar to that of the performer, someone who directly influences the actions in the performance; on the other hand, it can be the position of an 'influential spectator' or perhaps of a guarantor for the spectators. Everything said about the divergence between the performers' view and the spectators' view, about the contrast between them, about their accordance or even about the secrecy of them both, can also be affirmed with respect to the director, to his or her double inner theatre.

With respect to the director, the ambiguities of the meaning, or rather the superstition of the meaning, can become more immediate and acute. In the case of a performer's behaviour which is 'restored' by the director, or in the case of actions created in one context through improvisations or other means and used in another, the performer's discomfort due to the expropriation of the meaning can be felt in a particularly strong way: the decisions of the director recall the 'violence' of the spectator, becoming almost brutality. This violence is only imaginary, however, because it derives from the idea that there is only one single meaning possible in the performance, and that this meaning is the same for all the spectators. According to this idea, ideally the spectators would gain the maximum from the performer in

9. The ironical view of the spectator: Eleonora Duse, drawn by Olaf Gulbransson.

10. The ironical view of the spectator: kabuki *onnagata* Kikugoro as Koume (Little Plum). Caricature by Okamoto Ippei (1886–1948).

the moment they project their autonomous meaning onto his work, transformed by their eyes into a row of *signs*.

This view of theatrical life, which is afflicted with the anxiety to make oneself understood, can be replaced by another more dynamic and serene one: the gap between the view of the observers and the view of those who work in order to be observed may engender – through scenic tension – a multiplicity of meanings under the surface of those signs which are the basis of the accord between them.

In the material reality of the theatre, the divergence between the two views is normally practised in spite of commonplaces and ideals. But except in extreme and experimental cases, this gap remains tacit and hidden behind practices which correspond so much to theatrical customs that it seems that one ought not even to question their function.

In the case of a process based on materials created by the performers, elaborated and assembled by the director into a new organism, the relativism of the meanings which the performers, director and spectators attribute to the material is obvious, particularly if the pole of dramaturgical simultaneity is accentuated (cf. *Dramaturgy*, *Montage*, *Restoration of Behaviour*). This case, however, is not an exception. It brings to light something that is implicit in all theatrical professionalism, but which remains covered by the blanket of traditions that makes one look at the overall characteristics of the styles or conventions.

The relativism of meanings is more evident in those theatres that are not based on a written text and a firm tradition, but on a performance text and on individual and group experiences and visions. This is so because, in these cases, one of the constituent elements of the scenic work – which in theatres with consolidated traditions functions by means of implicit logic – is consciously reconstructed. This implicit logic is used with unconscious efficiency, almost in the way one speaks a mother tongue without being familiar with its structural elements.

We could ask ourselves whether, in the course of history, many technical devices and pragmatic solutions were developed also to guarantee a double view. For example, the rôle system typical of professional theatre from the seventeenth to the twentieth century in Europe, the Stanislavskian techniques and those that use his name, the use of improvisation to prepare materials for the performance. All these are procedures which – in their various cultural and environmental conditions – can free the performers from the predomination of the spectators' view, to which they would otherwise remain linked and would pilot them.

In autonomous and autodidactic theatres, the distance between the performers' view and that of the spectators – necessary for the artistic impact and safeguarded in various ways by the conventions of theatres from ancient traditions – is in general reconstructed and controlled. In such theatres, this distance is more evident than in ancient traditional theatres, but not because it is particularly accentuated. When, however, the wish to detach the performers' view from that of the spectators is expressed more obviously, this separation – which has always been ignored and denied by theatre ideology – produces amazement or scandal.

It created a scandal when it appeared in Stanislavsky's work. Anecdotes are still told today that give a clear picture of the 'bizarreness' and 'obsessions' of the great master of Russian theatre. They have to do with Stanislavsky's introduction into his performances of details that no spectator could see. For instance, precious objects which were so small and so concealed that only the actor could appreciate their value. The story is told of how he made an actor perform, in the wings, a character which was always spoken about in a particular play, but that never appeared on stage. In Chekhov's *Ivanov*, which contains certain important scenes between characters on a veranda and a woman who appears at the window of her house, Stanislavsky had a section of the room built in the wings just for the actress who had to appear at the window.

It is strange that episodes of this kind make us smile even today, so strong is our belief that theatre is the fruit of the 'view' of one eye only: the spectator's eye. And yet Stanislavsky's 'madness' is the sign of a profound rationality that has not yet been assimilated into theatrical practice.

Another example is training. Training is generally considered in a reductive way: as the sign of the performers' professionalism (they train every day, like a gymnast or a pianist), or as the sign of their ethical engagement (they do

11. The protesting spectator: fighting for room in an English theatre at the beginning of the nineteenth century (caricature print from 1821).

their exercises every day). Not enough value is given to the fact that training is – or can be – a factor of independence: the performer's independence vis-à-vis the director, independence of the continuity of his/her personal work in spite of the commitment in different productions, and also independence vis-à-vis the spectators.

Where training exists on a continual basis, it helps immerse the performer, or the aspiring performer, into the theatrical profession. It does even more: it integrates the performer into a tradition, be it vast or limited to the history of a small group. After a while, training ceases to have this function. Some performers, however, continue to practise training, constantly transforming it, always venturing out along new paths – a process that has nothing to do with the continual perfecting of virtuosity. In such a case, what is the training's function? It now no longer serves to integrate the performer into a profession. On the contrary, it makes it possible for him/her not to be completely integrated, defining an area of work not limited to the demands of the spectators and the performances.

Thus training transforms a practice – which seems always to be the same – into its opposite. Training can be turned from an instrument for integration into an instrument for non-integration, for independence. It makes it possible to work to fulfil the demands of a specific production while, at the same time, it helps the actor not to submit passively to those demands. These are all examples of the deep current which tends to safeguard the theatre's energy and impact by means of the distinction between the two views.

IX

It would be too easy to confuse the difference between the two views and their dialectic, with a pure and simple separation, that is, the absence of a dialectic.

There actually exists a *self-sufficient spectator* just as there exists a *self-sufficient performer*. There is no performance, however bad or insignificant, which cannot find a spectator who autonomously bestows on it values and meanings which he himself has elaborated while watching it. Many ingenuous observations have been made by self-sufficient spectators watching degraded theatre.

Similarly, there is no bad or insignificant performance in which a performer cannot live his/her views in a solitary way, without establishing any link with the spectator.

When there is no dynamic distinction, but an inert separation, performers and spectators meet at a mid-point of mutual disdain which can be flavoured with indifference, superiority or inferiority complexes, or animosity. The living dialectic between the two views is based, on the contrary, on mutual respect, on an interest in keeping the thread which links performers and spectators taut, yet without forcing them into unanimity.

A performance moves along a complex network of capillary veins which are profoundly justified by the performer and which therefore can assume the role of *signs* for the spectator. These *signs* can elicit meanings for the spectators, but they are not necessarily pre-established. There is a balance in the accord between the meanings for the performers and the meanings for the spectators, between a zone in which the clarity of the communication is essential, but which is different from that underlying zone where the two different views can diverge, determining the depth of the artistic and cultural impact of the performance. All this does not mean, however, that there is a casual and arbitrary deluge of meanings.

The consequence of the dynamic which I have tried to describe abstractly (but which is the very material of theatre) is that in the transition from the performer's work to the spectator's understanding there occurs a *peripety, a vicissitude of intentions and senses* (senses understood both as meanings but also what one feels).

This vicissitude makes theatre a living organism, not a replica conforming to external reality, and not a rite in which there is consensus: a laboratory where – given a known point of departure – an unpredetermined mental route develops.

Madame de Staël synthesised this situation when she recalled her attitude as a spectator at a particular performance in Germany. On the one hand, she knew the play's text and story; on the other hand, certain details, certain *things* done by the actors appeared to her eyes as *signs* to be scrutinised, because their meaning was not established by convention. She was obliged to observe what was happening on the stage with the same curiosity and desire to know as when she watched the unpredictable flow of the vicissitudes of life.

A theatre in which everything is predictable, which is codified and precisely de-codifiable by the spectator, is a laboratory that has stopped working. But a theatre that lets itself be seduced by the mirage which is opposite and specular to the foregoing (which maintains that the performer's views must always be analogous to those of the spectators) would also be a laboratory in ruins. It would fall prey to the superstition according to which everything that has a meaning for the performer can magically gain a meaning for the spectators.

This attitude is particularly destructive to art and we could define it as a nihilistic evaluation of the problem of the accord between performer and spectator. The independence of the performer's view from that of the spectator cannot come from separation, but – as has been emphasised – from a stronger contact. This independence can exist freely only in concomitance with a particularly strong constraint.

In conclusion, the Rorschach test can supply us with an example illustrative of this aspect of the problem. It helps summarise, by means of a new image, many of the themes that are inherent in the discussion of the two views.

When one wishes to refer to something which is devoid of meaning, and therefore open to all the meanings that can be projected on to it, one uses the example of clouds in the sky (as in the famous scene in *Hamlet*) or of stains on a wall (on which everyone, including Leonardo da Vinci, imagines and fantasises pictures and figures) or the example of the blots on a Rorschach test. But there is a huge difference between the first two examples and the third: the difference between arbitrariness and freedom, between daydreaming and imagination.

In the first two examples, all the work is done by the person who is watching, making use of something accidental in order to fall into a reverie. In the last example, that of the Rorschach test, there is no room for any kind of reverie. One's attention is fixed, and it is the imagination, that is, something precise, consequent and taut which is activated.

This happens because, faced with the Rorschach test blots, the observer is not abandoned to his own devices. His 'work' of giving an interpretation to the blot in front of him

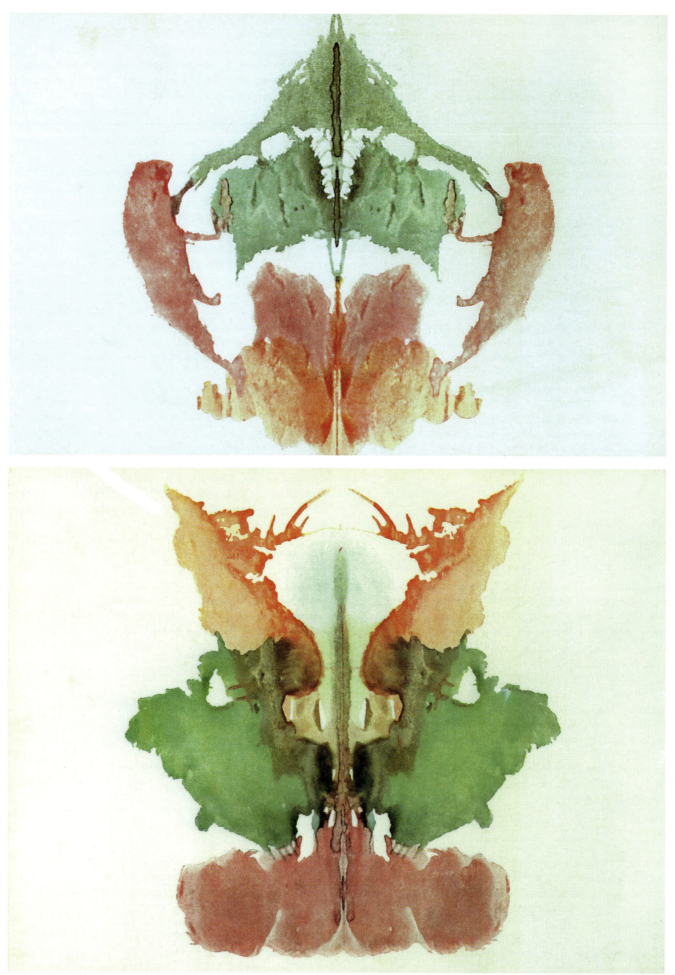

12–13. Plates VII and IX from Rorschach's *Psychodiagnostic.*

is related to and is interwoven with a long and accurate previous effort which has pre-established formally planned guidelines for his attention.

In his book, *Psychodiagnostics* (1921), Hermann Rorschach explains the method he used to prepare the material for his test, based on the free interpretations of blots. What Rorschach was looking for was exactly the opposite of accident. He made use of accident only as a point of departure, in order to make sure that he was not using signs with predetermined meanings. From that point on, everything had to obey a rigorous logic, the more rigorous in so far as it was independent of every consideration of the meaning which the blot could take on or have in the observer's view. Above all, the page on which the blot was made was folded in two in order to double the image. In acquiring a specular symmetry, the image also acquired a certain *necessity*. As performers know, if an error or something which happens accidentally in a performance is immediately repeated, it seems to become logical and gains a meaning in the spectator's eyes.

Thereafter, Rorschach and his collaborators chose certain of the images obtained from the blots folded in two; they eliminated all the images that did not have a harmonic spatial arrangement or that did not respond to particular conditions of spatial rhythm. If the image does not respect these conditions, writes Rorschach, it does not have plastic potential, and many observers reject these images, saying that they are "just blots", and refuse any attempt to interpret them'. It is interesting that the French translation of Rorschach's book employs the term *tableau* (painting) to describe what are usually referred to as 'formless blots', as if to emphasise how little influence accident had in their composition and how much influence artifice had.

From the initial selection of images which met specific spatial rhythm conditions, Rorschach made a further choice of a series of ten images, each one of which, in addition to having its own internal rhythm, became an integral part of a general rhythm determined by the sequence. It was a veritable *montage* established after many experiments: relationships were constructed between images in black and white and images in colour, alternations were set up between images easy to interpret and more difficult ones, between images that require an interpretation based on detail and those interpreted by considering the general comprehensive shape, on the space occupied by the blot or by the white interstices.

Finally, by means of a series of experiments, Rorschach and his team even established the meaning that each of the images had a certain probability of assuming. Very often, for example, Plate V, the one which most seemed to suggest its own meaning, was interpreted by observers as a bat. This nearly always happens. But not always and, above all, not necessarily. Sometimes it provokes a different and unexpected view which, when the test results are analysed, is defined as 'particularly good'.

This aspect of the Rorschach test demonstrates, almost like a model from a scientific laboratory, what can be achieved by establishing a dialectic relationship between two views that are strongly bonded to each other without an accord necessarily having been imposed between them. This is because Rorschach and his team, wanting to place the observer in a position which would enable him to see plants and animals, hunting scenes or family scenes, daily images or mythological pictures, worked neither on the basis of verisimilitude, nor with myth, plants and animals, but with rhythmic, apparently merely formal relationships. And their montage work was guided by accurate and tested views. But they were not attempting to convey these views. They worked on the spatial rhythms, on the assortment of colours, on symmetry, not in order to present spatial rhythms, assortment of colours and symmetry, but in order to elicit personal and unforeseen meanings.

14. Plate V from Rorschach's *Psychodiagnostics*: 'Often for example, task number five is interpreted as a bat, which it also seems to resemble'.

There exists a secret art of the performer. There exist recurring principles that determine the life of actors and dancers in various cultures and epochs. These are not recipes but points of departure that make it possible for an individual's qualities to become scenic presence and to be manifest as personalised and effective expression in the context of the individual's own history.

If we were to propose one single image to sum up all the recurring principles which are the basis of the actor's and dancer's pre-expressivity, it would be this: Salome, a Eurasian figure, between East and West, in St. Mark's Basilica in Venice.

The figure's gentle yet sprightly gait is due to the precarious balance produced by high-heeled shoes. A series of oppositions divide the body into planes and project its energy in various directions. This energy, neither masculine nor feminine but vigorous and soft at the same time, animates the chaste crimson tunic. The white vertical decorations dilate the body, whose tensions are retained, and yet flow in sinuous rhythm. The arms open asymmetrically: one hand claims victory, the other negates the weight which it is lifting. The mask-like severed head seems to duplicate the serenely pensive face.

And somewhere between this persona and the dancer's 'I', the cruelty which Artaud called 'rigour, perserverance and decision' seems to lurk.

This bibliography is a selection of books and essays concerning theatre anthropology and ISTA, as well as texts written from the perspective of theatre anthropology up to January 2005. It starts with all the previous editions of the dictionary as well as a series of collective works, with the name of the editor(s). The bibliography of Eugenio Barba is in alphabetical order.

Previous editions of the dictionary

N.S. ed., *Anatomia del teatro. Un dizionario di antropologia teatrale*, La Casa Usher, Florence 1983.

E.B. – N.S., *Anatomie de l'acteur. Un dictionnaire d'anthropologie théâtrale*, Bouffonneries, Lectoure, 1985.

E.B. – N.S., *Anatomía del actor. Diccionario de Antropología Teatral*, Editorial Gaceta, Mexico City 1987.

E.B. – N.S., *El arte secreto del actor*, Ed. Portico de la Ciudad de México & Escenología A.C., Mexico City 1990.

E.B. – N.S., *The Secret Art of the Performer. A Dictionary of Theatre Anthropology*, Centre for Performance Research, Cardiff, and Routledge, London and New York 1991.

E.B. – N.S., *The Secret Art of the Performer. A Dictionary of Theatre Anthropology*, Centre for Performance Research, Cardiff, and Routledge, London and New York 1993 (2nd reprint).

E.B. – N.S., *Enjya no hi gei. Engeki jinruigaku no jisho*, Parco Co. Ltd., Tokyo 1994.

E.B. – N.S., *The Secret Art of the Performer. A Dictionary of Theatre Anthropology*, Centre for Performance Research, Cardiff, and Routledge, London and New York 1995 (3rd reprint).

E.B. – N.S., *A arte secreto do ator. Dicionário de Antropologia Teatral*, Hucitec – Unicamp – Edusp, São Paulo 1995.

E.B. – N.S., *L'Énergie qui danse. L'Art secret de l'acteur*, Bouffonneries, Lectoure 1995.

E.B. – N.S., *Tajna Umetnost glumca*, Publikum, Belgrade 1996.

E.B. – N.S., *L'arte segreta dell'attore. Un dizionario di antropologia teatrale*, Argo, Lecce 1996.

E.B. – N.S., *L'arte segreta dell'attore. Un dizionario di antropologia teatrale*, Argo, Lecce 1998 (2nd revised reprint).

E.B. – N.S., *The Secret Art of the Performer*, Centre for Performance Research, Cardiff, and Routledge, London and New York 1999 (4th reprint).

E.B. – N.S., *Slovník Divadelní Antropologie. O Skrytém Umení Hercu*, Nakladastelví Lidové – Divadelní Ústav, Prague 2000.

E.B. – N.S., *Oyuncunun Gizli Sanati. Tiyatro Antropolojisi Sözlügü*, Ed. Cem Akas, Yapi Kredi Yayinlari, Istanbul 2002.

E.B. – N.S., *Sekretna sztuka aktora*, Ośrodek Badań Tworczości Jerzego Grotowskiego i Posukiwań Teatralno-Kulturowych, Wroclaw 2005.

E.B. – N.S., *L'arte segreta dell'attore. Un dizionario di antropologia teatrale*, Ubulibri, Milano 2005.

Collective works

Atzpodien, Uta, *Lernen zu lernen: Eugenio Barba, das Odin Teatret und die ISTA*, in *Theater der Zeit* 1, Berlin 2000.

Azzaroni, Giovanni ed., *Il corpo scenico ovvero la tradizione tecnica dell'attore*, Nuova Alfa, Bologna 1990 (texts by A. Appia, A. Artaud, E. Barba, B. Brecht, J. Copeau, E.G. Craig, E. Decroux, C. Dullin, S.M. Eisenstein, Y. Fukuoka, R. Laban, Mei Lanfang, V.E. Meyerhold, C. Sadoshima, K.S. Stanislavsky and M. Zeami).

Barba e o teatro antropologico, in *Inacen. Boletim informativo*, Instituto Nacional de Artes Cenicas 9/2, Rio de Janeiro 1987 (texts by E. Barba, L.O. Burnier, J.R. Faleiro, D. Garcia, C. Levi, Y. Michalski and R. Trotta).

Christoffersen, Exe ed., *At synliggore det usynlige*, Institut for Dramaturgi, Århus 1987 (texts by E. Barba, K.D. Kjeldsen, J. Risum, R. Schechner and E. Thomsen).

Cruciani, Fabrizio – Savarese, Nicola ed., *Hyphos* 1, special issue ISTA Salento, Lecce 1987 (texts by I. Babel, E. Bandiera, E. Barba, C. Bene, G. Di Lecce, N. Ginzburg, R. Kipling, F. Perrelli, M. Richard, J. Roth, L. Santoro, A. Savinio, V. Segalen, K. Stanislavsky and F. Taviani).

Cruciani, Fabrizio ed., *Historiografia teatral*, in *Mascara* 9/10, Mexico City 1992 (texts by A. Appia, A. Artaud, E. Barba, P. Cardona, R. Carreri, R. Carrió, J. Copeau, E.G. Craig, E. Decroux, S.M. Eisenstein, G. Guccini, F. Hoff, R. Laban, Mei Lanfang, V.E. Meyerhold, M. Oshima, S. Panigrahi, P. Pavis, C. Sadoshima, K.S. Stanislavsky, J.L. Valenzuela, J. Varley, T. Wethal and M. Zeami).

De Marinis, Marco ed., *Drammaturgia dell'attore*, I Quaderni del Battello Ebbro, Bologna 1997 (texts by E. Barba, R. Carreri, M. De Marinis, L. Masgrau, I. Nagel Rasmussen, P. Pavis, J. Risum, N. Savarese, M. Schino, F. Taviani, J. Varley and T. Wethal).

Hastrup, Kirsten ed., *The Performers' Village*, Drama, Gråsten 1996 (texts by K. Azuma, I Made Bandem, E. Barba, R. Carreri, K. Hastrup, R. Jenkins, S. Panigrahi, J. Risum, F. Ruffini, N. Savarese, M. Schino, F. Taviani, I Made P. Tempo, T. Chun-Lin, J. Varley and I. Watson).

Falke, Christoph ed., *Das Lernen zu lernen. ISTA International Schule für Theateranthropologie*, in *Flamboyant* 3, Cologne 1996 (texts by E. Barba, Ch. Falke, K. Hastrup, F. Taviani and J. Varley).

Filippetti, Renzo ed., *Materiali del lavoro sull'ISTA*, Documentazione 3, Centro di Iniziativa Teatrale S. Agata, Bologna 1987 (texts by E. Barba, M. Borie, P. Calcagno, P. Cardona, F. Coppieters, F. Cruciani, M. De Marinis, S. De Matteis, G. Di Lecce, P. Giacché, R. Molinari, F. Quadri, C. Ria, F. Ruffini, N. Savarese, F. Taviani and U. Volli).

Guccini, Gerardo – Valenti, Cristina ed., *Tecniche della rappresentazione e storiografia*, Synergon, Bologna 1992 (texts by E. Barba, R. Carreri, R. Carrió, F. Cruciani, M. De Marinis, F. Hoff, G. Guccini, M. Oshima, S. Panigrahi, P. Pavis, J.M. Pradier, C. Valenti, J.L. Valenzuela, J. Varley and T. Wethal).

Kowalewicz, Kazimierz ed., *Living in the Performers' Village*, Lodz University Press, Lodz 1999 (texts by J. Arpin, R. Avila, A. Max Hausen, S. Homar, K. Kowalewicz, D. Korish, L.A. Meambeh, I. Paggen Wabnitz, W. Pfaff, K. Spaic and C. Wolther).

Leabhart, Thomas ed., *Incorporated Knowledge*, in *Mime Journal*, Claremont 1995 (texts by M. De Marinis, K.

Hastrup, R. Jenkins and I.N. Catra, T. Leabhart, L. Pronko, F. Ruffini and J. Varley).

Pavis, Patrice ed., *La Dramaturgie de l'actrice*, in *Degrés* 97–98–99, Brussels 1999 (texts by E. Barba, R. Carreri, M. De Marinis, J. Féral, Y. Lorelle, Ll. Masgrau, I. Nagel Rasmussen, P. Pavis, J.M. Pradier, J. Risum, J. Varley and T. Wethal).

Pfaff, Walter – Keil, Erika – Schläpfer, Beat ed., *Der Sprechende Körper. Texte zur Theateranthropologie*, Alexander Verlag, Berlin & Museum für Gestaltung, Zurich 1996 (texts by E. Barba, M. Bauer, R. Barucha, P. Brook, E. Fischer-Lichte, D. Fo, J. Grotowski, J. Grädel, M. Mauss, W. Pfaff, J. Pfaff-Czarnecka, R. Schechner, and V. Turner).

Ruffini, Franco ed., *La scuola degli attori*, La Casa Usher, Florence 1981 (texts by K. Azuma, E. Barba, R. Bijeliac-Babic, T. Bjelke, M. Brauneck, T. Bredsdorff, T. Chun-Lin, J.J. Daetwyler, M. Delgado, X. Fabregas, B. Gale, J. Grotowski, A. Helbo, H. Laborit, N.R. Macdonald, S. Panigrahi, J.M. Pradier, N. Savarese, R. Temkine, I Made Pasek Tempo, A. Tordera, M. Watanabe, C. Weiler and W. Ybema).

Ruffini, Franco ed., *Le Théâtre qui danse*, in *Bouffonneries* 22/23, Lectoure 1989 (texts by E. Barba, M. Borie, P. Cardona, P. Giacché, P. Pavis, J.M. Pradier, F. Ruffini and F. Taviani).

Savarese, Nicola ed., *Terra d'Otranto*, special issue: *ISTA Salento. Dialoghi Teatrali*, Lecce 1987 (texts by A. Bandettini, E. Barba, L. De Luca, R. Durante, P. Giacché, C. Ria and F. Taviani).

Skeel, Rina ed. (1), *The Tradition of ISTA*, Filo/Univ. Estadual of Londrina, Londrina 1994 (texts by K. Azuma, I Made Bandem, E. Barba, N. Jacon, T. Chun-Lin, S. Panigrahi, F. Ruffini, N. Savarese, F. Taviani, I Made Pasek Tempo and J. Varley).

Skeel, Rina ed. (2), *A tradicâo da ISTA*, Filo/Univ. Estadual de Londrina, Londrina 1994 (Portuguese version of *The Tradition of ISTA*).

Taviani, Ferdinando ed., *Improvisation et Anthropologie Théâtrale*, in *Bouffonneries* 4, Lectoure 1982 (texts by K. Azuma, E. Barba, B. Colin, R. Guarino, S. Panigrahi, F. Ruffini, I Made Pasek Tempo and M. Watanabe).

Taviani, Ferdinando ed., *La Improvisación*, in *Quehacer Teatral* 2, Museo Arte Moderno y Centro de Investigaciones Teatrales, Bogotá 1984 (texts by G. Antei, F. Arenas, B. Balasz, A. Bandettini, E. Barba, E. Buenaventura, M. Chechov, J. Copeau, C. Dullin, W. Goethe, M. Gorki, R. Guarino, J. Monsalve, E. Piscator, C. Reyes, M. Sand, N. Savarese, K. Stanislavsky, E. Vakhtangov and B. Zakhava).

Taviani, Ferdinando ed., *L'Énergie de l'acteur*, in *Bouffonneries* 15–16, Lectoure 1987 (texts by E. Barba, P. De Vos, B. Kaquet, J.M. Pradier, F. Ruffini and M. Schino).

Watson, Ian ed., *Negotiating Cultures. Eugenio Barba and the Intercultural Debate*, Manchester University Press, Manchester and New York 2002 (texts by E. Barba, M. Bovin, I.N. Catra and R. Jenkins, F. Chamberlain, T. D'Urso, R. Jenkins, I. Nagel Rasmussen, M. Rubio, N. Savarese, M. Shevtsova, N. Stewart, F. Taviani and I. Watson).

Yarrow, Ralph ed., *Presence and Pre-Expressivity* 1, in *Contemporary Theatre Review* 6/4, Amsterdam 1997 (texts by F. Chamberlain, P. Pavis, J.M. Pradier and R. Yarrow).

General bibliography

Azuma, Katsuko
 – *Intervista*, by F. Ruffini, in Ruffini 1981.
 – *Entretien avec Katsuko Azuma*, by F. Ruffini, in Taviani 1982.
 – *Go Against the Rhythm of the Heart*, interview by F. Ruffini, in Skeel (1) 1994 (and in Hastrup 1996).
 – *Vá contra o ritmo do coração*, interview by F. Ruffini, in Skeel (2) 1994.

Bandem, I Made
 – *Tradition as Change and Continuity*, interview by E. Barba, in Skeel (1) 1994 (and in Hastrup 1996).
 – *Tradiçao como mudança e continuidade*, interview by E. Barba, in Skeel (2) 1994.

Bandettini, Anna
 ISTA 1986–1987, in *Teatro/Festival* 7, Parma 1987.

Barba, Eugenio
 – THE ACTOR'S TRADITION AND THE SPECTATOR'S IDENTITY: *Tradizione dell'attore e identità dello spettatore*, in *Hypos*, 1/1, Lecce 1987 (then in *Terra d'Otranto*, special edition, Lecce 1987); *The Actor's Tradition and the Spectator's Identity*, in Skeel (1) 1994.(and in Hastrup 1996); *A tradiçao do ator e a identidade do espectador*, in Skeel (2) 1994.
 – AN AMULET MADE OF MEMORY. THE SIGNIFICANCE OF EXERCISES IN THE ACTOR'S DRAMATURGY: in *The Drama Review* 156, New York 1997; *Un amuleto fatto di memoria. Il significato degli esercizi nella drammatugia dell'attore*, in De Marinis 1997; *Un amuleto hecho de memoria. El significado de los ejercicios en la dramaturgia del actor*, in *Teatro Siglo XXI* 4/3, Buenos Aires 1997; Arabic version in *El Masrah* 117–118, Cairo 1998; *Une amulette faite de mémoire. La signification des exercices dans la dramaturgie de l'acteur*, in Pavis 1999, and in P. Pezin, *Le livre des exercices*, L'Entretemps, Saussan 1999.
 – ANIMUS/ANIMA: in *Spillerom* 4, Oslo 1986; *Uomo-donna o Animus-Anima*, in *Teatro Festival* 5, Parma 1987; *Homme-femme ou Animus-Anima: l'énergie de l'acteur*, in Taviani 1987; *Mand-Kvinde eller Animus-Anima: skuespillerens energi*, in *Rap* 12, Copenhagen 1987 and in *At synliggøre det usynlige*, Institut for Dramaturgi, Århus University 1987; *La energía del actor: hombre-mujer o Animus-Anima*, in *Repertorio* 1, Querétaro 1987, *The Actor's Energy: Male-Female Versus Animus-Anima*, in *New York Quarterly* 1/3, Cambridge 1987, and in *ANT News* 19, Sydney 1986.
 – ANTHROPOLOGICAL THEATRE: *Teatro Antropologico*, in *Hypos* 1/1, Lecce 1987; *Teatro Antropológico*, in *Apuntes de Teatro* 95, Santiago de Chile 1987 (and in *Jaque* 177/4, Montevideo 1987; *Luz de ensayo* 2, Montevideo 1988); *Anthropological Theatre*, in *The Drama Review* 117, New York 1988; *Antropologisk Teater*, in E. B., *De flydende øer*, Borgens Forlag, Copenhagen 1989; *Teatro Antropológico*, in E. B., *Além das ilhas flutuantes*, Hucitec, São Paulo Campinas 1991.
 – CULTURAL IDENTITY AND PROFESSIONAL IDENTITY: in, Skeel (1) 1994 (and in Hastrup 1996); fragments in *The Soul of the American Actor* 4/4, New York 2002; *Identidade cultural e identidade profisional*, in Skeel (2) 1994; *Identidad cultural e identidad profesional: el sentido de la Antropología Teatral*, in *Mascara* 19–20, Mexico City 1995; *Kulturelle identität, professionelle identität*, in Falke 1996.
 – THE DILATED BODY: La Goliardica Editrice Universitaria, Rome 1985 *Il corpo dilatato*, La Goliardica

Editrice Universitaria, Rome 1985 (with the title *Il corpo stesso*, in *Sipario*, Milan 1988; fragments with title *Tebe dalle sette porte*, in the programme XXXIII Biennale di Venezia, 1985); *The Dilated Body: on the Energies of Acting*, in *New Theatre Quarterly*, 4/1, Cambridge 1985, *Den udvidede krop*, in *Årsberetning*, Institut for Dramaturgi, Århus University 1985 (fragments with the title *Thebens syv porte*, in E. Christoffersen, *Thebens syv porte*, Universitetsforlag, Århus 1986); *Le Corps dilaté*, in *Jeu 35*, Montréal 1985 (and in Taviani 1987); *El cuerpo dilatado*, in Maldoror 22, Montevideo 1986 (and in *Actes del Congrés Internacional de Teatre a Catalunya*, Institut del Teatre, Barcelona 1989); *The Dilated Body*, in *Kinopis* 6/4, Skopje 1992).

– EURASIAN THEATRE: *Eurasian Theatre*, in *The Drama Review* 119, New York 1988 (and in E. Fischer-Lichte ed., *Dramatic Touch of Difference (Theatre, Own and Foreign)*, Gunter Narr Verlag, Tübingen 1990; in R. Drain ed., *Twentieth Century Theatre*, Routledge, London and New York 1995; in E. B.,, *Theatre. Solitude, Craft, Revolt*, Black Mountain Press, Aberystwyth 1999); *Teatro Eurasiano*, in *Festival di Chieri*, Rosemberg & Sellier, Turin 1988 (and in E. B., *Teatro. Solitudine, mestiere, rivolta*, Ubulibri, Milan 1996); *Théâtre Eurasien*, in *Jeu 49*, Montreal 1988 (and in Ruffini 1989; P. Pavis ed., *Confluences*, Prépublications du petit bricoleur de Boir-Robert, Saint Cyr l'École 1993; in E. B., *Théâtre. Solitude, métier, révolte*, L'Entretemps, Saussan 1999); *Teatro Eurasiano*, in *Mascara 1*, Mexico City 1989 (and in *Tablas 1*, Havana 1990; in E. B. *Teatro. Soledad, oficio y revuelta*, Catálogos, Buenos Aires 1997); *Euro-asiatisk teater*, in E. B., *De flydende øer*, Borgens Forlag, Copenhagen 1989; *Teatro Eurasiano*, in *Adagio 4*, Evora 1991 (and in E. B., *Além das ilhas flutuantes*, Hucitec, São Paulo – Campinas 1991); Arabic version in *El Fenoun 42*, Cairo 1991 (and in , *The Theatre Cercles*, Baghdad 1998); *Teatr euroazyatycki, czyli szansa*, in *Dialog 8/38*, Warsaw 1993; *Avrasya Tyatrosu*, in *Mimesis 5*, Istanbul 1994; in E. B., *Teatro. Monazià, deziotecnia, ezeghersi*, Koan, Athens 2001.

– THE FICTION OF DUALITY: *La finzione della dualità*, in *Teatro Festival 10–11*, Parma 1988 (and in *Il Patalogo 11*, Ubulibri, Milan 1988); *The Fiction of Duality*, in *New Theatre Quarterly*, 20/5, Cambridge 1989; *La Fiction de la dualité*, in Ruffini 1989; *Dualitetens fiktion* in *Ritual & Perfomance*, Universitetsforlag, Århus 1993; *Fikcja rozdwojenia*, in *Opcje 1–2*, Katowice 1995.

– GRANDFATHERS, ORPHANS, AND THE FAMILY OF EUROPEAN THEATRE: in *New Theatre Quarterly* 74, Cambridge 2003; *Nonni e orfani. Una saga di famiglia*, in *Teatro e Storia 24*, Rome 2003; translations in: *Conjunto 129*, Havana, 2003; *Didaskalia 54–55–56*, Cracow, 2003.

– THE HIDDEN MASTER: *The Hidden Master*, in *Mime Journal. Words on Decroux 2*, Claremont 1997; *Il maestro nascosto*, in *Culture Teatrali 1*, Bologna 1999.

– INTRODUCTION TO THEATRE ANTHROPOLOGY: *Introduzione all'Antropologia Teatrale*, in *Scena 9*, Milan 1981 (and in E. B., *La corsa dei contrari*, Feltrinelli, Milan 1981); *Introduction à l'Anthropologie Théâtrale*, in E. B., *L'archipel du théâtre*, Bouffonneries, Lectoure, 1982; *Introducció a l'Antropologia Teatral*, in E. B., *Les illes flotants*, Edicions '62, Barcelona 1983; *Introdução à Antropologia Teatral*, in *Inacen 9/2*, Rio de Janeiro 1987.

– NATIONAL IDENTITY AND THEATRE ANTHROPOLOGY: *Identidad nacional y Antropología Teatral*, in *Antropomonis 1*, Buenos Aires 1996; *Identitat nacional i Antropologia Teatral*, in *Teatre, misteris i antropologia O*, Sitges 1991.

– ORGANICITY: *O-Effect. That which is Organic for the Actor / That which is Organic for the Spectator*, in *Mime Journal. Words on Decroux 2*, Claremont 1997 (and in *The Drama Review 157*, New York 1998); *O-Effect. Lo que es orgánico para el actor, lo que es orgánico para el espectador*, in *Funámbulos 2*, Buenos Aires 1999.

– THE PAPER CANOE: *La canoa de papel. Tratado de Antropología Teatral*, Escenología, Mexico City 1992 (and Catálogos, Buenos Aires 1994; fragments with the title *Apuntes para los perplejos (y para mí mismo)*, in *Mascara 9–10*, Mexico City 1992; fragments with the title *Antropología Teatral*, in *Primer Acto 263*, Madrid 1996); *La canoa di carta. Trattato di Antropologia Teatrale*, Il Mulino, Bologna 1993 (fragments with the title *Appunti per i perplessi (e per me stesso)* in Guccini – Valenti 1992; fragments with the title *L'azione reale*, in *Teatro e Storia 13*, Bologna 1992); *Le canoë de papier. Traité d'Antropologie Théâtrale*, Bouffonneries, Lectoure 1993 and L'Entretemps, Saussan 2004; fragments with the title *Antropologia teatru: geneza, definicja*, in *Dialog 86*, Warsaw 1993; *A canoa de papel. Tratado de Antropologia Teatral*, Hucitec, São Paulo – Campinas 1994; *The Paper Canoe. A Guide to Theatre Anthropology*, Routledge, London and New York 1994 (fragments with the title *The Genesis of Theatre Anthropology*, in *New Theatre Quarterly 38*, Cambridge 1996); *En kano af papir. Indføring i Teaterantropologi*, Drama, Gråsten 1994; fragments with the title: *Zapiski dla zaklopotanych (i dla siebie samego)*, in *Dialog 10/41*, Warsaw 1996; *De kano van papier. Verhandeling over Theaterantropologie*, PassePartout, Amsterdam 1997; *Ein Kanu aus Papier. Abhandlung über Theater-Anthropologie*, in *Flamboyant 7–8*, Cologne 1998 (fragments with the title *Wiederkehrende Prinzipien in Der Sprechende Körper*, Alexander Verlag, Berlin & Museum für Gestaltung, Zurich 1996); *Paberlaevuke. Sisse-juhatus Teatri-Antropologiasse*, Eesti Teatriliit, Tallin 1999; *Papírkenu. Bevezetés a színházi antropológiába*, Kijárat Kiadó, Budapest 2001; Korean edition: Moonhak-kwa-Jisung-sa, Seoul 2001.

– THE PARADOXICAL SPACE OF THE THEATRE: *Lo spazio paradossale del teatro*, in *Linea d'ombra 116*, Milan 1996; *Det paradoksale rum*, in *Politiken*, Copenhagen 1996 (and in *Årsberetning, Kulturministeriets udviklingsfond*, Copenhagen 2000); *O espaço paradoxal do teatro*, in *Cadernos do espectáculos 2*, Teatro Carlos Gomes, Rio de Janeiro 1996; *El espacio paradójico del teatro*, in *Festival Iberoamericano de Teatro*, Cadiz 1996.

– PEDAGOGICAL PARADOX: *Paradosso pedagogico*, in Ruffini 1981; *Pedagoski paradoks*, in *Prolog 50*, Zagreb 1981; *Le paradoxe pédagogique*, in Taviani 1982.

– PEOPLE OF RITUAL: *Il popolo del rituale*, in *Linea d'ombra 73*, Milan 1992 (and in *La costruzione della forma*, Università del Teatro Eurasiano, Padua 1992; in, E. B. *La canoa di carta*, 1993; in, E. B. *Teatro. Solitudine, mestiere, rivolta*, Ubulibri, Milano 1996); *El pueblo del ritual*, in E. B. *La canoa de papel* 1992 and 1994 (and in *Conjunto 94*, Havana 1993; in, E. B. *Teatro. Soledad, oficio y revuelta*, Catálogos, Buenos Aires 1997 and in *Teatro. Soledad, officio y rebeldía*, Escenología, Mexico City 1998); *Le peuple du rituel*, in E. B., *La canoë de papier*, 1993 (and in E. B., *Théâtre. Solitude, métier, révolte*, L'Entretemps,

Saussan 1999); *Ritualets folk*, in E. Christoffersen ed., *Aktuelle Teaterproblemer* 31, Institut for Dramaturgi, Århus University 1994 (and in E. B., *En kano af papir*, 1994); *O povo do ritual*, in E. B.,*A canoa de papel*, 1994; *People of Ritual*, E. B. in *The Paper Canoe*, 1994 (and , E. B., *Theatre. Solitude, Craft, Revolt*, Black Mountain Press, Aberystwyth 1999); *De mensen van het ritueel*, in E. B., *De kano van papier*, 1997; *Das Volk des Rituals*, in E. B., *Ein Kanu aus Papier*, 1998; *Rituaalirahvas*, in *Paberlaevuke*, 1999; *A rítus népe*, in E. B. *Papírkenu*, 2001.

– PERFORMANCE TECHNIQUES AND HISTORIOGRAPHY: *Prefazione* in Azzaroni 1990; *Notas sobre Antropología Teatral y técnicas de la representación historiográfica*, in *Espacio* 8, Buenos Aires 1990; *Performance Techniques and Historiography*, in Skeel (1) 1994 (and in Hastrup 1996); *Tecnicas da rapresentaçao e historiografia*, in Skeel (2) 1994.

– PRE-EXPRESSIVITY / IMPROVISATION: *Pre-expressivity / Improvisation*, in Skeel (1) 1994 (and in Hastrup 1996); *Pré-expressividade / improvisaçao*, in Skeel (2) 1994.

– THE STEPS ON THE RIVER BANK: in *The Drama Review* 4/38, New York 1994 (and in E. B., *Theatre. Solitude, Craft, Revolt*, Black Mountain Press, Aberystwyth 1999); *La scala sulla riva del fiume*, with the title *Il viaggio delle identità*, in *Il Patalogo* 17, Ubulibri, Milan 1994 (and in E. B.,*Teatro. Solitudine, mestiere, rivolta*, Ubulibri, Milan 1996); *La escalera a orillas del río*, in *Conjunto* 104, Havana 1997 (and in E. B., *Teatro. Soledad, oficio y revuelta*, Catálogos, Buenos Aires 1997 and in *Teatro. Soledad, officio y rebeldía*, Escenología, Mexico City 1998); *L'escalier sur la rivage du fleuve*, in E. B., *Théâtre. Solitude, métier, révolte*, L'Entretemps, Saussan 1999; Greek translation in E. B., *Teatro. Monazià, deziotecnia, ezeghersi*, Koan, Athens 2001; in E. B. *Teatr. Samotnosc, rzemiozlo, bunt*, Warsaw University, 2003.

– SILVER HORSE: *Caballo de plata*, in *Escénica*, special issue, Mexico City 1986 (and in E. B., *La canoa de papel*, 1992 and 1994); *Caballo de plata*, in Ruffini 1989 (and *Caballo de plata*, in *Teatro e Storia* 9, Bologna 1990; with the title *Il cavallo d'argento*, in E. B., *La canoa di carta*, 1993); *Cheval d'argent*, in E. B., *La canoë de papier*, 1993; *Cavalo de prata*, in E. B., *A canoa de papel*, 1994; *Sølvhest*, in E. B., *En kano af papir*, 1994; *Silver Horse*, in E. B.,*The Paper Canoe*, 1994; *Het zilveren paard*, in E. B., *De kano van papier*, 1997; *Silbernes Pferd*, in E. B., *Ein Kanu aus Papier*, 1998; Arabic translation in *The Theatre Cercles*, Baghdad 1998; *Hõberatsu*, in E. B., *Paberlaevuke*, Eesti Teatriliit, Tallin 1999; *Az Ezüst ló. Egy hetes munka*, in E. B., *Papírkenu*, Kijarát Kiadó, Budapest 2001.

– TACIT KNOWLEDGE: HERITAGE AND WASTE: *Tacit Knowledge: Heritage and Waste*, in *New Theatre Quarterly* 63, Cambridge 2000 (and in *Odin Teatret 2000*, Århus University Press, Århus 2000); *Conoscenza tacita: dispersione ed eredità*, in *Teatro e Storia* 20–21, Bologna 2000; *Cicha Wiedza: dziedzictwo i spustoszenie*, in *Didaskalia* 35, Cracow 2000; *Conocimiento tácito: herencia y pérdida*, in *Aula de teatro. Cuadernos de estudios teatrales* 18, Malaga 2001 (and in *Funámbulos* 14, Buenos Aires 2001); *Connaissance tacite: gaspillage et héritage*, in Anne-Marie Gourdon ed., *Les nouvelles formations de l'interprète*, CNRS, Paris 2004.

– THE THIRD BANK OF THE RIVER: *La tercera orilla del río*, in *Reencuentro Ayacucho*, Cuatrotablas, Lima 1988 (and in *Espacio* 4/2, Buenos Aires 1988; in *Conjunto* 78, Havana 1989, in E. B., *Teatro Soledad, oficio y revuelta*, Catálogos, Buenos Aires 1997 and *Teatro. Soledad, officio y rebeldía*, Escenología, Mexico City 1998)); *La terza sponda del fiume*, in *Teatro e Storia* 5, Bologna 1988, in E. B., *Teatro Mestiere, solitudine, rivolta*, Ubulibri, Milan 1996; *Flodens tredje bred*, in *Kritik* 87, Copenhagen 1989; *La troisième rive du fleuve*, in *Europe* 726, Paris 1989 (and in E. B., *Théâtre. Solitude, métier, révolte*, L'Entretemps, Saussan 1999); *The Third Bank of the River*, in *The Act* 1/2, New York 1990 (and in E. B., *Theatre. Solitude, Craft, Revolt*, Black Mountain Press, Aberystwyth 1999); *Trzeci brzeg rzeki*, in *Konteksty* 3–4, Warsaw 1991 and in E. B., *Teatr. Samotnosc, rzemiozlo, bunt)*; Arabic translation in *The Theatre Cercles*, Baghdad 1998; in E. B., *Teatro. Monazià, deziotecnia, ezeghersi*, Koan, Athens 2001.

– THEATRE ANTHROPOLOGY: *Anthropologie Théâtrale*, in *Degrés* 25, Brussels 1980; *Anthropologie Théâtrale*, in *Degrés* 29, Bruxelles 1982; *Antropologia Teatrale*, in *Il Patalogo* 3, Ubulibri, Milan 1981 (and in E. B., *La corsa dei contrari*, Feltrinelli, Milan 1981; E. B. *Aldilà delle isole galleggianti*, Ubulibri, Milan 1985); *Anthropologie Théâtrale*, in *Bouffonneries* 4, Lectoure 1982; *Theateranthropologie*, in R. Scholz – P. Schubert ed., *Körpererfahrung*, Rowohlt, Hamburg 1982 (and in E. B., *Jenseits der Schwimmenden Inseln*, Rowohlt, Hamburg 1985); *Antropologia teatru: krok dalej*, in *Dialog* 4/27, Warsaw 1982; *Theatre Anthropology*, in *The Drama Review* 94, New York 1982 (and in E. B., *Beyond the Floating Islands*, Performing Arts Journal, New York 1986); *Antropologia Teatral*, in E. B., *Les illes flotants*, Edicions '62, Barcelona 1983, (and in *Acto Latino* 0, Bogotá 1983; *Maldoror* 17–18, Montevideo 1984; E. B., *Las islas flotantes*, Universidad Nacional Autónoma de México, Mexico City 1983; E. B., *Más allá de las islas flotantes*, Gaceta, Mexico City 1986, and Firpo-Dobal, Buenos Aires 1987); *Al hayat al Masrahye*, in *The Theatre Life*, Ministry of Culture, Syria 1988 (and in *Masirat Al-muaksin*, Dar al Kinuz, Damascus 1995); *Pozorisma Antropologija*, in *Dometi* 72–73/20, Ljubljana 1993; *Theatre Anthropology*, in *Kinopis* 8/5, Skopje 1993; *Divadelní Antropologie*, in *Svet a Divadlo* 4, Prague 1994; *Tiyatro Antropolojisi*, in *Mimesis* 5, Istambul 1994.

– THEATRE ANTHROPOLOGY: FIRST HYPOTHESIS: *Theateranthropologie: über Orientalische und Abendländische Schauspielkunst*, in M. Braunek ed., *Teater im 20 Jahrhundert*, Rowohlt, Hamburg 1980, (and in *Jenseits der Schwimmenden Inseln*, Rowohlt, Hamburg 1985; *Antropologia Teatru: pierwsze hypotezy*, in *Dialog* 1/26, Warsaw 1981; *Theatre Anthropology: First Hypothesis*, in *Theatre International* 1, London 1981,(and in E. B., *Beyond the Floating Islands*, Performing Arts Journal, New York 1986); *Antropologia teatral, algunas hipótesis*, in *La Cabra* 33/35, Univ. Nacional Autónoma de México, Mexico City 1981,(and in E. B., *Más allá de las islas flotantes*, Gaceta, Mexico City 1986); *Anthropologie Théâtrale: premières hypothèses*, in E. B., *L'archipel du théâtre*, Bouffonneries, Lectoure 1982; *Antropologia Teatral: primeres hipòtesis*, in E. B., *Les illes flotants*, Edicions '62, Barcelona 1983; *Antropologia Teatrale: prime ipotesi*, in E. B., *Aldilà delle isole galleggianti*, Ubulibri, Milan 1985; *Antropologia Teatral: algumas hipótesis*, in *Teatro Universitario* 2, Rio de Janeiro 1986; *Teatriantropoloogia: ja selle toime (smane hüpotees)*, in *Teater, muusika, kino* 5, Tallin 1989.

– TRADITION AND FOUNDERS OF TRADITIONS: in Skeel (1) 1994 (and in Hastrup 1996); *La tradición y los fun-*

dadores de tradiciónes, in *Mascara* 15, 1993 and in *Mascara* 17–18, Mexico City 1994; *Tradizione e fondatori di tradizioni* e *La scala sulla riva del fiume* with the title *Il viaggio delle identità*, in *Il Patalogo* 17, Ubulibri, Milan 1994; *Tradiçao e fundadores de tradiçao*, in Skeel (2) 1994; *Traditions et fondateurs de tradition*, in *Marsyas* 31, Paris 1994; *Traditionen und traditionsgründer*, in *Flamboyant* 1, Cologne 1995.

– THE WAY OF REFUSAL: *La via del rifiuto*, in *Per 10 anni*, Centro per la Sperimentazione e la Ricerca Teatrale, Pontedera 1984; *La voie du refus*, in *Jeu* 33, Montreal 1984; *El camino del rechazo*, in E. Ceballos ed., *Técnicas y teorías de la dirección*, Escenología, Mexico City 1985 (and in *Maldoror* 22, Montevideo 1986); *La via del refús*, in *Estudis Escènics* 27, Barcelona 1985; *The Way of Refusal*, in *NCPA Quarterly Journal* 1–2/15, Bombay 1986 (and in *New Theatre Quarterly*, 16/4, Cambridge 1988); *Az Elutasítás Utján*, in *Kultura és Közosseg*, Budapest 1989; *Nægtelsens vej*, in E. B., *De flydende øer*, Borgens Forlag, Copenhagen 1989; *Caminho da recusa*, in E. B., *Além das ilhas flutuantes*, Hucitec, São Paulo-Campinas 1991.

– THE WAY OF THE OPPOSITES: *La course des contraires*, in *Les voies de la création théâtrale* 9, CNRS, Paris 1980 (and in E. B., *L'archipel du théâtre*, Bouffonneries, Lectoure 1982); *Modsætningerners spil*, Berg, Copenhagen 1980; *Komunikacija* (fragment), in *Prolog* 50, Zagreb 1981; *La corsa dei contrari*, in E. B., *La corsa dei contrari*, Feltrinelli, Milan 1981 (and in E. B., *Aldilà delle isole galleggianti*, Ubulibri, Milan 1985); *The Way of the Opposites*, in *Canadian Theatre Review* 35, York University 1982 (and in E. B., *Beyond the Floating Islands*, *Performing Arts Journal*, New York 1986); *La cursa de contraris*, in E. B., *Les illes flotants*, Edicions '62, Barcelona 1983; *La búsqueda de los contrarios*, in E. B., *Las islas flotantes*, Universidad Nacional Autónoma de México, Mexico City 1983 (and in E. B., *Más allá de las islas flotantes*, Gaceta, Mexico City 1986); fragment with the title: *Cuando el actor abandona los territorios conocidos*, in *Quehacer Teatral* 2, Bogotá 1984; *Bermerkungen über das Schweigen der Schrift*, in *Bermerkungen über das Schweigen der Schrift*, Verlag der theater-assoziation, Köln 1983 (and with the title *Der Lauf der Gegensätze* in E. B., *Jenseits der Schwimmenden Inseln*, Rowohlt, Hamburg 1985); *Dårlig far og dårlig sønn: om skuespillerens opplæring*, fragment in *Spillerom* 2, Oslo 1986; *Masirat al-mu-aksin*, Dar al Kinuz, Damascus 1995.

– WHAT IS THEATRE ANTHROPOLOGY?: *What is Theatre Anthropology*, in Skeel (1) 1994; *O que é Antropologia Teatral*, in Skeel (2) 1994; *Was ist Theateranthropologie?*, in Falke 1996; fragment with the title *International School of Theatre Anthropology*, Sofia 2000.

– *About the Invisible and Visible in Theatre and about ISTA in Particular: Eugenio Barba to Philip Zarrilli*, in *The Drama Review* 119, New York 1988.

– *Caballeros con espadas de agua*, in L. Masgrau ed., *Arar el cielo. Diálogos latinoamericanos*, Fondo Editorial Casa de las Américas, Havana 2002.

– *Carta de Eugenio Barba a Nitis Jacon*, in *Mascara* 19–20, México City 1995, with the title *Aquí no se puede hacer nada*, in *Arar el cielo. Diálogos latinoamericanos*, Fondo editorial Casa de las Américas, Havana 2002 (and in *Carta de Eugenio Barba a Nitis Jacon*, in *Cartas do FILO*, FILO, Londrina 1997; *Letter by Eugenio Barba to Nitis Jacon*, in *Cartas do FILO*, FILO, Londrina 1997).

– *Como surgiu a ISTA*, in Skeel (2) 1994.

– *La conferencia de Santiago*, in *Apuntes de Teatro* 99, Santiago de Chile 1989.

– *Le corps crédible*, in O. Aslan ed., *Le Corps en jeu*, CNRS, Paris 1993.

– *Elogio della boxe*, in *L'indice* 5, Rome 1995.

– *Et dramaturgisk grundprincip*, Årsrapport 2000, Danish Center for Culture and Development, Copenhagen 2000.

– *Exister avant de représenter*, in *Puck* 7, Les Ardennes 1994.

– *The Female Rôle*, in *The Drama Review* 110, New York, 1986 (and in Skeel (1) 1994; Hastrup 1996 and with title *O papel femenino*, in Skeel (2) 1994).

– *How ISTA Came into Being*, in Skeel (1) 1994 (and in Hastrup 1996).

– *Intervista a Volterra*, ed. by di P. Giacché, in Taviani 1982.

– *Lettera di Eugenio Barba a Marco De Marinis* in *Due lettere sul pre-espressivo dell'attore, il mimo e i rapporti fra pratica e teoria*, in *Teatro e Storia* 16, Bologna 1994.

– *O método Românico*, in *Cadernos de espectáculos* 2, Teatro Carlos Gomes, Rio de Janeiro 1996.

– *Prefazione* a Ruffini 1981.

– *The ripe action*, in *Mime Journal. Theatre East and West Revisited*, Claremont 2002–2003.

– *Il ritmo nascosto*, in *Corriere dell'UNESCO*, 4/1996, Rome 1996.

– *Sanjukta Panigrahi: In Memory*, in *The Drama Review* 158, New York 1998.

Barker, Clive
– *Developing a New Language*, in *Theatre International* 1, London 1981.
– *El ISTA de Bologna: premisas culturales*, in Cruciani 1992.
– *L'ISTA di Bologna: Rapporto della sesta sessione dell'ISTA*, in Guccini – Valenti 1992.

Bassnett, Susan
– *Anatomia del Teatro*, in *New Theatre Quarterly* 6, Cambridge 1986.
– *Tasks of Theatre Anthropology*, in *New Theatre Quarterly* 6, Cambridge 1986.
– *Perceptions of the Female Rôle*, in *New Theatre Quarterly* 11, Cambridge 1987.

Bjelác-Babíc, Ranka
– *Utilizzazione di un metodo scientifico nello studio dell'espressione sportiva e teatrale*, in Ruffini 1981.

Birringer, Johannes
– *Repetition and Revolution: Theatre Anthropology after Brecht*, in *Theatre, Theory, Postmodernism*, Indiana Univ. Press, – Bloomington and Indianapolis 1991.

Bjelke, Torben
– *Diario dell'ISTA di Bonn*, in Ruffini 1981.

Blum, Lambert
– *ISTA-Tagung in Holstebro 1986*, in *Theater Zeitschrift* 2, Berlin 1987.
– *Wachsamkeit und offene Freiheit des Körpers*, in *Tanz Aktuell* 3, Berlin 1988.
– *Von der Verantmortung individueller Freiheit*, in *Tanz Aktuell* 9, Berlin 1989.
– *Im Licht Gegenwärtiger Träume. Der klassische indische Tanz*, in *Tanz Aktuell* 2, Berlin 1992.
– *Odissi. Klassischer Indischer Tanz und Aspekte der Theaterantropologie*, Mime Centrum Berlin, Berlin 1992.

Borie, Monique
– *Eugenio Barba et son école*, in *Théâtre/Public* 38, Paris 1981.

– *Une pédagogie pour le théâtre de groupe*, in *Théâtre/Public* 46/47, Paris 1982.

– *L'Acteur: masculin, féminin*, in *L'Art du Théâtre* 7, Paris 1986.

– *Le Regard et l'autre, une école de l'acteur vivant*, in *Théâtre/Public* 76/77, Paris 1987.

– *Enseignement et création, un même chemin*, in *L'Art du Théâtre* 8, Paris 1987/88.

– *Anthropologie Théâtrale et approche anthropologique du théâtre*, in *Bouffonneries* 22/23, Lectoure 1989.

– *L'Acteur et la mémoire des origines*, in *Le Cahier de l'Herne*, Paris 1990.

Boudet, Rosa Ileana
– *Territorio de lo invisible*, in *Conjunto* 104, Havana 1996.

Bovin, Mette
– *Provocation Anthropology: Bartering Performance in Africa*, in *The Drama Review* 117, New York 1988.

Braunek, Manfred
– *Teatro come atteggiamento inscenatorio*, in Ruffini 1981.

Bredsdorff, Thomas
– *Det rejsende universitet*, in *Politiken* 2/5, Copenhagen 1996.

– *Lettera ad Eugenio Barba a proposito dell'ISTA*, in Ruffini 1981.

Cardona, Patricia
– *Crónica de un llamado*, in *Escénica*, special issue, Mexico City 1986.

– *Energie et vision du monde*, in Ruffini 1989.

– *Las primeras preguntas*, in Cruciani 1992.

– *Antropología Teatral*, in *Mascara* 19–20, Mexico City 1995.

– *Hombres y mujeres de acción escénica definen los principios comunes a las culturas teatrales del mundo*, in *Uno más uno* 28/5, Mexico City 1996.

– *Jerzy Grotowski hace crónica de su vida (I-II-III)*, in *Uno más uno* 7, 8, 9/6, Mexico City 1996.

– *Para sobrevivir el teatro debe saltar hacia lo invisible: Luis de Tavira en Copenhague*, in *Uno más uno* 31/5, Mexico City 1996.

– *Prendido dinamismo multicultural en Copenhague*, in *Uno más uno* 17/5, Mexico City 1996.

– *En el teatro no hay reglas, aunque todo nace en los pies y sube al cielo*, in *Uno más uno* 30/5, Mexico City 1996.

– *El teatro como afirmación de la identidad o puente de comunicación entre la diversidad*, in *Uno más uno* 29/5, Mexico City 1996.

Carreri, Roberta
– *The Actor's Journey: Judith from Training to Performance*, ed. by E. Christoffersen, in *New Theatre Quarterly* 26/7, Cambridge 1991.

– *Il viaggio dell'attore dal training allo spettacolo*, in Guccini – Valenti 1992.

– *El viaje del actor, del training al espectáculo*, in Cruciani 1992.

– *Territories of the Body*, interview ed. by I. Watson, in Hastrup 1996.

– *La dinamica degli equivalenti fisici*, interview ed. by L. Masgrau, in De Marinis 1997.

– *La dynamique des équivalences physiques*, in Pavis 1999.

Carrió, Raquel
– *Escrito en el espacio*, in *Mascara* 9/10, Mexico City 1992 (and in Cruciani 1992).

– *Scrittura nello spazio*, in Guccini – Valenti 1992.

Chamberlain, Frank
– *Presenting the Unrepresentable: Maeterlinck's* L'Intruse *and the Symbolist Drama*, in Yarrow ed. 1997.

Chatra, I Nyoman
and R. Jenkins, *Bacchanalian Hieroglyphs* in Leabhart 1995.

Chemi, Tatiana
– *'Mente' sapendo di mentire. Il concetto di Mente-Corpo nell'Antropologia Teatrale*, in *Porta di Massa*, special issue, Naples 2000.

Christoffersen, Exe
– *The Presence Radiated by the Actor-Dancer*, in *Nordic Theatre Studies*, Oslo 1989.

– *Yoricks Grimasse*, in *Teater Et* 79, Copenhagen 1996.

Coppieters, Frank
– *Eugenio Barba et son Ecole Internationale d'Anthropologie Théâtrale*, in *Alternatives Théâtrales* 6/7, Bruxelles 1981.

Cruciani, Fabrizio
– *A proposito della scuola degli attori*, in *Città e Regione* 3, Bologna 1981.

– *Il luogo dei possibili*, in Guccini – Valenti 1992.

D'Aetwyler, Jean-Jacques
– *Lettera a Eugenio Barba a proposito dell'ISTA di Bonn*, in Ruffini 1981.

Dasgupta, Gautam
– *Anthropology and Theater*, in *PAJ* 24, New York 1984.

De Marinis, Marco
– *Il Corpo artificiale. Biologia e cultura nell'arte dell'attore*, in *Prometeo* 4, Bologna 1986

– *Capire il teatro. Lineamenti di una nuova teatrologia*, La Casa Usher, Florence 1988.

– *A scuola con Faust (Riflessioni in forma di diario sull'Antropologia Teatrale)*, in Guccini – Valenti 1992.

– *Mimo e teatro nel Novecento*, La Casa Usher, Florence 1993.

– *Lettera di Marco De Marinis a Eugenio Barba*, in *Due lettere sul pre-espressivo dell'attore, il mimo e i rapporti fra pratica e teoria*, in *Teatro e Storia* 16, Bologna 1994.

– *From Pre-expressivity to the Dramaturgy of the Performer*, in Leabhart 1995.

– *The Mask and Corporeal Expression in 20th-Century Theatre*, in Leabhart 1995.

– *Comprender el teatro. Lineamentos de una nueva teatrología*, Galerna, Buenos Aires 1997.

– *Dal pre-espressivo alla drammaturgia dell'attore. Saggio sulla 'Canoa di carta'*, in De Marinis 1997.

– *Rifare il corpo. Lavoro su se stessi e ricerca sulle azioni fisiche dentro e fuori del teatro nel Novecento*, in *Teatro e Storia* 19, Bologna 1997.

– *En quête de l'action physique, au théâtre et au delà du théâtre: de Stanislavsky à Barba*, in Pavis 1999.

De Tavira, Luis
– *El teatro en una sociedad multicultural*, in *ADE* 56–57, Madrid 1997.

Delgado, Mario
– *Diario dell'ISTA di Bonn*, in Ruffini 1981.

De Vos, Patrick
– *Onnagata, fleur de Kabuki*, in Taviani 1987.

Elsass, Peter
– *Rapports sur les travaux de la deuxième session publique de l'ISTA*, in Taviani 1982.

Fábregas, Xavier
– *Lettera a Eugenio Barba in occasione dell'ISTA di Bonn*, in Ruffini 1981.

Falke, Christoph
– *Weites Land des Wissens*, in *Theater der Zeit*, 1996.

Falletti, Clelia
– *I labirinti dell'ISTA 1996*, in *Teatro e Storia* 18, Bologna 1996.

Féral, Josette
– *Le Texte spectaculaire: la scène et son texte*, in Pavis 1999.

Filippetti, Renzo
– *Il lavoro organizzativo: una lettera*, in Guccini – Valenti 1992.

Frechette, Carol
– *L'ISTA et le rôle feminin*, in *Jeu* 43, Montreal 1987.

Fredrikson, Hans
– *Antropologin som ingång till teatern*, in *Teater Tidningen* 78, Stockholm 1996.

Gagnon, Odette
– *En présence de la troisième session de l'ISTA*, in *Jeu* 39, Montreal 1986.

Gale, Barnaby
– *Diario dell'ISTA di Bonn*, in Ruffini 1981.

Garcia Muñoz, Francisco
– *Décima sesión internacional de la ISTA*, in *Primer Acto* 263, Madrid 1996.

Giacché, Piergiorgio
– *ISTA che scuola*, in *Scena* 9, Milan 1981.
– *La scuola di Barba e il teatro di gruppo*, in *Scena* 9, Milano 1981.
– *In Principio*, in *Teatro festival* 7, Parma 1987.
– *Antropologia Culturale e Cultura Teatrale*, in *Teatro e Storia* 4, Bologna 1988.
– *Mémoire sociologique*, in Ruffini 1989.
– *Teatro e antropologia. Note su una "canoa di carta"*, in *Linea d'ombra* 86, Milan 1993.
– *L'altra visione dell'altro. Un'equazione tra antropologia e teatro*, L'ancora del Mediterraneo, Perugia 2004.

Grotowski, Jerzy
– *Intervista*, ed.by F. Ruffini, in Ruffini 1981.
– *Lois pragmatiques*, in Taviani 1982.
– *Spannung und Entspannung mussen zusammenspielen*, in *Theater Heute* 9, Berlin 1982.
– *Tecniche originarie dell'attore*, Transcription of the lessons held in the Istituto del Teatro e dello Spettacolo dell'Università La Sapienza di Roma, Rome 1982–83.

Guarino, Raimondo
– *Une solitude attentive. Chronique de l'improvisation*, in Taviani 1982.

Guccini, Gerardo
– *Notas sobre la cultura del cuerpo en los cantantes líricos*, in Cruciani 1992.

Hanayagi, Kanichi
– *Intervista*, ed. by M. Oshima, in Guccini – Valenti 1992.
– *Entrevista*, ed. by M. Oshima, in Cruciani 1992.

Hastrup, Kirsten
– *The Motivated Body*, in *A Passage to Anthropology*, Routledge, London 1985 (with the title *Il corpo motivato*, in *Teatro e Storia* 17, Bologna 1995).
– *Incorporated Knowledge*, in Leabhart 1995.
– *Verkörperters Wissen*, in Falke 1996.

Helbo, André
– *Il "gioco" della terminologia*, in Ruffini 1981.

Hind, Tage
– *Naervaer i kraft af fravaer*, in *Tusind Øjne* 92, Copenhagen 1986.

Hoff, Frank
– *Rapporto della sesta sessione dell'ISTA*, in Guccini – Valenti 1992.
– *El ISTA de Bologna: premisas culturales*, in Cruciani 1992.
– *Zeami drammaturgo*, in Guccini – Valenti 1992.

Homar, Susan
– *Los susurros de la ISTA*, in *Conjunto* 104, Havana 1996.

Jenkins, Ron
– and I N. Catra, *Bacchanalian Hieroglyphs*, in Leabhart 1995.
– *A Hunger for Hieroglyphs*, in Hastrup 1996.

Jezier, Feliza
– *Desde los ojos de una americana del sur*, in *Conjunto* 104, Havana 1996.

Kaquet, Brigitte
– *Metadialogue*, in Taviani 1987.

Korish, David
– *Reflexiones de un constructor*, in *Conjunto* 104, Havana 1996.

Krøgholt, Ida
– *ISTA. At skabe deltagerens blik*, in *Teater Et* 79, Copenhagen 1996.

Laborit, Henri
– *Impressioni dal Simposio*, in Ruffini 1981.

Leabhart, Thomas
– *The mask as Shamanic Tool in the Theatre Training of Jacques Copeau*, in Leabhart 1995.

Mansur, Nara
– *Escalar el árbol de maple en otoño*, in *Conjunto* 111, Havana 1998.

Martinez Tabares, Vivian
– *Vivir la ISTA o el placer quimérico de apresar lo inasible*, in *Conjunto* 111, Havana 1998.

Masgrau, Lluís
– *L'uno e il multiplo. La drammaturgia dell'attore all'Odin Teatret*, in De Marinis 1997.
– *La dramaturgie de l'acteur à l'Odin Teatret*, in Pavis 1999.
– *L'interprétation de la partition*, in Pavis 1999.
– *La dramaturgie du personnage*, in Pavis 1999.
– *La dynamique des équivalences physiques*, in Pavis 1999.
– *La construction de l'extérieur*, in Pavis 1999.

Most, Henrik
– *We Are the World*, in *Teater Et* 79, Copenhagen 1996.

Muguercia, Magaly
– *Barba: trascender la literalidad*, in *Conjunto* 78, Havana 1989.

Munk, Erika
– *The Rites of Women*, in *PAJ* 29, New York 1987.

Nagel Rasmussen, Iben
– *La drammaturgia del personaggio*, interview ed. by L. Masgrau, in De Marinis 1997.
– *La dramaturgie du personnage*, in Pavis 1999.

Nakajima, Natsu
– *Butoh*, in *Spillerom* 61, Oslo 1997.

Noguera, Héctor
– *Castro y Barba: Teatro en la diversidad cultural*, in *Revista Apuntes* 96, Santiago 1988.

Omolú, Augusto
– *Omolú baila el silencio*, interview, in *Conjunto* 111, Havana 1998.

Oshima, Mark
- *Intervista con Kanichi Hanayagi*, in Guccini – Valenti 1992.
- *Entrevista con Kanichi Hanayagi*, in Cruciani 1992.

Panigrahi, Sanjukta
- *Intervista*, ed. by F. Ruffini, in Ruffini 1981.
- *Entretien avec Sanjukta Panigrahi*, in Taviani 1982.
- *La creazione della danza Odissi*, in Guccini – Valenti 1992.
- *Cinque maestri*, in Guccini – Valenti 1992.
- *Cinco encuentros*, in Cruciani 1992.
- Fragments with the title *Never Show Tiredness*, in Skeel (1) 1994 (and in Hastrup 1996).
- Fragments with the title *Nunca mostre cansanço*, in Skeel (2) 1994.
- *Five Meetings*, in Skeel 1994 (1) (and in Hastrup 1996).
- *Cinco encontros*, in Skeel (2) 1994.
- *L'ISTA di Bologna 1990*, in Guccini – Valenti 1992.

Pavis, Patrice
- *Dancing with Faust. A Semiotician's Reflections on Barba's Intercultural Mise-en-scene*, in *The Drama Review* 123, New York 1989.
- *Le Théâtre au croisement des cultures*, Librairie José Corti, Paris 1990 (English version *Theatre at the Crossroads of Culture*, Routledge, London 1992).
- *I testi dell'attore. Domande a Julia Varley*, in Guccini – Valenti 1992.
- *Los textos del actor*, in Cruciani 1992.
- *Da Stanislavskyj a Wilson. Antologia sulla partitura*, in De Marinis 1997.
- *Una nozione piena d'avvenire: la sottopartitura*, in De Marinis 1997.
- *Underscore: The Shape of Things to Come*, in Yarrow 1997.
- *Anthologie portative de la partition, de Stanislavsky à Wilson*, in Pavis 1999.
- *La Dramaturgie de l'actrice ou: 'voilà pourquoi votre fille est muette'*, in Pavis 1999.

Phelan, Peggy
- *Feminist Theory, Poststructuralism, and Performance*, in *The Drama Review* 117, New York 1988.

Pradier, Jean-Marie
- *L'ISTA o la 'maquette'*, in Ruffini 1981.
- *ISTA the First Session*, in *Theatre International* 1, Paris 1981.
- *Rapport sur les travaux de la deuxième session publique de l'ISTA*, in Taviani 1982.
- *L'Acteur: Aspects de l'apprentissage*, in *Internationale de l'Imaginaire* 6/7, Paris 1986.
- *Anatomie de l'acteur*, in *Théatre/Public* 76/77 Paris 1987.
- *L'Économie de la dépense*, in Taviani 1987.
- *Memoires extérieurs*, in Ruffini 1989.
- *Le Théâtre des émotions*, in *Evolutions Psychomotrices* 7, Paris 1990.
- *Les Corps séducteurs. Eugenio Barba et le «métier»*, in *Théâtre/Public* 11/12, Paris 1990.
- *Rapporto della sesta sessione dell'ISTA*, in Guccini – Valenti 1992.
- *La ISTA de Bolonia: premisas culturales*, in Cruciani 1992.
- *Verso un'estetica della stimolazione*, in Guccini – Valenti 1992.
- *De l'esthétique de la scène à l'étique du reseau*, in *Theatre/Public* 116, Paris 1994.
- *La Scène et la fabrique des corps*, Presses Universitaires, Bordeaux 1997 (extracts: *Fànic, fàllic, fàtic*, Universitat de València 1998).
- *The Pre-Expressive Level: A Mechanicist-Alchemist Concept?*, in Yarrow 1997.

Pronko, Leonard
- *Two Salomes and a Kabuki Montage: on Rereading a Dictionary of Theatre Anthropology*, in Leabhart 1995.

Revel Macdonald, Nicole
- *Lettera a Eugenio Barba in occasione dell'ISTA di Bonn*, in Ruffini 1981.

Risum, Janne
- *Verden vil bedrages: at forske i at se på opført fiktion*, in *Bunt* 9, Foreningen Nordiske Teaterforskere, Dragvoll, 1992.
- *The ISTA Circus*, in Hastrup 1996.
- *"Satori". Il rituale della sedia vuota*, in De Marinis 1997 (and in *Nordic Theatre Studies*, Oslo 1995).
- *Un habit bariolé: les acteurs de l'Odin*, in Pavis 1999.
- *A Study in Motley. The Odin Actors*, in I. Watson, *Performer Training. Developement Across the Cultures*, Harwood Academic Publishers, Amsterdam 2001.
- *Brechts "Kinesiske" Verfremdung. Hvordan og hvorfor*, in A. Scavenius – S. Jarl ed., *Sceneskift. Det 20 århundredes teater i Europa*, Multivers, Copenhagen 2001.
- *Mei Lanfang: A model for the Theatre of the Future*, in B. Picon-Vallin – O. Serbakov, *Meyerhold, la mise en scène dans le siècle*, Moscow 2001.
- *Female Look-outs*, in *Degrés* 107–108, Brussels 2002.

Ruffini, Franco
- *Gesto dello spettacolo/gesto del teatro: osservazioni sul training*, in *Quaderni di teatro* 2, Bologna 1978.
- *Ricordi e riflessioni sull'ISTA*, in Quaderni di teatro 23, Bologna 1984.
- *Antropologia teatrale*, in *Teatro e Storia* 1, Il Mulino, Bologna 1986.
- *Horizontal and Vertical Montage in the Theatre*, in *New Theatre Quarterly* 5, Cambridge 1986.
- *Antropologie Théâtrale*, in *Théâtre: modes d'approche*, Labor, Brussels 1987.
- *Le milieu-scène: pre-expression, énergie, présence*, in Taviani 1987.
- *'Il ruolo della donna' all'International School of Theatre Anthropology*, in *Teatro e Storia* 2, Bologna 1987.
- *L'attore e il dramma. Saggio teorico di Antropologia Teatrale*, in *Teatro e Storia* 5, Bologna 1988.
- *Theatre Anthropology*, in *Approaching Theatre*, Bloomington, Indiana University Press, 1991
- *El ISTA de Bolonia: premisas culturales*, in Cruciani 1992.
- *Rapporto della sesta sessione dell'ISTA*, in Guccini – Valenti 1992.
- *Precisione e corpo-mente. Sul valore del teatro*, in *Teatro e Storia* 15, Bologna 1993
- *Teatro e boxe. L'atleta del cuore nella scena del Novecento*, Il Mulino, Bologna 1995.
- *Mime, the Actor, Action: the Way of Boxing*, in Leabhart 1995.
- *Mime, Schauspieler, Action: die Kunst des Boxens*, in *Flamboyant* 2, Cologne 1995.
- *A Letter*, in Hastrup 1996.
- *I teatri di Artaud. Crudeltà, corpo-mente*, Il Mulino, Bologna 1996.
- *Antropologia Teatrale* e *Drammaturgia dell'attore*, in *Per piacere. Itinerari intorno al valore del teatro*, Bulzoni, Rome 2001.

Savarese, Nicola
  – *Diario caméra-crayon*, in Ruffini 1981.
  – *The Experience of the Difference: Eurasian Theatre*, in *Forum Modernes Theater Schriftenreihe,* Vol. II, Tübingen 1990.
  – *Teatro e spettacolo fra Oriente e Occidente*, Laterza, Rome – Bari 1992.
  – *Pourquoi l'Anthropologie Théâtrale?*, interview ed. by J. Féral, in *Jeu 68*, Montreal 1994.
  – *Work Demostrations at ISTA. Examples of Transcultural Dialogue*, in Skeel (1) 1994 (and in Hastrup 1996).
  – *Demostraçoes de trabalho na ISTA. Exemplos de diálogos transculturales*, in Skeel (2) 1994.
  – *Le dimostrazioni di lavoro all'ISTA come esempio di dialogo transculturale*, in De Marinis 1997.
  – *Teatro eurasiano. Danzas y espectaculos entre Oriente y Occidente*, Escenología, Mexico City 2001.
  – *Teatro eurasiano*, Laterza, Rome – Bari 2002.
  – *Towards Eurasian Theatre*, in *Theatre East and West Revisited, Mime Journal*, Claremont 2003.
Schechner, Richard
  – *Collaborating on Odissi*, in *The Drama Review* 117, New York 1988.
Schino, Mirella
  – *La recherche de l'invraisemblance*, in Taviani 1987.
  – *Ríen*, in *Mascara* 19–20, Mexico City 1995.
  – *Laughter at ISTA*, in Hastrup 1996.
  – *Shakuntala Among the Olive Trees*, in *Asian Theatre Journal* 1/13, Honolulu 1996 (and in De Marinis 1997.
  – *Le spectacle de la naissance. Les répétitions d'Eugenio Barba pour le Theatrum Mundi 'L'île des Labyrinthes'*, in G. Banu ed., *Les Répétitions*, in *Alternatives Théâtrales* 52–54, Brussels 1997.
  – *Teorici, registi, pedagoghi*, in R. Alonge – G. Davico Bonino ed., *Storia del teatro moderno e contemporaneo*, Vol. III, Einaudi, Turin 2001.
Seibel, Beatriz
  – *El Teatro Argentino y las Nuevas Técnicas Europeas*, in *Crear* 8, Buenos Aires 1982.
  – *Encuentro de Semiótica y antropologia teatral en Italia*, in *Espacio* 4, Buenos Aires 1988.
Stewart, Nigel
  – *Actor as Refusenik: Semiotics, in Theatre Anthropology, and the Work of the Body*, in *New Theatre Quarterly* 36, Cambridge 1993.
Taviani, Ferdinando
  – *Rapport sur les travaux de la deuxième session publique de L'ISTA*, in Taviani 1982.
  – *Un vivo contrasto*, in *Teatro e Storia* 1, Il Mulino, Bologna 1986.
  – *La danse occulte. Enseignements d'acteurs disparus*, in Ruffini 1989.
  – *Theatrum Mundi*, in Skeel (1) 1994 (and in Hastrup 1996).
  – *Theatrum Mundi*, in Skeel (2) 1994.
  – *What Happens at ISTA? Stories, Memories and Reflections*, in Skeel (1) 1994 (and in Hastrup 1996).
  – *O que acontece durante a ISTA? Histórias, memórias e reflexôes*, in Skeel (2) 1994.
  – *Was Geschieht? Geschichten, Erinnerungen und Reflexionen von den Treffen der ISTA (1980–1995)*, in Falke 1996.
  – *L'Amleto latente di Eugenio Barba ovvero quando Amleto si traveste da Don Giovanni*, in *Il patalogo* 19, Ubulibri, Milan 1996.

  – *Passagi e sottopassagi. Esercizi di terminologia*, in De Marinis 1997.
  – *Editoriale*, in *Teatro e Storia* 19, Bologna 1997.
  – *Taviani en la isla del teatro*, intervista, in *Conjunto* 111, Havana 1998.
  – *Artaud a voce sommessa*, in F. Ruffini – A. Berdini ed., *Antonin Artaud: teatro, libri e oltre*, Bulzoni, Roma 2001.
  – *Attore e attrice*, in *Enciclopedia del Cinema*, Istituto dell'Enciclopedia Italiana, Rome 2002.
Temkine, Raymonde and Valentin
  – *Lettera a Eugenio Barba in occasione dell'ISTA di Bonn*, in Ruffini 1981.
Tempo, I Made Pasek
  – *Intervista*, edited by F. Ruffini, in Ruffini 1981.
  – *Softness and Vigour*, in Skeel (1) 1994 (and in Hastrup 1996).
  – *Suavidade e vigor*, in Skeel (2) 1994.
Tordera, Antoni
  – *Sei riflessioni teoriche apprese con i miei muscoli*, in Ruffini 1981.
Turner, Jane
  – *Prospero's Floating Island: ISTA '96*, in *Asian Theatre Journal* 1/14, Honolulu 1997.
Tyszka, Juliusz
  – *Dziesiata Sesja ISTA*, in *Teatr* 11, Warsaw 1996.
  – *Dario Fo i Franca Rame wystepuja podczas ISTA*, in *Opcje* 1/20, Katowice 1998.
Valenzuela, José Luis
  – *Aldilà dell'Antropologia Teatrale*, in Guccini – Valenti 1992.
  – *¿Más allá de la Antropología Teatral?*, in *Mascara* 9/10, Mexico City 1992.
  – *Antropología teatral y acciones físicas*, Instituto Nacional del Teatro, Buenos Aires 2000.
Varley, Julia
  – *Una candela accesa fra le pagine dei libri,* in Guccini – Valenti 1992.
  – *Un vela prendida entre las páginas de los libros*, in Cruciani 1992.
  – *'Subpartitura': otra palabra útil y errónea*, in *Conjunto* 97/98, Havana 1994.
  – *A Candel Lit Amongst the Pages of Books*, in Skeel (1) 1994 (and in Hastrup 1996).
  – *Uma vela entre as páginas dos livros*, in Skeel (2) 1994.
  – *'Subscore': Yet Another Useful and Wrong Word*, in *Ilden i glasset. Aktuelle teaterproblemer 32*, Institut for Dramaturgi, Århus 1994 (and in *New Theatre Quarterly* 42, Cambridge 1995).
  – *The Pre-Expressive Family*, in Leabhart 1995 (and in Hastrup 1996).
  – *Die Prä-Expressive Familie*, in Falke 1996.
  – *La costruzione dell'esterno*, interview ed. by L. Masgrau, in De Marinis 1997.
  – *'Sottopartitura': ancora un termine utile e sbagliato*, in De Marinis 1997.
  – *La Construction de l'extérieur*, in Pavis 1999.
Vill, Susanne
  – *Ein Welttheater der Interkulturelle Kommunikation*, in *Wort und Musik* 15, Verlag Ursula Muller-Speiser, Salzburg 1992 (Polish version: *Swiatowy teatr interkulturowej komunikacji. Euroazjatyckie 'Theatrum Mundi' Eugenia Barby w Bolonii 1990*, in *Polska Sekcja Isme* 3/4, Warsaw 1993).
  – *Interakcyjna praca w teatrze ruchem, slowem i muzyka*, in *Polska Sekcja Isme* 1, Warsaw 1993.

– *Intermediäre Kreation in interkultureller Theaterarbeit. Aus der Werkstatt von Eugenio Barbas International School of Theatre Anthropology (ISTA)*, in *Arbeitsfelder der Theaterwissenschaft. Modernes Theater*, Gunter Narr Verlag, Tubingen 1994.

Watanabe, Moriaki

– *Tra Oriente e Occidente*, in Ruffini 1981.
– *Entre Orient et Occident*, in Taviani 1982.

Watson, Ian

– *Report on the fourth ISTA*, in *Canadian Theatre Review* 51, Toronto 1987.
– *Eastern and Western Influences on Performer Training at Eugenio Barba's Odin Teatret*, in *Asian Theatre Journal* 1, Honolulu 1988.
– *Towards a Third Theatre*, Routledge, New York, 1993.
– *Hacia un tercer teatro*, Ñaque, Ciudad Real, 2000.
– *Performer Training. Developments Across Cultures*, Harwood Academic Publishers, Amsterdam 2001.

Weiler, Christel

– and W. Ybema *Ricordi e riflessioni sull'lSTA*, in *Quaderni di teatro* 23, Bologna 1984.
– *An Attempt to Trace the Secret. One Aspect of Eugenio Barba's Theatre Anthropology*, in *Forum Modernes Theater Schriftenteihe*, vol. 2, Gunter Narr Verlag, Tübingen 1990.

– *Kulturelle Austausch: Theatrale Praktiken, Robert Wilson und Eugenio Barba*, Tectum Verlag, Marburg 1994.

Wethal, Torgeir

– *Dalle improvisazioni al Crossing*, in Guccini – Valenti 1992.
– *De la improvisación al Crossing*, in Cruciani 1992.
– *L'interpretazione della partitura*, interview ed. by L. Masgrau, in De Marinis 1997.
– *L'interprétation de la partition*, in Pavis 1999.

Yamaguchi, Masao

– *Rapporto della sesta sessione dell'ISTA*, in Guccini - Valenti 1992.
– *El ISTA de Bolonia: premisas culturales*, in Cruciani 1992.

Wunderrich, Veronica

– *Körper Philosophe: Eugenio Barba und das Odin Teatret. Theateranthropologie und die Dramaturgie des Schauspielers*, Edition Praesens, Vienna 2000.

Ybema, Walter

– *Diario dell'ISTA di Bonn,* in Ruffini 1981.

Zarrilli, Phillip

– *Collaborating on Odissi*, in *The Drama Review* 117, New York 1988.
– *For Whom Is the 'Invisible' Not Visible?*, in *The Drama Review* 117, New York 1988.

ACKNOWLEDGEMENTS

ISTA, International School of Theatre Anthropology

Directed by Eugenio Barba

Box 1283, 7500 Holstebro, Denmark.
Tel.: (+45) 9742 4777 – Fax: (+45) 9741 0482
E-mail: odin@odinteatret.dk – www.odinteatret.dk

ISTA, the International School of Theatre Anthropology, was founded in 1979. Conceived and directed by Eugenio Barba, it is based in Holstebro, Denmark. ISTA is a multicultural network of performers and scholars giving life to an itinerant institution whose main field of study is theatre anthropology.

ISTA holds open sessions periodically on the request of national and international cultural organisations which provide the necessary funding. Each session has a different theme defining a particular subject which is investigated through practical classes, work demonstrations and comparative analysis. Each time, a limited number of actors, dancers, directors, choreographers, scholars and critics can apply to participate.

ISTA's network is centred around a permanent core of European, American, Afro-American and Asian performers as well as scholars from various universities. This network meets, works and communicates not only during the public sessions, but also through mutual contacts, exchanges and initiatives, smaller closed work sessions and within the framework of the University of Eurasian Theatre whose open activity presents the results of ISTA's research.

During its twenty-five years of existence ISTA has been a laboratory for research into the technical grounding of the performer in a cross-cultural dimension. The objective of this methodological choice, deriving from an empirical approach, is the understanding of the fundamental principles which engender the performer's 'presence' or 'scenic life'.

Between 1979 and 2005 ISTA has organised fourteen international sessions with the following organisers:

Bonn (Germany) 1980: Hans Jürgen Nagel, Kulturamt der Stadt, Bonn.

Holstebro (Denmark) 1980: Odin Teatret.

Porsgrunn (Norway) 1980: Grenland Friteater.

Stockholm (Sweden) 1980: Teater Schahrazad.

Volterra (Italy) 1981: Roberto Bacci, Centro per l' Investigazione e Sperimentazione Teatrale di Pontedera.

Blois and Malakoff (France) 1985: Patrick Pezin, Bouffonneries, in collaboration with Nicolas Peskine, Compagnie du Hasard (Blois), Edith Rappoport and Pierre Ascaride, Théâtre 71 (Malakoff).

Holstebro (Denmark) 1986: Odin Teatret.

Salento (Italy) 1987: Giorgio Di Lecce, Cristina Ria, Mediterranea Teatro Laboratorio and Nicola Savarese, University of Lecce.

Bologna (Italy) 1990: Pietro Valenti, Centro Teatrale San Geminiano, Renzo Filippetti, Teatro Ridotto and the University of Bologna.

Brecon and Cardiff (Great Britain) 1992: Richard Gough and Judie Christie, Centre for Performance Research, Cardiff.

Londrina (Brazil) 1994: Nitis Jacon, FILO (Festival International de Londrina) and the University of Londrina.

Umeå (Sweden) 1995: Sven Sahlstrom and Chris Torch, Umeå Teaterforening and Riksteatern.

Copenhagen (Denmark) 1996: Odin Teatret and Trevor Davies, Copenhagen Cultural Capital of Europe '96.

Montemor O-novo and Lisbon (Portugal) 1998: Marco Abbondanza, Festival 7sois 7luas in collaboration with Montemor O-novo Municipality and the Gulbenkian Foundation.

Bielefeld (Germany) 2000: Siegmar Schröder, Theaterlabor Bielefeld.

Seville and La Rinconada (Spain) 2004: Ricardo Iniesta, TNT/Atalaya Teatro.

Wroclaw and Krzyżowa (Poland) 2005: Jaroslaw Fret and Grzegorz Ziólkowski, The Centre for Studies of Jerzy Grotowski's Work and for Cultural and Theatrical Research.

Invited artists

Argentina: César Brie, Pepe Robledo, Ana Woolf.

Bali (Indonesia): I Nyoman Budi Artha, I Dewa Ayu Ariani, I Made Bandem, Ni Ari Bandem, Ni Dewi Bandem, Swasti Widjaja Bandem, I Wayan Bawa, I Wayan Berata, Ni Nyoman Candri, I Nyoman Catra, Pino Confessa, I Made Djimat, I Nyoman Doble, Wayan Gatri, I Nyoman Jony, I Ketut Kodi, I Nyoman Kopelin, Desak Made Suarti Laksmi, Ni Wayan Latri, I Wayan Lantir, Ni Ketut Maringsih, Ida Bagus Nyoman Mas, I Wayan Naka, I Gede Surya Negara, Tjokorda Istri, Putra Padmini, I Ketut Partha, I Nyoman Punja, I Wayan Punia, Desak Putu Puspawati, Anak Agung Putra, Ni Made Putri, I Wayan Rai, Ni Made Sarniani, I Nyoman Sedana, Ni Wayan Sekarini, I Gusti Ayu Srinatih, Ni Wayan Sudi, Ni Ketut Suryatini, Desak Ketut Susilawati, I Ketut Suteja, I Wayan Suweca, Ni Nyoman Suyasning, I Gusti Nyoman Tantra, I Made Pasek Tempo, I Made Terika, Tjokorda Raka Tisnu, I Ketut Tutur, Ni Made Wati, Cristina Wistari.

Brazil: Antonios Carlos dos Santos Araújo, Bira Monteiro, Augusto Omolú, Clever da Paição, Jorge 'Funk' Paim, Jairo da Purificação, Ory Sacramento.

Canada: Richard Fowler.

China: Mei Baoju, Pei Yanling, Sun Zhong-Shu.

Denmark: Emil Ferslev, Nicolaj de Fine Licht, Palle Granhøj, Ivan Hansen, Stephen Pier.

France: Vincent Audat, Françoise Champault, Brigitte Cirla.

Germany: Gisela Cremer, Sonja Kehler, Natasha Nikprelevic, Ralf Raüker, Michael Vetter.

Great Britain: Clive Barker, Keith Johnstone.

India: Jagdish Burmann, Ileana Citaristi, Hamesh Kumar Das, Chinmaya Kumar Dash, Hemant Kumar Das, Hatmohan Khuntia, Kishore Kumar, Debi Prasad Mahanti, Kelucharan Mahapatra, Nityananda Mohapatra, Pradeepta Sekhar Mohapatra, M.P. Sankaran Namboodiri,

Raghunath Panigrahi, Sanjukta Panigrahi, Annada Prasanna Pattanaik, Mohini Mohan Patnaik, Bishnu Mohan Pradhan, Gangadar Pradhan, Jagdish Prasad Varman, K. N. Vijayakumar.

Italy: Sergio Bini, Orazio Costa, Dario Fo, Franca Rame.

Japan: Haruchiho Azuma, Kanho Azuma, Katsuko Azuma, Mari Azuma, Senkai Azuma, Shogo Fujima, Yoshikazu Fujisaka, Jutaiichiro Hanayagi, Kanichi Hanayagi, Sasakimi Hanayagi, Akiyaso Hirade, Choyuri Imafuji, Michi Imafuji, Kunitoshi Kineya, Sanshichiro Kineya, Shizuko Kineya, Naoyuki Kojima, Takae Koyama, Akira Matsui, Yasuhiro Miyata, Natsu Nakajima, Sae Nanaogi, Kosuke Nomura, Ryosuke Nomura, Mark Oshima, Taro Yamaguchi.

Odin Teatret: Kai Bredholt, Roberta Carreri, Jan Ferslev, Tage Larsen, Iben Nagel Rasmussen, Tina Nielsen, Isabel Ubeda, Julia Varley, Torgeir Wethal, Frans Winther.

Poland: Jerzy Grotowski.

Russia: Gennadi Bogdanov.

Sweden: Stina Ekblad, Ingemar Lindh.

Taiwan: Tsao Chun-Lin, Lin Chun-Hui, Tracy Chung, Helen Liu.

USA: Carolyn Carlson, Thomas Leabhart, Lisa Nelson, Steve Paxton.

Scientific staff and special guests

Ranka Bijeljac Babic, Eugenia Casini Ropa, Peter Chelkowski, Exe Christoffersen, Fabrizio Cruciani, Luis de Tavira, Johannes Fabian, Marco de Marinis, Peter Elsass, Clelia Falletti, Clifford Geertz, Kirsten Hastrup, Ronald Jenkins, Leszek Kolankiewicz, Henri Laborit, Eduardo Manet, Mbongemi Ngema, Zbigniew Osinski, Patrice Pavis, Jean-Marie Pradier, Kostanty Puzyna, Thomas Richard, Janne Risum, Franco Ruffini, Jonah Salz, Nicola Savarese, Richard Schechner, Mirella Schino, Wole Soyinka, Ferdinando Taviani, Susanne Vill, Ugo Volli, Moriaki Watanabe, Benito Zambrano.

Illustrations

Dorthe Kaergaard: 144, 176
Poul Østergaard: 71/22–23–24
Massimo Sarzi Amadé: 10, 199/11–12, 263
Shigetsugu Wakafuji: 6, 14, 39/19, 94/6–7, 195, 227/40

Photos

Fiora Bemporad: 12/20, 53/4, 103, 104, 105, 119/18–19, 120, 121, 210, 211/12–14, 224/29, 229/44
Peter Bysted: 71/28, 81/22
Pino Confessa: 77/13
Toni D'Urso: 1, 35/12, 69/10–11, 70, 71/25–27, 136/43–44, 159, 162/39, 207, 214, 215, 220, 231/51, 251/13, 254/24, 277/3, 279/5, 280/8
Christoph Falke: 29/11
Torben Huss: 12/23, 17/32, 35/13, 39/21, 42/35, 49/53, 53/3, 56/10, 72/1, 77/12, 78, 79, 80, 82, 83, 100, 133, 138, 157/26, 161/35, 199/10, 224/28, 228/43, 232/55, 234, 242/3, 251/12, 276, 277/2
Dana Kalvodova: 198/6-7-8, 263
Michèle Laurent: 257
Ingemar Lindh: 7, 11, 32/3, 45/43, 132/29, 183, 184/28–30–32–34–36, 213/18
Francesco Petroni: 49/52
Jan Rüsz: 71/26, 162/38, 225/32
Saul Shapiro: 18/35
Bernd Uhlig: 224/27, 247/17
Nicola Savarese: 13, 16/30, 19/37–38, 32/2, 35/10–11, 41/28, 42/32–33, 45/45, 72/2, 75, 81/21, 84, 85, 93/2, 94/4–5, 95/10–11–12–13, 96, 97/25, 98, 99, 126, 127, 129, 136/43, 140/1, 144/11, 145, 160/34, 181, 184/29–31–33–37, 194, 201/19, 204/31–32–33–34, 205, 223/25, 233, 243/8, 244, 248/1–2–3–4, 252, 253, 255, 265/43–44–45, 269, 283/14, 284/18, 286, 287

All other illustrations come from the archives of Eugenio Barba and Nicola Savarese.

EUGENIO BARBA (1936) Italian born, emigrated to Norway in 1954 where he worked as a welder and seaman. From 1961 to 1964, he followed Jerzy Grotowski's work in Poland, publishing the first book about him, *In Search of a Lost Theatre* (1965). In 1963, after spending six months in India, he published an essay on kathakali, a theatre form previously unknown in the West. In 1964 he founded Odin Teatret in Oslo, transferring it in 1966 to Holstebro (Denmark) as the Nordisk Teaterlaboratorium. He has directed thirty-two productions which have been regularly presented in Europe, Asia, North and South America. In 1979 he founded ISTA, the International School of Theatre Anthropology, an itinerant institution with actors, dancers, musicians and scholars interested in investigating the principles of scenic presence. He has written many books and articles, amongst which *The Paper Canoe. A Guide to Theatre Anthropology* (Routledge, 1994), *Theatre: Solitude, Craft, Revolt* (Black Mountain Press, 1999) and *Land of Ashes and Diamonds: My Apprenticeship in Poland* (Black Mountain Press, 1999). He has received numerous international awards and honorary doctorates.

NICOLA SAVARESE (1945) combines research into the past with direct participation in performance practice. He is specialised in ancient Greek and Roman theatre and in the complex dynamics of interaction between Western and Eastern performances. He has taught at the universities of Lecce, Kyoto, Montreal, Bologna and Rome where at present he is Professor of Theatre History. He has travelled widely in Asia, particularly in Japan where he lived for two years and has been Resident Guest Scholar at the Getty Research Institute in Los Angeles (1999). He has published *Il teatro aldilà del mare* (*The Theatre beyond the Sea*, 1980) and *Teatro e spettacolo fra Oriente e Occidente* (*Theatre and Performance between East and West*, Laterza, 1992) about the relationship between Western and Asian theatres. Other books: *Parigi/Artaud/Bali* (Textus 1996), *Il racconto del teatro cinese* (*The Tale of Chinese Theatre*, Carocci, 1997) *Teatro Eurasiano* (*Eurasian Theatre*, Laterza 2003), *Training* (Audino Editore 2004), *Te@tri nella rete. Arti e tecniche dello spettacolo nell'era dei nuovi media* (*Theatres on the Web. Arts and Techniques of Performance in the Era of New Medias*, Carocci 2004).

Note: Page numbers in italics indicate an illustration and/or information in a caption.

abacus: digital numeration *152*
absence 8, 194, *194*, 225
abstract mime 94
academic stage 271
Académie Royale de la Danse *226*
acculturation 219, *219*, 220, *220*
acrobatics 8, *9*, *49*, 168, 186; exercises *114*, 116–17; training 282, *282*, 284, *284*, *285*
acting: anatomy of *23*; and body 12–13; and dance 168; 'great actors' 208–9; organicity 206; performer's view 288–99; rôle types 274; Stanislavsky's system 170–3; technique 25, 219–20; Western theatre 103; *see also* scenic presence
action rhetoric 282, 284
actions: braking the action 88–90; and dramaturgy 66–9; 'physical actions' 112
Actors' Studio 280
Adam and Eve montage 180–2, *181*, *183*, *184*
Advayataraka Upanishad 28–9
Ahasuerus 54
Ahlstedt, Borge *275*
Aleksandr Nevskij (film) *178*, *179*
alienation effect 108, 219–20, 235
American Indians *150*, 151
amplification 268
anatomy 22–3, *37*
ancient Greece *10*, 106, *107*, 185; dance *186*, *188*; martial arts 230, *231*; tragedy 66, *189*; vase paintings *187*, *231*
animals 134, 227, *229*, *232*
animation: hands 154–5, *154*; opposition 195, *196*, 204, *204*; rhythm *245*
animus/anima 76–8, *79*, 87, *278*
anti-musical rhythm *245*
anti-traditional theatre 102–3
Antoine, André *272*
Aphrodite *see* Venus de Milo
Appia, Adolphe 24, 206, 209
apprenticeship 24–31, *36*, *278*; *see also* training
Après-midi d'un faun *188*, *226*
arabesque *15*, 35
aragoto 35, *36*
arangetram 30
Archer, William 165
archery *see* bows and arrows
Ardhanarishwara 19–20, *20*, 82
Aristotle 66
arms 95, *194*, 256
Arnheim, Rudolf 43, 216, 234
Art et l'instruction de bien danser, L' *226*
Artaud, Antonin 21, 108, *111*, 117, *199*, 206, 212, *213*
artificiality *see* acculturation; organicity
Asian theatre 185, 196, 222, 227–8; training 281, 284; and Western tradition 102–11, *188*, *190*; *see also* Balinese dance/theatre; Indian theatre; Oriental theatre
athletics 116–17
Atharva Veda 28
Attinger, Gustave 26
attitudes (classical ballet) 35
Aubert, René 134, *134*
audiences *see* spectators
Austin, Gilbert 152, *197*, 223, *224*

axé 211
Aztecs *6*, *54*, 200
Azuma, Kanho *228*
Azuma, Katsuko 11, *29*, *75*, *85*, *160*; balance 17, 40, *41*; costume *248*, *252*, *255*; face and eyes 126, *127*; omission 194, *194*; pre-expressivity *228*, *233*; rhythm 15, 16–17, *16*, *242*, 244, *244*; *tame* 84, *84*
Azuma, Mari *244*

Bakst, Léon 108, *142*
balance 9–10, 17, 32–51, 180, 268, 281; *see also* extra-daily balance; luxury balance
Balàzs, Béla 59
Balinese dance/theatre *6*, *111*; balance 35, *39*, *42*, *49*; codification 222; costume *248*, *249*; energy 75, *75*, 77, 81; face and eyes 123, 126, *127*, 136–7, 159; feet and walking 140, *140*, *144*; *gurus* *29*; hands 150, 159, *159*; *keras* and *manis* 11, *13*, 78, 81, *81*, 92, 126, *144*, 159, *159*; and martial arts 227, *228*; masks 136–7, *136*; oppositional movements *199*; organicity 207, *210*, 211; pre-expressivity *224*, 227, *228*; restored behaviour 235, 239; spinal column position 264, *264*; technique *262*; trance dances 239, *239*; and Western theatre 108, *111*, *199*
ballet (classical) *6*, 11, *15*, 17, 94, 108, *188*, 250; balance *10*, 35, *35*; hands and arms 161, *161*; notation 223, 226, 279; 'on point' 141, *141*; opposition 201, *201*; walking *142*, *143*; *see also* dance
ballet-comedies 186
Ballets Russes 108, *142*
Bandem, I Made 77, *136*, *159*, 220
Bandem, Swasti Widjaja *199*, *279*
Bando Tamasaburo 139
bapang *226*
Barba, Eugenio 62, 63, *190*, *269*; *animus, anima* 76–8, *278*; balance 32–5; face and eyes 123–4, 129; Grotowski on 268–9; *koshi* 75; on Meyerhold 118, 174–7; opposition 196; organicity 206, 212; pre-expressivity 216–20; rhythm 241–3, *276*; *Silver Horse* 63; tacit knowledge 121; on text *272*; training 276, 277–8, 281, 284, 286, *286*, *287*
Barbosa, Eduardo 60
barefoot dancers 140
baris 227, *228*
Barrault, Jean-Louis *213*
Barrymore, John *272*
Bassermann, Albert 267
Bateson, Gregory 239
Battleship Potemkin (film) *203*
Bauhaus movement 26, *222*
Bausch, Pina 212, *219*
Bawa, I Wayan *159*, *210*
bayadera 109
bayu 8, 72, 75, *77*
Bayuatmaja 77
beauty line 200
Beck, Julian *49*, 247
Bedhaya semang *42*
Beijer, Agne *164*, 168
being-in-life 59
belle courbe 93–5, *94*, *95*
Bengal: chhau dance 237–9
Benjamin, Walter 204

Bergman, Ingmar *275*
Berliner Ensemble 27, *46*, 266–7, *266*; *see also* Brecht
Bernhardt, Sarah 187, 208, *272*, *273*
bersilat *228*
bharatanatyam 31, 156, *235*, 236–7, *236*, 264, *264*
Bhattacharyya, Asutosh 237–9, *240*
Biezin, Ivan *247*
biological motions 244–5
biomechanics (Meyerhold): exercises 112, *115*, *116*, 117, 118, *119*; organicity 206, 212; and rhythm 246, *246*, *247*; shooting the arrow 100, *100*, *101*, 176
bios 7, 8, 12, 13; and *logos* 269; *see also* energy; scenic presence
Bjelàc-Babí100, Ranka 44–5
Blair, Preston 154–5, *154*, *196*, *204*
Blasis, Carlo *128*, 129, 141
Boccaccio, Giovanni 77
Bode, Rudolf *115*, *116*, 117
body: biological motions 244–5; decided bodies 16–17, *17*, 227, *284*; dilated body 52–61, 63–4, *65*, *84*, 225; double articulation 212; fictive bodies *16*, 17–18, 225, *225*; mechanics of balance 36–7; as microcosm 209; noh types 86–7; opposition 11, 12, 19; techniques 258–69; training 277–8; *see also* balance; daily techniques; exercises; extra-daily techniques; face and eyes; feet; hands
body architecture 233
body-in-life 52, 212
Bogdanov, Gennadi *100*, *101*, *119*, *247*
Böhm, Karl 27
Bohr, Niels 18, 22, 42
Bonaventura da Bagnoregio 290
Bonnard, Pierre 248
Booth, Edwin Thomas *270*
Bordier, Georgette 161, *161*
Borges, Jorge Luis: 'Dead Man' 60–1
Borodinskaya Studio 149
Boulez, Pierre *278*
Bowers, Faubion 110
bows and arrows 96, 97–100, *97*, *98*, *99*, *100*, *101*
boxing *115*, *116*, 117
Bragaglia, Anton Giulio 24
braking the action 88–90
Brandon, James 93, 110
Braun, Edward 177, 246,
breathing 15
Brecht, Bertolt 15, 27, *115*; alienation effect 108, 219–20, 235; *Brecht's Ashes* 18, *70*; *Caucasian Chalk Circle* 46–8; *Mother Courage* 18, *52*, 266–7, *266*, *267*, 269
Bresson, Robert 93, *178*, 191
bridge exercise 281, *282*, *283*
bridges on stage 148–9, *148*
Brook, Peter 207, *279*
Brun, Theodore 150
Bubus, the Teacher see Faiko
Buddha/Buddhist art 150, *153*, 217
bull-fighting 229
Bulwer, John 150, 151, *151*
Bunge, Hans Joachim 46–8, 267
Butoh dance *49*, 125
buyo dance 11, *41*, 103, *127*, 211, *242*, 248; energy 75, 84, *85*; *jo-ha-kyu* 16, 243–4

Callot, Jacques *34*, 168
Cambodian dance *111*, *218*
Candri, Ni Nyomen *220*
Cao Yu 108
capoera *232*
Carlson, Carolyn *161*
Carpentier, Georges *115*
Carreri, Roberta *35*, *120–1*, *133*, *220*, 277, 280
cartoons 154–5, *154*, 195, *196*, 204, *204*
Cassiodorus, Aurelius 150
Catandri, Filippo *152*
Celli, Giorgio 22
censorship: kabuki texts 110
centre of gravity 17, 35, 36, 37, 40
Cervi, Gino 59
cesta kara 75
Chandler, Billy Jaynes 60
Chang'an (Xian) 106, *107*
Chaplin, Charlie *76*, 176
character and rôle type 274
Chekhov, Michael *113*, 206
Cheyenne Indians 150
chhau dance *35*, 237–9, *240*
chikara 8, 72
children's art *57*, *58–9*, *59*, *60*
China: 'Tang exoticism' 106
Chinese dancers *221*
Chinese martial arts 228, *229*
'Chinese shadows' 106
Chinese theatre 11, 106, 108, *196*, 228, 251, 282, 284; *see also* Peking Opera
chirograms *151*, *152*, *197*
Ciaccona dance *149*
Cieslak, Ryszard *51*, *114*, *137*, *206*, 280, 282, 283
Claudel, Paul 108, 147, 289
codification 150–2, 161, 217, 222–3, 269; dance notation *223*, *226*, 279
Cohl, Emile 60
Colombaioni, Romano *114*
Comédie Française *128*, *187*
comedy: gesture *155*
commedia dell'arte 26, *81*, *149*, 199, *250*, *251*, 262; balance 10, 32, *32*, 45; codification 222; and dance 168, *169*, 186; energetic language *164*, *165*, *166*; nostalgia 185, 186, *189*
composition 178
concatenation 67–9, 273–4
concrete gaze 126
Confucius 72
Conrad, Joseph 288
Conselheiro, Antonio 61
Coomaraswamy, Ananda 108
Copeau, Jacques 24, 25, 26, *26*, 116, 117, 206, 209, *213*
Copiaus schools 24, 25
Coptic art *107*
Cornazano, Antonio 187, *226*
corral 147
costume *98*, *145*, 194, *240*, 248–57; *see also* make-up; masks; shoes
Cots, Toni *243*, 277
Covarrubias, Miguel *227*
Craig, (Edward) Gordon 24, 108, 206, 209, 233; *Hamlet* production *66*, 272; on Irving 10, 165–6, *167*
critics 288, 291
crying *289*
Cunha, Euclides da 60
Cynkutis, Zbigniew *137*

daily techniques 7–8, 11, 53, 152, 160, 187, 258, 268

Dalcroze *see* Jaques-Dalcroze
D'Amico, Silvio 26
dance 15, *42*, *249*, *250*; and balance 10, *41*, 43, *45*; and eyes 17–18, *18*, *124*, *125*; and grotesque 176; *gurus* and training 28, *29*, *30*; and Irving 165–6; and martial arts 230–1; notation *223*, *226*, 279; opposition 10–11, 12, 19, *204*; as technique 261–2, *262*; and theatre 10, 104, 168, 185–7, *226*; *see also* balance; ballet; rhythm
danda *232*
D'Annunzio, Gabriele 95, *95*
danza della spada 230, *231*
David, Jacques-Louis 167, *167*
deaf people *150*, *152*
decided bodies 16–17, *17*, 227, 284
Decroux, Etienne 7, 11, *11*, 12–13, 15, *32*, 45; *belle courbe* 93–4, *95*; energy in time with eyes *132*; exercises 117; mime and words 271; montage 181–2, *183*, *184*; omission 194; opposition *204*, *205*; organicity 212, *213*, 214; system of rules 6–7; use of masks 136
Delsarte, François 72, 155, *155*, *197*, 212
Denishawn *190*
dervishes 52, *250*, 262
Desak, Made Suarti Laksmi 77
déséquilibre *32*, 33, *40*, *43*
Desprès, Suzanne 272
devadasis 110, 237
Devi, Rukmini 29, *30*, 31, *236*, 237
Devrient, Ludwig 202
dhanu 96, 97, *97*
dialectics 58–9; *see also* opposition
diaphragm: extended position 81
Dickens, Charles 102
digital numeration *152*
dilation 52–65, 84, 225, 249, *249*
director's view 294–5
discus throwing 116, *117*
disorientation and dilation 59–60, 64–5
Djimat, I Made 211, *224*
Do-Jo 230
Dom drummers 237, 238
Domenico da Piacenza 187, *226*
Doré, Gustave *54*
double articulation 212–15
drama critics 288, 291
dramaturgy 66–71, 104, 112–21, 270–5; *see also* stage
Duchartre, Pierre Louis *164*
duel 230, *231*
Dullin, Charles 24, *26*, 27, 44, 108, 116, *132*, 209, 211, *213*
Duncan, Isadora 49, 108, *186*
Dürer, Albrecht *89*, 200
Durga, Lal 29
Duse, Eleonora 95, *95*, 295
Duval, Mathias-Marie *135*
Dyer, Carlus 223
dynamic balance 37, *37*, *38*, *39*, 43
dynamic immobility *see* immobility and energy

East–West theatre perspective 110
Ebreo, Guglielmo 187, *226*
Eibl-Eibesfeldt, Irenäus 134, *134*
Einstein, Albert 57
Eisenstein, Sergei 22, 27, *55*, *56*, 58, 67, 108, *115*, 118, *241*; on El Greco 68, 178, *178*, *179*, 180; montage 178, *178*, *179*, 180, *203*
Ekblad, Stina *53*
El Greco: *View of Toledo* 68, 178, *179*, 180
emotion 114, *129*, 130–5, 267
energetic language 164–9, *164*, *165*, *166*, 186

energy 10, 11, 13–14, 72–92, 175–6, 268, 277, 278; terms for 8–9, 18–19; *see also* immobility and energy
energy in time *132*, 194, 268
Engel, Johann Jacob 152, *222*
entrances 149, *149*, 198
entrechat *143*
equivalence 93–101, *181*, 194
Escher, Maurits Cornelis *55*
Essler, Fanny *143*
ethnology 134
ethos and training 278
Etruscan dancer *39*, 221
Etruscan discipline 216
Eurasian theatre 102–11, *106–11*, *190*
exercises 72, 73, 112–21, 138; *see also* acrobatics; biomechanics; martial arts; training
exoticism and Eurasian theatre 106, 108
expression, facial *129*, 130–5
'expressive gymnastics' *115*
extra-daily techniques 7–10, *11*, 258, 262, *263*, 268; acculturation 220; balance 8–10, 32, *34*, 35, *44*, 49; and dance 187, 262; energy 78, 92; equivalence 93–4; exercises 113; hands 150, 160; make-up 138, *139*; martial arts 227; 'negation principle' 56–7, 242–3; and spinal column 264; *see also* luxury balance

face and eyes 17–18, 122–39, 180, 289
Faiko, A.: *Bubus, the Teacher* 88–9, *88*, *90*, 243
fans *98*
feet *23*, 140–9; *see also* shoes; walking
Fé59, Elisabeth Rachel *208*
female impersonation 19, *250*, *251*; Indian dance 78, 82, *82*, *83*; kabuki 80, *139*; Peking Opera 72, *73*, 74–5, *158*; *see also* onnagata; *tan* actors
fencing 116
'fencing dance' *231*
fictive bodies 16, *17*–18, 225, *225*
fighting *115*, 116, *117*, 230–2; *see also* martial arts; stick fighting
Fiorilli, Tiberio *81*
Fischinger, Oskar *245*
flower path (*hanamichi*) *147*, *149*
flute *191*, 192
Flying Dutchman myth 54–5, *54*, 57
Fo, Dario 12, *14*, 103, *132*, *136*, 227, *227*, 269; virtue of omission 195, *195*
Fokin, Mikhail 108
Fossard, M. *see Recueil Fossard*
Fowler, Richard *162*
frasobliwy 206
Frisch, Max 294
Frittellino *32*
Fuchs, Georg 24, 209
Fuller, Loie 108, *155*, 176, *249*

gambuh 207
Gandhara art *107*
Garcia Lorca, Federico 229
gardens for sports 117, *117*
Garin, Erast 100, 155, *155*, 247
Garrick, David 110, *250*, 270
Gaugler, Hans *46*
Gautam (kathakali student) *82*, *83*
Gautier, Théophile 186
gaze *125*, 159; concrete gaze 126
gesture 150–63, 168, 217, 288, *289*; codification 150–2, 161, 217, 222–3; physiological analysis 44–5; plasticity 174–5; *see also* biomechanics
Giraudet, Alfonse *197*
Gladkov, Alexander 129, *272*

Gogol, Nikolai: *The Government Inspector* 88, 89–90, *89*, *137*, 247
Goldoni, Carlo *62*
Gopal, Ram 31
Gorchakov, Nikolai 24
Gorky, Maxim *163*
Gospel According to Oxyrhincus, The 60–1, *71*
gotipuas 82, *82*, *83*
Gozzi, Carlo 110, *189*
Graham, Martha *101*
Grand Guignol *90–1*
Grandville, Jean *245*
Granet, Marcel 263
Grasso, Giovanni *124*
Greece *see* Ancient Greece
grimaces *131*
grotesque 118, 175–6
Grotowski, Jerzy 51, 59, *114*, *142*, 249, 269; in China *190*; exercises *114*, 232; on expression 18; organicity 212, *214*; on technique 268–9; training 276, 280, *280*, 281, 282, *283*, 284, *285*
group expression 280, *280*
Grozdiev 247
Guerra, Rouy 60
Guglielmo Ebreo 186, 226
Guinness, Alec *275*
Gulbransson, Olaf *295*
gurus 28–31
Guthrie, Tyrone *275*
GVYRM laboratories 27
gymnastics *115*, 116, 117, *262*

Hacks, Charles *150*
hana 87
Hanako 106, 108, *111*
hanamichi 147, 149
Hanayagi, Kanichi *12*, *78*, *80*, *103*, 211, *242*
hanchement 200
hands 93, *95*, 150–63, 180, 222, 256; and eye movements 123, *123*, 159; *kanshu 193*, *193*
Hanuman 77
Hanxianzi *191*
Harlequin *81*, *164*, *165*, *166*, 168, *169*, 250, *251*, *282*
Harun ar-Rashid 106
hashigakari 148
hasta mudra 151, 156
hasta prana 156–7
hatha yoga *262*
Hauptmann, Gerhart 102
Hébert, Georges 117, *117*
Heine, Heinrich 54, *55*
Hellerau school 25–6, *115*, 116
hidup 211
high shoes *40*, *74*, *74*
hippari hai 10–11
Hiroshige 22
historiography 164–77, 185–6; *see also* nostalgia
Höffding, Harald 262–3
Hogarth, Burne 154, *154*
Hogarth, William 200, *200*
Hokusai: *Dance Lessons* 22, *23*; *Wave 21*, 22, *23*
Holder, Cristian *16*
Hong Shen 108
Hornbostel, Erich Maria von 261
House becomes a Chinaman, The (film) 60
hsin-i 229
Hu-Jeh 15
Hua To 228, *229*
Huang Zuolin 108
Hughes, Russel Meriwether 264
Hugo, Valentine *94*
Humphrey, Doris *199*, *204*, *242*

Ibsen, Henrik 102, *163*
Ichikawa Danjuro I *12*
Ichikawa Ennosoke *36*
icosahedron *223*
ikebana 14–15, *14*, *15*
iki iki 211
Ilar, Karel *275*
Ilinsky, Igor 176, *201*
imagination: and balance 44–5; dilated mind 53, 57, 62–5; fictive bodies 17–18, 225, *225*; *see also* thought
immobility and energy 84, *85*, 92, 116, *120–1*, 167, 168, 180, *206*; *mie* 130–2, *130*, *131*, 134, 138, *139*
improvisation 162, 269
inculturation 219–20, *219*, 234
independence of the organs 212, *214*
Indian theatre/dance 7–8, 17–18, 28, 82, 192, 248; apprenticeship 28–31; body architecture 233; female impersonation *78*, *82*, *83*; hands and gesture 150, *151*, 156–7; opposition 200–1; pre-expressivity *217*, *228*, 232; restored behaviour 236–9; and Western tradition 106, *109*, 110, *188*; *see also* kathakali theatre; odissi dance
individualism 280
Indo-Greek art *107*
inductive perception 234
intercultural training 279–80
International School of Theatre Anthropology (ISTA) 5, 19–20, 22, 104, 268–9
io-in 8
Ippei, Okamoto *295*
Ippitsusai Buncho *292*, *293*
ironical view of spectator *295*
Irving, Henry 10, *12*, 165–6, *202*
isolation 212
ISTA 5, 19–20, 22, 104, 268–9
Ito, Michio 108, *111*
Iyer, E. Krishna 237

Jaholkowski, Anton *232*
James, Henry 216
Japanese theatre *265*; costume *252*, *255*; fictive bodies 225; hands and gesture 160; *jo-ha-kyu* 16–17, *16*, 243–4; *ki-hai* 8, 18–19, *19*, 72, 75, *77*; 'killing the rhythm' 15, 244, *244*; and martial arts 228, 233; organicity 211; walking 146, 148–9; and Western theatre 108, 110, 146, 148, *173*; *see also* buyo dance; kabuki; kyogen; noh
Jaques-Dalcroze, Émile 26, *115*, 116, 117, *197*, 212
Jas 13, *75*, *81*, *81*, *126*, *127*, *144*
Javanese dance/theatre 42, 226, 264, *264*
Jelgerhuis, J. *155*
Jena, Ramani Ranjan 31
jesters *6*, *33*, *40*
Jindo Sitkim Kut *214*
Jnanananda ('mother guru') 28
jo-ha-kyu 16–17, *16*, 243–4
Joel *188*
Johansson, G. 244
Jones, William 106
Jousse, Marcel 241
Jouvet, Louis 26, *43*

kabuki theatre *6*, 8, *8*, *103*, 186, 202, 263, 284, 295; acrobatics 282, 284, *284*; *aragoto* and *wagoto* 35, *36*; censorship of texts 110; *Excerpts from the Plays* 23; face and eyes *19*, *128*, 129, *130*, *131*, 134, 138, *139*; female impersonation *80*, *139*; fictive body 225; hands and gesture 160; high shoes *40*;

lighting 130, *131*, 147; make-up 138, *139*; and martial arts 228, 230; *mie* 130–2, *130*, *131*, 134, 138, *139*; and montage 180; peepholes *292*, *293*; set design 248; *tameru* 13, 84; theatre interior *147*, 148–9
kacha 211
Kalakshetra dance school 29–30
Kalamandalam school, Kerala *36*, 102, *157*, 282, *283*
kalaripayattu 228, *228*
Kalidasa: *Sakuntala* 106, *190*
Kalvodova, Dana 198
kamae 93, 160, *160*, 233, *233*
kamen 136
kanshu 193, *193*
Kanze, Hideo 10, *289*
Kanze, Motomasa 225
Kaoru, Osanai 108, 110
karate *193*, *193*, 227
Karsavina, Tamara *101*
Kasar, Nana 31
kathakali theatre 102, *140*, 211, 222, 228; balance 35, *36*, *41*; exercises *122*, *123*, 138, 281; face and eyes 18, *123*, *123*, 138, *138*; female impersonation *78*, *251*; *gurus* 29–30; hands and *mudras* 156, *156*, *157*; omission *192*, *192*; spinal column position *264*, *264*; training 281, *282*, *283*
Kawamura, Kotaro *215*
Kawamura, Nobushige *215*
Keaton, Buster *72*
Keene, Donald 110
Kehler, Sonja 234
keras 11, *13*, *78*, *81*, *81*, 92, *126*, *144*, 159, *159*
Khokar, Mohan 237
khon dance 227
ki-hai 8, 18–19, *19*, 72, 75, *77*
Kichiwaemon, Kameko *13*
kikoro 8
Kikugoro *295*
'killing the rhythm' 15, 244, *244*
Kim Hong-do *41*
kimono 248, *255*
kinaesthetics 39, 43, 116–17, 175–6, 243
Kinesogram 44
Kirstein, Lincoln *141*, 223
Kiselë5, P. *89*
Kita School (noh) 10
Klee, Paul 59, *122*, *122*
kneeling positions 42, 265
knowledge: secret knowledge 279, *280*
koan 270
Koestler, Arthur 56
kokken 8
Komissarzhevskaja, Vera *175*
Komparu Zenchiku 86
Korean dance *41*, 211
koshi 8, 9, 10, 72, 75, 84
kris dance 239, *239*
Krishna *191*, 192, *192*, 221
Kuan Yin 217
Kusumo, Sardono W. *81*
Kum Kum Das 28
kung-fu 8, 11, 72–3, *74*, 92
kurogo 194
Kustov, Nicolai *101*, 247
kyogen theatre 8, 98–9, *98*, *134*, *145*, *181*, *255*

La Meri 264
La Scala, Milan 43
Laban, Rudolf von 26, 212, 222, 226
Labanotation 226
Laflotte, D.B. 187
Lairesse, Gerard de *151*

Lal, Durga 29
language 8–9, 210; *see also* energetic language; sign language
Larsen, Tage *280*
lasya 78, 82
Laukvik, Else Marie *162*, *254*
Leabhart, Tom *12*, *224*
learning: visual learning 122–3; *see also* apprenticeship; training
Lebedev (Calcutta theatre director) 110
Lecoq, Jacques *211*
legong dance *42*, 127
Leonardo da Vinci 39, *223*
Leroi-Gourhan, André *54*
li 58
lian-shan 84, 123, 130
lighting 130, *131*, *147*, 249
Lin Chun-Hui 126, *126*, *254*
Lindblom, Gunnel *275*
Lindh, Ingemar 93–4, *94*, *95*, 204, *204*, *205*
line of gravity 36, *37*
Ling, Dr (vocal specialist) *190*
Ling, Susanne *42*
'living marble' 166–7
Living Theatre of Khardaha 220
Living Theatre (New York) 49, 120, 247
Ljubimovka theatre *171*
logos and *bios* 269
lokadharmi 7–8, *8*, 11, 19
Lorca, Federico Garcia *229*
Lord of the Dance 34, 82
Lorde, André de: *The Telephone Call 90–1*
Lorre, Peter *249*
Lulli, Giovambattista 186, *226*
luxury (precarious) balance 32–3, *35*, *40*, *41*, *43*, *45*, *49*, *213*, 268

ma 16
Macuilxochitl *200*
Magarshack, David *163*
Magnani, Anna 76
Mahabharata 31, *226*, 237–8, *238–9*
Mahapatra, Kelucharan *30*, 82, *83*
maharajalilsana 217
maieutics 64
Makarova, Natalia 201, *201*
make-up 138, *138*, *139*
male impersonation 19, *79*, *85*
Malina, Judith *247*
Manet, Edouard *191*, 196
manis 11, *13*, *17*, 78, 81, *81*, 126, 159, *159*
Marceau, Marcel 9–10, *213*
Maria Theresa, Austrian empress 216
martial arts 116, 193, *193*, 195, 227–32, *227–30*, 233; *see also kung fu*; t'ai chi
Martinelli, Tristano *81*, 166
masks *134*, 136–7, *136*, 186, 200; chhau dance *35*, 237–9, *240*
matah 211
Matisse, Henri 39, *241*
Matsui, Akira *103*, *224*
maulavi 250
Mauss, Marcel 258–63, 268
Mayan dance/theatre 39, 251, *253*
Mead, Margaret 239
meaning of theatre 290, 292, 293, 294–5
Mei Baoju 72
Mei Lanfang 72, *73*, 74–5, 108, *132*, *158*, *177*
Meldolesi, Claudio 46, 266–7
memory 122–3, 164–9
Merleau-Ponty, Maurice 43
Meyerhold, V.E. 10, *12*, 59, 108, *174*, 206; braking the action 88–90, *137*; dynamic tableaux *175*; on eye movements 129; fission

in theatre 118, *119*; on Grasso *124*; grotesque 175–6; and Mei Lanfang *177*; oppositional movements *196*, *201*; organicity 206, 209, 213, 214; plasticity 173–4; and presence 166; rhythm *243*, 246; scenic rhythm 174–5, 213; sets 88, *89*, *149*, *243*; shooting the arrow 100, *100*, *101*, *176*; teaching 24, 25, *26*, 27, *27*; text and stage *272*; *see also* biomechanics
mi-juku 211
Michelangelo 155, 200; *David* 93, *93*
Michotte 43
mie 130–2, *130*, *131*, 134, 138, *139*
mime 9–10, 11, 15, 93–5, 224; *déséquilibre 32*, *33*, *40*, *43*; face and eyes *134*, *137*, 138; shadow test 204, *204*, 205, *205*; *see also* Decroux, Etienne
mind 171; dilated mind 53, 57, 62–5; *see also* imagination; thought
mise-en-scène 67, *272*
Mnouchkine, Ariane 257
modern dance 190, *197*, 219
Moholoy-Nagy, Sybil 28
Molière 173, 174, 186, *226*
Monsalve, Juan *286*, *287*
montage 99, 178–84, 191, *203*, 214, 299; and dramaturgy 67, 118; ecstasy of 58, 118
Morelli, Angelo 36–7, *37*
Morelli, Giovanni 37
moresca (morris dance) 230–1
Morrocchesi, Antonio 167, *167*, 222
Moscow Art Theatre *26*, 66, 174, *189*, *272*
motor activity 44–5
Mounet-Soully (Jean Soully Mounet) *187*, 211
mudras 107, 123, *123*, 150, *150*, 151, *153*, 156–7, *156*, *157*
mukna 228
muscular sense 36
musical background 88, *89*
Muybridge, Edward James 155
mystagmes 180

naka ya lethlake 191
Nakajima, Natsu *49*
Namboodiri, M.P. Sankaran *138*, *157*, *211*, 251
Nandikeshvara 150
naturalness 208–9, 219
natyadharmi 7–8, *8*, 11, 19
Natyashastra 228, 236, 237
nautch girls *109*, 237
'negation principle' 56–7, 242–3, 269
nei-kong 262
Nelson, Lisa *104*
Nemirovich-Danchenko, Vladimir *26*, 174
New York School of Visual Arts 154
ngidupan 211
Ni Nyoman Candri *220*
Nijinsky, Vaslav *143*, *188*, *226*
Nishi Honganji Temple, Kyoto *148*
Noel, Cayuqui Estage *200*
noh theatre 8, *9*, 11, *13*, *103*, *147*, 215, 279, *280*; energy 10, 75, 84; face and eyes 123, *134*, *289*; *jo-ha-kyu* 16–17, 243–4; masks *134*, 136, *136*; pre-expressivity 224, *225*, *225*; Skin, Flesh and Bone 21; spinal column position 264; theatre space 148–9, *148*; three types 86–7, *86–7*; views of weeping gesture *289*; walking 35, 146, 148–9, 268; *see also* kyogen theatre
Nomura, Kosuke 19, *93*, 99, *99*, 145, 180–1, *181*, 182, *184*, *254*, *265*
Nomura, Mannojo 10
North American Indians 150, 151
nostalgia 185–90; *see also* historiography
Noton, David 122–3

Noverre, Jean-Georges 141
nritta 150, 156
nritya 156
Nugini, Ni Made *207*
Nye, H. *202*
Nyegaard, A.C. *150*
Nyt Dansk Danseteater, Copenhagen *226*

obi 81
Odin Teatret 8, *50*, 60, 104; dramaturgy 69, *69*, *70*; exercises 116, *120–1*, *232*, 281, *282*, *283*; training 276, *276*, *277*, *280*, 281, *282*, *283*, *285*; *see also* Barba; *sats*; 'tae-tae' chain
odissi dance 6, *8*, 199, *248*, *263*; archery and equivalence 96, 97, *97*; balance 10, *32*, 35, 45; codification 223, *223*; energy *82*, *85*; face and eyes *126*, 129; *gurus* 28; hands and *mudras* 156, *157*; pre-expressivity 223, *223*; *rasa* 129; spinal column position 264, *264*
Ohno, Kazuo *105*, *115*, *125*
Okamoto Ippei *295*
Okamura Masanobu *147*
Okinawa 193
O55, L. 46
Olivier, Laurence *275*
omission 12–14, 191–5, 248
Omolú, Augusto 39, *56*, *210*, 211, 224, *225*, *232*
'on point' 141, *141*
onnagata 8, *80*, *139*, 180, *242*, *295*
Open Theatre 120
opposition 10–11, *12*, 19, 196–205, *213*, 268
organic effect 206
organic rhythm 276
organicity 62, 118, 120, 206–15, 219; Stanislavsky's system 170–3, 219
Oriental theatre 6–7, 102–11, 220; and martial arts 227–9; set and costume design 248–9; technique 268–9; training 276; Western view of 52, 67, 110; *see also* Asian theatre; Balinese dance/theatre; Japanese theatre; Peking Opera
'oriental theatres' 106, 110
Orientalism 106, 110
orixás 39, *210*, 211, 224
Orphan of the Family Zhao 106, *109*
otkaz 176, *177*, *196*, 246, *246*
Otojiro, Kawakami 106, 108, *111*
otsukaresami 8
Ouyang Yu-qian 108
Oxolotlan paesant theatre 220

pakka 211
Palucca, Gret *34*
Panigrahi, Sanjukta 7, 11, *82*, *105*, 211, *225*, *243*, *248*; absence 194, *194*; apprenticeship *30*, *282*, *283*; *Ardhanarishwara* 19–20, *20*; balance 10, *32*, 45; energy 19, *19*, *85*; equivalence 96, 97, *97*; face and eyes 126, *126*, 129; *tribhangi* 201, *201*
Panji cycle *226*
Pannikar, Chandu 29–30
Pantalone 34, *164*, 168, *169*
pantomime 151, 248
parampara 31
Paris Conservatory 222
Parvati 82
Pascal, Blaise 178, 191
Pasek Tempo, I Made 11, *17*, *29*, *136*
pataka mudra 156
pause-transitions 242, 243, *243*
Pavlova, Anna 108
Paxton, Steve *104*
Paz, Octavio 74
peasant theatre 220

pedagogy 24–8, 281; *see also* training
peepholes *292, 293*
Pei Yanling *17, 35, 49, 79*
Peirce, Charles S. 290
Peking Opera 186, *263*; acrobats *9*, 282; balance *35, 49*; costume 248, *249, 254, 256, 256*; energy and immobility 84, 130; face and eyes 123, 126, *126*, 138, *138*; female impersonation *72, 73*, 74–5, 158; hands and gesture 158–9, *158*; 'in the dark' scenes 248; make-up 138, *138*; male impersonation *79*; opposition 11, *196, 198*; props 248, *254*; shoes *40, 74, 74*; spinal column position 264; stage design *198*; training 74–5, *74*, 281, 282, *282, 283*
pentjak dance 228
perezhivanie 62–3, 64–5, 171–2
performance text 66, 67, 69, 104, 118, 279, *279*
performer's view 288–99
peripeteia 54–5, 57–8, 63–4, 118, 120
personal expression 280
personification techniques 171–2
Petipa, Marius 141
'physical actions' 112
physiognomic displays 131
Piacenza *see* Domenico da Piacenza
Picasso, Pablo 93, *111*, 191, *272*; *Guernica* 93, 266, *267*
Pier, Stephen *53*
Piermarini, Guiseppi *43*
Pierrot *256*
Pillai, Muthukumara 31
Piscator, Erwin 266
Pissarro, Camille 196
Planck, Max 57
plasticity 174–5
Plato 230, 241; *Dialogues* 64–5
plié 35, *35*, 227
plots 67, 273–4
Plutarch 106
pneuma 18–19, 75
Polaniy, Michael 121
Polycletus 200
'poor' text 271–2, 273–4
Poseidon 231
poses *217*
power centre 40
Pradier, Jean-Marie 244–5
pragmatic laws 268–9
prana 8, 19, 72, 75
precarious balance *see* luxury balance
pre-expressivity 14, 104, 216–34, 255, 269; and dilated mind 62, *63*; pre-expressive nucleus 60; Stanislavsky's system 172–3; *see also* energetic language
pre-interpretation 234
presence *see* scenic presence
'process logic' 218
Proletkult schools 24
Pronko, Leonard 110
props 248, *251, 254*; *see also* weapons
prostitution: Indian temple dancers 237
psycho-technique 218
Pulcinella *256*
puppet theatre *see* shadow theatre
Purificaçao, Jairo da *232*
Purulia chhau dance *35*, 237–9, *240*
pyrrhic dance 230, *231*

Rachel (Elisabeth Rachel Félix) *208*
Racine, Jean *187, 189*
Raghavan, V. 237
Rajkh, Zinaida *272, 273*

Rama 78
Ramayana 226, 237–8
Rame, Franca *163*, 202
Rameau, Pierre *161*
Raphael 200
rapid eye movements 122–3, *122*
rasa 129
Rasmussen, Iben Nagel *18*, 19–20, *50*, 92, *92*, 220, 232, 269, 276
Raüker, Ralf *247*
Ravana 238, *240*
reassemblage 213–14
Recueil Fossard engravings *164, 165, 168, 169, 251, 282*
Reddi, Dr Muthulakshmi 237
reflex excitability 246
rehearsals: restored behaviour 236
Reichel, Kathe 47, *48*
Reinhardt, Max 24, *25*, 209
relaxation and contraction 268
repertory text 271
Requeno, Vincenzo 151, *152*
restored behaviour 180, 191, 235–40
'result logic' 218
'return to life' 62–3, 64–5, 171–2
rhythm 15, 241–7, 276, 278; braking the action 88–90; organic rhythm 276; scenic rhythm 174–5, 213; standing in rhythm 92
'rich' stage 271–2, 273–4
Rilke, Rainer Maria 95
Ripellino, Angelo Maria 175
Ristori, Adelaide *208*, 209
ritual *214*, 235, 236
Rocha, Glauber 60
Rodin, Auguste 106, *111*; *Cathedral 153*; *L'Homme qui marche* 95, *95*
rôle types: and character 274; noh 86–7, *86–7*; and performers 280
Roman empire 106, *107*
Roman inscription 289
Rorschach test 297–9, *298, 299*
Royal Theatre, Turin *146*
Rubenstein, Ida *97*
Ruggeri, Ruggero *219*
rules: Oriental theatre 6–7, 222; Western theatre 6–7, 25, 26, 35, 222; *see also* codification

saccades 122–3, *122*, 180
Sacchi (acrobatic dancer) *49*
Sachs, Curt 261, *262*
Sacre du printemps, Le 94, 188
sadhana 29
sadir nac 236, 237
Sadoshima Dempachi 18
Said, Edward 110
Saint-Denis, Michel 108
Saint-Denis, Ruth *188, 190*
Salome 300, *301*
salutation 265
Salvini, Tommaso 174, *208*
sampun wayah 211
Sangeet Natak Akademi, New Delhi 238
Sano, Seki 108, *111*
santai 86–7
Sarabhai, Mrinalini 31, *237*
Sarniani, Ni Made *207*
sats 92, 113, 116, *120–1*, 268–9, 277
Savarese, Nicola 130–2
Sawamura, Sojuro 9, 10
'scan path' 122–3
Scaramouche *81*
scenic behaviour *208*, 278
scenic bios 223

scenic presence 52, 62, 72, 75, 92, *229*; and energetic language 164–9, *164, 165, 166*; and organicity *206, 207*, 208–11, *208, 213, 215*; total presence 277–8
scenic rhythm 174–5, 213
scenic tradition 102
Schall, Ekkehard 27, *46*, 267
Schechner, Richard 67, 68, 180, 191
Schlemmer, Oskar 222
schools *see* pedagogy; theatre schools
score and subscore 112, 113–14, 236
Scott, Adolphe Clarence 110
sculpture 200
second nature 206
secret knowledge 279, *280*
Selacia 76
self-expression 280, *280*
semiology 290–1
Seneca 216
set design 88–91, *88, 89, 149, 243*; *see also* stage
sexes 19, 104; *animus/anima* 76–8, *79, 87*, 278
shadow test 204, *204*
shadow theatre 106, *109*, 226
Shakespeare, William: *Hamlet* 66, 68, 270, *272, 275*; and Irving 166
shakti 8, 19, *19*, 72
shamanism 45, 211, *214*, 236, 279
shan-toeng 84
Shanghai People's Theatre 108
Shankar, Ravi 29
Shankar, Uday 108
Sharaku 130
Shaw, George Bernard 102, 108, 165
Shawn, Ted 101, *188, 190*
shinmyong 211
Shirabioshi 19
Shishi 194, 252, *253*
shite 8
Shiva Ardhanarishwara 19–20, *20*
Shiva Nataraja 34, 82
Shiva's Cosmic Dance 188
shoes *40, 74, 74*, 140, 141, *143*
Shoyo, Tsubouchi 108
shui xi 256
shun 8
Siddharta 129
Siddons, Henry 152, 222
Sieffert, René 16–17
sign language *150*, 151–2, *151, 152*
signs and theatre 290–1, 292, 297
'silent scream' 266, *267*
Silk Road 106
simplification 12
simultaneity 67–9, 273–4, 295
Singer, Milton 236
Sklovskij, Viktor 27
Slepjanov, I. *88*
sloping stages *43*, 89–90, *89*
Socrates 230
soft energy (*anima*) 76–8, 278
Sogdian dance *41*
Sojuro, Sawamura 9, *10*
Sololev, Vladimir *149*
Sophocles: *119*, *Antigone* 187, *Philoctetes* 279
'space-time' 277
Spain: *corral* 147
spectators 104, 147, 206, 234; and kinaesthetics 116–17, 175–6; view of 288–99
spinal column 47, 252, 264, *264, 265*, 266; and emotion 267; and eyes 128, 129, *129*; training 277, 281, *282, 283*
spirit 18–19, 75

spoken drama in Asia 108
spontaneity 212, 219, 269
sports and exercises *115*, 116–17
Staël, Madame de 297
stage: kabuki theatre *147*, 148–9; noh theatre bridges 148–9, *148*; peepholes *292, 293*; Peking Opera *198*; sloping stage *43*, 89–90, *89*; and text 270–5; view of theatre *294; see also* set designs
'stage business' 13
stage servants 8, 194, *194*
Stalin, Joseph 61
standing position 36, 44, 84, *85*, 92, 116
Stanislavsky, Konstantin Sergeyevich 24–5, *46*, *67*, 108, *163, 170, 171, 173*; dilation 62–5, *62–5*; organicity 170–3, 206, 209, 212, 214, 219; performer's view 296–7; pre-expressivity *216*; restored behaviour 236; rhythm 244; scenic presence 166–7, 170–3; standing in rhythm 92; subtext 112; 'system' 170–3, 219, 274; teaching 23, 24–5, *24, 25, 26, 26, 27*; training 280
Stark, Lawrence 122–3
statics 36–7
Stato-Kinesogram and Kinesimeter *44*
Steckel, Leonard *46*
Steinberg, Saul *55*
Steiner, George 266
stick fighting *116*, 228, 232
stilt walking 74, 75, *251*
Stormare, Peter *275*
Stowe, Harriet Beecher: *Uncle Tom's Cabin* 102
Strindberg, August 55, 182, *184*
studios and pedagogy 25, 26–7
subscore 112, 113–14
subtext 112
Sudbinin, S.N. *163*
Sukeroku *40*
Sulerzhiski, Leopold 25
sutradhara 233
Suzuki, Tadashi 146, *146*, 148
sword dances 230, 231
synthetic rhythm *245*
Szondi, Peter 273

tabi 146
tacit knowledge 121
Tadashi Suzuki Company *146*
'tae-tae' chain *210*
Tagore, Rabindranath 110, *111*
tahan 11
t'ai chi 84, 229
Tairov, Aleksandr *189*
takhousarol 228
taksu 8, 75, 211
tame 13, 84, *84*
tameru 13, 84
tan actors 72, *73*, 74–5, *74*
tandava 78, 82
'Tang exoticism' 106, *107*
Taoist gymnastics *262, 263*
Tarzan illustrations 154, *154*
Taviani, Ferdinando 72, 274
taxu 72
Taylor, Frederick 177
teaching *see* gurus; pedagogy; training
Teatr Laboratorium *232, 280, 281, 282, 285; see also* Grotowski
Teatro alla Scala, *see* La Scala

technique 25, 219–20, 258–69, 276
temperament and sexes 19
temple dances in India 236–7
Tempo, I Made Pasek *see* Pasek Tempo
tempoz 88–9
tennis 116
text 66, 67, 68, 104, 279; and stage 270–5
teyyam dance *135*
Thai dance *38, 227*
theatre: combination of text and stage 270–1; views of 288–99
Théâtre, Le (journal) *187*
Théâtre du Soleil *257*
theatre anthropology 6–20
Théâtre Antoine, Paris *272*
theatre schools 24–6
Theatre of Sources 269
theatre-institution 271
theatres (buildings) *146, 147; see also* stage
Theleur dance notation *226*
Thevenaz, Paulet *197*
thought 57–8; *see also* peripeteias
thumbs: expressivity 155, *155*
Tian Han 108
Todaiji Temple Buddha *153*
toeng 8
Tommaseo, Niccolò 185
topeng 136, 248
Toporkov, V.O. 92, *173*, 244
Torch, Chris *247*
total presence 277–8
Toulouze, Michel *226*
town criers *192*
tradition and Eurasian theatre 102–11
tragedy 106, *155*
training 74–5, 276–87, 297; *see also* apprenticeship; exercises; pedagogy
Trance and Dance in Bali (film) 239
trance dances 236, 239, *239*
transcultural theatre 269, 279–80
transverse flute *191, 192*
'tre-tre' exercise sequence *120–1*
Tretiakov, Sergei M. 108, *115*
tribhangi 32, 35, *37, 41*, 92, *97, 192*, 200–1, *200, 205, 264*
trompe-l'oeil 149
ts'ai chi'ao 40, 74, *74*
Tsao ChunLin *282, 283*
Tsukiji Shogekijo 110
tsura akari 131
Turkish theatre 109; *see also* shadow theatre
Turner, Victor 236
twin logics 58–9

uslovny 174–5

Vajravarahi *200*
Vakhtangov, Eugeni 24, *33, 189*, 206, 209, *217*
Valencia, Tórtola *124*
Van der Decken, Captain 54–5
Van Hamal, Martine *17*
Vargas Llosa, Mario 61
Varley, Julia *120–1, 210, 250, 277*
vase paintings *187, 231*
Vatsyayan, Kapila 236
Veda 28
Venilia 76
Venus de Milo 95
Verfremdungseffekt 108, 219–20, 235

verisimilar acting 208
Verry, Pierre 9–10
Vestris, Gaetano *226*
Vieux Colombier (Copeau) 24, 25, *26, 27*
views of theatre 288–99
vigorous energy (*animus*) 76–8, 278
Vijayakumar, K.N. *78, 251*
vinaya 29
virasa 8
visual learning 122–3
visual perception of spectator 234
Visvarupadarshanam *221*
vocal sounds 98
voice training 276
Voltaire: *The Orphan from China* 109

Wagner, Richard 54–5
wagoto 35
Wakafuji, Shigetsugu *227*
waki 8
walking *142, 143, 145, 146, 146*, 148–9; and energy 92, *92*; Irving's walk 165–6; opposition *198*; *tan* actors 74, *74, 75*; technique 261, 267, *268; see also* feet
Wandering Jew 54, *55*
Watanabe, Moriake 8, 225
water sleeves 256, *256*
wayah 211
wayang kulit 226
wayang wong 77, *226, 264*
weapons 193, *193*, 228, *230, 231; see also* bows and arrows; stick fighting
weeping 289
Weigel, Helene 46–8, *47, 52*, 266–7, *266, 267*
Wells, Herbert George 288
Western theatre tradition 24–8, 102–11, 230–2, 281
Wethal, Torgeir *232, 285*
White, C. 28
Wiesenthal, Grete *33*
Wigman, Mary *101, 202*
Willumsen, J.E. *178, 180*
Wiratini, Ni Made *49*
Woolf, Virginia 20
working languages 210
World Exhibitions 106, 108, *111*
Wrestler, The (Olmec statue) *74*
written text 66, 67, 68, 104, 279, *279*

Xochipilli *200*

Yacco, Sada 106, *111*
yakshagana costume *248*
Yeats, W.B.: 'dancing plays' 108, *111*
yoga *262, 263*
Yogjakarta, sultan *226*
Yoshi, Hijikata 110
Youge, A. *202*
yugen 19, 72

Zacconi, Ermete *90–1*
Zakhava, Boris 24
Zeami Motokiyo 17, 19, 21, 86–7, *86–7*, 129, 149, 258, 276, *280*
Zen 23, 270
Zhang Pengchun 108
Zhang Yunxi *198*
Ziryab 106
Zorn, Friedrich Albert *143*